The Grammar of Politics and Performance

This volume brings together important work at the intersection of politics and performance studies. While the languages of theatre and performance have long been deployed by other disciplines, these are seldom deployed seriously and pursued systematically to discover the actual nature of the relationship between performance as a set of behavioural practices and the forms and the transactions of these other disciplines.

This book investigates the structural similarities and features of politics and performance, which are referred to here as 'grammar', a concept which also emphasizes the common communicational base or language of these fields. In each of the chapters included in this collection, key processes of both politics and performance are identified and analysed, demonstrating the critical and indivisible links between the fields. The book also underlines that neither politics nor performance can take place without actors who perform and spectators who receive, evaluate and react to these actions. At the heart of the project is the ambition to bring about a paradigm change, such that politics cannot be analysed seriously without a sophisticated understanding of its performance. All the chapters here display a concrete set of events, practices and contexts within which politics and performance are inseparable elements.

This work will be of great interest to students and scholars in both International Relations and Performance Studies.

Shirin M. Rai is Professor in the Department of Politics and International Studies at the University of Warwick, UK.

Janelle Reinelt is Professor in the School of Theatre and Performance at the University of Warwick, UK.

Interventions
Edited by Jenny Edkins
*Aberystwyth University and Nick Vaughan-Williams,
University of Warwick*

The Series provides a forum for innovative and interdisciplinary work that engages with alternative critical, post-structural, feminist, postcolonial, psychoanalytic and cultural approaches to international relations and global politics. In our first 5 years we have published 60 volumes.

We aim to advance understanding of the key areas in which scholars working within broad critical post-structural traditions have chosen to make their interventions, and to present innovative analyses of important topics. Titles in the series engage with critical thinkers in philosophy, sociology, politics and other disciplines and provide situated historical, empirical and textual studies in international politics.

We are very happy to discuss your ideas at any stage of the project: just contact us for advice or proposal guidelines. Proposals should be submitted directly to the Series Editors:

- Jenny Edkins (jennyedkins@hotmail.com) and
- Nick Vaughan-Williams (N.Vaughan-Williams@Warwick.ac.uk).

'As Michel Foucault has famously stated, "knowledge is not made for understanding; it is made for cutting" In this spirit The Edkins – Vaughan-Williams Interventions series solicits cutting edge, critical works that challenge mainstream understandings in international relations. It is the best place to contribute post disciplinary works that think rather than merely recognize and affirm the world recycled in IR's traditional geopolitical imaginary.'
Michael J. Shapiro, University of Hawai'i at Manoa, USA

Critical Theorists and International Relations
Edited by Jenny Edkins and
Nick Vaughan-Williams

Ethics as Foreign Policy
Britain, the EU and the other
Dan Bulley

Universality, Ethics and International Relations
A grammatical reading
Véronique Pin-Fat

The Time of the City
Politics, philosophy, and genre
Michael J. Shapiro

Governing Sustainable Development
Partnership, protest and power at the world summit
Carl Death

Insuring Security
Biopolitics, security and risk
Luis Lobo-Guerrero

Foucault and International Relations
New critical engagements
Edited by Nicholas J. Kiersey and Doug Stokes

International Relations and Non-Western Thought
Imperialism, colonialism and investigations of global modernity
Edited by Robbie Shilliam

Autobiographical International Relations
I, IR
Edited by Naeem Inayatullah

War and Rape
Law, memory and justice
Nicola Henry

Madness in International Relations
Psychology, security and the global governance of mental health
Alison Howell

Spatiality, Sovereignty and Carl Schmitt
Geographies of the nomos
Edited by Stephen Legg

Politics of Urbanism
Seeing like a city
Warren Magnusson

Beyond Biopolitics
Theory, violence and horror in world politics
François Debrix and Alexander D. Barder

The Politics of Speed
Capitalism, the state and war in an accelerating world
Simon Glezos

Politics and the Art of Commemoration
Memorials to struggle in Latin America and Spain
Katherine Hite

Indian Foreign Policy
The politics of postcolonial identity
Priya Chacko

Politics of the Event
Time, movement, becoming
Tom Lundborg

Theorising Post-Conflict Reconciliation
Agonism, restitution and repair
Edited by Alexander Keller Hirsch

Europe's Encounter with Islam
The secular and the postsecular
Luca Mavelli

Re-Thinking International Relations Theory via Deconstruction
Badredine Arfi

The New Violent Cartography
Geo-analysis after the aesthetic turn
Edited by Sam Okoth Opondo and Michael J. Shapiro

Insuring War
Sovereignty, security and risk
Luis Lobo-Guerrero

International Relations, Meaning and Mimesis
Necati Polat

The Postcolonial Subject
Claiming politics/governing others in late modernity
Vivienne Jabri

Foucault and the Politics of Hearing
Lauri Siisiäinen

Volunteer Tourism in the Global South
Giving back in neoliberal times
Wanda Vrasti

Cosmopolitan Government in Europe
Citizens and entrepreneurs in postnational politics
Owen Parker

Studies in the Trans-Disciplinary Method
After the aesthetic turn
Michael J. Shapiro

Alternative Accountabilities in Global Politics
The scars of violence
Brent J. Steele

Celebrity Humanitarianism
The ideology of global charity
Ilan Kapoor

Deconstructing International Politics
Michael Dillon

The Politics of Exile
Elizabeth Dauphinee

Democratic Futures
Revisioning democracy promotion
Milja Kurki

Postcolonial Theory
A critical introduction
Edited by Sanjay Seth

More than Just War
Narratives of the just war and military life
Charles A. Jones

Deleuze & Fascism
Security: war: aesthetics
Edited by Brad Evans & Julian Reid

Feminist International Relations
'Exquisite Corpse'
Marysia Zalewski

The Persistence of Nationalism
From imagined communities to urban encounters
Angharad Closs Stephens

Interpretive Approaches to Global Climate Governance
Reconstructing the greenhouse
Edited by Chris Methmann, Delf Rothe & Benjamin Stephan

Postcolonial Encounters in International Relations
The Politics of Transgression in the Maghreb
Alina Sajed

Post-Tsunami Reconstruction in Indonesia
Negotiating normativity through gender mainstreaming initiatives in Aceh
Marjaana Jauhola

Leo Strauss and the Invasion of Iraq
Encountering the Abyss
Aggie Hirst

Production of Postcolonial India and Pakistan
Meanings of partition
Ted Svensson

War, Identity and the Liberal State
Everyday experiences of the geopolitical in the armed forces
Victoria M. Basham

Writing Global Trade Governance
Discourse and the WTO
Michael Strange

Politics of Violence
Militancy, international politics, killing in the name
Charlotte Heath-Kelly

Ontology and World Politics
Void Universalism I
Sergei Prozorov

Theory of the Political Subject
Void Universalism II
Sergei Prozorov

Visual Politics and North Korea
Seeing is believing
David Shim

Globalization, Difference and Human Security
Edited by Mustapha Kamal Pasha

Imagining World Politics
Sihar & Shenya, a fable for our times
L.H.M Ling

International Politics and Performance
Critical aesthetics and creative practice
Edited by Jenny Edkins and Adrian Kear

Memory and Trauma in International Relations
Theories, cases, and debates
Edited by Erica Resende and Dovile Budryte

Critical Environmental Politics
Edited by Carl Death

Democracy Promotion
A critical introduction
Jeff Bridoux and Milja Kurki

International Intervention in a Secular Age
Re-enchanting humanity?
Audra Mitchell

The Politics of Haunting and Memory in International Relations
Jessica Auchter

European-East Asian Borders in Translation
Edited by Joyce C.H. Liu and Nick Vaughan-Williams

Genre and the (Post)Communist Woman
Analyzing transformations of the Central and Eastern European female ideal
Edited by Florentina C. Andreescu and Michael Shapiro

Studying the Agency of being Governed
Edited by Stina Hansson, Sofie Hellberg Maria Stern

Politics of Emotion
The song of Telangana
Himadeep Muppidi

Ruling the Margins
Colonial power and administrative rule in the past and present
Prem Kumar Rajaram

Race and Racism in International Relations
Confronting the global colour line
Alexander Anievas, Nivi Manchanda and Robbie Shilliam

The Grammar of Politics and Performance
Edited by Shirin M. Rai and Janelle Reinelt

War, Police and Assemblages of Intervention
Edited by Jan Bachman, Colleen Bell and Caroline Holmqvist

Re-Imagining North Korea in International Politics
Problematizations and alternatives
Shine Choi

On Schmitt and Space
*Claudio Minca and
Rory Rowan*

Face Politics
Jenny Edkins

Empire Within
International hierarchy and its imperial laboratories of governance
Alexander D. Barder

The Grammar of Politics and Performance

Edited by
Shirin M. Rai and Janelle Reinelt

LONDON AND NEW YORK

First published 2015
by Routledge
2 Park Square, Milton Park, Abingdon, Oxon, OX14 4RN

and by Routledge
711 Third Avenue, New York, NY 10017

Routledge is an imprint of the Taylor & Francis Group, an informa business

© 2015 selection and editorial material, Shirin M. Rai and Janelle Reinelt; individual chapters, the contributors

The right of Shirin M. Rai and Janelle Reinelt to be identified as authors of the editorial material, and of the individual authors as authors of their contributions, has been asserted by them in accordance with sections 77 and 78 of the Copyright, Designs and Patents Act 1988.

All rights reserved. No part of this book may be reprinted or reproduced or utilised in any form or by any electronic, mechanical, or other means, now known or hereafter invented, including photocopying and recording, or in any information storage or retrieval system, without permission in writing from the publishers.

Trademark notice: Product or corporate names may be trademarks or registered trademarks, and are used only for identification and explanation without intent to infringe.

British Library Cataloguing in Publication Data
A catalogue record for this book is available from the British Library

Library of Congress Cataloging-in-Publication Data
The grammar of politics and performance / edited by Shirin M. Rai and Janelle Reinelt.
    pages cm. – (Interventions)
Includes bibliographical references and index.
1. Communication in politics–Social aspects. 2. Persuasion (Rhetoric)–Political aspects. 3. Theater–Political aspects.
4. Performing arts–Political aspects. I. Rai, Shirin, editor of compilation. II. Reinelt, Janelle G., editor of compilation.
JA85.G74 2014
320.01'4–dc23   2014019766

ISBN: 978-0-415-71650-5 (hbk)
ISBN: 978-1-315-87987-1 (ebk)

Typeset in Times New Roman
by Sunrise Setting Ltd, Paignton, UK

Contents

List of figures	xi
Notes on contributors	xii
Acknowledgements	xv

1	Introduction JANELLE REINELT AND SHIRIN M. RAI	1
2	Performing democracy: roles, stages, scripts JOHN PARKINSON	19
3	Performance at the crossroads of citizenship JANELLE REINELT	34
4	'I am an American': protesting advertised 'Americanness' CYNTHIA WEBER	51
5	Characterization and systemic gender violence: the example of *Laundry* and the figure of the mother in Irish culture LISA FITZPATRICK	67
6	Theatricality vs. bare life: performance as a vernacular of resistance SILVIJA JESTROVIC	80
7	Becoming a democratic audience ALAN FINLAYSON	93
8	Street arts, radical democratic citizenship and a grammar of storytelling SUSAN C. HAEDICKE	106

x *Contents*

9   Tahrir Square, EC4M: the Occupy movement and the dramaturgy of public order   121
SOPHIE NIELD

10   Temporality, politics and performance: missing, displaced, disappeared   134
JENNY EDKINS

11   Performance and politics: ceremony and ritual in Parliament   148
SHIRIN M. RAI

12   Bringing the audience back in: Kenya's Truth, Justice and Reconciliation Commission and the efficacy of public hearings   162
GABRIELLE LYNCH

13   Betrayal and what follows: rituals of repentance, healing and anger in response to the church sexual abuse scandal in Ireland   183
JOSHUA EDELMAN

14   Closet grammars of intentional deception: the logic of lies, state security and homosexual panic in cold war politics   198
JAMES M. HARDING

15   Afterword: sovereign and critical grammars   217
MICHAEL SAWARD

Bibliography   226
Index   248

Figures

4.1	Elvira Arellano	58
4.2	José Matus	58
4.3	Phil McDowell	59
4.4	Saul Arellano	59
8.1	Mouton de Vapeur, *Les Quiétils*	109
8.2	Jeanne Simone, *Le Parfum des Pneus*	112
11.1	Parliament of South Africa	150
11.2	Parliament of India	151
11.3	Westminster security, UK Parliament	152

Contributors

Joshua Edelman is Fellow in Research and Enterprise at the Royal Central School of Speech and Drama, University of London, and holds a Ph.D. from Trinity College, Dublin. He writes on theatre and performance in the religious and political systems of the contemporary West. He is the co-editor of *Performing Religion in Public* (Palgrave, 2013), and is founding co-convenor the Performance and Religion Working Group of the International Federation for Theatre Research.

Jenny Edkins is Professor of International Politics at Aberystwyth University. She is author of *Missing: Persons and Politics* (Cornell University Press, 2011), *Trauma and the Memory of Politics* (Cambridge University Press, 2003) and *Whose Hunger? Concepts of Famine, Practices of Aid* (University of Minnesota, 2000). She is co-founder, with Adrian Kear and Mike Pearson, of Aberystwyth's university-wide research centre, Performance and Politics International (PPi), and co-editor with Kear of *International Politics and Performance: Critical Aesthetics and Creative Practice* (Routledge, 2013).

Alan Finlayson is Professor of Political and Social Theory at the University of East Anglia. His research interests include the theory and history of political rhetoric, political ideologies and democratic theory. He is an Associate Editor of the journal *Contemporary Political Theory* and a co-editor of the series 'Rhetoric, Politics and Society' published by Palgrave.

Lisa Fitzpatrick completed her Ph.D. on postnationalism and contemporary Irish theatre at the Graduate Centre for Study of Drama, University of Toronto. She teaches at the University of Ulster. Her research is mainly engaged with issues of representing violence on stage, Irish women's writing, and feminism in Ireland. She has published in *Performance Research, CTR, Modern Drama*, and *L'Annuaire Théâtral*. Her edited collections *Performing Violence* and *Performing Feminisms in Contemporary Ireland* are with Carysfort Press.

Susan C. Haedicke is Associate Professor in the School of Theatre, Performance, and Cultural Policy Studies at University of Warwick in the UK. She has published several articles and book chapters on street arts since 2006 and, most recently, a book titled *Contemporary Street Arts in Europe: Aesthetics and*

Politics (2013). She has co-edited *Political Performances: Theory and Practice* (2009) and *Performing Democracy: International Perspectives on Urban Community-Based Performance* (2001).

James M. Harding is Professor of Theatre and Performance Studies at the University of Warwick in the UK and will join the Department of Theatre and Performance Studies at the University of Maryland, College Park in the fall of 2014. He is the author of *Ghosts of the Avant-Garde(s)* (University of Michigan Press, 2013), *Cutting Performances: Collage Events, Feminist Artists and the American Avant-Garde* (University of Michigan Press, 2010) and *Adorno and a Writing of the Ruins* (SUNY, 1997).

Silvija Jestrovic is Associate Professor in the School of Theatre, Performance and Cultural Policy at the University of Warwick (UK) and a playwright. Her books include *Theatre of Estrangement: Theory, Practice, Ideology* (University of Toronto Press 2006) and *Performance, Exile, 'America'* co-edited with Yana Meerzon (Palgrave Macmillan, 2009). Her latest monograph, *Performance, Space, Utopia: Cities of War, Cities of Exile*, was published by Palgrave in 2012.

Gabrielle Lynch is an Associate Professor of Comparative Politics at the University of Warwick, and her research interests include ethnic identities and politics, elections and democratisaton, and transitional justice and local reconciliation efforts with a particular focus on Kenya. Gabrielle has published numerous journal articles and book chapters, and her first monograph, *I Say to You: Ethnic Politics and the Kalenjin in Kenya*, was published by the University of Chicago Press in 2011.

Sophie Nield teaches theatre and film at Royal Holloway College, University of London. She has published widely on questions of space, representation and theatricality in political life and the law, and on the performance of borders of various kinds: the international border, the former site of the Berlin Wall and the problem of the corpse in representation. Recent work has appeared in *Contemporary Theatre Review*, *Performance Research* and *Moving Worlds*.

John Parkinson is Professor of Politics in the Centre for Governance and Public Policy, Griffiths University, Australia. He works at the intersection between normative democratic theory and critical policy studies, especially deliberative democracy and the public sphere. His recent work includes *Democracy and Public Space* (Oxford University Press) and *Deliberative Systems: Deliberative Democracy at the Large Scale* (Cambridge University Press) edited with Jane Mansbridge, Harvard. His next book is with André Bächtiger (Luzern) called *Mapping and Measuring Deliberation* (Oxford University Press, forthcoming).

Shirin M. Rai is Professor in the Department of Politics and International Studies, University of Warwick. She directed a Leverhulme Trust funded programme on Gendered Ceremony and Ritual in Parliament (2007–11). Her research interests are in gendered analyses of performance and politics, political institutions and governance and the political economy of development. She is the author of *The Gender Politics of Development* (Zed Books/Zubaan Publishers, 2008) and editor of *Ceremony and Ritual in Parliament* (2010). She is the co-founder, with Janelle Reinelt, of the Warwick Politics and Performance Network.

Janelle Reinelt is Professor of Theatre and Performance at University of Warwick. She was President of the International Federation for Theatre Research (2004–7). Her most recent book is *The Political Theatre of David Edgar: Negotiation and Retrieval* with Gerald Hewitt (2011). She received the 'Distinguished Scholar Award' for lifetime achievement from the American Society for Theatre Research (2010) and in 2012 she was awarded the Excellence in Editing prize with Brian Singleton for their Palgrave book series, 'Studies in International Performance'.

Michael Saward is Professor of Politics and International Studies at the University of Warwick. He is the author of *The Representative Claim* (Oxford University Press, 2010) and co-editor of *Enacting European Citizenship* (Cambridge University Press, 2013).

Cynthia Weber is Professor of International Relations at the University of Sussex, UK, and a documentary filmmaker. Her work critically engages various forms of hegemony, particularly those found in US foreign policy, gender and sexuality and constructions of US Americanness.

Acknowledgements

We would like to thank the Performance and Politics Network at the University of Warwick (WPPN) in which we first held the conversations that led to this book, and all the scholars and students who participated in the four inaugural colloquia. Thanks to the contributors for their original and thought-provoking essays. In addition, we thank our series editors Jenny Edkins and Nick Vaughan-Williams for their encouragement and support of the project, and our Routledge editor Peter Harris and his staff for helping us produce the book in a felicitous and timely fashion. Also we would like to thank Francesca Chiu for editorial work on the bibliography. Thanks to Marvin Carlson for advice with the introduction, Susan Haedicke for allowing us to use her photograph for the cover art, and especially to Michael Saward for agreeing to read the manuscript and write an Afterword for the book.

1 Introduction

Janelle Reinelt and Shirin M. Rai

All human knowledge takes the form of interpretation.
(Walter Benjamin[1])

Wherever you go, you will see a polis.
(Hannah Arendt[2])

This volume brings together a set of essays that work in the interstices of the disciplines of politics and theatre and performance studies. This intervention takes place against the backdrop of contemporary disillusionment with political processes and democratic institutions and actors, addressing in particular those scholars who are inclined to give up on some major categories of political struggle such as interests, representation, identity and redistribution. The languages of theatre and performance have long been deployed by other disciplines such as psychology (Freud's primal 'scene'), sociology (Goffman's 'backstage'), anthropology (Turner's 'liminal', Singer's 'cultural' and Bateson's 'ritual' performances) and politics (Aristotle's spectator/citizen and Lukes's 'political ritual'). This attribution often remains at the level of metaphor and has not been pursued systematically in the discipline of politics to discover the nature of the cross-over between performance as a set of behavioural practices and the transactions of these other realms.

Rather than take these for granted, we investigate the relationship between politics and performance to discover structural similarities we are calling 'grammar'. Designed to mean that certain features of political transactions shared by performances are fundamental to both provenances, the concept of grammar also emphasises the common communicational base or language of these fields. Neither politics nor performance can take place without actors who perform and spectators who receive, evaluate and react to these actions. Moreover, the notion that one can study and describe the 'grammar' governing politics (which will always involve performance) as well as the 'grammar' governing performance (which will always involve politics) is a provocative idea which we hope will give rise to further research on the complex and fluctuating relationship between these two terms. There is another more direct objective in this work as well: to bring practical political processes back into theatre and performance studies, from where they have been somewhat displaced in recent years by a variety of less defined and definitely less partisan thematics and stylistics (as we discuss further on in this Introduction). Additionally, we argue that political thinkers need to consider a dramaturgical and performative[3] analysis such that politics cannot be analysed seriously without a sophisticated understanding of its performances. While theatre scholars have often cited political thinkers from Plato and Aristotle forward, politics scholars have rarely engaged reciprocally. Our authors, however, are equally chosen from both disciplines, developing a dialogue between fields and strengthening our claim that performance and politics are co-constitutive even if distinct.

We regard theatricality and performance more fundamentally as indispensable and unavoidable components of democratic politics. As Reinelt (2006) argues, 'this time – our time – is aggressively theatrical ... the present historical moment is in fact specifically and technically theatrical and performative'. Thus beyond the grammar which operates between politics and performance, the historical specificity of this time intensifies the affinities. The essays that were chosen for this volume display a concrete set of events, practices and contexts of special concern to the present: e.g. crises of legitimacy and the role of ritual in the face of the Catholic Church's abuse scandal (see Edelman, in Chapter 13), or the questionable efficacy of certain forms of political protest after 9/11(see Nield, in Chapter 9), or the tension in instruments of transitional justice in Truth, Justice and Reconciliation Commissions (see Lynch, in Chapter 12).

This is not, of course, the only historical conjuncture governed by a 'performance culture'. Scholars have written extensively about the performative power of the state and of social movements throughout history. Indeed, we highlight a portion of this scholarship further on. But this contemporary moment addresses our lifetime and therefore, as a matter of personal urgency, we respond to the political necessity that confronts us by exploring ideas for better governance and the theatrical possibility of its imagining.

Why 'grammar'?

A grammar is a set of recognisable rules or codifications that facilitate communication. However, grammar shifts and changes over time, and thus allows for a space to re-form and re-enact rules through everyday subversion of some codes and renegotiation of others. This definition is part historical, part literal, and implicitly metaphorical. The earliest grammars were found in Iron Age India, and in the West in Hellenic Greece. Children are taught grammar in primary schools (or at least they used to be), where they learn parts of speech and sentence construction. More recently, emphasis has shifted from the prescription of grammar to its description – informed by the practices of actual language speakers and the evolution and indeed instability of grammar's governing structure. If we deliberately look for a looser, more flexible formulation, Merriam Webster gives a broad definition as its fourth place citation: 'the principles or rules of an art, science, or technique "a grammar of the theater"; also: a set of such principles or rules'.

When Kenneth Burke wrote *A Grammar of Motives* in 1945, he evoked 'grammar' to mean 'the basic forms of thought ... that are exemplified in the attributing of motives' (p. xv). He used the term to connote that this highly questionable and ambiguous matter – motives – could be understood and grasped through an orderly formal structure of attributes. He was seeking to ground his commentary on a strong set of principles common to his subject – motives.

Kenneth Burke is a deliberate choice for an interlocutor. Throughout a long and productive life as a multi-disciplinary thinker working at the interface of literature, sociology and philosophy, Burke carved out a unique theory of 'dramatism' that attempted to provide a methodology for analysis of realms other than the theatrical. He serves the purposes of this book because he wanted to find flexible and yet durable categories of thought to highlight the connections between elements of social experience. He was one of the first theorists to insist that the text or the performance needed to be analysed in relation to its audience and its socio-political context (what he called its scene). He was influenced by Aristotle's ideas about rhetoric and believed that the act of persuasion in political speech elicited a complex set of possible responses on the part of its recipients (cf. Parkinson's Chapter 2). And although he used the term 'grammar' to describe his interpretative principles in *A Grammar of Motives*, he also believed that parts of speech and grammar would always be trumped by the particular social context of their employment. He considered communication a form of action, and his emphasis on symbolic action, seen in retrospect, seems like a version of 'the force of the performative' (although he had no truck with J. L. Austin or other linguistic philosophers who were prominent in his time).

Burke referred to 'drama': the term did not have quite the exclusive emphasis on text and formal script characteristics that it does today, 'drama' having lost out in the hierarchy of objects of study in the contemporary discipline of theatre and performance studies. In Burke's thought, 'dramatism' 'invites one to consider the matter of motives from a perspective that, being developed from the analysis of drama, treats language and thought primarily as modes of action' (p. xxii). Here we can see how his sense of the dynamics of the theatrical set-up seemed to him descriptive of the communication act itself. He put forward five terms he called 'the pentad' as his grammatical basic categories: Act, Scene, Agent, Agency, Purpose. This seemingly fixed system of alternating elements was also, however, informed by Burke's insistence on the presence and the value of ambiguity. Recognising that any categories he named would not always deliver a straightforward or total explanatory power, he writes that what he wants '*is not terms that avoid ambiguity, but terms that clearly reveal the strategic spots at which ambiguities necessarily arise*' (p. xviii; emphasis in the original). In a particularly prescient claim for the purposes of our own investigation in this volume, he writes:

> Instead of considering it our task to 'dispose of' any ambiguity by merely disclosing the fact that it is an ambiguity, we rather consider it our task to study and clarify the *resources* of ambiguity. For in the course of this work, we shall deal with many kinds of *transformation* – and it is in the areas of

ambiguity that transformations take place; in fact, without such areas, transformation would be impossible.

(p. xix; emphasis in the original)

Remembering him in our title, we also recognise him in the spirit that animates our present work – it is precisely in the ambiguities where politics and performance intersect that we might find the possibility of (political) transformations. This is what Sophie Nield argues in her chapter on the Occupy movement, and what James Harding teaches us about the logics of lying that govern security and surveillance regimes. If we are turning away from Burke's dramatic pentad or his specific form of analysis and interpretation, we honour him in seeking to create our own grammar that catches the overlapping but ambiguous motives of politics and performance.

We approach the conjunction of 'politics and performance' in search of a set of principles that can anchor our interdisciplinary investigations. Holding the conviction that there are good reasons why it makes sense to consider politics and performance as inter-related discursive and embodied practices, we set out to identify what some of these structures in common might be, remaining mindful of the ambiguity of the overlap and its potential for transformation. To begin with the most obvious, both politics and performance require publics and exist to affect their constituencies in aggregate form, whether through laws and policies or through providing certain (often aesthetic) experiences in common. However, just as grammar is constantly evolving and adjusting to the stimulus of its actual usage, politics is similarly processual, defining itself in sometimes revolutionary, sometimes incremental transactions and signature practices. In this it participates in the fundamental features of performance: performances are actions, events, or behaviours that are relational and self-conscious (Schechner 2003; Carlson 2003; Balme 2008; McKenzie 2001). 'Any action that is framed, presented, highlighted or displayed is a performance' (Schechner 2003). Key to its structure is reflexivity: to perform is to be aware of the act of doing something, and to show doing it. Performance always bears the traces of this reflexivity – it 'knows' it shows. Not all performance is confined to individual subjects – institutions also perform when they demonstrate their power in particular scenarios or appearances: the 'halls of justice' utilise literal and metaphoric space to identify a precinct where justice theoretically prevails (Resnik and Curtis 2011). All performances are transactional – between the performer(s) and the spectators or recipients of the act.

In the chapters that follow, our authors identify a number of features that constitute this hypothetical grammar, draw on a range of political thinkers in their case studies and engage in disciplinary debates to push beyond available formulations. This volume thus lays the foundation for an ongoing collaboration between these discrete fields.

A partial genealogy

Although this book is a contemporary study, it is useful to highlight some of the work that has preceded us and the efforts of scholars who have recognised the important relationship between our two keys terms in the history of both disciplines. Starting with 'Classical Greece', both politics and theatre/performance studies have paid significant attention to the relationship between Greek theatre and politics. Aristotle and Plato provided theoretical starting points for a series of topics in which it is all but impossible to disassociate politics from theatre: mimesis, representation, spectacle, citizenship, rhetoric, leadership, participation and polis. Civic festivals containing performances were clearly ceremonies of the Athenian state, and it is difficult if not impossible to separate out the aesthetic concerns of the one from the governance concerns of the other.

Thus one strand of theatre scholarship that leads towards our present study might begin with *Aeschylus and Athens: A Study in the Social Origins of the Drama* (1946) in which Marxist scholar George Thomson first put forth an analysis of Athens in relation to class relations and Aeschylus as a key to this understanding (also see Vernant's work on Greek society (1974)). In the 1990s, John Winkler and Froma Zeitlin (1990), and Simon Goldhill and Robin Osborne (1999) argued explicitly for a political reading of the Greek theatre and a theatrical understanding of democracy. Winkler and Zeitlin's collection stressed the civic ceremony of theatre and the way as an institution it bore civic status, while for Goldhill and Osborne, the role of citizen was linked to participation – and often to display; moreover citizens deliberated as part of audiences. More recently, we note that David Wiles (2011), writing on theatre and citizenship, opens with a first chapter on Athens, and concludes with a meditation on the public sphere and theatre's place within it today, while Nicholas Ridout grounds his conviction that 'the polis might itself be constituted in the action that is the making of theatre' in a certain vision of Athenian democracy as social praxis (2013: 16).

'Early modern England', the period marked by the Tudor monarchs, Shakespeare and eventually civil war is a second logical site to look for scholarly recognition of the inextricable links between politics and performance. Indeed, many Shakespeare courses started by asking students to read E. M. W. Tillyard's *The Elizabethan World Picture* (1943). However, theatre historians' archival work on the playhouses and companies, and 'New Criticism' based on close readings of texts (but little context), were the dominant trends in Shakespeare scholarship – until the rise of 'New Historicism' circa 1980 placed a methodological emphasis on the socio-political context of works of art leading to exciting new scholarship that followed up on this theoretical stance. Stephen Greenblatt's *Renaissance Self-Fashioning* (1980) and Jonathan Dollimore and Alan Sinfield's *Political Shakespeare: Essays in Cultural Materialism* (1985) were landmark publications, and over the next decade were joined by Orgel and Keilen (1999) and Howard (1994), among others. Shakespeare scholarship, in fact, became a stage for playing out the culture wars that marked the British and American academies in the 1980s and 1990s.[4] In recent years, Shakespeare scholarship has turned to global politics and the ways Shakespeare has been appropriated by a range of nations and contexts, as well as the politics of transnational cultural exchange. (Examples include Kennedy (1993), or more recently Litvin (2011). Julia Lupton is probably closest to our conceptualisation of the relations between politics and performance in her equal immersion in Shakespeare studies and contemporary political problems: in her latest book (2011), she marshals Arendt and Agamben to discuss political questions of life and living such as friendship, and elections, concluding with an epilogue on 'defrosting the refrigerator', a return to Arendt's notions of *oikos* for purposes of Shakespearian refashioning.

The modern period gave us Brecht and Beckett, arguably the two most influential Western playwrights of the twentieth century. While Beckett resisted any socio-political programme, Brecht's overt desire for a politically engaged theatre led to scholarship that mined links to Marx, Althusser and Benjamin (Willett 1977; Giles 1998; Kruger 2004; Carney 2005; Rokem 2009). Augusto Boal, with his own idiosyncratic readings of Aristotle, attempted to create political theatre as a tool of struggle for the oppressed, and has been widely influential across the globe with his ideas of Forum Theatre and Legislative Theatre (Cohen-Cruz and Schutzman 1993; Emert and Friedman 2011). No contemporary survey of modern theatre would omit Brecht, nor more recently Boal. Both men wrote extensively about their ideas and their theatre, so their primary texts remain the most important sources.

Turning to the politics literature, while there is no unified history of engagement with performance and theatre scholarship, the different subfields within politics have made various connections, depending on their focus. Of course, Plato and Aristotle took positions on the role of performance and its audience – Plato's scepticism condemned both, fearing an erosion of deliberative politics and the dethroning of reason; Aristotle on the other hand found the citizen/audience a site of catharsis for politics in the democratic city-state. But in contemporary debates on democratic theory, performance makes an appearance fairly recently, largely inspired by social anthropological work on the performance of ritual. For example, Stephen Lukes (1975) noted the importance of performances of ritual in both the politics of integration and fragmentation of polities. Political symbolism has been another focus of attention in political analyses alert to performance and its affects. As Michael Walzer pointed out, 'Politics is an art of unification; from many, it makes one. And symbolic activity is perhaps our most important means of bringing things together, both intellectually and emotionally' (1967: 194). Aesthetic effects of political performance have been a third strand of engagement since the Situationist movement, led by Guy Debord, developed the idea of the performance of capitalism through the concept of the spectacle (1999). The reproduction of capitalist social relations through the globalisation of taste through control over media and advertising has figured in the cultural economy of capitalism literature (Debord 1999; Appadurai 1990; Chomsky and Herman 1994). Rhetoric and language, speech and music also made entry into political analyses to reach back to the Durkheimian concept of 'charismatic leadership' but also its rejection through counter-rhetorics and disruptions performed by 'audience'/citizens (Finlayson 2007; Ilie 2003). And finally, politics and international relations scholars have examined the performance of state institutions, not just in terms of their efficacy, but also their performative reach, which can shore up or undermine their legitimacy (Kertzer 1988; Hobsbawm and Ranger 1992; Lukes 1975; Shils and Young 1953).

This opening up of behavioural and normative politics to performative scrutiny allowed political scientists to explore the mobilisation of power through staging state events – the colonial durbars in India (B. Cohen 1992), Fascist and Soviet parades (Falasca-Zamponi 2000), the opening ceremonies of parliaments (Armitage, Johnson and Spary in Rai and Johnson 2014), the performance of international politics at summits (Reynolds 2007). The rhetoric of political leaders and representatives has been scrutinised to suggest the importance of speech in/as performance in political institutions (Finlayson 2007; Ilie 2003). It also allowed the exploration of counter-performances by and of individual actors and social movements. For example, Achille Mbembe's work on the delegitimation of state authority through public political humour: 'the subject's deployment of a talent for play and a sense of fun which makes him homo ludens par excellence [...] enables subjects to splinter their identities and to represent themselves as constantly changing their persona' (Mbembe 1992: 6). The claim to representation is often also challenged through cartoons, the telling of jokes and teasing those who make such claims (Shehata 1992: 75). Political and cultural theorists have also analysed contemporary governance – of both markets and the state: they have pointed to 'the colonized social circuits that comprise spectacle – including confidence in the market and the state, and an identification with commodity culture – and [have noted] that to disrupt spectacle may have great and unpredictable consequences' (Stallabrass 2006: 90). And in the international political economy literature, global capitalism has been analysed, via Debord, as dependent on the society of the spectacle in which citizens and consumers become culturally produced subjects capable of receiving the performances of politics and the market (Brassett and Clarke 2012: 4). Thus, following in Gramsci's footsteps, the unpacking of political hegemony has opened up politics and international relations as disciplines to the promise of a performative reading of their subjects.

What we have tried to demonstrate through our partial genealogies of scholarship linking politics and performance is that there is a historical trajectory of scholarship in both fields which has preceded the present volume. If our efforts differ from those we have highlighted, this difference manifests mostly in the appeal to interdisciplinary engagement. For all their use of political theorists' ideas, theatre and performance studies scholars speak mostly to their own disciplinary context; so too with politics. The emphasis on cross-over is our proposed way forward.

The current state of play

Recently there has been a manifest interest in the conjunction of politics and performance in both disciplinary fields – or at least in redefining their relationship to each other in light of new pathways of thought and modes of understanding. Twenty-five years after the collapse of 'really existing socialism' put paid to the cold war and its binary formulations of ideology and economics, a number of scholars and artists are searching for fresh approaches to the globalizing thrust of neoliberalism. The key political forms of theatre in the twentieth century were clear strategies of intervention into contemporary political struggles through various theatre works that sought to create and represent a mass political subject, a capitalism-resistant sociality and an aesthetics that, while extremely rich and varied (from epic to surrealist for example), appealed to its audiences in terms of a collective address. Now, performance scholarship has preferred to reject 'messages' (let alone didactics), settled meanings, direct political polemics – all of these seen as being alternately crude and heavy-handed or insulting and oppressive for audiences who need emancipation from discursive engagement perceived as harangue. We are thinking here of Hans-Thies Lehmann's postdramatic critique (2006), but also of Alan Read's rejection of 'political theatre' (2008), or the explicitly anti-identitarian position of Matthew Causey and Fintan Walsh in their recent collection *Performance, Identity and the Neo-Political Subject* (2013). Much of this work is in debt to a group of philosophers who have become dominant in scholarly discourse across a number of fields – especially Rancière, Badiou and Agamben, as well as Žižek, Deleuze and Nancy. While each has his own specific system of thought, they share a critique of identitarian politics and multiculturalism, a desire to recover a form of universalist ethics (though not necessarily Kantian) and a rejection of political negotiation leading to any of a number of 'c' words (e.g. coalition, compromise, consensus) because in this 'post-political' time, these political strategies have become associated with the hegemonic (the UK coalition government, for example). In embracing these thinkers, scholars believe they are moving to a more radical form of political theory, one which will challenge the ability of capitalism under globalisation to thrive on the appropriation of identities for the production of profits. A sample of this thinking, for example, posits that

> What is emerging on the streets, as well as within academic discourse, is a strong sense that identity-based struggles are politically limited, and that a different type of grounded collective action is in order. We are at a stage where neo-liberal culture has absorbed any agency that politicized identities were once presumed to have. Capitalism sees in the fracturing of identity a wonderfully lucrative commercial project, to the extent that it does not simply respond to identitarian distinctiveness but cultivates it for its own purposes.
> (Causey and Walsh 2013: 2)

A leftist version of this argument is that identities essentialise differences and that identity is more easily folded into capitalist social relations than solidarities of class that cut across such a politics. This thinking was at the heart of the feminist debate between Nancy Fraser and Judith Butler in the 1990s. Fraser argued that redistributive politics addresses the economic structure while recognition politics addresses issues of identity, which are important but not reducible to structural redistribution that she sought to foreground (1995, 1997). For her part, Butler was insistent that Fraser's perspectival dualism allowed issues of recognition to be trumped by those of economic distribution (1997). In her intervention in this debate on identity, culture and redistribution of power, Iris Marion Young explicitly addressed the politics of Fraser's dualist approach: 'Fraser's opposition of redistribution and recognition, moreover, constitutes a retreat from the New Left theorizing which has insisted that the material effects of political economy are inextricably bound to culture' (1997: 148; see also Butler 1997).

This scepticism about identitarian politics appears somewhat ironic in light of the history of identity politics in the civil rights movement, the anti-apartheid movement and in second-wave feminism when discrete identities were articulated precisely in order *not* to essentialise and therefore homogenise race and gender, in a political struggle to gain recognition and political rights for those who had been invisible within the category 'citizen', and had been discriminated against under laws that did not recognise them as equal and sovereign subjects (see Young 1990).

While Fraser's recent attack on feminism as the 'handmaiden of capital' (2013) suggests that this is an ongoing debate, especially at this time when neo-liberalism has coopted many identities to market-related ends, this also makes the urgency of rethinking strategies to empower political subjects undeniable. In the essays collected here readers will find how identity categories continue to structure real political struggles (see Weber or Fitzpatrick or Lynch) as well as encountering circumstances when transcending identity categories offers some tangible rewards (see Haedicke and Edkins). In almost any case, however, where political struggle involves the need to put forward the claims of some as equal to the claims of the dominant many, it is through affiliating with designated subjects in acts of collective solidarity that the political process gains traction. Furthermore, in neglecting to historicise the role of identity in the political struggles of many countries, many ages, this scholarship often 'throws the baby out with the bathwater' in its desire to be current and radical. A serious and committed political artist or scholar must needs grapple with the differential naming of causes, groups and categories of beings that finally are understood as 'identities'. Even within the new emergence of post-human discourse, the privileging of animals and critique of anthropomorphism is itself a form of identity politics – the pig counts as much as the human while not being human.[5] The interest in returning to notions of a universal subject, so visible in much of this work, neglects or appears not to think it matters if the new post-identitarian subject papers over the very differences it seems to bind together.

Part of the energy in the new scholarship on politics and performance comes from the desire to radicalise and refresh both the politics of art and the art of politics. For theatre and performance scholars, especially given the emphasis within Performance Studies on marginal or dissident figures and ideas, this has meant what we might call a romance with dissensus, highlighting Rancière's heavy influence on this thinking (Rancière 2010; see also Davis 2013). Performance Studies has historically defined itself as 'radically democratic and counterelitist' (Pelias and Van Oosting 1987), preferring scholarship that shows how performances can disrupt or contest dominant hegemonies (good) rather than how performances might consolidate or strengthen hegemonic positions or formations (bad). In the current climate of impatience with many traditional political concepts, it is perhaps not surprising to find a de-politicising and ahistorical move to aestheticise and personalise art and its political form. Where a previous generation was suspicious of aesthetics as a dodge for politics and a way of continuing an unexamined valorisation of an elite white canon, some scholars today have reintroduced aesthetics as a forgotten and essential discourse that brings the creative faculty of the imagination back to the table.

This is exciting and valuable as far as it goes, but it will not and cannot replace an engagement with the material and social structures of power and governance that politics has always been 'about'. As Reinelt wrote with Joseph Roach in the introduction to their *Critical Theory and Performance* in 1992, 'We did not include a section on the pure aesthetics of performance, transcending the realm of ideology, because we could not imagine one' (2). This was a provocation at the time, but in the new millennium, it is only too possible to recognise a realm of aesthetic analysis that considers itself political but does not engage in the collective concrete struggles of pragmatic politics. Where this new theory eschews an older interest in activism and coalition building, it emphasises individual response-ability and dissensual refusal to participate in codified political practices (such as parliamentary reform, or electoral politics, or relief aid). Collectivity is maligned as much as consensus. Further, this formulation of an aesthetic politics overlooks, as Rai has argued, the politics of 'a) the production of art and b) [of] ... state-capital relations in this production – their focus remains the social and individual consumption of art' (2014). The politics and the materiality of aesthetic production and consumption are then separated and depoliticised.

A recent book illustrates this desire to make aesthetics central in order to reanimate the relations between performance and politics – but not as an interdisciplinary project. In *International Politics and Performance: Critical Aesthetics and Creative Practice* (2013) Jenny Edkins and Adrian Kear write what might be seen as a direct challenge to this present volume:[6]

> This way of thinking – emphasizing the need to think through politics and performance as modes and practices of aesthetic thinking, and to think them together as modes and practices of aesthetic politics – is in stark contrast to an alternative 'interdisciplinary' approach, which remains primarily interested instead in elaborating the performance dynamics of politics (their ritual incarnations and modalities of practicing citizenship) and the ways in which performance addresses politics and 'the political' through staging and interrogating its processes. In this empirically restricted view, we're still in the territory of examining 'performances about' political events, histories, experiences, etc. on the one hand, and explaining political events in terms of the logic of performance on the other. Whereas in this volume we see performance and politics as 'folded' in myriad and complex patterns, interanimating one another as domains of political subjectivation and creative practices undertaken by aesthetic subjects, a more conventional approach might be to see them as operating in 'dialogue'.
>
> (2013: 8)

There are a number of points to be made here, but the most important is that the oppositional axis set up between these two types of approaches is contrived and forced. It is not clear what the difference is between dialogue and 'interanimation', nor between being folded into complex patterns and sharing a set of identifiable features or principles – except that the first turn of phrase, being 'folded', pulls in from Rancière a larger theoretical argument that exceeds this quotation,[7] and that the second (searching for identifiable features or principles) is a perfectly useful and valid procedure which is denigrated without evidence or illustration of fault. Furthermore, in this formulation, aesthetics can provide a cloak for an effete and sophisticated realm of sensibility next to which dialogue, debate and even conflict appear prosaic and so passé!

What does one find when one turns to the essays collected together by Edkins and Kear – do they manage to avoid 'examining "performances about" political events, histories, experiences, etc. on the one hand, and explaining political events in terms of the logic of performance on the other'? We will comment only on two contributions but could engage most of the essays in a similar fashion. Kear's own essay for the collection is a brilliant encounter and response to an exhibition of works by Chilean artist Alfredo Jaar, but in the process, he is both examining performances about discrete (political as well as aesthetic) events and making use of the logic of performance as an explanatory principle – the tension between representation and presentation, for example, or the conceit of 'staging' that marks the section heading, 'Logics of Staging'. Diana Taylor's essay looks at passionate protest in relation to Mexico's contested election of 2006. Analysing embodied engagement as political performance (as she has done throughout her career), Taylor is the consummate scholar who excels at 'elaborating the performance dynamics of politics'. She develops a striking notion of 'animatives' in opposition to performatives in which animatives evoke the individual passionate but 'messy' protests of individuals and performatives are, in the Austinian sense, expressions of codified legitimacy – in this case the Electoral Commission's declaration of the winner of the election. Yet Taylor herself critiques the exclusivity of her terms: 'Performatives and animatives only ever work together – nothing pronounced means much without the re-action of those addressed or invoked. The terms call attention to different political acts, uptakes and positionalities encompassed by the broader word, performance' (88). We submit that Taylor's work is precisely the kind of work we engage in our own volume – concrete political events and situations and the way that performance structures and complicates our understanding of them. (See Edleman and Lynch for related chapters on ceremonies of healing in our volume.)

Indeed, while it would be our contention that *The Grammar of Politics and Performance* overlaps in important matters of subject and perspective with *International Politics and Performance: Critical Aesthetics and Creative Practice*, we would also point to significant differences in what we find important in this project, and in particular in what goals we might be pursuing through this work. We do in fact aspire to interdisciplinary dialogue in search of common ground to form an ongoing partnership between politics and performance scholars that might strengthen the insights of each discipline. As might be expected, we resist those aspects of Rancière's thinking that emphasise only rupture and emancipated singularity, agreeing with Peter Hallward: 'Rancière's emphasis on division and interruption makes it difficult to account for qualities that are just as fundamental to any sustainable political sequence: organization, simplification, mobilization, decision, polarization, taking sides, and so forth' (2006: 126). On the other hand, we recognise the importance of Rancière's thought and his contribution to rethinking many areas of political and theatrical expression – several of the essays in our book make productive use of his ideas (see Haedicke, Nield, Finlayson and Edkins). What we contest strongly is to rule out a focus, in addition to dissensus, on building and sustaining movements, organisations, or even institutions that can aim for producing better governance and struggle for social justice. We believe that it still makes sense to analyse the performance dynamics of politics in parliaments, citizenship laws and practices, electoral contests and mainstream theatre *as well as and alongside of* attention to the aesthetics of protest or the affect of particular micropractices of resistance, or experimental art and theatre (see Mouffe 2007). While Rancière's (2004) consideration of the promise of art (the distribution of the sensible) as a mode of equality in the Kantian sense is helpful in reading current modes of politics, we also need to remind ourselves of other readings – of Bourdieu (1984) for whom art is framed in and reproduces the distinctions of social class and of Gorz in understanding the place of aesthetics in the production of subjectivity in this current time of neoliberal capitalism (2004). Further, as Rai has argued elsewhere, 'the insights developed by postcolonial theorists trying to understand not only the role that art played in the political movements of independence but also how the form that art takes is framed by the histories of colonial inequality, nationalist aspirations and collective imaginaries of freedom and modernity' are important in our political reading of aesthetics (Rai 2014: 3; Mitter 1995, 2007; Guha-Thakurta 1992; Sachs 1983). We therefore harbour a suspicion of too much emphasis on aesthetics because of the historical collusion between aesthetics and hierarchies of taste and judgment. We discuss aesthetic matters all the time – every time we describe style, dramaturgy, affect. However, we argue, 'Aesthetics' begins to re-establish an autonomous modality that we do not embrace – for political reasons. In this, we are closer to Bourdieu than to Kant, to Mouffe than to Rancière. In the next section we bring together these debates on politics, performance and aesthetics, on democracy and representation, on space and the publics and audiences, to suggest the grammar that takes shape when we bring these into one frame.

The grammar that emerges

Democracy works through the assertion and affirmation of claims to represent others. Such 'representative claims' (Saward 2010) require cultural performances deploying varied resources, not least ceremony and ritual (Rai 2010 and in this volume). Performing claims to represent is not a marginal curiosity or epiphenomenal aspect of a more fundamental idea of representation – rather, it creates and reinforces representation itself. Representation is not so much institutionalised as performed. In traditional social science research, when representation is analysed in the context of institutionalised political structures, or institutions embedded in social structures, the performance of both institutions and structures is often overlooked, taken for granted, undervalued. Overlooking the performative processes through which claims are made opens a gap in democratic theory that this volume begins to fill. We would suggest the 'claim to represent' is the first grammatical principle that we shall isolate and highlight.

The claim to represent is common to both performance and politics, especially in democracy. Performances claim to stand in for or enact reality – sometimes presenting it directly or in a condensed and framed version, but even then unable to shake off their relation to mimesis, which is of course the representation of reality that Plato considered a mere copy of a copy, giving theatre its originary bad name.[8] In traditional theatre pieces the presence of character, scene, plot and spectacle supports a 'making' that for Aristotle was the core dramatic creative work – world-making, we might say. Beyond such theatre pieces, performance frames a reality which it is not, and yet also is, in a double-time that Herbert Blau has captured so eloquently in his many books (e.g. *Take Up the Bodies: Theatre at the Vanishing Point*, 1982). The abiding tension between modes of performance that privilege representation or presentation is itself evidence of the imbrication of representation in all performance. Derrida is perhaps the most eloquent here.[9]

For politics scholars, representation is part and parcel of most struggles over appropriate governance. We become aware of representative politics only through the mode of performance through which individuals and institutions (actors) make claims to represent and affect their audience (represented). Some claims are factual – 'I am British' because 'I have a British passport'. Others are identitarian – 'Britishness' is a claim that encapsulates a particular understanding of identity politics, political history, a social positioning that is recognisably inscribed in the public imaginary and a relational matrix which might place 'the British' in contrast to 'the Other' (see Rai 2014). The claim to representation itself comprises a connective tissue of relations – between actors and politicians and those they represent, but also between actors in the 'limelight' and those who perceive their claims and accept or reject them – their audience. The different repertoires of performance that we have access to and their recognition/reception as legitimate are influenced by the broad social relations of class and gender, ethnicity and language – by the *habitus* that shapes our choices (Bourdieu 1991). Like the other elements of grammar described here, the representative claim interlocks political processes with theatrical ones at a corporeal level of processual dynamics. Jeffrey Alexander, for example, has outlined a cultural pragmatics of social performance that travels from ritual to performance and back again – from 'de-fusion' to 're-fusion' of performative elements that make for stories that are convincing and therefore powerful and fundamentally believable (2006: 32–7). A materialist understanding of political performance, however, focuses on the harnessing of material bodies, rituals and ceremonies, sounds and voices with great effort and labour to generate a political syntax that is both accepted and challenged by different audiences (Rai 2014). Thus, there is a growing awareness among politics scholars that the interactions between performance and its reception generate politics. All of the chapters collected here manifest this connection, although it is not the explicit focus of some.

A second element of the grammar of politics and performance manifests in regimes of appearance in relation to power, presence and visuality. Performance makes visible (although its doubleness also hides or covers over). This aspect of performance connects to political struggle around both heightened spectacle and clandestine acts, ceremony and ritual, and the role of public space as a staging ground for political legitimacy and contestation. A number of our chapters address this visual/spatial crux of power manipulation, especially Harding and Lynch who write in relation to their topics, respectively, about the power of deliberate lack of transparency and the impact of inadequate public space.

Third, identity in its relation to power and to belonging is dependent on performance to enact the roles that can be recognised and acclaimed as legitimate or illegitimate. While citizenship is a central category in several of our essays (Weber, Reinelt and Fitzpatrick for example), Parkinson looks at roles more generally in relation to everyday political processes, and Jestrovic urges us to see personal identity as a weapon against political despair when 'bare life' was replaced by performances of everyday life in Sarajevo under siege during the Bosnian War (1992–6). In a kind of counterpoint, Edkins draws our attention to 'missing persons' in order to argue that a missing person is an absent presence who cannot appear 'on stage' and that a progressive politics of personhood-as-such must resist the objectification of administration or governance that proceeds from 'naming, recognition, presence, visibility, identification, or exhumation'.

If these are the main areas around which our writing circulates, each essay in the volume features its own understanding of the grammar it is describing. The order of the essays attempts to place side by side authors whose ideas may stimulate additional associational thinking, but there is not any real need to read them in order, for they circle back on each other at many points of possible intersection. And although certain political thinkers appear often in this writing, in the final analysis, there is not one unified philosophy or 'school of thinking' dominating the volume, which we view as a positive indication of the possibilities of the overall enterprise. We begin the volume with an essay about the most practical and literal aspects of the imbrication of politics and performance. John Parkinson claims that performance is unavoidable in democracy, and organises his argument around three features: actors and the roles they play, the stages required for certain democratic acts and the scripts which govern political expression. This chapter provides a broad overview of the topic, and contextualises it in terms of prevailing theories of democracy and politics scholarship.

The next four chapters are concerned with the performance of citizenship. Janelle Reinelt begins with an analysis of the way issues of citizenship manifest in today's global world, and links theatrical performances to the task of imagining new relations between and among citizens. Following Etienne Balibar's call for new worksites of democracy, she proposes the theatre as one arena for building an appropriate and pluralistic republican citizenship. Cynthia Weber examines 'how citizenships and nationalisms [are] constructed, connected, and contested in the post-9/11 US'. The chapter describes two performances: the first is a Public Service Announcement (PSA) deployed by the American Ad Council to secure American solidarity and identity after 9/11; the second is Weber's own counter-performance deconstructing its 'diversity-patriotism' and which features and insists upon the legitimacy of citizens deliberately targeted or occluded in the PSA. Her documentary, *I am an American: Video Portraits of Unsafe US Citizens* interrupts and interferes with the 'performative grammars of citizenship and nationalism', manifesting as a form of citizenship protest, and certainly of talking back to power.

Lisa Fitzpatrick's account of a particular theatrical performance, *Laundry*, is presented as a provocation to Irish citizens to confront their complicity with Irish state violence against the 30,000 women who were incarcerated in the Magdalene Laundries. Reviewing the history of collusion between church and state in the characterisation of the female body and motherhood during the formation of the Irish Free State, Fitzpatrick claims that 'the characterization of "immoral" women as dangerous to the body politic' became normalised over time and persists to this day within Irish political discourse. Based on her own experience at the performance, the appeal of the theatrical piece to its audiences as citizens is foregrounded.

Finally (in this section) Silvija Jestrovic offers a moving account of the citizens of Sarajevo who performed everyday behaviours as political acts during the Bosnian War, 'creating a cultural public sphere, in conditions where the collective and individual *self* was [...] deprived of acting as an active political agent'. Jestrovic considers a range of practices, including cultural events, as unfolding 'a vernacular grammar' that resisted both the official languages of political conflict in the global media and the reduction to bare life that the situation under siege threatened. Agamben and Arendt offer her the means to highlight how the citizens of Sarajevo began to create a public sphere out of their personal subjectivities and everyday actions – 'a self-conscious framing of behavior for viewing by others'.

Jestrovic's essay leads directly to the next four chapters which foreground the public sphere and the staging space of political performances. All four draw on Rancière for key theoretical insights; two of the essays, by Susan Haedicke and Sophie Nield, address efforts to transform hegemonic forms of behaviour: Haedicke posits street arts as a site of dissensus where art creates a 'grammar of storytelling' that can counter 'abstract ideas about freedom, equality, and citizenship', constructing a frame for 'new perceptions and concepts'. Her chapter leads back to the chapters on citizenship as well as contributing to the analysis of public space as staging ground for resistance. Nield is concerned with explicit protest protocols, and what she describes as 'the dramaturgy of public order'. Nield argues that, while power manifests through symbolic and theatrical means, the politics of legibility has served to regulate protest by reducing and controlling its means of expression. Calling once again on Arendt (along with several other theorists such as Lefebvre and Žižek), Nield develops her own unique account of the Occupy movement's theatrical doubling as it performed private life in public space, a form of both practice and symbol: 'It translated itself into a representation of what it actually was'.

Alan Finlayson's chapter sits within the field of rhetorical theory, and concerns the audiences for political performances as 'the people' who need to reflect upon the performances and recognise themselves in 'plebiscitary' rhetoric in order to interpret and judge. He insists that the public staging of political claims affords 'the people' an opportunity to 'see itself and reflect upon who it is, has been and might become'. For Finlayson, speaker, topic and audience are not isolated elements but relational parts of a performance.

Jenny Edkins's contribution complements but also challenges these chapters in that she questions the value of visibility if it is confined within the policing action of governmentality. She writes about missing persons, 'You cannot tell that someone is missing by looking at them. A person is only ever missing in relation, when they are missed by someone else.' A missing person cannot take the stage, only the demand for the particular person to appear can be made visible. All attempts to represent the missing person are subject to reduction as objects of administration or governance.

The last four chapters are concerned with rituals and ceremonies of state and church. They span official events of parliaments, extraordinary bodies such as Truth and Reconciliation Commissions, attempts to heal the crisis of legitimacy of the Catholic Church's sexual abuse scandal and the grammar of state security and intelligence gathering. Beginning with Shirin Rai's overview of ceremony and ritual, the protocols of each and their relationship to performance is described and applied to a number of state occasions and processes. Rai makes a useful distinction between the hyper-visibility of ceremony and the normalised visibility of ritual that is sometimes overlooked because of its everyday performances. This observation plays back among the other essays, contextualizing, for example, Jestrovic's chapter on Sarajevans' 'vernacular grammar' or Finlayson's discussion of what kind of rhetoric benefits 'the people' in exercising their judgements about political speech. It also sets ups some frames for the following chapters.

Gabielle Lynch writes about Kenya's Truth, Justice and Reconciliation Commission and the reasons why it has not been perceived as successful as, for example, South Africa's TRC. Key to her chapter is the role of audience – if it is missing, if it is uninvolved with the proceedings, it is difficult to create the relational conditions for transformation essential to their success. Her analysis of the Kenya ceremonies is that, using Rai's dichotomy, they slipped too often into ritual. The necessary national drama that would command widespread audiences to identify with the testimony was missing – the spaces were not symbolic of the whole body politic, the media coverage was spotty and non-existent in too many cases, and the audience present in the spaces of the proceedings was often lacking in both official presence and ordinary people's attention.

Joshua Edelman's analysis of the Catholic Church's response to the sexual abuse scandal in Ireland uses the vocabulary of ritual throughout, but contains an interesting distinction between the ceremonial efforts of the church hierarchy and rituals designed to embrace the vernacular of everyday Roman Catholic observances and the victims and families of the wider church. Edelman's chapter also contextualises its discussion within Habermas's work on political legitimation, and is especially interested in the agon between religious and political authority. He cites the way the state and church have been joined in the history of the Irish Republic (which can remind readers of Fitzpatrick's discussion), and questions the efficacy of secular and religious modes of reasoning to accomplish tasks of solidarity, healing and reconciliation across a schism of church and state.

The final chapter applies these concerns of state power and ritual to state security and the intelligence community. James Harding begins with the assertion that 'lying is as transactional as it is performative', and is the bedrock of state security and intelligence agency practices. Following a theoretical analysis of the definitive traits of lying and its imbrication with performance, he critiques a grammar of state security and intelligence gathering that turns on the justification of lying to 'those who have no right to know'. He presents a case study of the historical figure Colonel Alfred Redl, an Austrian double agent at the turn of the twentieth century. When he committed suicide in 1913, it turned out he was also a closeted homosexual. Harding looks at his after-life as a negative exemplar presented to the 1950 hearings on the security risks of homosexuals in government in the US, an offshoot of Macarthyism, and also at the theatrical representation of his life in John Osborne's play, *A Patriot for Me* (1966).

In the last chapter of the book, Mike Saward provides a commentary on the rest of the chapters taken as a whole, organised around a distinction between what he calls sovereign and critical grammars. Written from the perspective of a politics scholar and theorist of democracy who has also been attentive to performance studies and has incorporated performance research in his own work, Saward closes the collection on a note of sustained integrative thinking about our disciplines and our shared concerns.

This book is an attempt to engage in interdisciplinary dialogue that goes beyond the polite acknowledgement of academic efforts to think beyond our disciplinary paradigms. The essays show a wide array of connections between and among vocabularies, concepts and methods of approaching our topic. Hopefully the stimulus of this work will provoke further investigation of distinguishing features of performative politics, and will lead to sustained engagement across academic divides, producing new articulations of the grammars of politics and performance.

Notes

1 From a letter to Christian Florens Rang, 9 Dec. 1923, quoted in Susan Sontag's introduction to *One-Way Street and Other Writings* (1997), 18.
2 *The Human Condition* (1998), 198.
3 We use 'performance' to designate any single and complete act, event, or behaviour as it is contextualised by its relationships. Performances are reflexive actions, events, or behaviours that are relational and self-conscious (Schechner 2013). 'Performativity' is

18 *Janelle Reinelt and Shirin M. Rai*

treated as a philosophical term, following Austin, Derrida and Butler, used to designate the 'reiterative power of discourse to produce the phenomena that it regulates and constrains' (Butler 1993: p. xii). Sometimes, it is used as an adjective to indicate a holistic dimension of the noun it modifies; e.g. 'performative analysis' means an analysis involving a performance studies lens carrying aspects of both performance and its power to produce effects.

4 Gender, race, sexuality – all the issues of identity politics – played out in Shakespeare criticism, and there were also conservative critics who thought this was a great mistake. For instance, see Bloom (1996).
5 For some interesting performance studies work that addresses the subject of pigs, see Rae (2011), Edkins and Kear (2013: 4–7) and Parker-Starbuck (2008).
6 And indeed, a note in their manuscript just following this quotation mentions our volume along with one other as an explicit example. See Edkins and Kear (2013: 14).
7 See above for the full development of Edkins and Kear's point of view here, based on Rancière (2004, 2010) and also elaborated in Chapter 2.
8 Plato's theory of mimesis and objections to theatre can be found in the *Republic*, books 2, 3 and 10 (1989). For a recent contemporary discussion of mimesis which moves from Plato and Aristotle to theories of 'memetics' in evolutionary biology and genetics, see representation/presentation binary in performance, see Potolsky (2006).
9 Derrida (1978: 292–316) wrote of the impossibility of 'pure theatre' in Artaud's sense – the impossibility of avoiding repetition, and therefore representation in theatre's doubling apparatus.

2 Performing democracy
Roles, stages, scripts

John Parkinson

Introduction

Metaphors of the stage are commonplace when it comes to democracy. We talk of political 'actors' and 'audiences', 'backstage' politics and potential leaders 'waiting in the wings'. But with few exceptions, democracy scholars treat such talk as mere metaphor. They do not think that democracy really *is* a performance, with all the dramatic norms and paraphernalia that go with that. Indeed, in an era in which highly rationalist models of democracy dominate, many scholars would recoil from a dramatic account, linking performance and drama with insincerity, strategising, manipulation and 'spin'.

This chapter argues that while a performative account of democracy comes with some normative dangers, it nonetheless illuminates important issues that current democratic theory is blind to. In particular, it draws attention to three features: the distinction between democratic actors and the roles that they play; the idea that certain democratic acts require particular kinds of staging; and the degree to which democratic performance is scripted. These points help us make sense of some institutions and practices in democratic societies that current orthodoxy finds difficult to accommodate.

The discussion begins with a brief history of performative accounts of politics before setting out a number of roles that must be played in any democratic society. Real democracies assign actors to those roles in all sorts of different ways, with some actors taking multiple roles, others just one. This variety does not necessarily undermine the democratic quality of the institutions in question, a point that helps us make some illuminating comparative evaluations of the democratic arrangements we find in the real world, and a point that challenges elements of standard deliberative democratic theory. The discussion then turns to questions of democratic stages, where I argue that the performance of some democratic roles has quite specific staging requirements, something that challenges the view that democracy can shift online without suffering significant loss. The penultimate section concerns democratic scripts, and reveals both strengths and weaknesses that come with particular approaches to ritualising politics.

The resulting account has much in common with work that calls for more inductive democratic theory, theory that attends to democracy as it is actually *performed*, rather than as it is ideally conceptualised.[1] The aim, therefore, is not to promote a new model of democracy; it is to take the idea of performance seriously, and use its elements to highlight issues in the comparative study of democratic institutions that otherwise go unremarked on in mainstream democratic theory.

Performative approaches in politics

Thinking of politics in performative terms has a long history. In ancient Greece, politics and drama were commonly seen as equivalent enterprises, both requiring the same rhetorical skills to move an audience (Hindson and Gray 1988: 31). When the *ecclesia*, the assembly of all Athenian citizens, moved from the Pnyx to the Theatre of Dionysus in the fourth century BC, the equivalence was made even clearer. This view persisted well into the early-modern period. Public figures were often 'dramatists, courtiers, scholars and politicians' rolled into one, while monarchs commissioned public spectacles to dramatise and legitimate their rule (Walker 1998: 1; see also Backscheider 1993; Barker 2001). One finds echoes of this view in Edmund Burke, who draws repeated attention to the idea that parliament is a great, dignified 'theatrical exhibition hall for dramatic talents' (Hindson and Gray 1988: 28), full of actors acting out a grand play.

By contrast, drama is now a problematic label at a time when democratic theory is concerned with rationality and communicative competence. Drama carries with it an implication of insincerity – the suspicion is that one is putting on a show in order to manipulate, not to communicate honestly (Harrington and Mitchell 1999: 1). Thus drama is viewed with the same suspicion that some deliberative theorists like Chambers (1996) and Spragens (1990) have viewed rhetoric. However, not all view rhetoric with suspicion. Dryzek, for example, adapts a distinction between 'bridging' and 'bonding' from the social capital literature to argue that certain kinds of rhetoric have essential roles in forming linkages between differently situated people (2010). At a more micro-level, O'Neill argues that rhetoric is an essential part of interpersonal communication, and overcomes the normative worry by arguing that people in real deliberations are perfectly capable of making rational judgements about rhetorical claims (1998). To think otherwise is to worry, along with religious literalists, about the 'lies' told in the theatre, as if audiences were not sophisticated enough to distinguish between fictional stories and the 'truths' they convey.

While some branches of political scholarship have abandoned serious comparison between drama and politics, others have not. Most obviously, there is a strong tradition of precisely this kind of analysis in political communication, particularly the work of Edelman (1988, 1995); and the study of new social movements, especially Tilly (2004, 2008). Scholars in other fields have also highlighted the linkages. Whitehead stands out for his use of features of drama – conflict, leadership, persuasion, narrative tension and resolution, dramatic time, motives, character development and public/private personas – as an analytic framework for understanding democratic transitions (Whitehead 1999). In policy studies, there is a rich thread of scholarship that has analysed the policy process as a battle between competing narratives, with good guys and bad guys, tragedy and comedy, and the selection of salient facts to bolster or undermine particular storylines.[2] Among these, Hajer argues that policy stories are not merely narrated but performed, staged and dramatised, because this is what political communication in a 'mediatised' age demands (Hajer 2009). The modern media does not merely transmit words; it transmits still and moving pictures, taken by journalists and passers-by, on television cameras and mobile phones or captured on security cameras and shared on newspaper websites and YouTube alike. In that environment, intentional communication becomes highly performative, and Hajer spends much time showing the degree to which political images are the intended or unintended results of a scripted performance, in which issues of staging, lighting, audience access, symbolism and interaction between actors are all important.

It is important to stress that for the majority of these writers, narrative structures and dramaturgy are not mere heuristic devices to explain political processes; it is how politics really proceeds (Street 2001: 36). They argue that political actors make sense of the world in dramatic terms because it is the tool that allows them to attempt 'to create order and structure in potentially unstable situations' (Hajer 2009: 54); without this tool, complexity would overwhelm us – we would literally not know where to start. This is therefore more than an empirical point about how people in the real world communicate; it is a theoretical point about the conditions of democratic communication.

However, while performance is not optional, the choice of performative style is, and here Young (2001), Sanders (1997) and others are surely right to highlight the degree to which certain sites and styles of performance tend to be privileged over others in political contests: the conference room over the bar room, and the committee room over the creche, for example. To enter into political debate, therefore, is to participate in a clash of which issues to narrate, a clash of performative styles, a clash of attempts to cast people as villains and heroes, a clash of what facts and values count as salient to the story, and to challenge attempts to close political contests with some variant of 'and they lived happily ever after'; or perhaps, following Stone's analysis of policy stories (2002: 138), 'and they would have lived happily ever after had it not been for the interference of X' – insert the appropriate bogey-man.

Democratic roles, actors and audiences

What, then, are the roles that need performing in democracy? Drawing on my own model of democratic institutions, which emphasises functional role separation, and the emerging field of 'deliberative systems' theory,[3] we can distinguish the following:

- articulating interests, opinions and experiences;
- making public claims

- defining collective problems or defending existing arrangements
- requesting action or inaction on collective problems
- expressing, setting and defending norms, and
- making claims on public resources;

• deciding what to do, or what not to do, to address public claims,
    - including weighing up options;
• scrutinising and giving account for public action and inaction.

I distinguish between general articulation of interests, opinions and experiences on the one hand, and making specific public claims on the other, because the former does not automatically imply the latter, yet is an important resource for the latter. As Kingdon (1984) points out, there are many issues and conditions that attract our attention, but not every one of them comes with a demand for collective action in response. In his terms, this is what separates a 'condition' (that there are rich and poor, for example) from a 'problem' (that we ought to do something about the differences in income, or opportunities, say, between rich and poor). It might be objected that therefore mere 'articulation' should be left out of a list of democratic roles – it is, at least on a classic liberal account, pre-political. I do not need to rehearse here the long tradition of criticism of the classic liberal account – Cohen (1996) provides an excellent overview – but just want to highlight the case for taking the realm of everyday discourse seriously because it gives public claim-making its foundation in lived experience (e.g. Fraser 1992; Mansbridge 1999). That is in addition to its value in encouraging people to talk about conditions that they might want to raise to the status of 'problem'.

Given the political equality criterion of democracy, these are roles that all members of the demos should be able to play to some degree. However, in a large-scale society, there is necessarily a division of labour, and thus some role specialisation. This may not simply be a matter of rationality and efficiency but necessary for achieving what in Britain is now called 'joined-up' decision-making, ensuring that issues are considered in the round, relative to other public claims, rather than piecemeal (cf. Kateb 1981). Given that some specialisation is necessary, we can add the following roles, some of which will be more often than not performed by representatives, whether elected, selected or self-appointed (Saward 2010), some of which will be undertaken by everyone. Those representative roles are:

• re-presenting experiences, opinions and interests to other representatives;
• making, checking, accepting and challenging claims to represent (Saward 2006);
• leading
    - proposing ends and means, norms and standards;
• communicating decisions and reasons to other members of society;
• making claims to public office and non-official leadership roles, and deciding between competing claimants.

The first supplementary role includes making actors in the formal public sphere aware of the narratives and claims circulating in the informal public sphere, and vice versa. This is particularly a role for attentive publics, Schudson's (1999) 'monitorial citizens', journalists, bloggers and advocacy groups, but also artists (dramatists, even), competing political parties (one of whose roles is to look for chinks in their opponents' argumentative armour), even the formal scrutiny role of bodies like the Audit Office or the Committee on Standards in Public Life in the UK. This in turn leads to a distinction between the full-time role of the managers of such organisations, and the part-time role of other individuals who may devote a great deal of time and resources to supporting a cause on a regular basis, or who may take only an occasional interest, responding with time and money, voice or vote when an issue that concerns them closely is brought to their attention.

There are, of course, many other things that governments and states do, such as enforcing law and providing other public goods. But these are things that governments of all stripes do; they do not emerge from the requirements of democracy per se. I also do not mean to imply that representation roles automatically map onto a centralised, hierarchical form of state organisation. Formal public spheres exist at fairly local levels too, in the shape of parish, town and district councils, for example. Equally, deliberative systems can form around a particular issue in a particular place, with ad hoc institutions set up to deal with it (Parkinson 2006: 177). It is a mistake to equate the formal public sphere with central legislatures alone.

It is important to separate democratic roles from the actors who perform them. For one, single actors can play multiple roles: this is commonly the case with elected representatives who not only have private and public roles to keep separate, but who also can have multiple public roles as party members, constituency representatives, government members and so on. This helps make sense of the sources and nature of the competing demands on elected representatives, something that traditional principal-agent models struggle to account for (Mansbridge 2003; Rehfeld 2009). For another, consider the important democratic role of scrutinising the legislative programme of governments. In many countries, this scrutiny role is played primarily by an upper house; in others, it is played by subcommittees of the legislature; in yet others, it is played by courts, or legislative analysts' offices (as in some US states), or academics, or quangos, or any number of other appointed and self-appointed watchdogs. Now, effective scrutiny requires independence from those people whose actions are being scrutinised, which tends to mean independent resources and tenure – one's ability to scrutinise the powerful is seriously compromised if one owes one's job to those same powerful individuals. In the United States, this is a reason why the members of the Supreme Court are appointed for life – no President can remove judges whose decisions he or she does not like. In the United Kingdom, the House of Lords performs a similar role: life tenure frees up members to scrutinise the government's programme, regardless of who actually secured them their ermine robes. While hardly a complete justification for the present House of Lords, this provides at least *some* logic to what would otherwise be a puzzling feature of British democracy: the unelected nature of the upper house. It is most puzzling when seen in isolation and when seen from the point of view of deductive democratic theory; when considered from the perspective of roles in a democratic system, it makes a great deal more sense, although is certainly not beyond improving.[4] The point is that while roles and actors have many linkages – it would not do to have too young an actor playing the 'four score and upward' King Lear, and it would not do to have a government crony playing the role of Chief Justice – there is still a great deal of room for creativity and local tradition in assigning democratic roles to individuals and institutions. Therefore, I do not propose to provide a detailed cast list to match the dramatis personae above: the precise actors assigned those roles will vary from context to context, with some actors performing a single role, others playing several.

The final point to make about democratic roles concerns the audience. It is a commonplace observation in dramatic theory that no theatrical 'event' can exist without the audience; it is always aimed at communicating with or involving someone, and those others co-create the event not just through their reactions but their mere presence (Sauter 2000). Likewise, democratic performance, especially claim-making, is always directed at an audience, persuading others to think something or do something. However, modern democratic theory and practice does not distinguish well between performers and audience. For example, in what Elstub (2010) calls first and second generation models of deliberative democracy, oriented around the ideal speech situation, participants are alternatively speakers and listeners, all engaged together in the attempt to achieve mutual understanding. Move beyond even fairly small numbers of participants, however, and some role specialisation emerges, with the majority taking a supporting role, or a seat in the stalls, while the few occupy centre stage. When that happens, communication can become less about achieving mutual understanding with one's interlocutors, more about persuading the audience, depending on where the decision-making power lies. For example, no one, I imagine, would expect a debate between a group of presidential candidates to result in one of the leaders being persuaded by something another said, stroking his chin thoughtfully and responding, 'There is something in what you say, I shall have to reconsider my position.' Rather, the aim of such events is to convince the audience that one's ideas are right (logos), to engage their emotions on your side (pathos) and to convince them of your good character (ethos – to use Aristotle's categories of rhetorical proof), at the expense, rather than to the mutual benefit, of one's opponents. Furthermore, the primary audience may not even be in the same room. This was clearly the case with a deliberative poll in Australia: some of the expert witnesses and some of the small-group spokespeople in the televised plenary question-and-answer sessions realised that their primary audience was not their fellow panellists or randomly selected participants in the chamber, but the television audience. Some, therefore, and completely rationally, chose to play to that gallery rather than engage in micro-deliberative reasoning together (Gibson and Miskin 2002). The point to emphasise here is that in large-scale democracy, even though the audience might not be physically present at all, and even though the performance might be conveyed to them by virtual means, their virtual presence nonetheless affects what kind of performance is undertaken, and the imperative of reaching them determines the choice of stage: it must be highly visible, or made so by attracting media attention.

Democratic staging

The physical settings of democratic performance have been given very little attention by mainstream political scientists and theorists. Those who discuss 'democratic architecture' tend to mean the institutional arrangements, not bricks and mortar (e.g. Reynolds 2002); those who look at public space mean it metaphorically, not literally (e.g. Hénaff and Strong 2001; Reynolds 2002; Nagel 1995). A performative account of democracy, however, helps reveal some reasons why it is a mistake to ignore the physical settings of democracy.

Maarten Hajer argues that it is meaningless to seek a general account of links between political acts and their appropriate scenes, drawing on Kenneth Burke's idea of the 'scene-act ratio' (Burke 1969; Hajer 2005, 2009). He argues instead that it is only worthwhile looking at how particular ratios are constructed in particular cases. Of course, the scene-act ratio involves more than just scene and act – there is also actor, audience, script, time, author and so on – and I agree with Hajer that what links these elements is highly variable and interdependent; but high variability does not mean that there are *no* limits within which the variation takes place. We can therefore theorise what those limits might be, and this section offers some thoughts on the settings appropriate to particular democratic roles.

The first democratic role is narrating political issues, in which citizens form not only their own views but also distribute opinion and storylines through the system as a whole. When it comes to the performance of this role, the staging possibilities are very wide indeed. At the informal end of the deliberative system, it happens in homes, pubs, clubs, at work, in the street, wherever people interact. At the formal end, it happens when witnesses are called to give evidence to parliamentary committees, or when representatives narrate stories about the impact of policy on those they represent. It happens virtually too, in magazine and newspaper stories, in documentaries, in blogs and other online forums; but it happens in physical settings too. Indeed, one of the ways that we might be able to tell whether we have a healthy democracy is the degree to which the narratives that are told at street level are conveyed, represented, in formal decision-making moments, so that decision-makers know how it feels to be on the receiving end of the decisions they make.

An important point arises here. Private political narrative is more than casual interaction, something that is indicated by the frequently encountered taboos in many cultures about discussing certain topics with strangers. In Britain, for example, there is a strong taboo against talking about money, sex and politics even with fairly close friends. During a research visit to Chile, I found that people approach political topics extremely warily, partly because of their recent history of deadly political conflict but also because of a more general reticence to talk about potentially conflict-generating topics too quickly, before one has had a chance to establish some grounds of trust and friendship with that person. I suspect this is universal: a great deal of, and in some cultures most, private talk is about establishing and maintaining social relationships, not sorting out the problems of the world. This is related to the points that Sunstein (2002: 176) makes about group polarisation, an effect in part of 'people's desire to maintain their reputation and their self-perception', which reinforces the tendency of people to socialise and deliberate with the like-minded rather than those with differing experiences, in isolated 'deliberative enclaves' rather than as fellow members of a single demos. This has both positive and negative consequences: positive for subaltern groups whose experiences might easily be swamped in the wider public sphere by the stories of the majority, negative in terms of encouraging extreme views to develop without the moderating influence of engagement with alternative points of view.

When we expect narration to happen across the boundaries of experience and enclave, or when we expect conflict to arise, we tend to move narration to particular designated settings where conflict can be encouraged yet contained, to place it in a more formal setting, with formal rules of engagement to civilise conflict, perhaps controlled by a mediator or chairperson. This can be fairly hierarchical and formal, as with committees that operate in conjunction with setting norms of having a dignified, sometimes raised, place for the chairperson; or fairly egalitarian, with participants sitting in a circle but still using a moderator to encourage norms of respect.

All this is to show that the limits of the scene-act ratio when it comes to the narration of experience depend on whether the experience being narrated involves conflict with others present at the same time, which in turn depends on local norms about what constitutes acceptable and unacceptable topics of normal, unmediated interaction. When it is 'safe' topics with friends or strangers – the weather, say – the range of possible stages is extremely broad; when it is 'unsafe' topics with friends, the range is narrower, more private, because of the risk of causing conflict with others nearby; when it is unsafe topics with strangers present, it is narrower still, moved to committee rooms or other neutral territory like library rooms, or ritualised in the form of demonstrations or public hearings. These points present a challenge to the too-quick equation of publicness with open, unrestricted encounters between strangers that is found in sections of the urban theory literature (e.g. Lofland 1998; Madanipour 2003; Sennett 2002). I have argued that as an empirical matter the narration role, for one, does not work that way. Sunstein provides a further argument that enclaves can be normatively valuable from the perspective of subaltern groups, helping them create spaces in which they can narrate their experiences and interests without being swamped by the experiences of dominant groups.

Incidentally, note how different this is from narrating experience in virtual settings. On the radio or online, people do not worry so much about offending each other because they are not physically present: they cannot pick up on body language, cannot be physically attacked, often cannot even be personally identified because of the use of online identities, and thus can get away with casting the other as a one-dimensional opinion-carrier rather than a flesh-and-blood person with feelings, goals and interests. This is one reason why I think that physical public space is a necessity in democracy, and that a purely online, virtual democracy is an unrealistic vision – physical presence helps activates the ethical dimension of democratic, public interaction. The other reasons are (1) to do with the fact that the visual media, both traditional and 'new', rely on images of physical events; mere 'talking heads' are not sufficient to communicate the impact of an event; (2) that the rhetorical presentation of a representative's ethos requires physical cues and staging; and (3) that physical performance has an 'impressive' effect, giving citizens cues as to how seriously to take a set of claims (Parkinson 2012).

The second democratic role, making public claims, has much in common with narration, and thus shares elements of its scene-act ratio. Indeed, it is important not to think that the roles require *separate* stages: clearly, a particular setting can and often does involve all the roles, with people narrating experience, perhaps on the basis of claims that that experience is representative of some wider group, in order to back up claims for action on one's own behalf as well as on behalf of others. Still, the specific act of making public claims requires that the rest of the public is paying attention somehow, and that in turn implies another set of restrictions on the range of possible settings. Thus scene-act ratios are neither identical for different democratic roles, nor entirely separate, but have areas of overlap.

We can think about the settings for making public claims in direct and indirect ways. In small-scale groups where all the members of the relevant demos can physically gather together in one place, public claims can be made directly in front of the assembled masses, as in the Athenian *ecclesia* or the Swiss *Landsgemeinden* (Reinisch and Parkinson 2007). In large-scale societies, the demos simply will not fit into the agora anymore, so claim-makers either require mediated ways of making the whole public aware of their claims, in cases where the whole public still is the final decision-making authority (as in referendums, say), or require ways of making representatives aware, in cases where decision-making power lies with a representative body of some sort. These requirements overlap: in a democracy, part of what makes a decision-maker take notice of a claim is to convince them that the wider public has noticed and takes it seriously too.

The stages for such activity are not unlimited. In any of these cases, simply 'talking among yourselves' in out-of-the-way places will not do – getting noticed and taken seriously is what matters, which means that claims need to be made in publicly visible and accessible places. Most obviously, groups can organise demonstrations at sites of power or sites of symbolic importance, perhaps adding a march from one site to another. The more people who turn out, the bigger the impact, recalling the importance of numbers as a short-cut to calculating the significance of a point of view. It is relatively easy for decision-makers to dismiss letters to the editor as the rantings of a few cranks, much harder to dismiss millions demonstrating in the streets. It could involve spaces that the media regularly monitor anyway, because they are spaces where the powerful and decision-makers gather: legislatures, courts, meeting venues for the G-8 or the World Economic Forum. It could involve stunts designed to attract the television cameras – remembering that news is about the unusual, the extraordinary, not the commonplace – such as environmentalists scaling smokestacks, or disability activists chaining themselves to inaccessible buses, although the 'taken seriously' requirement sometimes means that movements face difficult choices about when to behave soberly and engage with the powerful, and when to throw the toys out of the cot. For some, a reasonably successful strategy is to split themselves into collaborative and insurgent wings, one wearing suits and sober miens, the other causing the stir that gets the suits invited round the table (Barnes and Oliver 1995; Dryzek et al. 2003). But for all these approaches, visibility is paramount. This can present particular challenges in some cities. In Minneapolis, with its raised network of 'skyways' connecting downtown buildings, it is hard for public demonstrators to attract the notice of fellow citizens walking one or two levels above street level; in Bangkok the situation is often reversed, with marchers having to use elevated roads, passing fairly harmlessly over the heads of their fellow citizens below (Byers 1998; Dovey 2001). There are places where access to symbolic sites is strictly limited or controlled, as in London where the already-limited space for protest is being even more constricted by security barriers, permit systems and heavy policing.

It is instructive to consider the 2011 uprisings in the Middle East in light of these thoughts. Because of the undeniably important roles that online and mobile tools performed in gathering and organising demonstrators, media commentators and activists dubbed these the 'Twitter' and 'Facebook Revolutions' (Zuckerman 2011). But what is noteworthy is that, while social media performed many functions, one of their most important was to gather and coordinate people *in physical space* – Tahrir Square, Pearl Roundabout, the streets of central Tunis, Benghazi and so on. Those regimes that fought focused first of all on recapturing those stages, attempting to shut down dissenting performances and thus remove the very thing that the cameras feed on. Therefore these were Facebook revolutions only in part; at their core, they were remarkably familiar rebellions, with people confronting each other and contesting the right to occupy and make their claims on very specific stages.

When it comes to the decision-making role in large-scale democracy, I tend to the view that binding collective decisions are best made by elected representatives in legislatures or councils, or directly by referendum. In the case of elected representatives this is because their hold on office is dependent on the pleasure of their constituents; other kinds of representative, like the self-appointed or randomly selected, cannot be held accountable for their actions so easily, and so should not hold the power to make decisions that are binding on the rest of us. In the case of referendums, it is because of the clear act of consent to a specific proposal that such mechanisms entail (Parkinson 2006). Here too the setting range is narrower again. We need not get quite so carried away as Burke who thought that parliament should be 'imposing and majestic. It should overwhelm the imagination of the populace, and awe them into acquiescence. The arena should be the architectural summit of human achievement, vast, impressive and sublime' (Hindson and Gray 1988: 31).

Just being a regular meeting place – the main town square in the case of the Swiss *Landsgemeinden* cantons – imbues a site with meaning and dignity beyond the everyday (Parkinson 2009; Rapaport 1982). This is important for two reasons. The first is that the staging signals to people that the event matters, that the decisions reached there have an impact on thousands, even millions of people. The rituals of seriousness cue us in to taking the proceedings seriously, although that could also be a good reason for ditching some of the regalia worn in the UK parliament, simply because they no longer signify serious and dignified to most onlookers, but outdated, out of touch and doddery.

The same applies to voting: I think it is useful that one has to go physically to another public building – a school, or a church, a village hall or council office – and go through the physical performance of an act of voting, because it helps reinforce the importance of the action. Voting for one's leaders or a ballot proposition has much more impact on the lives of one's fellow citizens than voting on the latest C-list celebrity game show or shopping online, and it is important to mark that difference by an appropriate performance, such as having to turn out to a polling booth, or come to the town square on *Landsgemeinde* day. The action and the setting impresses people with a toned-down, ideally more egalitarian, but still somewhat Burkean sense of significance, and should not, in my view, be replaced by the option of clicking a mouse or pushing the red button. Making voting easier in these ways might, I suspect, have the unintended consequence of making it seem less significant, and in this respect the rituals of the formal public sphere have some value.

The other reason is hinted at by something else Burke says: that being a member of a legislature means that one is 'on a conspicuous stage, and the world marks our demeanour' (Hindson and Gray 1988: 21). When considering the fourth, scrutiny role of democracy, is it is a significant advantage to have a single, readily identifiable and prominent stage on which the powerful must perform. It puts the powerful under the 'spotlight' and keeps them there. This, I suspect, is one reason why people find the existence of 'off-stage' political actors so troubling. It is not just that these people are unelected yet still influential, not just that they are hard to hold accountable for their actions, but that they cannot be clearly seen on the stage, that they cannot be located in a physical sense and thus have the light of publicity shone on their words and actions.

Democratic scripts

I have already argued that democratic performance has much to do with the presentation and conflict of narratives. The final substantive point to explore is the idea that these narratives are to a large extent formalised, standardised, scripted. These scripts both help and hinder audiences in their understanding of democratic politics. On the positive side, they help an audience understand what kind of drama is being enacted, and thus not only give clues about how the story is likely to play out, but also what their role is likely to be, what the access points are. This can *aid* participation – as an immigrant, for example, I know well that it is when one is unfamiliar with the scripts of public life that one is most hesitant about stepping in and playing a part. When those scripts are constantly changing, access becomes hard even for insiders. On the negative side, however, scripting makes it easier for public life to become habitual, and to draw on symbolism that, for the most part, is not reflected on. Thus democratic scripts can overwhelm substantive argument and critical engagement, encouraging performance and participation that is merely formal, disguising the real location of power and decision-making.

Those few scholars who have looked into matters of democratic scripting have tended to focus on the rituals of the formal public sphere – the obviously ritualistic, such as the opening of parliament, and slightly less so, such as Prime Minister's Question Time, as well as the rest of the arcane mysteries of parliamentary procedure. Even those polities that stage binding collective decision-making in much less grandiose style, such as the *Landsgemeinden*, nonetheless surround them with dignifying rituals that have remained largely unchanged for hundreds of years.

However, even the informal public sphere has its scripts, scripts which help make any given performance understandable to a particular audience (Wilentz 1985), and one of the clearest examples of this is the scripting of public protest. The script usually has stage directions: because one of the purposes of protest is to cloak claims in the symbols of authority, protest sites are often full of the symbols of nation and authority: Mexico City's Zócalo (Plaza de la Constitución), for example, or Washington's National Mall, London's Parliament Square, or Plaza de Mayo in Buenos Aires: standing in any of these spaces, one is surrounded by the facades of presidential palaces and town halls; there are national flags flying from gigantic central flagpoles or from the roofs and balconies of the surrounding buildings, bowsprits of the ships of national enterprise. These spaces help people cloak themselves and their claims with the same symbols and dignity that the powerful do when claiming the symbols and status of high office.

Often we find that protest takes scripted routes. In Athens, there are two: one heads down Stadiou Avenue to Syntagma Square then and back up Panepistimou (University); the second starts on Alexandras Avenue then proceeds down Patissiou to Omonia Square. The scripts specify many other familiar elements: banners and effigies, costumes and masks, chants and songs, marshals with loudhailers, platforms, public address systems and speech-making. In some places there is ritual combat, with police and black-clad youths deploying their usual props: riot shields, batons, tear gas and water cannon versus cobblestones, boots, slogans and the odd molotov cocktail.

All this ritualisation has clearly positive effects and negative ones. On the positive side, protestors dignify their claims by linking them visually with the symbols of the state and nation, or reinforcing more particular partisan identities. Regularity also has benefits when it comes to people joining in. Organisers do not need to give Mexicans detailed explanations of where exactly to gather – one just knows that big marches start at the roundabout of El Ángel on La Reforma and heads to the Zócalo. However, therein too lies one of the problems, and it is a big one. Because of the ritualisation, it is easy to pay no attention to the actual claims being made – 'There go the communists again', rather than 'Oh, a protest about wages' – or to greet the umpteenth protest march down La Reforma this month with a shrug, or not even have it register because one sees the same sight every other day of the week. Likewise, there is a clear problem in that the dominant mode of policing protests, based on risk assessment, tends to classify all public claim-makers as potential petrol bombers, with sometimes-devastating consequences for the vast majority of peaceful protestors and innocent bystanders alike. This is despite the overall reduction in the violence of police–protestor interactions since the 1960s (della Porta and Reiter 1998; Soule and Davenport 2009).

In response, many protest organisers try to turn to new sites or new methods. However, some organisers positively encourage a degree of ritualisation. One example is Hong Kong. The territory's citizens have long been seen as politically apathetic, and yet since 1989 Hong Kongers have regularly commemorated the Tiananmen Square massacre on 4 June, while 1 July marches began in 1997 with the return of Hong Kong to PRC control, and have a different theme every year. The march that really put 1 July on the calendar, as it were, was the 2003 event which attracted an estimated half-million people protesting the 'anti-sedition' Article 23 of the Hong Kong Basic Law. To almost everyone's surprise, the protest was successful in forcing the abrogation of the law, and since then the old 'apathetic Hong Kong' cliché has been harder to sustain (Cheng 2005, see also Lam 2004). But the important point here is that while the protests have become ritualised in the sense that they happen in the same places on the same days every year, they are not *daily* occurrences, and thus do not become part of the landscape. On the contrary, they become more like a public festival, things that happen just a few times a year, things that are looked forward to, that are written into journalists' diaries and thus generate column-inches in the press and blogosphere for weeks before and afterwards. They are regular, ritual reminders to liberal Hong Kongers of the dangers of an overwhelming state. Their very regularity keeps them in the news and in people's hearts and minds, but they are not so frequent as to become ignored.

Conclusions

This chapter began with the view that drama is not as antithetical to democracy, including deliberative democracy, as it is often portrayed. On the contrary, it is an essential part of democratic communication. Because political experiences and claims are communicated in narrative form, to deny narrative a normative place in democratic theory is to deny the demos its voice. Because the demos is made up of embodied beings who take up space, democratic role playing is itself a physical act. Because the media, new and old, rely to a large extent on pictures of these physical events for copy, communication relies on the physical performance of democratic roles.

I have chosen to focus on three aspects of democratic performance: the roles that democracy requires be played as distinct from the actors that play them; the stages they use; and the scripts they follow. The role/actor distinction is crucial, because it helps makes sense of features of democracy that other approaches struggle to account for, and I noted three examples. First, it helps make sense of the sources and nature of the competing demands on elected representatives in a way that standard analyses of representation cannot. Second, it helps make sense of some institutional oddities because it focuses on the particular roles that institutions and actors within them play in a given democratic system, rather than expecting each and every institution to meet all the democratic desiderata at once, as is often the case when scholars evaluate particular institutions against the usual sets of democratic criteria and inevitably find them wanting. Third, it introduces an actor/audience distinction that otherwise standard deliberative theory is blind to, and thus avoids placing impossibly demanding participatory requirements on the shoulders of citizens, or impossibly demanding legitimacy burdens onto individual institutions.

The reflections on audience led to a consideration of staging, which is almost entirely off the radar of political scientists and theorists, focused as they are on non-physical aspects of political institutions and procedures. On this point I have gone further than Hajer and argued that the performing of certain democratic roles requires particular kinds of stages. For narrating experience, there are very few limits, although dominated groups of people may value having protected spaces in which their voices are not continually drowned out by the majority. In those cases, when we expect narration to happen across the boundaries of experience and enclave, or when we expect conflict to arise, we tend to move narration to designated settings where conflict can be encouraged yet contained; to place it in a more formal setting, with formal rules of engagement to civilise conflict, perhaps controlled by a mediator or chairperson. When public claims are made, then it is essential that the staging is highly visible and accessible, either to the public as a whole or to the media, and in this respect it is troubling from a democratic point of view to note that current approaches to policing protest are limiting the ability of citizens to make themselves visible in this way. For binding collective decision-making and scrutiny, the stage requirements are even narrower: single, highly visible and somewhat (but not overwhelmingly) dignified stages such that citizens are cued into taking it seriously, and such that they allow citizens monitoring political life to focus the spotlight of publicity on proceedings. This in turn has a clear deliberative democratic benefit: publicity provides deliberative democracy with its ethical underpinnings, its disciplining force.

The 'dignity' of formal democratic stages led finally to a consideration of the degree to which democratic performance is scripted and ritualised. This point is perhaps the most familiar to scholars of political communication and new social movements but is still remarkably off the radar of most democracy scholars. On this point I was less sanguine about performance's normative status. While there are benefits of ritualisation in terms of ease of participation and legibility to the audience, the downsides are significant. These are mainly to do with the loss of impact on the broader public sphere that comes with frequency: if every attempt to make a claim on public attention uses the same technique in the same location, the cameras stop turning up and passers-by stop noticing, a case of familiarity breeding not so much contempt as indifference. The exception I noted was Hong Kong's 1 July marches which, while highly variable in turnout over the years, have nonetheless become something of an annual public festival, devoted not to the cultural or spiritual realms, but the political – an important achievement in allegedly apathetic Hong Kong. The point is this: public claim-makers need to use a variety of scripts and variety in their scripts, if they are to be effective in attracting attention and stimulating debate.

However, the overall aim has been analytic, not normative. It argues that a performative account of democracy opens our eyes to aspects of real-world democratic activity that presently dominant strands of democratic theory are blind to. If, along the way, the idea of dramatic performance has shed some of its pejorative connotations, then so much the better. My claim is that performance is unavoidable in democracy. That is not just an empirical statement about how people in the real world communicate but also, as I argued earlier, a theoretical point about the prerequisites for communication. It is certainly the case that a performative account brings with it some normative worries, and the scripting discussion highlighted one of those, but even in that case the problematic features can be managed in practice by alert political actors. Even if those normative worries are severe, however, a theory of democracy that responds to those worries by ignoring democracy's performative aspects is, I hope I have demonstrated, an incomplete theory.

Notes

1 See e.g. Dryzek (2000); Fung (2003); Mansbridge (2003); Saward (2003) and Smith (2009).
2 A thread that includes Dunsire (1973); Fischer and Forester (1993); Hajer (2005); Hood and Jackson (1991); and Stone (2002).
3 Parkinson and Mansbridge 2012. Mansbridge (1999) is generally credited as the origin of systems thinking in deliberative democracy. Other work in this mode includes Bohman (2007); Dryzek (2010); Goodin (2005, 2008); Goodin and Dryzek (2006); Hendriks (2006); Saward (2003) and Thompson (2008).
4 Parkinson (2007). Let me stress this: being in favour of appointment to the House of Lords does *not* mean being in favour of the hereditary peerage or party patronage. I simply mean that appointment for life shores up the scrutiny function in a context where it is otherwise weak. See also Wright and Gamble (1999).

3 Performance at the crossroads of citizenship[1]

Janelle Reinelt

Politics is the activity of attending to the general arrangements of a collection of people who, in respect of their common recognition of their manner of attending to its arrangements, compose a single community [...] This activity, then, springs neither from instant desires, nor from general principles, but from the existing traditions of behaviour themselves. And the form it takes, because it can take no other, is the amendment of existing arrangements by exploring and pursuing what is intimated in them.

(Michael Oakeshott 1962: 112)

Citizenship is a hinge between the several overlapping spheres in which postmodern people live their lives, and a cornerstone concept in political theory as an essential component of democracy. In its aspects of role-playing, performing, representing and social agency, it is also central to the relationship between politics and performance. While the initial relevance of this discussion to performing arts practices may not be immediately clear, several recent developments in our field are implicated in or related to citizenship discourses. First, the term 'political theatre' has become increasingly weakened or even discarded by some scholars, thus losing its appeal to the social gathering power of theatre as one element of the public sphere. The civic traction that the characterisation 'political' can bring to the performing arts has been lessened by the seeming trivialisation of art, on the one hand, and the gravitas of world-historical events on the other. While to be in opposition to a ruling system seemed possible and efficacious for artists in a cold war era of binary thinking, opposition seems less likely than a kind of resistance-without-programme in an era of globalisation and neo-liberal assimilation. The experience I will describe here registers anxiety about losing track of the world in this new situation; the meaning of being a citizen also threatens to slip away.

Second, a new universalism, whether imagined through a thinker such as Alain Badiou (Wickstrom 2012), or through a version of neo-Kantian cosmopolitanism (Rebellato 2009) is being linked to the disparagement of identity politics as 'over', no longer relevant to a progressive performance practice (Read 2008; Causey and Walsh 2013).[2] (These ideas often draw support from a cluster of thinkers such as Judith Butler and Wendy Brown in the US, Badiou, Jacques Rancière and Giorgio Agamben in Europe). The application of these ideas to performance means that the critical attention to matters of race, class, gender and sexuality in performance (representation in both its aspects as mimesis and as political standing-in or counting-for) that has marked Anglo-American scholarship in the field for the last thirty years is now perceived as either misguided or outdated.

Third, the extremely influential discourse of postdramatic theatre, as described by Hans Thies Lehmann in his 1999 study, *Postdramatisches Theater*, has circulated throughout theatre and performance scholarship, shifting attention away from any direct connection between theatre and political life outside the theatre, and turning attention inward to the processes of the theatrical apparatus itself and its internal politics: 'It is not through the direct thematization of the political that theatre becomes political, but through the implicit substance and critical value of its *mode of representation*' (emphasis in the original; Lehmann 2006: 178).[3]

I intend to return to these points of view in theatre and performance scholarship, but will first proceed with a personal reflection on events drawn from the summer of 2011 to invoke the critical barometer of citizenship in relation to this experience. In the years since this summer snapshot, many aspects of these events have continued to exacerbate toxic conditions at the intersection of governance and citizenship around the globe.

Mid-summer 2011

I am struck by the dizzying array of claims made on my attention in the nightly news: the same week in July I flew back to California from my school-year home in London, the phone hacking scandal was in the headlines as Rupert Murdoch was called to account before a committee of the British Parliament. Meanwhile, the fight in the US Congress over raising the debt ceiling resulted in hourly bulletins and special speeches from the White House or the Capitol, as President Obama and the leaders of Congress jockeyed for power and influence domestically while playing for high stakes internationally as well (a scene which came to be overly familiar during the next two years). Two weeks later, the slaughter in Norway of young people attending a political summer school exploded across our screens, while simultaneously dire famine reports from Somalia and amateur video footage of the Syrian military attacking civilians competed for attention. One hardly knew where to look, and the chance that any one of these critical events might slip away from consciousness in the force of the barrage seemed obscene but imminent.[4]

Some of the confusion and vertigo I describe can be explained with reference to problems of citizenship. The performance of political leaders in the name of citizens in the US and UK, the specific attack on and destruction of citizenship witnessed in the Norwegian killings, the invasion of citizens' privacy in the hacking scandal and the struggle to overthrow tyranny in the name of new democratic movements in Syria (as well as Libya and throughout the Arab world) can all be understood as political struggles with serious consequences for citizenship through highly theatrical performances of power. Knowledge of these actions circulates through theatrical images and sound-bites that call attention to their performative force and their mediated dramaturgy. Each of these 'stories' creates effects far beyond their particular location or circumstances: the attack on multiculturalism and 'cultural Marxism' in Norway by a right-wing Christian extremist chimed with elements of the ideology of the conservative Christian right in the US and could be heard in the widespread debates about the value of multiculturalism throughout Europe as well.[5] Young people risking their lives to change their political systems across the so-called 'Arab Spring' demonstrated the exclusions of sovereignty in the existing regimes, demanding citizens' rights to participate in shaping their futures. The humanitarian crisis of staggering proportion in Somalia was/is due in part to a dysfunctional government involved in civil war. As refugees fled into Ethiopia and Kenya, nations that were themselves facing precarious situations, the issues of citizenship took on a different proportion, poised between what Agamben has characterised as 'bare life' and the necessity of moving beyond restrictive political categories in the face of such dire threats to human lives. In the years since, most of these alarming events have become permanent fixtures of our news scene, and many places such as Syria and Somalia have continued to degrade.

In the discussion that follows, I will return to the role of theatre and performance studies more directly, but first I want to further interrogate the problems of imagining citizenship as a functioning political category for a global age.

Where/who are the people?

Etienne Balibar, writing specifically about the breakdown of representative democracy in contemporary Europe, has argued persuasively that we are facing a crisis of sovereignty, the heart of which is the '*disappearance of the people*, both as an instance of symbolic legitimation and as an instance of real control' (emphasis in original). Tracing a similar attenuation of law, that situation becomes dire: 'But with neither people nor law there can only exist a phantom public sphere, a *regression* and not a progress in relation to the history of democratic states' (emphasis in the original; 2003: 160). Although Balibar is speaking about Europe and the particular difficulties of sovereignty and law he perceives in the pan-European situation, the 'disappearance of the people' and a 'phantom public sphere' are aspects of our contemporary predicament at the level of much smaller units of sociality and also at the global level.

This is a political crisis because it involves a breakdown in the instruments through which citizens constitute and are constituted by their participation in various activities that together perform self-governance and democratic belonging. Whether experienced in local or national contexts or again in transnational dimensions, the symptoms of this crisis can be found not only in the exclusion of large segments of a population from the protections of the state in which they live (as in the case of Somalia and Syria and also for many other immigrants, refugees or asylum seekers), but also in the civic disengagement of the disaffected 'silent majority' who choose not to take up their interpellation as citizens.[6]

In addition to the exclusions and disaffiliations within local or national polities, the conditions of global mobility and transience also lead to complex negotiations of multiple relations to place and space across vast territories, and to proliferating identifications with and relations to others living alongside one or across the world. At this dispersed level too, the absence of 'the people' or the inability to imagine one holds back the development of effective political strategies, while neo-liberal economics invades every aspect of global culture with a reductive homogenisation, and while the public sphere, increasingly conceptualised as web space, not only excludes many from its scene but also seems to posit advertising and commodification as its principal languages.

Theories of citizenship and identity

In Western citizenship theory, there have been two dominant traditions: classical civic republicanism emphasises citizenship as belonging, with its ideas of a common good, public spirit, care for the community and participation in civic and political life as a citizen's duty. The other tradition is modern liberalism with its emphasis on individual rights and private interests, in which citizenship is seen as a legal status held equally with others.[7] On this model the individual is the bearer of citizenship rights and the nation state is the guarantor of citizenship. This later liberal concept was dominant throughout most of the twentieth century until it came under pressure from both globalisation and multiculturalism. As Anupama Roy writes,

> In the changing contexts of the late twentieth century, viz., globalization, transnational migration, multicultural national populations, etc, the manner in which citizenship has been understood so far has been redefined. In this context it has become acceptable to talk of the ideas of (i) global/world citizenship with its basis in human rights that delink the relationship between citizenship and the nation-state, the hitherto uncontested unit of membership, and (ii) differential rights and differentiated citizenship for members of cultural groups which gives them rights not only as individuals but also as members of groups, their rights depending also on this group membership and catering to their special needs.
>
> (2005: 21–2)

It is evident that this recent type of thinking has more in common with republican concepts than liberal ones, especially insofar as participation and care for the community are highlighted. Indeed feminist thinkers who focus on the ethics of care and the dissolution of the public/private distinction have been instrumental in articulating this view of citizenship. As early as 1990, Iris Marion Young, for example, coined the term 'differentiated citizenship' to mean that members of certain groups should be accommodated not only as individuals but also through their group, arguing that the 'attempt to create a universal conception of citizenship transcending group differences is fundamentally unjust because it oppresses historically marginalized groups'.[8]

However, rather than the inclusive politics that Young and others (e.g. Lister 2003) draw from this way of thinking, republican conservatism has reacted strongly against the presence of strangers in their midst by emphasising exclusionary criteria for who is able to be counted as a citizen in the first place. This is in part due to the permanent tension between inclusion and exclusion inherent to the concept. As politics in many Western countries have swung to the right, immigration laws have tightened while citizens have argued that immigrants and refugees will take up resources needed by the native citizens. Here, ideas of common good and care for the community are turned against outsiders as a way to keep them out. Fortress Europe has been especially susceptible to this thinking as its social welfare infrastructures crumbled, especially in the early months of financial recession with the collapse of the Irish, Greek and Portuguese economies.

Meanwhile, neo-liberal regimes operating at the transnational level, but also strengthened through the accommodations national governments have made to global business, have determined that liberal citizenship as a concept has become even more individualised and cut off from any social demands, leaving it almost solely a juridical category. This kind of position fits well with a neo-liberal strategy of individual self-interest and market dynamics, where citizenship only means legal protection, and the basic membership card is further attenuated by the 'mask', to use Roy's suggestive theatrical term, which covers over any contextual, cultural or historical differences under the law – this is what in reference to India she calls the 'power of dissociation', the hegemonic requirement of dissociation since the political community into which the members enter after shedding their ascriptive identities is already marked as male, upper class, upper caste, Hindu or white. 'In these circumstances formal citizenship rights cannot influence the conditions that render the possession of citizenship ineffective, if not worthless' (Roy 2005: 238). Here we see clearly the critique of universalism in relation to citizenship – it covers over the characteristics which may require different treatment in order to be just or equal. However, as compelling as group rights and well-marked differences are for the achievement of justice and equality, there are also problems inherent in the republican position; this has been evident in the debates concerning multiculturalism.

The competing views of citizenship have been deeply imbricated within the discourses of multiculturalism. Multiculturalist advocates have questioned this primacy of the masked, rights-bearing individual because it disadvantages those who belong to minority communities. However, multiculturalism as state policy has also been seriously critiqued, and not just from the right: what has been called 'the silo effect' is allegedly created whenever the state separates out its citizens for different treatment on the basis of ascriptive characteristics.

Multiculturalism in the context of citizenship

To see how both the right and the left might object to multiculturalism, we need to recognise that there are two distinct meanings of the term. The difference needs to be recognised between multiculturalism as a description of a state of affairs (a mix of diverse people living together in proximity) and as a normative policy or value to be pursued through political means (a programme of multiculturalism): they are not identical. For many ordinary people, however, this distinction is not clear, and furthermore it is sometimes deliberately blurred in political discourse for rhetorical effect. This occurred in the UK in winter 2011, when Prime Minister David Cameron proclaimed that multiculturalism had failed and should be abandoned.[9] In a critical speech given in Munich in February, he engaged in a blanket condemnation which not only attacked the previous Labour government's policies but also rejected the state of affairs of multiculturalism on the ground – this is what made it a right-wing and reactionary pronouncement, not the criticism of actual policy (which is indeed open to objections).

By blurring the lines between a policy and a description of a state of affairs, Cameron rejected the de facto everyday living arrangements of multicultural Britain. In fact, it was actually worse – he made this pronouncement in a speech about getting tough on terrorists, and he suggested that tolerance of Islamist extremists had been the result of a policy of multiculturalism. In narrowing the scope of multiculturalism to Muslims and further to Islamists, he not only targeted these groups, but he also covered over or masked the large numbers of non-Islamist Muslim and non-Muslim citizens who have immigrated to Britain from former colonies or Eastern Europe and who have had some stake in the creation and improvement of a multicultural society. Some citizens for as many as three generations would now lose the attention and care of a conservative coalition government rejecting multiculturalism. This is the argument from the left in support of multiculturalism.

However, the deployment of multiculturalism as concrete government policy is rightly open to criticism for its ill-conceived approach to the nation's communities. While New Labour under Tony Blair made multiculturalism state policy in the 1990s, that did not necessarily turn out to benefit multiculturalism as a life practice. New Labour policies are open to such criticisms as inattention to poor white working-class disadvantage when instituting specific programmes designed to benefit immigrant or multi-racial groups; promoting certain community leaders or groups as spokespersons for a cultural constituency they may not actually represent; delegating to these leadership groups responsibility for keeping the peace on the streets rather than engaging deeply with any problems; and conceptually creating the silo effect (or separatism) that the policy of multiculturalism should instead break down. These are the main features of the critique of multiculturalism as a failed policy, although a more reactionary form of criticism simply holds that multiculturalism has failed because no cohesion exists to which all British citizens adhere, a view which inevitably sets up an insider-us and an outsider-them.

Kenan Malik, a political journalist born in India and brought up in Britain, is a more reasoned critic of multiculturalism, but an outspoken and absolute one. Writing in the wake of the 7/7 bombings in London by 'home-grown' terrorists from northern cities, Malik blames a long process of creating a discourse and practices in which culture became more important than politics:

> Over time, what became subcontracted out [...] was not simply the provision of welfare but political authority too. Rather than appeal to Muslims as British citizens, and attempt to draw them into the mainstream political process, politicians and policy-makers came to see them as people whose primary loyalty was to their faith and who could be politically engaged only by Muslim 'community leaders.' It was a policy that encouraged Muslims to view themselves as semi-detached Britons – and that inevitably played into the hands of radical Islamists.
>
> (2009: 76)

For Malik, multiculturalism shifted the emphasis from politics and democratic processes to cultural differences, creating cultural divisions where there might have been negotiated settlements on political grounds.

Thus to summarise the tensions within contemporary citizenship so far is both to recognise the increasing pressure from neo-liberalism to deny any contextual or cultural markers beyond individual legal status on the one hand, and on the other to acknowledge the dangers of identity-based demands for differential citizenship based on particularities which run the risk of becoming themselves ossified in ways that oppress individuals who are considered deviant within their groupings – such as gay persons within Muslim communities, for example – or alternatively by empowering leadership cadres that do not represent their constituencies or who lead the constituency into polarisation instead of negotiations with the other groups and individuals who make up the polity. The situatedness of each individual's experiences produces uneven meanings and values of citizenship, and this is precisely what citizenship theory needs to account for. As Engin Isin and Patricia Wood write,

> Rather than regarding citizenship and identity as antinomic principles, we recognize the rise of new identities and claims for group rights as a challenge to the *modern* interpretation of universal citizenship, which is itself a form of group identity. Instead of either eradicating or flattening the tension between citizenship and identity, we aim to make a productive use of it. We seek a new conception of citizenship [...] with an emphasis on the practice of democracy, that would meet the needs of a diverse citizenry facing the challenges of advanced capitalism.
>
> (1999: 4)

Of course how to imagine this new practice has proved difficult. This is perhaps where theatre comes in (and other art forms as well) – its great capacity is to imagine and stage some of this lived citizenship. We will come back to this point.

Global site of multiple affiliations

This account of how citizenship, whether republican or liberal, can still foreclose the inclusivity of its promise has thus far been illustrated only at the national or metropolitan level. When we think globally, another set of contradictions come into view which intersect with these territorial concerns. Migration studies, diaspora studies and studies of globalisation have all documented the dramatic changes in the mobility of large numbers of people and their multiple affiliations with place and identity as a result of a fluid and often increasing set of identifications and networks. While multiple passports and rapidly shifting circumstances have attenuated postmodern mobile individuals' connections to heritage, place and birth culture, some poor citizens in the West have experienced 'staying put' or 'being stuck' – not benefiting from globalisation's mobile possibilities. While some mobile individuals are forced or even coerced into the movement that characterises their lives, others have taken advantage of what Aihwa Ong (1999) calls 'flexible citizenship' to negotiate an agency based on multiple passports and no concrete affiliations to place or community, a kind of hyper-liberal world citizenship. Republican citizenship might criticise this lack of responsibility and participation in the common good but these global subjects might feel that they have justly escaped the entrapments of the states in which they live by restricting their involvement to the legal status of their passport entitlements.

The privilege of mobile elites contrasts sharply to those who have no choice and who either have no rights and are reduced to bare life, as Agamben theorises, or those who are stuck in situations which do not recognise their identities or their disadvantage, but treat them solely as equal under the law. The articulation of universal theories of human rights and other liberal theorisations of masked difference under a supposed common status of human being or world citizen can be made compatible with neo-liberalism's emphasis on securing human rights only in support of free enterprise, and does not take into account the situated and multiple lives and identities of these world citizens. Maurya Wickstrom details how human rights have been linked to 'business, capitalism, and the construction of the *homo economicus*' (2012: 9). Cosmopolitanism, then, with its gesture toward theorisation of a global (republican) ideology of participation and mutual care, can often be squeezed into a (neo-)liberal pathway for those who wish to by-pass the messy affiliations of political obligations in order to create an 'entrepreneurial subject'.

Thus at the global level, there are few support structures for civic virtues or actions, and inclusion into the privileges of mobility is both limited and potentially depoliticising.

Theatre as a democratic worksite

Any new political initiatives concerning citizenship will need to take into account these intersecting but disparate issues of both exclusion and deliberate disaffiliation in addressing its tasks. Here, I return to Etienne Balibar who develops the idea of 'worksites of democracy'. What he advocates is, in a neo-Gramscian move, 'a "war of position" or gradual construction of a new historical hegemony, that is both a new way of thinking, a new collective "common sense", and interacts between multiple interventions stemming from both civil society and the public sphere' (Balibar 2003: 172). Where this differs from cosmopolitanism is that 'democratic work requires determinate matter and not just an ethics and juridical norms, and this sort of matter is only given in situation'. The situation, both locally and globally, is that 'individuals and groups can neither separate nor get along at will' (Balibar 2003: 173). This why we all need to engage in a political practice of citizenship-in-the-making. Balibar's four worksites are concerned specifically with the predicament of Europe:

1 The question of justice, which is juridical but also involves legislation, protection for individuals and groups, ways and means of attacking corruption, and many other matters.
2 Trade union struggles in relation to efforts to recognise social activity as labour, a valuing of productive labour as the production of sociality as well as goods and services.
3 The democratisation of borders.
4 Concerning culture, the effort to find an answer to language differences that affirms 'translation' as the medium of communication and the key language above all others in contrast to monolingual national languages and especially educational systems.

Worksites can be seen as situated within the European context, but with various adjustments would no doubt be useful foci in other concrete situations around the world. Some questions of justice and employment conditions lend themselves to multi-sited initiatives; networking across borders as well as local workgroups is also possible.

I would like to propose the theatre as a possible worksite for democracy and citizenship in Balibar's sense.[10] The kind of negotiation of determinate matter among social actors he identifies as key to the worksite idea is precisely the sort of embodied repertoire available in theatrical performance. The theatre's contribution to the public sphere is limited to its local impact, from one point of view, but as performances travel, and keeping in mind Balibar's emphasis on translation, theatre also contributes to sectors beyond the local, even to the global, as it circulates. Some performances become more influential than others, certainly, and performance scholars themselves help widen their impact by bringing public attention to some performances through our academic networks, what we might think of as our own form of a counterpublic, in Michael Warner's sense.[11] The public sphere functions by amassing a number of strands of discourse around certain topics, thus like the million tweets at the moment of the Japanese earthquake (also in 2011), a number of theatre pieces engaging with, for example, citizenship, when circulated along with other forms of discourse, films, essays, demonstrations, art exhibits, committed journalism – all manner of expressions – can create a buzz or a circle of attention where political negotiation by what might almost constitute a people materialises. This is the zone of politicality in public space, whether virtual or concrete.

This idea of 'worksites' in theatre is also one answer to Hans-Thies Lehmann's sense of the impossibility of theatre engaging directly with politics. One of his strongest convictions is that the mediatisation of news leads to the 'erosion of the act of communication' (Lehmann 2006: 184). Because of the bombardment of images such as I described in the summer of 2011, the connection between sender and receiver in the circulation of signs is broken, according to Lehmann. 'The basic structure of perception mediated by media is such that there is no experience of a connection among the individual images received but above all no connection between the receiving and sending of signs; there is no experience of a relation between address and answer.' He calls for theatre to develop 'a politics of perception, which could at the same time be called an aesthetic of responsibility (or response-ability)' (Lehmann 2006: 185).

While the basic social situation of the theatre lends itself to the kind of attention to the communication circuit that Lehmann favours – through both its immediacy and its liveness – this is not the only ground of politics that theatre as a democratic worksite offers. Indeed, the contrast between highly mediatised and live events has already been questioned and undermined, and I think there is no going back.[12] It makes more sense to see theatre conducting its investigations and interventions alongside of but also in tension with other nodes in a communications network. From its embodied and concrete practices and representations of possible ways of 'attending to arrangements' theatre can modify or challenge, or possibly even sometimes support, other information or modes of knowing that are addressing the polity. Not always will theatre be transgressing taboos (*pace* Lehmann 2006: 186); there may be situations where contributing to paths of compromise, incorporation of seemingly irreconcilable differences or the negotiation of relations between the state of what is and what might be is its proper task. The insistence that art can only be transgressive and individual seems like a legacy of romanticism.[13] To write, 'Theatre itself would hardly have come about without the hybrid act that an individual broke free from the collective, into the unknown, aspiring to unthinkable possibility; it would hardly have happened without the courage to transgress borders, all borders of the collective' reveals a conception of theatre within a particular ideology of individual artistic greatness and *via negativa* that hardly seems to match up with the reference to Brecht's *Fatzer* that Lehmann is quoting in support of his point that the 'unquantifiable singular' is the key attribute of art (Lehmann 2006: 178–9).

Politics is to be found in the necessary constant evaluation of and negotiation with the relations of power as they occur in our daily lives – both micro and macro relations of power – challenging, deconstructing or transgressing these structures but also modifying, improving or sustaining them (not all relations of power are unjust; not all terms of relation are non-negotiable). The identification of meaningful instances of these negotiations and the imagination of new possibilities for alternative arrangements can both critique the world-as-is and suggest a future world-as-might/should be. The courage and energy to engage in this practice of politics is what I imagine to be produced in Balibar's democratic worksites; theatre that can re-energise a commitment to 'keep on keeping on' with the daily struggle to give some affirmative horizon to this work is a theatre that might not shrink its ambitions to merely examining its own apparatus or breaking taboos in order to 'create playful situations in which affects are released and played out" (Lehmann 2006: 186). Indeed, theatre fully engaged in this imaginative task demonstrates the common grammar of politics and performance.

In citing distrust of the instrumental rationality that has been the basis of neoliberal economics and philosophy, Lehmann and other champions of 'affect' call for a new cultivation of spontaneous impulses and extremes of emotion as a way to build a political capacity for judgement and action outside of predetermined, suspect 'rational preconsiderations' (Lehmann 2006: 186). While I can value this possibility for theatre's engagement with politics, it should not be its only mode of engagement. One does not have to embrace Habermas in order to think that certain uses of logic, reason and argumentation are precisely what have been missing from the public sphere and globalised media.[14]

Staging discrete identities

From what I have been arguing here, it is probably obvious that I do not think identity politics are exhausted for use on stage. Theatre is a site where concrete individuals appear in embodied practices before others. To say that the critical markers of situated identities are no longer useful on stage or in our performance analyses only abdicates the struggle in the trenches to manoeuvre the determinate matter before us. As in liberal citizenship theory, it masks difference and favours the hegemonic. To take just one example, the idea that 'colour-blind casting' will mask colour in performance has always been wrong-headed because, like liberal citizenship, it tries to pretend that all humans would experience the dramatic situation in the same way regardless of – in this case – race or ethnicity. While it is quite true, as Lehmann has written, 'That politically oppressed people are shown on stage does not make theatre political' (Lehmann 2006: 178), it is also quite true that if certain persons are not represented on stage at all, they will not find themselves recognised within the social surround as legitimate (political) subjects. If theatre managers do not take account of what sorts of people attend their performances, no attention will be paid to the absence of certain demographics. If public discourse no longer analyses differences among citizens, who will notice inequalities or have the language to describe and address them?

On the other hand, this is not an argument for a message-laden theatre of old, driven by a static political ideology. Simple stagings of difference certainly do not go far. It *is* an argument, however, for a pluralistic space of aesthetics and experiment which can embrace a number of styles and types of democratic art. Rather than arguing about what the ideal performance might be, could we not celebrate a plurality of effective stagings of politics, joining audiences in creating these as worksites of citizenship? (Or to refer to the subject matter of this volume, to exercise the common grammar that allows the theatre and politics to mutually articulate democratic possibilities?).

A multiple and hybrid engagement

Here are three examples from the British context, chosen because they differ from each other and yet together address some of the issues concerning citizenship I have raised in this chapter. While the first displays a conscious identity politics, the second might be seen as universal and cosmopolitan in its underlying thrust. The third experiments in ways that I think Lehmann would approve – the politics of perception within theatre and emotional affect as a heuristic device. My contention is that only taken together – all three types of aesthetic engagement with politics – can we begin to figure theatre as a worksite of democracy and a space where appropriate citizenship for our global age might be cultivated. Moving back and forth between and among these theatrical events, weighing them up, comparing and contrasting, feeling their entailments and questioning their premises, spectators might be said to be doing the work of citizenship, whether fully conscious of it or not.

To begin with the most traditional and least postdramatic example, David Edgar's play, *Testing the Echo*, written for Max Stafford Clark's Out of Joint theatre company, toured around the UK in 2008, from Salisbury to Edinburgh to Warwick, to Birmingham, to London. This play took up the ongoing debates on citizenship and being British, characterising a multicultural society struggling with the issues and values surrounding life in Britain. It was a response to what Edgar perceived as a reactionary entrenchment against newcomers after the 7/7 bombings. The separatism of cultural communities, especially religious communities, seemed to many people to have been the 'seedbed' of terrorism. People were fragmented, lacking a sense of belonging to Britain, so the argument went, and as long as they had no allegiance or identification with Britain, they were susceptible to attempts to betray it. Edgar recognised that people become British citizens for many reasons, and that affiliation is shaped through many pathways and relationships of kith and kin. In the subject matter of this production, readers will recognise the republican citizenship issues of identification with, and care and responsibility to, the community as well as the multicultural debates described above.

Edgar is probably the epitome of the thesis-driven, narrative-based, coherent argument-making political writer, but this play departs considerably from his previous profile.[15] While it has a dramaturgical shape and a set of characters, it does not have a strong narrative and most certainly does not put forward a sustained thesis, or even a point of view beyond the careful balancing of legitimate but diverse values and experiences, captured in the phrase repeated by several characters after expressing something they feel deeply, 'Although for you I'm sure it looks different.' If the play has a political goal, it is to enable its audiences to consider how differently positioned subjectivities might find themselves engaged in attending to the arrangements of democracy, citizenship, family, workplace

46   *Janelle Reinelt*

and the law. *Testing the Echo* was based on interviews conducted with people who were studying to take their citizenship test or enrolled in citizenship classes. It also includes quoted versions of several texts produced to describe Britishness or to give a 'potted' version of British history and communal life to newcomers. Eight actors play multiple roles, cast across race and ethnicity, to represent a cross-section of people who might be seeking citizenship, plus a teacher of English for Speakers of Other Languages (ESOL) and her family, and some 'native' co-workers of a candidate for citizenship. Edgar dramatises the different reasons people might seek citizenship, and spectators can come to understand that identifying with a community of citizens is dependent on mutual recognition and participation in valued activity. Anti-universalist, identity-specific and engaged directly with a political topic – I think there is still a place for this type of political theatre, within a range of progressive performances.

The second example comes from an experimental theatre company in Birmingham called Stan's Cafe. They devise their work collectively, but with leadership from James Yarker, and they perform both locally and on tour, including internationally. The performance I describe here is about global citizenship, but it does not address this directly, but instead through what it asks audience members to imagine about themselves and others. 'Of All the People in All the World' is an installation with actors and some audience interaction. 'It uses grains of rice to bring formally abstract statistics to startling and powerful life. Each grain of rice equals one person and you are invited to compare the one grain that is you to the millions that are not.'[16]

Prior to the performance a team of performers carefully weighs out quantities of rice to represent a host of human statistics such as

- the populations of various towns and cities
- the number of doctors, or the number of soldiers in various places or situations
- the number of people born each day, the number who die
- all the people who have walked on the moon
- deaths in the holocaust.

These rice grains as statistics are arranged in labelled piles creating a series of landscapes of rice. The statistics and their juxtapositions can be moving, shocking, celebratory, witty and thought-provoking. The company adapts the show to the place of performance, adding exhibits that have local meaning and also ones that emerge in the global surround as critically important. If it were being produced in July 2011, it might have featured the number of people lost in the Japanese Tsunami, for instance. The amount of rice used varies according to which version is performed, too. For *Of All the People in All the World: UK* it uses 1,000 kg of rice to represent 60,000,000 people. *Of All the People in All the World: Europe* uses 12,000 kg. The performers dress in costume and are present weighing and counting rice during the performance, and can be asked questions and interact with the visitors. The impact of the piece will be different for everyone, of course, but it does conjure up a meditation on how to conceptualise the people and the world in relation to one's own subjectivity. It arguably appeals to a universalist conception of liberal citizenship and cosmopolitanism through its grains of rice. As Dan Rebellato describes it, citing the production as a specific example of the cosmopolitan art he advocates:

> *Of All the People in All the World* feeds the cosmopolitan imagination, giving us new ways of grasping the enormity of the world, and the imagination feeds our perception of the exhibits, as we invest – in a somewhat theatrical way – the blank uniformity of each rice pile with personality and significance.
> (Rebellato 2009: 74)

The third example is the controversial performance of Tim Crouch's *The Author* from 2009 at the Royal Court and 2010 at the Edinburgh Festival where it was especially popular and the subject of avid public discussion, blogging and social networking. It takes place among the audience, and indeed the audience is asked to judge its own viewing practices. Crouch describes the play on his website thus:

> *The Author* is a play about what it is to be a spectator and about our responsibilities as spectators. It explores the connection between what we see and what we do. I feel strongly that we have lost a thread of responsibility for what we choose to look at. *The Author* uses only words to show us things and sometimes the things those words show us are disturbing. It is not a play for children but it IS a play for audiences.
> (Crouch website)

Without disclosing all the play's strategies, because the whole point is for the audience members to confront their own feelings and choices in the face of what they are experiencing in the moment, I will say that I think the link to these citizenship discussions is that it challenges the disaffiliation of liberal citizenship or flexible citizenship that trades on its passports but does not take up responsibility for the communities with which it is linked. In other words, it is addressed precisely to the bourgeois audience of the mainstream public sphere, many of whom refuse the republican aspects of citizenship's care for the common good. At the same time, it is profoundly metatheatrical and asks about what transpires on stage and what constitutes an ethical mode of reception or attendance at such a spectacle. That the particular theatre audiences who attended this play reacted so publicly through a variety of social media and face-to-face debate is a measure of its provocation. It is clearly postdramatic, and it addresses Lehmann's call for emotional confrontation and transgression. Audiences' perceptions are precisely the subject of the performance.

Although all three of these pieces could be said to negotiate the concept of citizenship in ways that Balibar would approve, what excites me is thinking about them together – and moreover, positing them as overlapping and relational as their best or most significant impact. By thinking how *The Author* confronts our own voyeurism and complicity in refusing responsibility alongside the meditation of Stan's Cafe, a more complex effect is achieved. If *Testing the Echo* introduces a notion of multiple modalities and intentionalities of citizenship, it also suggests concrete embodied lives which can come to haunt the grains of rice representing the abstract humans to whom we are related in the global village, and it intersects with *The Author* in interesting ways since at the swearing-in ceremony toward the end of the play, the candidates who come together act as a social group to prevent the interruption of the ceremony and ensure one of the group members is able to complete her swearing-in. This is a spontaneous act among people who do not know each other but act together in a singular moment of decision. It is one answer to the predicament of *The Author*: you can choose to stay, or you can choose to go, or you can choose to try to stop what is taking place. The theatre, then, as a worksite for constantly processual, changing performance(s) of citizenship, can address multiple positions and contradictions using a myriad of aesthetic means. It can contribute to the public sphere by offering its public performances to join with other sorts of interventions by similar and different publics to negotiate the determinate matter of our everyday local and global lives. It can engage politics by feeling political, and stimulating political thoughts and actions, and by attending to the arrangements of our ongoing sociality. As it participates in those arrangements, it is part of the grammar of politics and performance.

Conclusion

The challenge of this chapter has been to try to understand the conditions under which we live our lives together in a global time which is also resolutely local and spatial. The quotation with which I began, Michael Oakeshott's somewhat convoluted description of being embedded in social practices and manoeuvring to try to assess them, imagine alternatives and negotiate the difficult 'amendment of existing relationships', expresses what I understand the nature of 'politicality' to be – the ongoing and inescapable relations of individuals and groups and their sticky messiness. It also involves relations of power, but these are not separated into a clinical political sphere – no, the relations of power are imbricated in every social practice, and the way we experience and react to those relations, together and alone, makes up the living grammar of everyday life as well as world-historical events.

This being the case, theatre cannot help but be saturated with politics. What it inevitably shows its audiences are sets of these 'arrangements' and the attempts humans make to amend or reconfigure them. This much seems inescapable but it does not mean that the theatre will necessarily succeed in illuminating or advancing any betterment of these amendations. That is rather the challenge, especially in our time, a global time which suffers from all the problems discussed here.

It means seeing theatre as a part of a multiple and hybrid social engagement, peopled by a variety of publics, and making its contribution not as a huge stand-alone event or artefact, but rather as a communication node within a network of highly varied and sometimes contradictory nodes that together make up public discourse. Its efficaciousness is not solitary – theatre cannot change the world – but it can and sometimes does work towards change alongside the other multiple avenues of public expression.

Looking at citizenship as a constantly evolving and changing concept, conditioned by many factors and subject to dramaturgies of savagery as well as hospitality, I have argued that the issues of belonging, exclusion, representation, role play and responsibility that circulate through different iterations of citizenship have something in common with theatre's own repertoire of gestures, its own structural troubles with spectacle and viewing, visibility and invisibility, reason and affect. This is the shared 'grammar' of our lives in common.

Finally, this has also been an attempt to persuade scholars not to shut down the claim to theatre's deep involvement in political matters, not to deny that it sometimes imagines or criticizes or brightens our pathway, not to give up on searching for new theatrical manifestations of strategies for living together.

Notes

1 This chapter is revised and updated from a version that first appeared in English and in Serbian in the journal *TkH: Journal of Performing Arts Theory* (2012). It was the lead essay in a special issue on 'Politicality'. I am grateful to Ana Vujanović and the *TkH* editorial collective for permission to reprint it here.
2 Mauyra Wickstrom (2012) provides a trenchant critique of the ways humanitarianism, human rights discourses and much of what used to be called 'political theatre' has played into the strategies of neo-liberalism, using Badiou to shape her primary theoretical framework; Dan Rebellato (2009) advocates universalism, meaning that 'the same principles are valid for everyone', and defends this against arguments based on diversity in relation to Complicité's *Mnemonic* (1999); Alan Read, perhaps the most polemical of this group of scholars, writes, almost as an aside, that the orthodoxy of identity politics is 'exemplified by the evocation of minorities who have become fetishized for their ability to deliver political credibility to any discourse in search of a victim' (2008: 9).
3 I will be quoting from the English translation by Karen Jürs-Munby.
4 There were many other important things going on that summer as well – and I mention here only the ones that exerted the strongest claims on me in a particular week as a political subject and as a citizen, whether of a nation or the world.
5 Anders Breivik has been widely reported as identifying his motives as anti-Muslim and anti-multiculturalism, which he sees as cultural Marxism. See e.g. Marquiez and Ferran (2011).
6 This term, 'silent majority', was popularised by Richard Nixon in 1969 who described the non-active average citizen in the US context who did not participate in politics or public discourse, in contrast to the radical elements around them who participated in demonstrations against the Vietnam War and other social movements.
7 The genealogies of these citizenship theories can be traced to Greece (republicanism) and Rome (liberalism), following a conventional historical trajectory.
8 Quoted in Roy 2005: 239. Young's full theory of difference can be found in *Justice and the Politics of Difference* (1990).
9 At a security conference in Munich on 5 Feb. 2011, David Cameron criticised state multiculturalism as a 'failed policy'. For a summary and a clip, see BBC News (2011).
10 Of course, the concept of a 'worksite' is built on the notion of productive creative activity as a form of labour, and Nicholas Ridout's recent book argues persuasively that 'work' is the capitalist form of necessity, whatever its guises, and that 'passionate amateurs' might best escape the regulation of wage labour and the cooption of their love of

theatre (2013: ch. 2, 'Of Work and Time'). I recognise Ridout's critique, and I suspect he would also recognise the ambiguous but real value in Balibar's concept of worksites for democracy.
11 'Counterpublics are defined by their tension with a larger public. Their participants are marked off from persons or citizens in general. Discussion within such a public is understood to contravene the rules obtaining in the world at large, being structured by alternative dispositions or protocols, making different assumptions about what can be said or what goes without saying' (2002: 56–7).
12 I am referring here, e.g. to Philip Auslander's seminal work, *Liveness* (1999).
13 I use romanticism as a pejorative here, but recognise the rehabilitation of 'anti-capitalist romanticism' in Ridout as a legitimate reconsideration of term. The difference is that I am talking about a conservative and elite concentration on the individual while Ridout is addressing the tendency to look back to a previous ideal age (which is often a myth) in order to critique the present and gesture to a possible futurity (2013: 7–11).
14 For my own form of negotiation with Habermas on the functions of the public sphere, see Reinelt (2011).
15 For more on Edgar, see Reinelt and Hewitt (2011).
16 From the Stan's Café website.

4 'I am an American'
Protesting advertised 'Americanness'

Cynthia Weber

Introduction

How are citizenships and nationalisms constructed, connected and contested in the post-9/11 US – performatively, affectively and visually – and how do their relationships figure 'Americanness'? This chapter suggests that among the ways citizenships and nationalisms figure Americanness is through the performative grammars of public service advertising campaigns, which are both theatrical and political in equal measure, with a specific focus on the American Advertising Council's 'I am an American' campaign from 2001.

As Evelyn Alsultany (2007) has pointed out, advertising was a strategy used by the American Advertising Council (among others) to figure patriotic post-9/11 US identities as racially and ethnically diverse yet nationally unified. Taking Alsultany's work as its point of departure, this chapter tracks how Americanness was advertised in the 'I am an American' campaign. It does this by focusing specifically on how the Ad Council's 'I am an American' public service announcement (PSA) attempts to 'not so much represent society *as it is* but society as it *should* be' (Cronin 2004: 113) through its advertising of what Alsultany calls 'diversity-patriotism', a patriotism that makes the celebration of diversity its foundation for affecting feelings of national unity. For a nation that envisions itself as a melting pot in which individual differences melt into insignificance when US citizens identify with the US nation, diversity-patriotism is a highly charged affective technology of patriotism that attempts to performatively bring into being the diversity-patriots and the US nation that it celebrates.

Running counter to the idealized notion of a unified Americanness that it advertises, but also embedded in its performative grammar, the PSA uses visual, aural and editing techniques to construct a complex, mobile system of differentiation that marks some US citizens with what might be called 'safe forms of Americanness' and other US citizens with 'unsafe forms of Americanness'. If safe US citizens are US citizens whom the PSA imagines as easily melting into the PSA's advertised ideal of a diverse yet unified Americanness, then unsafe US citizens are those US citizens whom the PSA marks with differences that cannot or will not melt into this ideal of advertised Americanness.

These unsafe US Americans and their unsafe forms of Americanness expose what Barbara Johnson calls 'the critical difference' that keeps an identity like the

United States of America from corresponding to its image of itself, in this case as a patriotically diverse melting pot (Johnson 1980). More generally, unsafe citizens point to the limits of the liberal promise of inclusion through citizenships and nationalisms that persistently invent distinctions between good citizens and bad citizens, labelling them as 'meltable' or 'tolerable diversity-patriots' or 'safe' on the one hand and 'unmeltable' or 'unpatriotic, intolerably dangerously different (potential) enemies' or 'unsafe' on the other. The figuring of some citizens as unsafe leads us to question how perceived racial, ethnic and cultural differences figure political subjectivity, since they highlight how what is assumed to be a unified, coherent sovereign national political subjectivity fragments into various forms of national sovereignties and 'cultural citizenships'. These perceived 'cultural' differences locate unsafe citizens beyond the bounds of what the sovereign nation will tolerate because it locates unsafe citizens beyond the bounds of patriotism (Brown 2006; Weber 2008). As such, 'cultural citizenship' marks not only the limits of what the sovereign nation-state perceives as patriotic; it locates intolerably different citizens as justifiably beyond the bounds of their sovereign entitlement to the state's security and safety. This is a problem that is every bit as acute today with the congressional passage of a bill that would allow for the indefinite detention of US citizens on US soil[1] as it was in the immediate aftermath of September 11, 2001.

The visual and aural focus of the Ad Council's 'I am an American' campaign is on safe US citizens. As a protest project, I created a practice-based project called '*I am an American*'*: Video Portraits of Unsafe US Citizens* that takes mainly unsafe US citizens as its visual and aural focus. After introducing and analyzing the Ad Council's 'I am an American' PSA, I introduce my alternative 'I am an American' project and the visual, aural and editing techniques it employs to contest and complicate the Ad Council's performative grammars of citizenship and nationalism and to examine how unsafe US citizens refigure Americanness. I conclude by critically reflecting upon both projects as illustrations of 'citizenship protests' and what these projects might tell us about citizenships, nationalisms, Americanness and political subjectivity.

The American Ad Council's 'I am an American' Public Service Announcement

On September 21, 2001 – ten days after 9/11 – the American Ad Council launched its 'I am an American' advertising campaign (Ad Council 2004a). The campaign featured 30 and 60 second Public Service Announcements (PSAs) broadcast on US television in which a montage of US citizens of various ages, races, religions and ethnicities look directly into the camera and declare 'I am an American' while emotive American music in a style reminiscent of Aaron Copeland's work plays in the background. The US motto appears on the screen, first in Latin, then in English – 'E Pluribus Unum', Out of Many, One. The final shot is of a young girl – possibly Arab, possibly South Asian, possibly Hispanic. She rides her bike in Brooklyn Bridge Park across the river from where the Twin Towers used to be.

Protesting 'Americanness' 53

Smiling broadly, the little girl waves a US flag. According to the Ad Council (which is the leading producer of PSAs in the US),[2] the 'I am an American' campaign 'helped the country to unite in the wake of the terrorist attacks' by 'celebrat[ing] the nation's extraordinary diversity' (Ad Council, 2004a).

The 'I am an American' PSA illustrates how US national sentimentality (Berlant 1991, 1997, 2008) and the technologies of mechanical reproduction (Benjamin 1969; Anderson 1983) combine to produce what Evelyn Alsultany calls 'diversity-patriotism', whereby racialized groups are temporarily incorporated into the imagined community of 'Americans' to the point that '[d]ifference is identified as defining the nation' (2007: 598). The cinematic strategies the PSA employs to achieve this diversity-patriotism are masterful. It saturates the visual space with a diversity of sharply focused unnamed US Americans and softly focused familiar American backdrops, like a fire station in lower Manhattan or the Golden Gate Bridge in San Francisco. It saturates the aural space with the repetitive yet performatively varied mantra 'I am an American' uttered with an array of accents, inflections and intensities. It sets these visual and aural representations to the emotive American music 'Short Trip Home' by Edgar Meyer that has a Coplandesque quality to it. And it literally spells out what its message is – 'E Pluribus Unum', Out of Many, One – a phrase that, according to the makers of the PSA, communicates 'out of many faces, religions, geographical backgrounds, and ethnicities, we are one nation' (Ad Council 2004b).

By employing these cinematic strategies, the 'I am an American' PSA constructs not only difference but the ideal of the *tolerance of difference* as the foundation of the modern US nation (Brown 2006; Weber 2007), as if the US identity announced in the original US motto 'E Pluribus Unum' (which in 1776 referred to the uniting of different US colonies into one Federal system) always referred to the 'melting' of individual racial and ethnic differences of US Americans into the united citizenry of the United States and as if this melting and the acceptance of all those melted into this pot by all US citizens were a long-ago accomplished fact (Berlant 1997; Fortier 2008; Marciniak 2006). Textually, aurally and visually, the PSA achieves this rhetorical feat by attempting to solve what R. B. J. Walker refers to as the three problems facing the authorization of the sovereign nation-state – the need to resolve the relationships between (1) the universal and the particular, (2) the self and the other and (3) space and time (Walker 1990).

The PSA resolves the universal/particular problem by attaching to the sign 'America' a plurality of visible, individual bodily differences (skin colour, age, sex, accent) of US American citizens while at the same time denying these individual citizens any invisible, private signs of difference (their names, their lived histories, their easy or complicated relationships with the US state). The PSA resolves the self/other problem by appearing to dissolve all differences – visible and invisible – within the sameness of the US melting pot, while it nonetheless excludes or leaves ambiguous differences that might disturb the national melting pot ideal. For example, apart from two ambiguous individuals who might be either Arab or Muslim but cannot be definitively identified as such, the PSA includes 'no visible markers of anything Arab, Muslim, or Sikh' (which is misread as Muslim by some US Americans), 'no veil, no mosque, no turban, no beard; no distinctive Arab, Muslim or Sikh clothing; no Arab accent' (Alsultany 2007: 598). In this way, Alsultany concludes, 'the Ad Council affirms the binary between "the citizen" and "the terrorist"' (2007: 598) both inside and outside the US nation-state. Finally, the PSA resolves the space/time problem by domesticating a particular identification – the claim to be 'American' – within the United States rather than within the larger continent that goes by this name and by excluding histories past and present that might make this claim contingent. It does this not only by deploying famous US landmarks as backgrounds in some shots. It also does this by excluding any unambiguous signs of Indigenous Americans in the PSA, a population that even today is not containable in the national imagery of either a territorial state like the United States or within the modernist history of progress narrated through the melting pot myth (Sollors 1996; Shaw 2007).

Through these aesthetic and political strategies, the advertising strategy of the 'I am an American' advertisement is invisible because the timeless ideal of an American that the PSA sells to US Americans hardly seems like a product to many of its consumers. As I detail below, for many US viewers of the PSA this emotive mosaic of modern US citizenship is so overwhelming that the PSA's obvious exclusions that would challenge its frame of reference are not strong enough to disrupt the PSA's emotional impact in the moment of its viewing. Indeed, on one level the PSA seems to be about having an emotional impact on emotionally impacted 9/11 US citizens. More specifically, the PSA seems to be designed to rechannel US American emotions towards a united citizen ideal and away from a troubling grief, mourning and melancholia (Gilroy 2006; Maira 2010) that got US citizens stuck on difficult questions like 'Who are we?' and 'Who might we become?', questions implied in that other question that circulated in the US media as *the* question of 9/11 – 'Why do they hate us?' (Sardar and Wyn Davies 2003; Weber 2006).

Instead, the Ad Council's 'I am an American' PSA participates in transforming this 'bad grief' into a state-sponsored and therefore (from the state's point of view) socially responsible form of 'good grief' – a kind of cathartic release *from* the challenges of US identity posed by 9/11.[3] For the PSA seemed to be telling US Americans *not* to think about what it means to be a US citizen after 9/11 outside of the PSA's frame of reference, even though this was arguably the very time US Americans ought to have been asking questions about America and American citizenship.

That the PSA succeeded in moving many US citizens from a state of not knowing what to think or to feel into a cathartic embrace of their presumed tolerance of difference as the foundation of the US nation is evidenced by the many 'heartening emails' the Ad Council received in response to the campaign, including this one: 'When the twin towers came crashing down, I didn't cry. Like everyone else, I was in shock. When I saw your PSA "I am an American", I did cry. Thank you for putting forth the best and the most appropriate PSA ever' (Ad Council 2004b). This response was not unique. The Ad Council received so many messages of thanks and support for this campaign that it 'complied [them] in a booklet and sent [the booklet] out to volunteers who helped with the project' (Ad Council 2004b).

The effect of these many conscious or unconscious aesthetic, political and affective strategies is a PSA that aesthetically reifies the illusion of a unified US national citizenry, one that has just enough content to give it resonance with individual US citizens but that is empty enough to make it presumably universalizable among all US citizens, but not to non-US Americans. As such, the PSA's repeated declaration 'I am an American' hails US Americans to identify with their nation and with the specific type of US citizen it constructs – one who recognizes that 'what it is that makes the US nation so unique' is its foundational claim to difference (Ad Council 2004b). More than this, though, the PSA hails these US diversity-patriots to perform this illusion in practice, on behalf of their state and their nation, to literally and metaphorically wave the flag.[4] For as Walker reminds us about the sovereignty of nation-states, 'Absolute authority has itself no absolute ground to stand on. What counts is the degree to which people can be persuaded to underwrite the sovereign power' (Walker 1990: 8). Considered in this way, the PSA is an instance of what might be called nationcraft as citizencraft (to paraphrase Richard K. Ashley's famous phrase 'statecraft as mancraft'; see Ashley 1989) in that it exemplifies how political nationalism is localized not only through legal and juridical practices (as Lauren Berlant convincingly claims; see Berlant 1991) but also through particular aesthetic practices that make the body and the citizen indivisible.

It is on the basis of this specific yet universalizable construction of a collective US national identity in which body is nation, diversity is identity, and tolerance is patriotic citizenship that the PSA hails every US citizen to actively tolerate those differences that compose this 'America'. But because of the necessary exclusions and ambiguities the PSA employs to assemble this ideal 'America', what the PSA also does is remind US Americans of how distinct they are from those whose differences – foreign and domestic – cannot be melted into this 'America'. It is these differences that the PSA implicitly instructs US Americans not to tolerate, for these are the differences embodied by those who presumably hate 'us'.

In this respect, then, the PSA not only draws a line between the normative white or normatively melted US citizen and the threatening Muslim, Arab, or Sikh terrorist, as Alsultany argues (2007: 598). By representing some 'culturalized' differences as acceptable and failing to represent other 'culturalized' differences at all, the PSA encourages a more amorphous, unanchored fear of any difference – not only racial and religious but also indigenous, sexual and political, for example – that was not clearly represented in the PSA.[5] For by failing to represent these additional differences as melted into the US ideal of itself, the PSA leaves open the possibility that these, too, might be threatening to US citizens and the US nation-state now or in the future. In this way, the PSA even more narrowly draws a line around what Alsultany calls 'the limits of cultural citizenship' (2007: 596). And it is only within the limits of this narrowly drawn, acceptable cultural citizenship that US citizens are hailed by the PSA to transform the aesthetic illusion propagated by the PSA of a united (albeit exclusive) US national identity into a practical fact.

Contrary to its intended purpose of preventing 'a possible backlash against Arab Americans and other ethnic groups after the [9/11] attacks' (Ad Council

2004a), the PSA helps to organize a US national imaginary in which some but not all bodies are equated with the US nation, some but not all differences are equated with US identity, and some but not all forms of tolerance are equated with patriotic citizenship. In so doing, the PSA simultaneously anchors itself in a celebration of diversity on the one hand and a fear of difference on the other. For as Anne-Marie Fortier so persuasively argues, even though individuals, societies, nations and states regularly conflate the two, the celebration of diversity does not necessarily equate to the celebration of difference. Rather, the celebration of diversity often explicitly refuses difference and thereby refutes the politics of difference (Fortier 2008). It is through this simultaneous conflation of diversity with difference and strategic separation of these two terms that the PSA effectively constructs a complex, mobile system of differentiation in which some differences mark citizens as 'safe citizens' and others mark them as 'unsafe citizens'. 'Safe citizens' are those citizens whose differences can, through their citizenship performances, be made to normatively conform to national ideals during the War on Terror historical moment so that they not only pose no threat to their state but, rather, they defend their state from threats by confirming these national ideals. In contrast, 'unsafe citizens' are those citizens who either will not or cannot make their differences normatively conform to the national ideals of this particular historical moment, making them real or potential threats to 'unifying' national ideals and to the US state itself (Weber 2008).

It is these unsafe citizens – US citizens who are beyond the limits of US cultural citizenship – who are cautioned by the PSA to keep their 'culture' (a euphemism for 'disturbing differences') private so that their differences do not endanger the US nation-state (Brown 2006). For if these unsafe citizens do not melt into/mesh with the US image of itself after 9/11, they are likely to find themselves on the wrong side of the us/them divide, whether they are 'American' or not. In this sense, the 'I am an American' PSA is not only a celebration of US diversity-patriotism; it is a warning to 'different' US Americans to align with the national side by keeping what could be their disturbing cultural differences private or face the consequences. As such, the PSA reinforces the message President George W. Bush made before a Joint Session of the US Congress the day before the 'I am an American' PSA was broadcast – 'Either you are with us or you are with the terrorists' (Bush 2001). For even though President Bush's words were directed to foreign nations that harbour terrorists, his words, like the 'I am an American' PSA, attempt to persuade US citizens to underwrite the sovereign power of the US state in its War on Terror or face the possibility of having US sovereign power unleashed against them.

Filming the fear of difference[6]

The multimedia project '*I am an American*': *Video Portraits of Unsafe US Citizens* was crafted in response to the Ad Council's 'I am an American' PSA.[7] The project explores the complicated meanings and practices of citizenship, identity, tolerance, nationalism, patriotism, justice and memory woven into and around the seemingly simple declaration 'I am an American'. It does this by recounting the experiences of some US citizens who after 9/11 would not or could not normatively conform to the ideal of 'safe citizenship' the PSA hailed them to embody and enact.

The films, photographs and feedback commentaries that compose this project originated in a series of on-camera interviews I began in 2005 with a wide range of US Americans about their experiences as citizens in the post-9/11 US. Some of the individuals I interviewed were involved in US foreign wars in Iraq and Afghanistan, others were involved in US domestic wars on immigration primarily at the US–Mexico border, and still others were caught up in the security and immigration crossfire of the War on Terror as a sort of collateral damage. These individuals ranged from patriotic soldiers who served in the Iraq War to patriotic Muslims who found themselves detained as alleged enemy combatants; from undocumented immigrants to the US citizens who either track them and turn them over to US Border Patrol or who offer them humanitarian assistance; and from indigenous US Americans living on both sides of the US–Mexico border who are subjected to extraordinary surveillance by US Border Patrol, or Hurricane Katrina evacuees whose needs too often failed to register as urgent in the post-9/11 US, to artists and activists who found themselves suspected of practicing terrorism or aiding terrorists.

These individuals, their stories and how these stories are performed through my project can be understood as enactments of citizenship protests generally and often as immigrant protests specifically, as Tyler and Marciniak define it, because they question the capacity of citizenship to capture how political subjectivity functions. These stories are told from the perspectives a number of very differently situated protesters – some who are immigrants, some who insist they are not immigrants and some who are struggling to become immigrants. Let me give an example of each of these types of stories, which highlight tensions among continental vs. sovereign Americanness, indigenous vs. settler Americanness and consenting vs. contesting patriotisms, respectively.

The story of Mexican citizen and immigrant rights activist Elvira Arellano and her US citizen son Saul highlights some of the tensions around immigration and birthright citizenship that Tyler and Marciniak discuss (2013). This is the story of an undocumented economic migrant to the US who worked in Chicago's O'Hare airport and who was discovered to have been using a false social security number when the US tightened up its immigrant checks on airport workers after 9/11. Elvira received a deportation order which she defied, claiming that to deport her would effectively mean deporting 8-year-old Saul, who was born and raised in the US. Elvira lived with Saul in sanctuary in a Chicago church for one year. When she left sanctuary, she was deported. She and Saul now live in Mexico.

Another story is that of indigenous rights activist José Matus. A Yaqui tribal member and director of the indigenous rights group Alianza Indigena Sin Fronteras/ Indigenous Alliance Without Borders, José tells of how the US–Mexico border crosses what are traditional Yaqui tribal lands. Over the years, this has led to the dismemberment of the Yaqui nation, with part of it in the US and part of it in

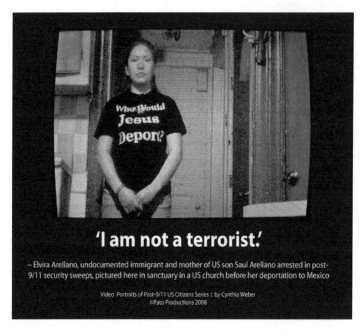

Figure 4.1 Elvira Arellano (courtesy of photographer Cynthia Weber © Pato Productions).

Figure 4.2 José Matus (courtesy of photographer Cynthia Weber © Pato Productions).

Figure 4.3 Phil McDowell (courtesy of photographer Cynthia Weber © Pato Productions).

Figure 4.4 Saul Arellano (courtesy of photographer Cynthia Weber © Pato Productions).

Mexico. José works with other indigenous rights activists to insure the free passage of Yaqui tribal members across the US–Mexico border, whatever their US or Mexican citizenship. But because of increased border security measures in this region, José explains that Yaqui nation members coming from Mexico into the US are often treated with the same suspicion as undocumented economic migrants coming into the US. José's immigrant protest is against the idea that Indigenous Americans are being treated like immigrants. As he puts it, 'We didn't cross the border. The border crossed us'.

And then there is the story of Phil McDowell, a former sergeant in the US Army. A college graduate, Phil enlisted in the military after 9/11 because he believed that 'the US was a beacon of light in the world and that we were a good society'. By the time he deployed, the US was at war with Iraq, a war for which he saw no legal or moral justification. Even though he objected to the US war in Iraq, Phil served out his four-year term. Deciding not to re-enlist, Phil got his separation papers, cleared base and took his vacation days. A few days before his vacation was over, Phil was stop-lossed. 'Effectively, I was drafted and told I had to go back to Iraq'. Unable to continue to serve in a war he believed was illegal and immoral, Phil deserted the army and sought asylum in Canada. 'I never thought I'd be a political refugee from the United States', says Phil.

I asked each interviewee to narrate their story, reflect upon their experiences of citizenship and patriotism after 9/11, create a pose (with the US flag if they so chose) that epitomized their experiences and encapsulate their experiences into a sentence that included the words, 'I am an American'. I edited the resulting thirteen major interviews into thirteen short documentary films.

Each of my thirteen documentary films begins with the emergency call between fire fighters on their way to the Twin Towers and their Command Post:

> Firefighter to Command: The World Trade Center Tower Number One is on fire. The whole left side of the building … it's just a huge explosion.
>
> Command to Firefighter: 10-4. All units stand by at this time.

As this exchange plays, the name of the film's title character fades up. A few seconds later, the words 'I am an American' fade up below the name. Then the action starts. Over the next three and a half minutes, the title character narrates their story in their own words as a variety of still and moving images roll across the screen. The typical arc of each story goes like this – normal life before 9/11, how 9/11 changed the character's life for better or usually for worse, how this change was adjusted to or resolved and how all of this makes the character reflect on US citizenship and what it means to be a US American. After this narration, each film cuts to the title character looking directly into the camera and saying not only 'I am an American' but explaining what kind of US American they are. So, for example, Phil McDowell says 'I am an Iraq War Resister, and I am an American'. Saul Arellano says, 'I am the son of an immigrant without papers, and I am an American'. And another Indigenous American I interviewed, Ofelia

Rivas, says, 'My nation is divided by an international border, and I am an O'odham American'.

As in the Ad Council's original PSA, I end each of my films with a version of the US motto. But instead of displaying the motto in its original form, I turn the motto around so that 'E Pluribus Unum' – Out of Many, One – becomes 'Ex Uno Plures' – Out of One, Many. This reversal is not meant to suggest some revaluing on my part between the One and the Many or a redirecting of the process of transformation between the One and the Many. Rather, it is meant 'to expose the unreliability of the code' (Keenan 1997; also see Barthes 1995; Weber 1999) upon which the US national imaginary of the tolerance of difference is founded. Combining this reversed/reversible motto with films that, by R. B. J. Walker's description of them, 'capture the dilemma of a national sovereignty caught between classical sovereignty and biopolitical sovereignty' (Walker 2007), the overall effect is to demonstrate how the US state can at any time – and does during the War on Terror – change direction, rewrite its foundations and potentially put in jeopardy the Many who are not protected by the always historically contingent promise of the One. This means that those in the safe 'One' may at any time find themselves in the unsafe 'Many'.[8]

Just as in the Ad Council's PSA, my reversed/reversible US motto fades up onto a black screen as a cacophony of US voices repeat all or part of the line 'I am an American'. The final image in each of my films is of the title character looking directly into the camera while (in most cases) holding the US flag. As the film cuts from the US motto to this 'flag shot', the cacophony of voices resolves with an anonymous US voice saying 'I am' and the title character in voice-over saying 'American'. Each film then fades to black, and the credit sequence begins.

I used the materials from these short documentaries to produce an alternative 'I am an American' PSA that quite literally speaks back to the original PSA. Like the Ad Council's one-minute PSA, my one-minute PSA features each of my title characters looking directly into the camera and declaring 'I am an American' while the emotive Americana music of Edgar Meyer plays in the background. Structurally, declaratively, aurally, cinematically and affectively, my PSA deliberately mimics the Ad Council's PSA. But twenty seconds into my PSA, my PSA confounds expectations because my characters go on to declare (as they do in their individuals films) just what kind of US American they are – an Iraq War resister, a political refugee *from* America, a wrongly suspected bioterrorist. From this point on, my PSA also includes explicit markers of racial, ethnic, religious and political differences that are excluded from the Ad Council's PSA. These include shots of a clearly identifiable Muslim character praying in a mosque, of a clearly identifiably Indigenous character posing next to a banner with the emblem of her nation on it (as opposed to the US flag) and of a political protest that features a sign that reads, 'I won't trade my humanity for patriotism'. Finally, as in the individual films, my PSA ends with a twist on the Ad Council's ending, with my characters saying 'I am an American' while the inverted US motto fades in and out.

The final shot of the Ad Council's PSA is of a smiling, brown-skinned little girl waving a US flag. She seems to embody the PSA's post-9/11 affirmation of the tolerance of difference and the promise of carrying this tolerance into our melted American Dream-like future. In contrast, the final shot of my PSA is of a visibly unhappy Saul Arellano waving a US flag, just as he did at his mother Elvira Arellano's press conference in which she announced she was taking sanctuary in a US church to defy her deportation order. As viewers learn from the four-minute film about Saul and Elvira, Elvira was deported when she left sanctuary after a year, and Saul eventually joined her in Mexico. Both because this 8-year-old US citizen had his childhood cut short by political circumstances and because he was in his mother's words 'effectively deported' with her to Mexico, Saul can be read as embodying the post-9/11 American Nightmare experienced by those US Americans whose differences are not tolerated.[9] If read in this way, the future Saul's image predicts is not one that is celebratory of difference and diversity-patriotism but mournful of how some differences are always placed beyond tolerance, especially in times of patriotic fever. Saul's image, then, can be read as announcing (to borrow a turn of phrase from Sara Ahmed) that while all US citizens are part of 'America', 'being "in it" does not mean we are all "in it" in the same way' (Ahmed 2000: 171; also see Lewis 2004).[10]

Nor, as this final image of Saul suggests, do we all feel the same way about being in it. In making these different 'feeling states' (Fortier 2008, 2010) explicit, my PSA attempts to make an affective break from the Ad Council's PSA. For my PSA it meant to play itself out in a different affective register than does the Ad Council's PSA, one which lingers in/on 'bad grief' and the difficult questions it poses to 'America' and 'Americans' after 9/11 rather than affectively attempting to transform this 'bad grief' into a state-sponsored 'good grief' that might release US citizens from the post-9/11 challenges of US identity. As such, my PSA is meant to mark how affect is politically and aesthetically mobilized on behalf of a state-sanctioned national fantasy while suggesting the possibility for new mobilizations of affect, aesthetics and politics, ones that might refigure the complex relationships among citizenship, identity, tolerance, nationalism, patriotism and memory to make them more just and more politically responsible to populations both within and beyond nation-states.

Viewed as a collection, these fourteen films are meant to convey a sense of what Barbara Johnson calls 'the critical difference' that keeps any identity from corresponding to its image of itself (Johnson 1980). That critical difference is surely expressed in the disjuncture between the lived reality of US citizenship for unsafe US citizens during the War on Terror measured against the ideal of the tolerance of difference as the foundation and lived reality of the US nation-state.[11] But in expressing that critical difference, the films suggest yet another critical difference. This is the radical disjuncture between the citizen and the human – a disjuncture that, according to Kant, need not exist in the modern liberal nation-state because the modern liberal nation-state makes being a good citizen the basis for being a good human (Walker 2007).

It is this equation of the good citizen to the good human that the Ad Council's PSA circulates when it attempts to represent the tolerance of difference as the foundation of diversity-patriotism. But because the Ad Council's PSA organizes the US national imaginary by disavowing many differences in the name of one national ideal of tolerance and censuring many differences in the name of one national idea of justice, the Ad Council's PSA effectively forecloses on a whole range of expressions of humanity that cannot or will not be confined within the limits of diversity-patriotism. The effect of this foreclosure is that the Ad Council's PSA fails in its representation of the good citizen as the good human.

My project is dedicated to communicating this failure so that it can be known, felt and remembered in ways that not only potentially refigure what it means to be an 'American' but also what it means to be a citizen and a human more generally. For as Judith Butler (paraphrasing Emanuel Levinas) explains, 'For representation to convey the human ..., representation must not only fail, but it must *show* its failure' (Butler 2004; also see Managhan 2008).[12] By reminding us, as R. B. J. Walker puts it, that 'the modern compromise in political life is that we are citizens first and humans second' (Walker 2007), my fourteen films not only contribute to chronicling the violence and injustice required to make this compromise work on behalf of the modern nation-state. They hopefully suggest that, because the US state (like any state) reserves for itself the power to determine who among its citizens is 'safe' or 'unsafe' and to reverse this decision at any time, this modern liberal compromise of humanity for citizenship is a compromise too far. This is not only because citizenship can never guarantee one's safety (meaning there is no such thing as a 'safe citizen' from the citizen's point of view; Weber 2008). More importantly, this is because citizenship not only cannot but willfully does not guarantee one's humanity, much less the humanity of those who are not among the 'One'.[13]

Critical reflections

If the Ad Council's 'I am an American' PSA is a protest *for* citizenship, can my alternative 'I am an American' project be understood as a protest *of* citizenship? Answering this question is not straightforward because of how my project uses and apparently reaffirms the phrase 'I am an American'. As such, one might suggest that my project celebrates both citizenship itself as a regulative ideal of political subjectivity and US citizenship as the most sought-after brand of national citizenship far more than it offers 'a protest against citizenship' (Derrida 1994b: 240–1).

These criticisms of my project are not without merit, particularly when one considers the individual films on their own, rather than the films as a collection. Yet if individually the films often express a desire to be included within a unified national ideal of a coherent liberal Americanness – to protest *for* citizenship – collectively these films protest *against* citizenship by challenging notions of coherent liberalism, coherent nationalism, or coherent Americanness and the performative grammars that enable them. So while both examples of advertised Americanness discussed in this chapter might be understood as citizenship protests, whether they are for citizenship or against citizenship depends upon how they perform advertised Americanness.

Evelyn Aslultany clearly grasps this performative function of advertising in her critique of the Ad Council's PSA in terms of how it attempts to sell 'diversity-patriotism' to the post-9/11 US citizenry. From Alsultany's perspective, it seems that the Ad Council's PSA 'does not so much represent society *as it is* but society as it *should be*' (Cronin 2004: 113), even if, as she points out, how the US 'should be' for the Ad Council is one in which the limits of cultural citizenship are narrowly drawn. Alsultany's observations sit nicely within Anne Cronin's work on the performative function of advertising more generally. For, as Cronin argues, advertising functions performatively by offering consumers not only products but 'promotional beliefs' and 'invested understandings' that perform divisions in the social order and frame classificatory regimes in relation to their consumption habits, which in this case are about consuming the 'diversity-patriotism' of the US nation (Cronin 2004).

As a protest against citizenship, my 'I am an American' project appears to be in a different register than the Ad Council's original 'I am an American' PSA. For if the Ad Council's PSA takes unified US nationalism as the pre-given basis upon which to sell 'diversity-patriotism' to a unified US citizenry, my 'I am an American' project puts this pre-given category under erasure. It does this by asking, for example, if it means the same thing for an undocumented continental American migrant to the US like Elvira Arellano to say 'I am an American' as it is for a documented legal immigrant to the US to say this same thing. It shows a curiosity about why it is that an Indigenous American like Ofelia Rivas refuses to say 'I am an American', opting instead to say 'I am an O'odham American', with O'odham being the name of her tribal nation. More broadly, it ponders how race, class, sexuality, gender and indigenity performatively come into existence in relation to the seemingly simple declaration 'I am an American' in ways that not only identify with the US and with citizenship but also simultaneously disidentify with citizenship through their creative reidentifications with the phrase 'I am an American'. What this means is that my 'I am an American' project offers what Cronin might call a different 'matrix of transformation' in relation to how the advertised and consumed subjectivities of 'America' and 'American' are performatively constructed, connected and contested (Cronin 2004), to the point that nationalisms and indeed citizenships might be reimagined.

By inviting the uninvited, unsafe US citizen to make a claim to the United States of America, then, my 'I am an American' project just might begin to expose how ill-equipped the concept of citizenship is to function as a universal framework for political subjectivity. The effect might well be to shame some specific post-9/11 legal enactments of US citizenship, if not the concept of citizenship itself. Understood in these terms, the performances of citizenship protest in this project may not amount to endorsements of US citizenship in its post-9/11 form or of citizenship more generally. Rather, they might be read as shaming gestures (Souweine 2005: 534) that provide some future grounds from which to oppose citizenships, nationalisms and how they figure Americanness (Parenti 2003) by aiming 'to expose the banal violence of citizenship *as regimes of control*' (Tyler and Marciniak 2013).[14]

Notes

1 I am referring to the National Defense Authorization Act, which at the time of this writing was passed by both Houses of Congress and threatened with a presidential veto.
2 For historical background of the Ad Council, see <http://www.adcouncil.org/About-Us>.
3 My inspiration for thinking about 'good grief' and 'bad grief' in relation to this project was sparked by a presentation by Gaye Chan and Nandita Sharma at the Melancholic States conference at Lancaster University. My use of these terms, however, bears no resemblance to how they used these terms and is not one that they endorse. See Chan and Sharma (2007).
4 On the hail, see Althusser (1971).
5 For example, the US singer Pat Boone labelled gay rights activists working to overturn California's ban on gay marriage as 'sexual jihadists'. Writing about these activists in the context of the November 2008 Mumbai terrorist attacks, Boone commented, 'What troubles me so deeply, and should trouble all thinking Americans, is that there is a real, unbroken line between the jihadist savagery in Mumbai and the hedonistic, irresponsible, blindly selfish goals and tactics of our homegrown sexual jihadists. Hate is hate, no matter where it erupts. And by its very nature, if it's not held in check, it will escalate into acts vile, violent and destructive'. See Boone (2008).
6 Thanks to Kate Nash for articulating this form of words to describe my project.
7 Films from my 'I am an American' project can be viewed at <http://www.iamanamericanproject.com>. For a book-length elaboration of the project, see Weber (2011).
8 In his generous commentary on this project, R. B. J. Walker elaborated this point in grander terms, arguing that my project makes visible 'the reversibility in all modern claims to subjectivity' (Walker 2007). And if modern subjectivity is reversible, then the modern promise of progress and meaning the nation presumably guarantees cannot be insured.
9 Saul and Elvira's case is a complicated one. In my collection of films and in my PSA, it is not meant to represent how all foreign mothers of US children were treated by the US government, either before or after 9/11. Rather, because each film is shot as much as possible from the perspective of the person telling that story, the film about Saul and Elvira represents Elvira's perspective on their situation, a perspective Elvira did much to popularize before, during and after her sanctuary stay with Saul.
10 Ahmed's quote refers to her description of a globalized economy of difference, not to any particular national economy of difference. But because the US national economy of difference is a colonial and post-colonial economy of difference, Ahmed's point applies to the US.
11 Another way to think about this is through the notion of what Homi Bhabha calls the split that is inherent in writing the nation. As Bhabha explains, 'In the production of the nation as narration there is a split between the continuist, accumulative temporality of the pedagogical, and the repetitious, recursive strategy of the performative. It is through this process of splitting that the conceptual ambivalence of modern society becomes the site of *writing the nation*' (Bhabha (2004); also see Bhabha (1990) and Stephens (2008, 2010)).
12 Thanks to Tina Managhan for bringing Butler's formulation of this point to my attention. See Managhan (2008).
13 Barbara Johnson's ideas of critical difference follow on from Jacques Derrida's idea of 'differance'. In this context, both Johnson and Derrida agree that to construct singularity and deny difference is a violent act. It is worth quoting Derrida at length on this point. As he puts it, 'As soon as there is the one, there is murder, wounding, traumatism. The one guards against the other, it protects itself from the other. But in the movement of this jealous violence it compromises in itself its self-otherness or self difference. The difference from within one's self, which makes it one. The one as the other. At one and the same time, but in the same time that is out of joint. The one forgets to remember

itself to its self. It keeps and erases the archive of this injustice that it is, of this violence that it does. The one makes itself violence, it violates and does violence to itself. It becomes what it is, the very violence that it does to itself. The determination of the self as one is violence' (Derrida 1996).

14 An earlier version of this chapter was published in 2013 as '"I am an American": Protesting Advertised "Americanness"', *Citizenship Studies*, 17(2): 278–92. This research was supported by grants from the British Academy and the Leverhulme Trust. My generous network of friends and family helped these funds go further and enabled me to self-fund the final four films in this series by providing accommodation, food and transportation whenever they could. They include Lucy Suchman, Andrew Clement, Monique Fortier, Roxanne Doty, Spike Peterson, Candy, Heather, and Max Ogle, Cheryl Hill, Nigel Clark, Shelia Rye, Chris Olofson and as ever Chuck, Nina, Lindsay and Seth Clovis. Additional grants from the Lancaster University Faculty of Arts and Social Sciences and from the Lancaster University Friends Association helped to fund the production of still images for exhibition. My greatest debt is to those people featured in this project – Lupe Denogean, Phil McDowell, Jamine Aponte, Fernando Suarez del Solar, Cindy Sheehan, James Yee, Greg and Glenda Avery, Chris Simcox, Elvira and Saul Arellano, Shanti Sellz, José Matus, Ofelia Rivas, Julia Shearson, Abe Dabdoub, Will Potter and Steve Kurtz.

5 Characterization and systemic gender violence
The example of *Laundry* and the figure of the mother in Irish culture

Lisa Fitzpatrick

Historian Maria Luddy writes, 'The idealization of motherhood was a significant feature of the rhetoric of politicians in the new Irish State [in the 1920s]; the female body and the maternal body, particularly in its unmarried condition, became a central focus of concern to the State and the Catholic Church' (2007: 80). This 'focus of concern' is apparent in the laws and practices introduced by the first governments of the Irish Free State (founded 1922); the discourses in circulation in the media and in government and church communications in the decades before and after the founding of the state, and in the Irish Constitution of 1937. It persists, differently framed, in current political debates in Ireland around reproductive rights, where it seems at odds with the generally good status of women; and has recurred with heightened intensity following the tragic death of Savita Halappanavar in October 2012.

It is difficult at present to consider attitudes to women and maternity in Irish politics without thinking of Halappanavar, who presented at University Hospital Galway with the symptoms of an early 'inevitable miscarriage'. The Irish Constitution states that 'The State acknowledges the right to life of the unborn and, with due regard to the equal right to life of the mother, guarantees in its laws to respect, and, as far as practicable, by its laws to defend and vindicate that right' (40: 3: 3). Because there was a foetal heartbeat, Mrs Halappanavar's pregnancy could not be terminated until either the baby died, or her medical condition deteriorated to the point of death, despite her and her husband's repeated requests for an abortion. She miscarried without medical intervention over a period of three days, and died afterwards of septicaemia and organ failure.

In July 2013 the Irish government passed new legislation. The Protection of Human Life During Pregnancy Bill allows medical intervention to save the mother's life, based on the judgement of two doctors or, if the risk is because the mother is suicidal, on the judgement of three doctors including a psychiatrist. The legislation is based on the Supreme Court ruling in the 'X Case' in 1992, in which a teenager pregnant by rape was refused permission to leave the country to have an abortion in England. It was not until 2012 that legislation to address the ruling on the 'X Case' was proposed. The months of debate about this very minimal legislation has foregrounded yet again Irish society's official attitudes to women, motherhood and the 'unborn' (there is some evidence that government's attitudes are more conservative than those of the population). However this is only one example of medical practices that subordinate the mother to the foetus. There have been other recent cases where the woman's right to refuse medical interventions like the induction of labour have been weighed against the baby's right to life.[1] At times even future, as-yet-unconceived, children have been preferred over the best maternal care: women with obstructed labour were sometimes subjected without their consent to symphysiotomies[2] in preference to Caesarean sections, a practice that continued into the early 1990s in some hospitals. Survivors of this practice were left with limited mobility and in chronic pain but, crucially, since there is no scarring to the uterus there is no limit on the number of subsequent pregnancies the mother can deliver.[3] And individual cases – like 'X' or the Kerry Babies case of the 1980s – have repeatedly foregrounded contradictions between public expressions of revulsion at abortion, the ready availability of abortion services in the United Kingdom for women who can afford to travel there and the practice of infanticide which appears from the Kerry case to have been quite common at least until the 1980s, if not still today.

  I would argue that this set of contradictions that denigrates individual women while idealizing the concept of motherhood emerges from a characterization of women as a class and the accompanying promulgation of a set of beliefs and knowledges about women, by the Irish State and the Catholic Church acting in partnership, particularly during the period of nationalist uprising and the decades following the foundation of the state. I use the concept of characterization, normally used in literary and dramatic discourses, to describe the construction of the figure of the 'mother' as a subject, in political and other official discourse. This characterization is accomplished discursively, and recent historical analyses have explored archival sources to trace the history of women and sexuality in modern Ireland. It is also accomplished also through the use of iconography, public practices and the marginalization of women in public life. Characterization in theatre provides the spectator 'with a means of seeing and/or imagining a dramatic world and thus creating a *reality-effect* by contriving to produce the credibility and verisimilitude of the character and his [sic] actions' (Pavis 1998: 52). At its simplest this is achieved in two main ways: by scripting the character's actions and words, and by scripting the other characters' responses in actions and words. This process of scripting the fictional world (both the production of a written script and the script's function as outline for the theatrical performance) is a useful analogy for the discursive creation of a new 'Ireland', a post-independence state that is evoked with wide-ranging references to Catholic moral teaching, an Edenic pre-colonial Ireland, heroic myths and legends, nationalistic conceptions of gender roles, Victorian puritanical attitudes towards sexuality and poverty, ultramontane Catholicism and a post-colonial sense of cultural inferiority. This scripting process established narratives of power and authority for the new state, and characterized its citizens according to conservative notions of class and gender. Through this process of characterization, continuing into the present, the subject is fixed within a set of potential meanings, narratives and actions and a set of affective, social and political responses to the subject are formed and authorized. Thus a narrow set of meanings and of approved behaviours becomes attached to the character called 'mother'. The interrogation of this characterization is a recurring theme in contemporary women's writing in Ireland.

Affectively, the discourses about female sexuality and maternity in the 1920s and 1930s are primarily expressive of disgust, anger and shame at the (female) agents of immorality. In giving voice to and encouraging such affects, they helped create the conditions for the abuse of vulnerable sections of the population and systemic practices of violence against women. Žižek describes systemic and symbolic violence as often underlying individual actions, shaping the contexts and the pressures to which the individual is subject (2009: 1). Both are classified as objective forms of violence that operate seemingly without agency and thus reflect an unchangeable status quo. These forms of violence are apparent when hegemonic structures and institutional power and authority become corrupt and reliant on repressive measures to sustain themselves, or engage with repressive measures to sustain normative social values and structures (2009: 10–12). Relating Žižek's terms to the characterization of the mother draws upon discourses that characterize 'unchaste' women as dangerous to the state and the moral life of the nation, if they are not strictly controlled.

My starting point for this piece of research was an immersive, site-specific show called *Laundry*, performed by Anu Productions in October 2011 as part of the Dublin Theatre Festival. The production used a set of staging strategies to examine the systemic and symbolic nature of the violence enacted by the state upon the bodies of women incarcerated in the Magdalene Laundries: an estimated 30,000 women over the course of the twentieth century.[4] Many of these women were unmarried mothers; some were victims of rape, incest or sexual abuse, and some were orphaned or illegitimate girls who had grown up in state care and whose uncertain antecedents rendered them likely to 'fall into sin' or to 'lead others to sin'. The Laundry, on Sean McDermott Street just a few blocks from O'Connell Street in Dublin's north inner city, was run by the Sisters of Our Lady of Charity of Refuge. The Laundry finally closed in 1996; the last woman was admitted there in 1995. The naming seems like a double irony, the first the name of the Order and the second, that these streets were named after the executed leaders of the 1916 Uprising, with its Proclamation of a Republic that 'guarantees religious and civil liberty, equal rights and equal opportunities to all its citizens, and declares its resolve to pursue the happiness and prosperity of the whole nation and of all its parts, cherishing all the children of the nation equally'. The staging strategies used by Anu draw attention to the systemic and symbolic nature of the abuse represented by the Laundry, and the complicity of the state and population in the violence. This opens opportunities for a debate about the current, as well as the historical, characterization of women in independent Ireland's national imaginary.

Witnessing the performance

Performances of *Laundry* are scheduled for each half-hour and I hurry up O'Connell Street, turning onto Cathal Brugha Street, walking fast; even though

I know Dublin well I am not entirely sure where the building is, or if anyone will know it if I ask for directions. I see the Festival's mobile office outside a large brick building that is clearly locked up and that blends into the cityscape. There are chipped white-painted metal railings around it and the sash windows are dirty and opaque. The two smaller windows beside the dilapidated dark red double doors are barred and I can see bars on the inside too, and there is a grille set in the door. The architecture and details, like the carvings on the building of crosses and of the Virgin and Child over the door and the cross on the roof, identify it as a convent. Buildings like this are part of the urban landscapes of Ireland, functioning as schools and hospitals as well as convents and former laundries. There is nothing about this building that would make me look twice; it is large and slightly ominous yet simultaneously so familiar as to be invisible. There are two other spectators waiting outside and we stand together by the door. We are all women. We make some conversation but not much; I have the feeling we should stand quietly, like supplicants or penitents, though there is nothing explicit to suggest that. The metal grille sometimes grinds open and eyes are visible, staring at each of us in turn. There is nothing friendly in the gaze. Whenever the grille opens we fall silent. It is uncomfortable to be watched by someone whose face I can't see; I feel awkward and self-conscious. Then there is a flurry of activity: the bolts scrape loudly back and the door opens, and two women rush out, one of them a young woman in uniform with downcast eyes holding a bundle of laundry. The uniformed woman seems afraid; she moves rapidly, pushes the first woman into a taxi, throws in the laundry and hurries away across the street. Another young woman, also in uniform, gestures us in without looking at us. We enter into a small square hallway and the door is bolted loudly behind us. The women all wear a uniform that resembles a convent school uniform with a shirt and tunic. Their hair is scraped back, their faces are unsmiling and their eyes cast down.

Three doors open from the hallway: a cell on either side, and another bolted door straight ahead. We are separated: one of my fellow spectators goes into either cell, and I am left in the hallway with the woman by the door who gives me a bucket of whitish liquid to hold. The smell of carbolic is overpowering. I stand in silence in the hallway for a while and then the woman turns quickly to me and whispers that the bucket contains breast milk. Her sudden movements suggest that she is imparting secrets and mustn't be caught talking. I don't know what to say in response; I feel disoriented by the intimacy of the performance style and trapped in the narrow space. She grabs the bucket from me and pushes me into the first of the cells, gesturing the other spectator out.

The bucket of breast milk is a grotesque object, one that reappears later in the performance, and the first in a number of moments that draw attention to the nature of the violence perpetrated by the Laundry system. The industrial, metal bucket and the quantity of liquid it contains suggests mass production and the depersonalization of a profound biological bond. The babies can be fed by anyone, with milk taken from any or all mothers; the maternal bond is neither nurtured nor cherished. The intimate, interior nature of breast milk is negated and thereby abjected in this representation of a bodily fluid expressed and hauled by workers: the warm intimacy of the breast is transformed into the trappings of the machine. The lack of hygiene implicit in this also signifies the lack of regard for mother or baby.

Moving from the hallway into the first cell, I find a young girl, obviously pregnant, struggling and pleading wordlessly with her unresponsive father in a scene I recognize as him signing her into the Laundry (I recognize it from *The Magdalene Sisters*, but also from my own absorbed embodied knowledge of women's value and remembered youthful dread of accidental pregnancy). I am so close to them that the despairing girl's hair lies on my knees as she crouches rocking in her chair. The door is unbolted and I am beckoned out and pushed into another cell, where a young man (a brother? a boyfriend?) sits waiting for a girl. He asks me the time. He has been waiting for hours and nobody will let him see her, nobody will answer his questions. The reported histories of the Magdalene Laundries include testimonies from men who went looking for their sisters or girlfriends and were told that the person they sought was no longer there; this was not always true. The young man becomes agitated and hits the wall, shouting. The door is unbolted and he is pushed back inside by the uniformed girl, and I am beckoned out again into the lobby. Now the door into the building is opened, its bolts scraping loudly; I walk through, the door bangs closed behind me, the bolts scraping and slamming closed again.

It is very, very cold in the building and the light is chilly and hard. There is nothing soft to be seen: no carpets, no cloths: just hard bare surfaces. A filing cabinet stands with its drawers partially open and I can see that it is full of carbolic soap, and cards with names on them, and swatches of women's hair attached to the cards. A uniformed girl circles the cabinet watching me, unsmiling, wary. She is reciting the names of women in a litany that seems to neither begin nor end. She leans towards me and whispers four names, urgently, asking me to remember them: this is another secret; she asks me on two separate occasions. Then the door to the right opens and a heavily pregnant, uniformed girl beckons me in. She sits on a chair and watches silently and impassively as a young woman with bandaged breasts unfastens the bandages and indicates that I should hold one end of the cloth. Unwinding herself, she then steps naked into the tin bath and sits, shivering. Beyond the room a baby howls and her body convulses in response. Apart from the screaming child, all is silent. The room is full of the buckets of the same whitish liquid I was told was breast milk: it is a like a scene from some terrible, grotesque dairy with this vulnerable soft body exposed to the gaze of the spectator. The young woman emerges from the bath and gestures to me to hold the cloth, and she winds her body until she is bound once more. I do not know what else to do so I hold the cloth. What else can I do? I try to seem kind, comforting, but the women do not respond. Again, I am gestured from the room and across the hall into another room, this one with five uniformed women who use dance and abstract movement to respond to the spoken texts of the many human rights policies and declarations that these institutions contravened: policies on torture, unjust imprisonment, rights to liberty and justice.

The bolts scrape back, doors open, I move through and they slam and are locked behind me, an aural representation of imprisonment as I move deeper and further into the building. There is a chair set facing a floor to ceiling mirror. I sit, looking at myself and at the wall behind me. Then the light shifts and behind the mirror I can see a young woman moving slowly towards me. As she moves along the line that links her to me, the changing light shows her, then me, eliding one to the other, a palimpsestic human. As she draws close to the glass she implores me silently, through her gestures, to acknowledge that I saw her, to remember her, to tell others that she is there.

Though shaken by the encounter with the young woman and by the performance's evocation of the random circumstances that situated each of us on either side of the mirror, I have to move swiftly to engage with the next moment of performance. There is a walkway from the hall into the chapel, and it is covered in (human) hair which is silky under my fingers but also shocking: pleasantly tactile but conceptually distressing. Another young woman approaches me, coming very close to take my arm and whisper if I can hear her baby crying: I can. She pulls me to a wall with a peephole drilled into it, nudging me to look through. I see a windowless room full of empty cradles. She brings me back to the church. Inside the doorway is a stained-glass window set in a large alcove. Taking up a bundle of sheets, she climbs into the alcove and mimics the Virgin in the image, clutching the sheet to her breast in place of her missing baby. Her madness evokes distress in me: again, an uncertainty about what to do, how to respond to this image of maternity idealized in juxtaposition with maternity punished and denied. An older woman, also uniformed, hurries forward, reaching up to the girl to coax her down, begging me not to report them. I say of course I won't. She leads me into the chapel she asks if I will sit with her a while. We genuflect and sit in the pew. When we're seated she offers me a boiled sweet, and asks if she can hold my hand. I take a sweet and say yes, she can hold my hand. The warmth of her hand and the sweetness of the candy are immensely comforting; I hadn't realized how lonely this experience is. She tells me that she left the Laundry to marry but that after her husband died she asked to re-enter, because she was afraid to be on her own. It's not so bad here, she says; and when she is dead everyone will remember her and pray for her, won't they? I say yes. I don't say, no: you'll be buried in a mass grave, possibly undocumented; it will be as if you never lived at all.

The older woman tells me to go into the confessional on the other side of the chapel and I cross to it and enter. Inside it is larger than I expected, as the compartments have been removed. A uniformed girl is drawing on the wall and whistling; she catches my eye, stops, giggles. Women are not supposed to whistle; it makes the Virgin Mary cry, she says; I remember old women saying that when I was a child. She tells me a secret. She sketches herself an imaginary, fitted dress with cuffs, and high heels for her feet. Then on tiptoes she approaches me and asks me to dance. We waltz gently. She asks me if she looks nice and I tell her, 'You look lovely'. She laughs, and the door opens; she jumps back. A young woman with a grim, downcast expression comes in, and gives her a warning glance as she beckons me out, and takes me into the sacristy behind the altar. This woman begs me to help her escape. She will accompany me out of the building saying she is helping to carry my laundry. I am given a pile of sheets and she takes another pile; she then pushes me out of the sacristy. We hurry back through the church – pausing again to genuflect – and out across the walkway. A girl unbolts the first set of doors and we pass through. The bolts slam home behind us. We hurry through the next set of doors, and the next: out into the street: sunlight and fresh air.

In the street the girl pushes me into a waiting taxi with the sheets. My driver, an actor, offers a potted history of the neighbourhood as he drives me to a local laundrette where I iron sheets with two other spectators and hear stories of the laundry. After a while, the taxi returns and brings us back to the front of the Convent building. We are each presented with a bar of carbolic soap wrapped in brown paper, with our names and the date on it. Then we get out of the car and are back in the centre of the city. It feels like a release. I sit with a cup of tea for a long while and write down the details of the performance, feeling an urgent need to tell everything that I have seen. This urgent need to speak about the performance is one that other spectators have also commented upon.

History and context

Laundry is the second in a series of four site-specific, archaeological performances devised by the interdisciplinary team at Anu Productions under the directorship of Louise Lowe. They are archaeological in the sense that the performances uncover the history of a particular square mile in inner-city Dublin – the Monto district famous from the 'Circe' chapter in Joyce's *Ulysses* – and the research identifies 'potentially transferable concepts' and uses these, intertwined with historical reenactment and with a strong emphasis on documentation, to engage with performance that explores the everyday use of the site over the period of about a century. Other works in the series include *World's End Lane* (2010) and *The Boys of Foley Street* (2012), with *Vardo Corner* which premiered as work-in-progress in October 2013. Although the other pieces were also critically acclaimed, *Laundry* met with a tremendous emotional response apparent in blog postings and social media, selling out all performances, and winning the Irish Times Theatre Award for Best Production that year. Lowe describes her aim as 'a forensic examination of space. Translating all the many levels of experience into performance, so that the performance speaks to the space and reflects the space and encapsulates the truth of that space; the lives of people who have inhabited it, its history' (Keating 2009).

Although the whole series is concerned with examining dispossession and impoverishment, *Laundry* takes the maternal body as a central focus, and the work repeatedly presents images of motherhood that draw attention to contradictions between a rhetoric that glorifies motherhood, and social practices that denigrate it. Images of maternity denied and abjected recur throughout the performance: not only the buckets of breast milk, but the young girl abandoned by her family and signed into the convent; the girl with the bandaged breasts which suggests mastitis, which was often left untreated; the sound track of screaming babies, and the empty cribs glimpsed through the peephole. Perhaps most poignant is the distressed girl seeking her lost child, then standing against the rich stained-glass window mimicking the Virgin, clutching a bundle of soiled sheets in place of a baby.

By juxtaposing these performed images of maternity denied with the religious iconography of the stained-glass window and the carved Virgin and Child above the convent door, the performance draws attention to social and cultural attitudes towards maternity as well as the violence of the Magdalene Laundries. These attitudes are at the heart of the focus on the female body that Luddy's work addresses. The published materials to which she and other historians refer may reflect differing degrees of severity towards the unmarried mother or 'fallen' woman, but the overall attitudes remain constant. The *Irish Ecclesiastical Record* for example published multiple articles during the 1920s and 1930s, mostly by clergy, on the 'unmarried mother'.[5] Some of them express pity for the 'poor creatures' (Devane 1924: 173), and Revd Devane expresses anger and disgust at the disparity in treatment between the women and the men, describing it as 'this unchristian dual standard' and demanding that 'we set man and woman equal before the law of the land for their parental responsibilities, as they are equal before the law of God for their moral fall and sin' (1924: 174). All the commentaries, however, ultimately focus on the woman. A harsh, punitive response that leaves mother and baby entirely destitute is judged to be unworkable because of the danger of 'Souperism': that is, Protestants will offer charity ('soup') and the mother and child will fall victim to proselytizers, lose their religion and so lose all hope of salvation.[6] Thus most of the commentators recommend some kind of provision for the woman and her child, at least until the child is weaned and can be fostered.

Devane, whose writings suggest that he has a keen sense of natural justice and a generally charitable attitude to the women he writes about, suggests a system of refuge that is in fact identical with the abuse perpetrated by Magdalene Laundries (1924: 183). However, he also argues strongly for the raising of the age of consent and proper protection of the growing girl, judging Irish law to be deficient. Historian Diarmuid Ferriter draws attention in his recent work to an absence of legal measures at the time to protect young girls and women against sexual violence, and to startlingly high rates of infanticide throughout the early decades of the state (2009: 119–27). Ferriter offers evidence that infanticide was treated quite leniently by the courts and by officials who often sympathized with the mother's plight. Regarding the treatment of victims of sexual violence he comments that the blame for sexual crime was frequently attributed to the victim rather than to the perpetrator (2009: 127). Thus the female citizen's rights were held in a precarious balance where the appearance of immodesty in her speech or behaviour could lead to her characterization as an immoral and corrupting element. These facts sit in stark contrast to the rhetoric of Ireland as a pious country where 'moral ideals stand high and have a strong influence on the life of the nation' (Sagart 1922: 147).

Texts from the early part of the twentieth century characterize the unmarried mother as an innocent, foolish girl who has made a mistake and can be rehabilitated, or as an 'imbecile', not capable of taking responsibility for herself, or as vicious (Sagart 1922: 148–9). Class is highly significant in this classification.

Middle-class girls tend to be characterized as foolish but not immoral, and if their pregnancy is managed discreetly Sagart suggests they may even marry respectably thereafter. Unlike working-class girls, they should not be subjected to the humiliations of confinement in a state institution. This class prejudice is evident as a strand running through the gendered discourse, which reserves public shame and disgrace for working-class women. And despite Devane's critique of the double standard, he does advise that unmarried mothers be 'made to think deeply on their sin, and to realize what a woman has done when she has lost her virtue and her honour' (1924: 179). There is no equivalent level of shame for the man, who as Devane acknowledges is likely to be treated as a 'cavalier' (1924: 173).

The texts insistently use terms like 'shame' and 'disgrace' ambiguously, as verbs as well as nouns: the unmarried mother not only feels shame, she is shamed and this shaming is public and is intended, as Sagart says, to induce 'fear in their neighbours' souls' (1922: 145). Shame is different from guilt because it is intercorporeal, Sara Ahmed argues; it is guilt that has been witnessed by another, made public and which has consequences in the public world. Ahmed writes that shame 'secures the form of the family by assigning to those who have failed its form the origin of bad feeling (You have brought shame on the family)' (2004: 107). This observation is borne out in the narratives of women consigned to the Magdalene asylums, whose families disowned them as a means of preserving what remained of the family honour. Allied with shame is disgust, a response to the shamed one; the disgust is evoked by the possibility of contamination. Although in this case the contamination is moral, it is heightened by the inclusion of other possible 'contaminants' such as poverty, destitution, intellectual disability or mental illness. Historians of the period repeatedly point to the characterization of marginalized citizens as contaminating to public moral health, and as likely to corrupt others. Sagart writes, 'This whole subject [of the unmarried mother] is of extreme importance, concerning as it does the preservation of a strict standard of moral life in the nation, and the saving from utter ruin of the faith and morality of so many Catholic girls.' He suggests that priests and Catholic lawyers (the former all male, the latter likely also all male) should work together to develop a response (1922: 152–3).

This characterization of women is strongly influenced by Roman Catholic religious practice. The iconography of the Virgin that is apparent throughout the space in *Laundry* is a common sight in Ireland, even today. The invisibility and inaudibility of respectable women recommended by some commentators should to be read alongside the Irish culture of devotion to the Virgin Mary, which was evident not only in private religious observances but also in the grottoes and altars to the Virgin that are still visible in villages and housing estates as well as in church grounds,[7] and Marian processions during May (which still take place, but no longer as large-scale events). The emphasis on the Virgin as both mother and virgin provides a locus around which normative constructions of feminine roles as virgin (daughter) and (married) mother can cluster.

However, signifying practice is unstable and the potential for the respectable woman to fall into sin was ever present. Religious characterizations of women as morally inferior, prone to sexual temptation, or as temptresses leading men to sin emphasized the need for external control of women's sexual behaviour. This characterization of female purity as bound into the moral health of the country,[8] and the characterization of unmarried mothers and prostitutes as sites of contagion (Luddy 2007: 89), are a form of symbolic violence. Slavoj Žižek defines symbolic violence as 'embodied in language' and involving 'the imposition of a certain universe of meaning' (2009: 1–2). Bourdieu similarly describes it as the least recognizable form of violence, calling it 'a gentle violence, imperceptible and invisible even to its victims, exerted for the most part through the purely symbolic channels of communication and cognition (more precisely, miscognition), recognition, or even feeling' (2001: 1–2). The rhetoric of female sexual purity as necessary to the health and future of the nation disguises the violent repression that is its end through the ostensible exaltation of women as the inspiration of masculine heroes and the mothers of the nation. This is not a peculiarly Irish phenomenon: Joanne Nagel argues that the depiction of women in European nationalist histories shows that, while 'female fecundity is valued in the mothers of the nation, unruly female sexuality threatens to discredit the nation' (1998: 256).

Žižek describes systemic symbolic violence as often underlying individual actions, shaping the contexts and the pressures to which the individual is subject (2009: 1). Both are classified as objective forms of violence that operate seemingly without agency and thus reflect an unchangeable status quo. These forms of violence are apparent when hegemonic structures and institutional power and authority become corrupt and reliant on repressive measures to sustain themselves, or engage with repressive measures to sustain normative social values and structures (2009: 10–12). Relating Žižek's terms to the Magdalene story draws upon discourses that characterize 'unchaste' women as dangerous *to the state* if they are not strictly controlled. Respected community figures like the local doctor or the parish priest were normally engaged in the committal of the pregnant woman to a mother and baby home or a laundry, thereby endorsing the practice with a performance of well-educated, professional authority, while the gender power relations at work (men incarcerating women) reinforced and were reinforced by religious and cultural beliefs about the proper relative status of the sexes. It only adds to the characterization of sexually active women as mad or criminal that the police were involved in catching those who escaped and returning them to the laundries. As a further means of control, the new state enacted legislation that limited married women's access to economic independence and bodily integrity. Legislation limited married women's right to secure employment outside the home (repealed in the 1970s), criminalized the sale or import of contraceptives (repealed in the 1980s) and offered no legal provision for divorce (introduced in 1996). But legal controls are less effective than internalized social and cultural attitudes, and the characterization of women by the state and church was part of a set of discourses within the society about religious belief, a deeply puritanical anxiety about family respectability, officially sanctioned disgust towards an economic underclass and disgust with sexuality, sin and therefore with the too-carnal bodies of women. The corresponding lack of sympathy or empathy with women deemed to have fallen spiritually, socially or sexually is evident in the history of the Magdalene Laundries.

The affective response to *Laundry* – in the press, online, in academic conferences and in conversation – was extraordinary. Why was this? The Magdalene Laundry used in the performance is only a few short blocks from a main thoroughfare. Like all the laundries, it operated as a business, and church, state and local citizens used its services. Moreover, they sent their daughters, sisters, cousins, aunts there: these institutions were usually staffed with women from local families. Well into the 1980s it was common practice to send an unmarried, pregnant daughter away until the baby was born and given up for adoption, and families that decided to support their disgraced daughters were feted on national television (RTÉ's *Late Late Show* hosted more than one discussion on the matter). Everybody knew. The spectators, I would suggest, were shocked by the performance's representation of the suffering of the women and the culpability of the community. The performance engendered fright (*Schrecken*) as Lehmann explains it: as a moment of responsibility (2006: 143) or response-ability, in Oliver's terms (2001: 5).

The use of a former convent as venue allowed members of the public to see a space that was closed and forbidden: a space normally accessible only to the consecrated and the Magdalene women. The building therefore emerged from its invisibility within the cityscape to become a space inhabited by individuals who interact personally with the audience members so that afterwards the performance has the feeling of a lived experience. The physical, sensory experience of walking through the space, and the positioning of the audience member as witness to the re-enactment of injustice, and repeated appeals by the performers to remember, remember them, remember they were there, creates a spectator experience that encourages the audience members to reflect upon this history, the structure of the state that allowed it to happen and their complicity with it in the moment of performance. Through this, the complicity of the society as a whole in the full scandal of the laundries, and the whole state apparatus of 'containment', becomes visible and tangible. *Laundry* is both a document and an imaginative exploration of this apparatus.

By representing the women as imprisoned, but not apparently by anyone – or perhaps, by each other and by us, the representatives of the outside world, and by removing the immediate agents of repression from the performance – *Laundry* foregrounds ways in which this violence invisibly supported cherished nationalist imaginaries and governmental structures, and prompts reflection on the complicity of the general population and the attitudes to women and sexuality that motivated this violence. The women in the laundries became the scapegoats to carry the sexual crimes and misdemeanours of the whole population.

The violence represented in *Laundry* is the logical end point of, and a performative element in, the characterization of women in the political discourses of the first half of the twentieth century. The symbolic and systemic violence of these discourses made visible in moments of live performance correspond to longitudinal political practices that characterized female citizens according to their sexual status. *Laundry* documents and makes visible a particular thread in the history of the Irish State. In doing so, it draws attention not only to the abuse of unmarried mothers and their children but also to the social and cultural attitudes that tolerated it. By removing representations of the nuns who ran the laundry from the performance, Anu Productions make visible the operation of objective forms of violence and prompt the audience to question the state's use of repressive measures to create normative social relations. By implicating the audience, not only in the moment of performance but – more powerfully – as part of the social system that approved and perpetuated the violence, the production raises questions about the ongoing characterization of women in Irish society and culture. The actions that resulted from these characterizations, in particular the emergence of a system of incarceration and of vanishment from public sight and discourse marks the architecture of Irish cities, the structures of Irish families and the lives of an estimated 30,000 citizens whose civil rights were so easily set aside. The characterization of 'immoral' women as dangerous to the body politic becomes a way of normalising the expulsion of problematic elements, whose main threat was to economic practices of landownership, and the nationalist narrative of the Irish nation. I would suggest that its affect is not only strong because of the sad history that it reveals, or because of the staging strategies that foreground the culpability of the state and the population in this violence. Rather, it is because the lingering scars of this early characterization of Irish women as either moral (mothers) or immoral (and dangerous) can be seen to persist in contemporary political discourse around women's reproductive rights in Ireland. The female body and the maternal body recur as a focus of concern to the state and the church in the early twenty-first century.

Notes

1 One such case is reported on the website of Hayes Solicitors. See <http://www.hayes-solicitors.ie/news/courtaskedtobalancerightsmotherunbornchild.htm> accessed Sept. 2013.
2 Symphysiotomy is a medical procedure which severs the pubic bone in order to enable birth when labour is blocked. It was widely used in Ireland instead of Caesarian procedures because the woman could bear additional children. However it also leads to chronic pain and incontinence, and it was widely performed without consent.
3 The organization Survivors of Symphysiotomy (SOS) have been campaigning for compensation for women disabled by the practice: <http://www.sos-symphysiotomy.com>
4 Histories of the Magdalene Laundries can only be partial, because as James Smith notes, 'no such history can exist until the religious congregations afford scholars access to their archival records' (2007: p. xvi). Useful sources include Frances Finnegan's *Do Penance or Perish* (2001) James M. Smith's *Ireland's Magdalene Laundries and the Nation's Architecture of Containment* (2007) and Steve Humphries's Channel 4 documentary *Sex in a Cold Climate* (1998).
5 A selection of articles from *The Irish Ecclesiastical Review* includes, Rev. R.S. Devane, S.J. 'The Unmarried Mother: some legal aspects of the problem I and II' published in 1924, 55–68 and 172–188 respectively; 'How to Deal With the Unmarried Mother' by Sagart (a pseudonym meaning priest); 'The Unmarried Mother' by Sir Joseph Glynn; 'The Souper Problem in Ireland' by Rev. M.A. McInerny, O.P. Other interesting contextual material in the same journal includes Rev. Cornelius Lucey, 'The Problem of the

Woman Worker' and Rev. J. McCarthy, 'A Report on Abortion'; and Rev. M. Garaghy S.J., 'Idols of Modern Society'.

6 On the dangers of 'Souperism', see Sagart, and Rev. M.A. McInerny, O.P.
7 In 1985 during a period of political upheaval and instability, the statue of the Virgin Mary in a grotto in rural Cork was seen to move. The phenomenon then spread across the country. The phenomenon is analysed in Colm Toibin, 1985.
8 Luddy quotes from a number of sources and directs the reader to *The Irish Catholic Directory and Almanac* for 1920 and 1927; the pamphlets of the Office of the Irish Messenger also offer interesting insights into Catholic teaching of religious doctrine at the time. This particular linking of female purity to the future of the nation is reported in *The Irish Independent* 12 May 1926 n.p.

6 Theatricality vs. bare life
Performance as a vernacular of resistance

Silvija Jestrovic

Following the breakdown of Yugoslavia, in the early 1990s, the besieged city of Sarajevo, pieced together through news reports and images, entered our living rooms and our imaginations. Sarajevo became a synecdoche of the conflict in Bosnia and the iconic site of war and suffering. Theatrical terminology was frequently used in the local media to describe the war as 'theatre of cruelty' and 'theatre of the absurd', while 'Waiting for Godot' became the favourite metaphor for the position of citizens in the besieged city. These performance metaphors have seldom been further explored, hence they did not do much more than contribute to the framing of Sarajevo as a site of passive suffering, mute and frozen in its *historical paralysis* (Wertenbaker 2001), while mediated through voices of politicians, journalists and Western intellectuals. Nevertheless, there was something intuitively correct in this toying with performance metaphors to describe the various dimensions of the war.

In his illuminating book, *Blue Helmets and Black Markets*, Peter Andreas applies Erving Goffman's theatrical tropes of 'front stage action' and 'back stage action' to the situation in besieged Sarajevo and the war in Bosnia. For Andreas, performance as a metaphor is also an epistemological tool through which to see the various aspects of the Bosnian conflict better. Goffman's notion of 'back stage action' gave Andreas the conceptual tool to look beyond the undeniable but often simplified 'front stage action' of suffering and ethnic violence. By including the concept of 'back stage action', Andreas was able to explore key aspects of the siege such as the war economy and the incipient criminalization of the city that mainstream media (local and global) so deftly sidestepped. The notion of performance uncovered the structures of the conflict, its various players and its ambiguous relational dimensions. Moreover, against the dominant trope of suffering and ethnic strife, the resilience of the city, that is, its *normalcy*, its cultural production and its performances in everyday life, were also relegated to the back stage domain. In other words, some of the 'back stage actions' were, somewhat paradoxically, taking place on actual theatrical stages.

In this chapter I am interested in looking beyond performance as a metaphor and as an epistemological tool, and into performance as a set of artistic and everyday practices that both generate symbolic meanings and function as actions. These actions formulate not only a performance language, but also a unique 'grammar' of political resistance. Using Sarajevo under the siege as an extreme case scenario, I will explore how performance practices unfold to make the microhistory of the city within and against the grand narratives inscribed by various conflicting voices, including local and international media. I will argue that forms of everyday life in Sarajevo during the siege, as well as artistic performances in and about the city, established a vernacular of political resistance to talk back, both in relation to the politics of war and to its depiction in the world media. Forms of everyday behaviour, as well as artistic practices, became political acts creating a cultural public sphere, in conditions where collective and individual *self* was, presumably, reduced to bare life, in Giorgio Agamben's terms – hence, deprived from acting as a political subject. Performance, through its various embodied practices, is viewed as the key factor in recreating and reformulating the roles of civic institutions that were – metaphorically and actually – reduced to rubble and where the role of citizen as an active political agent was diminished. The embodied language of performance and structures of artistic practices establish a public civic space, offering somewhat paradoxically, both an escapist outlet from the grim reality of the war-torn city and a language through which to articulate and retrieve political agency. Through range of performance practices – from rituals of everyday civic life to cultural events – unfolds a vernacular 'grammar' that resists, at least temporarily, the official language of the political conflict and the lingua franca of the world media.

In the introduction to his collections of testimonials about theatre in Sarajevo during the war (*Teatar u ratnom Sarajevu: 1992–1995*), Darko Diklić provides a summary of the cultural activities during the siege:

> [...] in this period 3,102 artistic and cultural events took place or on average 2.5 events per day! The Sarajevo Philharmonic orchestra performed 48 concerts in Sarajevo and in Europe. On February 5th, when 66 people were killed and 199 wounded in the Markale massacre, the Sarajevo String Quartet performed its hundredth concert and continued performing until the end of the war. Yahudi Menuhin, Zubin Mehta, Jose Carreras ... gave guest performances. Fifteen writers were killed during the war, while, at the same time 263 books were published. Although 18 visual artists were killed, exhibits where taking place all the time during the war – a total of 177 in six city galleries and in a number of improvised venues. [...] Despite the fact that 10 filmmakers were killed, 156 documentary and short films were produced during the war. Almost at the very beginning of the war MESS (*Male i eksperiemntalne scene Sarajeva*) inaugurated the Sarajevo Film Festival. (When a foreign journalist asked Haris Pašović 'Why a film festival during the war?', he would answer: 'And why a war during the film festival?!'). In Sarajevo theatres, 182 performances premiered and over two thousand shows were performed that half a million people saw. There were also countless other artistic and cultural events, the festival *Sarajevo Winter* (Sarajevska zima), Fama, La Benevolencia etc.
>
> (Diklić 2004: 10)

This account testifies that Sarajevo was not just a city of passive suffering where very little was going on aside from destruction and the day-to-day struggle for survival. It also provokes us to think that these performance events in nearly impossible circumstances were not just mere curiosities, but vital acts of structuring urban life and of meaning making amidst the chaos of war. I would argue that these performative utterances of the city became a form of activism, similar to what Butler has described as 'breaking out' of the frame in her analysis of the circulation of images of torture at Abu Ghraib and the poems by the prisoners of Guantanamo:

> The conditions are set for astonishment, outrage, revulsion, admiration, and discovery, depending on how the content is framed by shifting time and place. The movement of the image or the text outside the confinement is a kind of 'breaking out', so that even though neither the image nor the poetry can free anyone from prison, or stop a bomb or, indeed, reverse the course of the war, they nevertheless do provide the conditions for breaking out of the quotidian acceptance of war and for a more generalized horror and outrage that will support and impel calls for justice and end the violence.
>
> (Butler 2009: 11)

Cultural production in Sarajevo was a form of *breaking out* of the confinement that the siege had imposed both literally – central Sarajevo and some other parts of the city were sealed off – and metaphorically. Showing how power manipulates the terms of appearance, Butler compares the notion of 'breaking out' both to a prison break and in relation to the concept of 'frame' – meaning both the context within which a content is organized and in the sense of being framed.

In his introduction to the *Metastases of Enjoyment*, Slavoj Žižek calls for an expansion and alteration of the frame within which the tragedy of Sarajevo has been read and understood in a manner that is akin to Butler's notion of *breaking out*:

> [...] reporters compete with each other on who will find a more repulsive scene – lacerated child bodies, raped women, starved prisoners: all this is good fodder for hungry Western eyes. However, the media are far more sparing of words apropos of how the residents of Sarajevo desperately endeavour to maintain the appearance of normal life. The tragedy of Sarajevo is epitomized in an elderly clerk who takes a walk to his office everyday as usual, but has to quicken his pace at a certain crossroads because a Serbian sniper lurks on the nearby hill; in a disco that operates 'normally', although one can hear explosions in the background; in a young woman who forces her way through ruins to the court in order to obtain a divorce so that she can start to live with her lover; in the issue of the Bosnian cinema monthly that appeared in Sarajevo in 1993 and published essays on Scorcese and Almodóvar...
>
> (Žižek 1994: 2)

Butler's notion of *breaking out* and Žižek's expanding of the frame concern not only our frame of understanding, but also the frame of utterance. In other words, performance does not only emerge here as a phenomenon that shows how better to read and understand the besieged city, but it also emerges as an act of living, a way of life – a modus vivendi in the besieged city.

Bosnian theatre director Haris Pašović asserts that the cultural production in Sarajevo 'was not some unique feature of Sarajevans and that it would have happened in other places since this is a human reaction to dehumanised circumstances. Primarily, it is an anthropological dimension rather than a special trait of our people' (in Diklić 2004: 205). He points out common traits in the cultural activity of Sarajevo during the war with the recent history of other cities including the siege of Leningrad and of the Warsaw ghetto during World War II. One might also add the Theresienstadt concentration camp where inmates, most of them highly educated, were given some resources and a certain degree of freedom enabling a form of urban life and activity to flourish under extreme circumstances, until most of the inhabitants got deported to the death-camps. Although the comparison between Nazi concentration camps and the siege of Sarajevo is, as Pašović himself admits, limited and problematic for a number of reasons, it is relevant to our attempt to grasp how theatre, performance and cultural activity in the besieged city shaped the meaning and acts of being a citizen. The urge to perform – 'to communicate through action that is framed, presented, highlighted or displayed' (Schechner 2003: 2) – is not only the anthropological will to play, but often also a need for political expression. How and under what circumstances could performances of everyday life and artistic performances become political acts? How do they form a counter discourse in relation to the language of political violence? How do performance and cultural production shape the grammar of political resistance? How do these performances renegotiate the 'grammar' of private and public sphere, personal and political? Why is it possible to talk about theatre, performance and rich cultural production in the context of Sarajevo and Theresienstadt, for example, but much less so in the context of, say, Auschwitz? The answer inevitably brings Giorgio Agamben's notions of bare life and the camp into discussion. To what extent did the besieged Sarajevo embody Agamben's concept of the camp and to what extent was life in the city a bare life?

Bare life

In formulating his notion of bare life, Agamben's point of departure is the ancient Greek distinction between *zoe* 'which expressed the simple fact of living common to all living beings (animals, humans, or gods), and *bios*, which signified the form or manner of living peculiar to a single individual or group' (Agamben 2000: 3). He then identifies his notion of a naked life as a 'presupposed common element that is always possible to isolate in each of the numerous forms of life' (Agamben 2000: 3). This possibility to isolate the axiomatic bare life from other forms of life is, in some instances and on its political level, akin to Butler's concept of framing through which some lives appear less grievable than others. As Agamben illustrates, drawing from ancient Greek and Roman law, a bare life is one that can be taken but cannot be sacrificed – in other words, a life framed so that it appears devalued in all its aspects except as confirmation of the political power that rules over it. Agamben writes:

> The state of exception, which is what the sovereign each and every time decides, takes place precisely when naked life – which normally appears rejoined to the multifarious forms of social life – is explicitly put into question and revoked as the ultimate foundation of political power. The ultimate subject that needs to be at once turned into the exception and included in the city is always naked life.
>
> (Agamben 2000: 5–6)

The street scenes from Sarajevo that regularly appeared in media reports and that constituted the everyday reality of the city illustrate to a great extent what bare life looked like. Hungry people and stray dogs wandering through city ruins in search of food always under the watchful eye of the enemy sniper; water queues, filth and stench, and spilled brains on the pavement – all suggest life reduced to literal survival in Agamben's terms:

> Biological life, which is the secularized form of naked life and which shares its unutterability and impenetrability, thus constitutes the real forms of life literally as forms of survival: biological life remains inviolate in such forms as that obscure threat that can suddenly actualize itself in violence, in extraneousness, in illness, in accidents. It is the invisible sovereign that stares at us behind the dull-witted masks of the powerful who, whether or not they realize it, govern us in its name.
>
> (Agamben 2000: 8)

In the images from Sarajevo, one can clearly see the actualization of naked life through political violence. As other bodies in extreme circumstances that are both physical and political, the suffering bodies of Sarajevans remind us of the intrinsic link between biological life and politics, since even the tendency to separate the body from its political dimension is essentially about power. Hence, even if we talk about biological life as a secularized naked life, we are still, following Foucault's line of reasoning, talking about a form of biopolitics.

For Agamben, inasmuch 'as its inhabitants have been stripped of every political status and reduced completely to naked life, the camp is [...] the most absolute biopolitical space that has ever been realized – a space in which power confronts nothing other than pure biological life without any mediation' (Agamben 2000: 41). A camp is the materialization of the state of exception that is often invoked through the rhetoric of protection from a threat that needs to be isolated. In this sense, the rhetoric of protection is the common denominator in a variety of historically very different camp contexts – from colonial wars to Nazi death-camps, and from the camps of the most recent wars in the Balkans to Guantanamo. Agamben somewhat provocatively points out that 'we will have to admit to be facing a camp virtually every time that such a structure is created, regardless of the nature of the crimes committed in it and regardless of the denomination and specific topography it might have' (Agamben 2000: 41–2). Aspects of Sarajevo, a city that clearly had features of a camp, resembled Theresienstadt. According to the argument of Bosnian Serbs, the three-year-long siege of the city, an invocation of a state of exception, was justified in order to protect its folk from the Muslim population that was perceived as both a physical and a political threat. The material conditions of the siege, more often than not, reduced life to mere survival.

On the one hand, the images and footage of Sarajevo that were widely circulated through media outlets often epitomized bare life. Indeed, we saw starved, wounded, suffering bodies of Sarajevans, like all other suffering bodies, used in a variety of political scenarios but stripped of any political status. On the other hand, Sarajevo could not be fully reduced to the notion of city-camp space inasmuch as the life of its citizens was not a naked life at each and every moment of the siege. All the examples of cultural production, and some aspects of everyday public and private life in the city, could be read as forms of resistance to naked life. Sarajevo was a place of tension and ambiguity rather than a mere embodiment of political violence. The city was and was not a camp; life in Sarajevo was and was not naked. That is what makes Sarajevo truly interesting as a case study. The inhabitants resisted the violence of naked life in a variety of ways – from performing civic roles and duties and maintaining social rituals such as weddings and funerals, to vibrant cultural production. The possibility to counteract naked life with other forms of life enabled Sarajevans to have agency – to find ways to assert their rights and responsibilities as citizens.

It goes without saying that the possibility of resistance and ambiguity could never have emerged in Sarajevo without a certain degree of freedom, individual autonomy and safety. These are the axiomatic minimal conditions without which resistance to bare life would be impossible. Whereas these axiomatic conditions existed in Sarajevo and Theresienstadt, enabling a communal life, including various forms of performances and cultural activity, they were fully revoked in places like Auschwitz. Haris Pašović also talks about the physical circumstances without which theatre in the city would not have been possible:

> If it wasn't for those defending the city we wouldn't be able to perform downtown, because the *chetniks* would have physically entered the city [...] This was one set of circumstances. Otherwise they would have come into the city and made us leave as had happened in Prijedor, Banja Luka, Srebrenica, etc. [...] Thus our audience was in a way also these fighters who defended the city. In the morning they would be on the front line, in the afternoon they would come to see our performances – not all of them, but quite a good number. In that sense, our audience enabled us to perform.
>
> (Diklić 2004: 201–2)

In the ecological triad of individual psyche, collective self and the city, there is a direct relationship between physical space and freedom. The axiomatic condition for theatre and performances to take place in the city was essentially based on relative degrees of physical distance from the forces that invoked the state of exception. In some parts of the city, the proximity between a person running down the street and the hillside sniper fire was no more than 50m – close enough to have to run for your bare life but far enough away to have a chance to escape. Although the siege imposed some aspects of the camp onto the city, the state of exception was never fully materialized. Back alleys, basements, secluded courtyards and gardens, tucked away houses, apartment building corridors and underground spaces enabled a city-within-the-city to sustain itself more or less under the radar of sniper-fire and mortar shells. Even under the siege conditions, the city asserted itself in opposition to the camp status. It emerged as an ambiguous space – at one and the same time controlled and uncontrollable. In his novella, *Apocalypse from the Recycling Bin* (*Apokalipsa iz recycle bina*), poet, writer and former soldier in the Bosnian Army, Faruk Šehić, describes his encounter with Sarajevo in December 1995 when, with a group of soldiers, he entered the city:

> It felt as if life here doesn't exist at all. Only grey buildings dotted with shrapnel, grey pavement, grey streetcar tracks. Ghastly was the feeling of standing in the street in the hope of seeing something alive. The silence that filled the Sarajevo air was worse than all the fighting I went through as a solder of the 5th corpus. Desolation was getting into my sleeves like the winter cold. What I saw and felt was surrealism in the real world, escaped from within book covers, painting frames, and film screens. In that moment I had only one wish, to get on a bus and out of this dead city.
>
> The first place where I encountered a living soul was the coffee house Cinema. Here the colour black was intimate and warm. [...] Then I discovered the true image of the city, hidden and vibrant in secluded coffee houses and clubs where everything unfolded as if the outside world did not exist. In addition to the Cinema, Obala, Kuk, and Lisac were also open and many more invisible ghettoes. If any city lived its underground life, it was Sarajevo during the siege. The entire city was a vast underground gallery with an astonishing instinct for life and joy. There was no anger and no anxiety, we were all still embalmed[1] by the war, when life is celebrated most.
>
> (Šehić 2008: 263–4)

This description captures what it was that made Sarajevo different from Theresienstadt: the latter, despite its cultural activity and some degree of internal autonomy, remained a strictly controlled space – a camp. In contrast, the Sarajevo siege – justified by the political and military enforcement of a state of exception – never truly materialized as a camp. In the case of Theresienstadt, a minimal axiomatic degree of freedom and safety was temporarily granted to the inhabitants by the sovereign power (following Agamben's thought, a 'sovereign' is the one who authorizes a state of exception) and subsequently revoked. Although

Theresienstadt mimicked a city in its layout and in its cultural life, its inhabitants were no longer citizens – they were inmates. In the case of Sarajevo, the physical and political circumstances were very different as central Sarajevo was besieged, but not occupied.[2] In the 'underground life' of the city, which could never be fully contained by the state of exception, the inhabitants alone reclaimed their safety, freedom and agency asserting their status and role as citizens.

Theatricality

In opposition to his concept of bare life, Agamben sets up the notion of *form-of-life* to describe life as that which 'can never be separated from its form, a life in which it is never possible to isolate something such as naked life' (Agamben 2000: 4). According to Agamben, intellectuality and community are intrinsically linked to life being constituted as a form-of-life: 'Intellectuality and thought are not a form of life among others in which life and social production articulate themselves, but they are rather *the unitary power that constitutes the multiple forms of life as form-of-life*' (Agamben 2000: 11). In her critique of the refugee figure, which plays a central role in Agamben's discourse on naked life and camp, scholar Patricia Owens turns to Hannah Arendt and to performance practice. She suggests that the possibility of resistance is not in the effort to reclaim 'bare life', but is 'wholly dependent on the ability to forge a public realm grounded on the appropriate distinction between nature and political artifice, between human life and political world' (Owens 2009: 569).

Naked life presupposes the collapse of private and public spheres into one another, while the notion of form-of-life necessitates the opposite – a formation of public sphere. Throughout the siege, Sarajevans reclaimed the public sphere in a multiplicity of ways including theatre productions, performances on the ruins of cultural institutions, publishing the newspaper *Oslobodjenje* and radio programmes such as *Zid*. When public institutions had either been destroyed or deemed unsafe, the public realm moved to private spaces. Filmmaker Nihad Kreševljaković reminisces about the *mobile university* that often took place in his own backyard:

> Lectures and discussions took place under an apple tree in our garden where there is a gorgeous view of Sarajevo. A few American and local professors gave lectures in a variety of disciplines including art, architecture, history, etc. Everything started within the project 'Beba Univerzum' organised by MESS and FAMA.[3] Suada Kapic[4] had an idea to create a mobile university where university lecturers would come to various spaces to give accessible, public lectures in their area of expertise. Tvrdko Kulenović[5] gave a lecture in Svrza's house, while all the other lectures took place in ours because it was easier to organise them. Behija Zlatar, Boris Minavić, and Mila Kuposović talked about the history of Sarajevo. Dževad Jezbašić talked about railways, Professor Numić lectured on Ancient philosophy. William Hunt's lecture was on the Vietnam war, while John Fine and Robert Donia[6] talked about the

Medieval Bosnian state. All these lectures included discussions where both experts and the wider public participated. Erika Munk gave a lecture,[7] and Vanessa Redgrave talked about her life and acting in general. More than 200 people came, filling every bit of space in our garden. All of this happened in '94 in the midst of the besieged, bombarded, and tortured city.

(In Diklić 2004: 145)

This example illustrates Arendt's and Owens's notion of resistance by which '*bare life* is repudiated and a new, worldly community is formed around resistance to injustice: that is, when individuals *begin to create public space between them*' (Owens 2009: 577–8). Owens also recognizes that a certain element of artificiality, which we might identify as theatrical, is essential in this process, when she writes:

To engage in political action is to participate in founding and sustaining a common political world that can last longer than a natural human world. This is partly a matter of the inherent artificiality of politics. To speak and act in public is to wear a kind of 'mask' – a public persona that is 'given and guaranteed by the body politics' not the natural body.

(Owens 2009: 578)

I would argue that, in the case of Sarajevo, both the creation of the public sphere and Agamben's 'intellectuality as antagonistic power and form-of-life' (Agamben 2000: 11) more often than not sustained itself through communal theatricality. This theatricality encompassed different aspects – from putting a performance on stage to everyday communal encounters where people used jokes, jests and occasional enactments to give both meaning and distance to their situation. Theatricalization of everyday life – as self-conscious framing of behaviour for viewing by others – emerges as a means of making and maintaining a public sphere. Theatricality, both as a communal experience of some form of theatre and performance and as the theatricalization of everyday life, was a way of meaning making – of inserting thought into the violence of naked life.

Nihad Kreševljaković's film, *Do You Remember Sarajevo?* clearly depicts the role of theatricality as a means of resistance to bare life. It is a deliberately rough-cut documentary that features various episodes from everyday life in the city during the siege with commentary from the author's friends, neighbours and family. The film starts in the early days of the war and captures a voice from Sarajevo television calling for citizens to film the reality unravelling around them as a mode of witnessing. Kreševljaković's camera bears witness to first attacks on the city and to the confusion and dismay of the citizens. It depicts the siege from the perspective of citizens as they watch grenades fall on the city from their apartment windows or, as they squat, panic-struck, in underground shelters. The footage from the early days of the siege is often shaky as the filmmaker moves quickly to safety or to film another attack. Voices around him are shouting: 'Look what they are doing to the city!' 'It hit Hotel Europe! Hotel Europe is burning ...'. Kreševljaković continued to film the city and its citizens throughout the siege and edited the film after the war was over. As the siege wore on, however, the life that the filmmaker was documenting was no longer solely epitomized by looks of fear, panic and bewilderment. It becomes apparent that the inhabitants are no longer completely caught in their altered reality, but rather are able to step back and comment on their situation with a sense of distance, often with dark humour. Distance and humour are particularly important here as they not only become strategies of reflecting on the given conditions, but also presuppose a choice of frame within which the reality is represented. The film depicts the siege of Sarajevo from the perspective of the besieged, and although the subjects are at times simply caught on camera, they also often address the camera or perform for it – to some degree choosing the frames and strategies of their own representation. Most of the interviewees have an almost gestic[8] approach to Kreševljaković's camera as they offer surreal reflections on the city or dead-pan commentaries. One of them, called Ibro, appropriates a mock attitude of a wise-elder of the community when talking about life in the besieged city: 'It's nice to be without anything, we have no worries. We are relieved. I recommend to everybody: don't accumulate too many things. And always have a bag with the most necessary things ready in case someone chases you out one day ...'. The documentary also depicts kids playing joyfully amongst the ruins, the opening of the Sarajevo film festival and a wedding. In the wedding sequence, the expected wedding imagery is mixed with some extraordinary elements in which this civil ritual takes place. It is a modest affair, but everybody is nicely dressed and the guests enjoy the party very much, singing *Guantanamera* to the accompaniment of a guitar player. When the elegant and cheerful group passes by shattered buildings and façades pockmarked by shrapnel, one of the guests looks slightly alarmed. Another reassures him: 'Don't worry, there are no snipers here, just grenades!' Everybody bursts out laughing. In another wedding scene, one of the guests takes both a bouquet of flowers for the newlyweds and a first-aid kit out of the trunk of his car. Lifting the first-aid kit in front of the camera, he grins and says: 'Just in case'. Perhaps more than bearing witness to the atrocities of war, this film shows how theatricality and performance became a vital part of the relationship between public and private realms, not only through various forms of cultural production, but also as aspects of daily life.

In this context, humour emerges as a means of distancing and a vital strategy of meaning making that necessitates some degree of theatricality in everyday life. Nikolai Evreinov, a member of Russia's avant-garde who was interested in the theatricality of everyday life, ascribed to it the somewhat anthropological traits ingrained in a shared impulse or will to play. Interestingly, Evreinov's notion of theatricality as a necessity, no different from the need for food and water, is not that far removed from Pašović's:

> It wasn't at all extraordinary that we made theatre during the war. It was extraordinary that the siege lasted as long as it lasted or whatever it was that was happening. It was extraordinary to bomb a city, to kill people. That was

extraordinary. Making theatre and making bread is nothing out of the ordinary. That's normal for people to do.

(In Diklić 2004: 205)

Kreševljaković, too, makes a similar observation that has somewhat anthropological roots:

> In a sense, there was no distance between the stage and the audience in theatre. Of course, if a performance was put on in a theatre there was physical distance between the stage and the auditorium. But there was this feeling of community that has blurred all the divides. Everybody was a participant and we all felt safe although more often than not this was an illusion. In general, I think that theatre, for reasons unknown to me, has a specific power that became particularly evident during the war. For example, in my neighbourhood children gathered and started making performances. Nobody brought them together or asked them to do it. They decided on their own to play theatre.
>
> (In Diklić 2004: 142)

Evreinov emphasized that the notion of transformation lies at the core of theatricality. It is a rejuvenating principle that restores the sensation of life. He urges us not to be ourselves, and goes back to a pre-theatrical time when 'primitive' people realized that in addition to the conscious, waking *I*, there was a second *I* that existed in dreams. 'Without seasoning, without the salt of theatricality, life was a dish we would only eat by compulsion' (in Golub 1984: 52). Cultural production in the city, performances in theatres, dark humour and the theatricality of everyday life enabled this transformational potential of theatricality to take place.

The case of Sarajevo offers a possibility to rethink the notion of reclaiming Agamben's bare life through two seemingly disparate, but essentially linked spheres – the public realm (Arendt, Owen) and theatricality (Evreinov). Theatricalization becomes an integral part of the public sphere and, thus, a means of counteracting the reduction to bare life where all forms of life become only one – survival. A sequence in Kreševljaković's film, *Do You Remember Sarajevo?* depicts an utterly surreal scene from daily life: a young man in full skiing gear, glides masterfully through the streets of Sarajevo. His skiing through the city is both a practical way of getting around and a commentary – a unique site-specific performance of navigating the streets of a city left without public transportation and under the always-watchful eyes of enemy snipers. The next scene takes place in a private home with two friends. They announce that this was a skiing championship and that their friend – whom they decide to call Alberto Tomba, after the famous Italian ski champion – is the winner. As a reward, he gets half a kilo of powdered milk, while the runner-up is awarded a half-eaten piece of feta cheese. When one of them asks: 'Where is the second runner-up?' they look around before quickly remembering 'he is dead of course'. Finally, the three young men pretend to stand on a pedestal while singing the Italian anthem. Their short, dead-pan improvization instantly reverses the situation they are in – and the absurdity of their existence in besieged Sarajevo has at least temporarily lost its hold over them. In other words, by performing the absurdity of life in Sarajevo, they reclaim the imposed condition, albeit temporarily, and place it under the control of theatricality.

On an individual level, which clearly influences the public realm, there is a certain kinship between the three young men who turned their experience of a snow-covered, besieged Sarajevo into a home-made show about a skiing competition, and a seemingly very different example, Christoph Schlingensief's opera-oratorio, *The Church of Fear* (2009), where the famous German director staged and performed his own terminal illness. Both performances are made in circumstances where individuals are threatened by the imposition of bare life. Moreover, in both cases the resistance emerges through invoking a kind of public realm and through the interplay of theatricality and performativity. By bringing the process of his own illness and death to centre stage, Schlingensief masterfully blurs the lines between reality and performance. In this case, he also inserts the private into the public, not so much to blur the lines, but to create a shared communal experience as a means of reclaiming life as a form-of-life. The three young men in Sarajevo theatricalize their daily navigations through the besieged city by staging a mock public event – the skiing competition – in their own living room. Through theatricalization, they transform an everyday episode into a commentary on their own existence in the city. Using dark humour, they also make a sophisticated and a painful link to Sarajevo's past identity in the global context – as the host city of the 1984 Winter Olympic games. The absurdity of this performance lies largely in its enactment of a grand, public event in a small living room – seemingly without the public. But we must not forget Kreševljaković's camera that bears witness to this performative commentary and eventually brings it back to the public realm.

Through this possibility to comment, which lies at the core of the concept of public sphere, *zoe* is distinguished from *bios*, and the resistance to naked life takes place. In a sense, bare life could be understood as a form of life deprived of its impulse to theatricality, stripped of its ability to play (in Evreinov's sense of the term). It is a form of life that is denied the possibility of commenting on its own situation – deprived of the distancing through which life acquires meaning. Through both performance-making and through the self-fashioning of daily life, theatricality in Sarajevo became a means of individual and collective commentary – a transformative self-reflection and a form of agency. Agamben writes:

> [...] human beings – as beings of power who can do or not do, succeed or fail, lose themselves or find themselves – are the only beings for whom happiness is always at stake in their living, the only beings whose life is irremediably and painfully assigned to happiness. But this immediately constitutes the form-of-life as political life.
>
> (Agamben 2000: 4)

In another sequence of Kreševljaković's film, a young man stands in a sun-filled street of besieged Sarajevo, looks into the camera and says the most unexpected thing: 'Sometimes I'm so happy'. I believe him.

Notes

1. I have translated 'embalmed' literally ('balzamovani' in the original). In the local jargon the word can also mean *intoxicated, being in an altered state*, which is what it means in the context of the quoted paragraph. I have decided to go with the literal translation because of the duality that the meaning of this word evokes – dead, yet preserved.
2. However, this applies to downtown Sarajevo and certain neighbourhoods where most of the cultural activity was taking place. The city was essentially divided, so there were suburbs that were controlled by Serbian forces and neighbourhoods cut off from the rest of the city.
3. MESS is the acronym for the Sarajevo Festival of Small and Experimental Stages, that Haris Pašović had resurrected during the war. MESS was responsible for a variety of cultural projects in the besieged city and remains active. The FAMA collective was involved in a number of projects during the war including the publication of the Sarajevo Survival Guide. More recently, FAMA has launched an interactive museum of the Sarajevo siege. See <http://vimeo.com/23039488>.
4. Suada Kapic is a Bosnian author and activist.
5. Tvrdko Kulenovic is a well-known Bosnian author and academic.
6. John Fine and Robert Donia are American history professors who published extensively on the history of Bosnia and Herzegovina. See Fine *et al*. (1994).
7. Erika Munk's lecture was on theatre in extreme circumstances.
8. Gestic is meant here in the sense Bertolt Brecht has defined his notion of gestus: a gesture that contains an attitude – a gesture, which is the gist, often political, of the action or argument.

7 Becoming a democratic audience

Alan Finlayson

Introduction

In this chapter I argue that the presence of ritualised performances in politics is not necessarily a sign of societal immaturity or corruption. In democratic societies 'the people' are in charge – but who they are and what they stand for is ambiguous, contested and subject to revision. The public staging of political claim and counterclaim may afford an opportunity for 'the people' to see itself and reflect upon who it is, has been and might become. In political spectacles the audience is part of the performance – its source and object – and through the act of judging may also become a subject.

The chapter begins with some general reflections on the prevalence of ritualised political performances. I then examine some of the ways in which political theorists can be anxious about audiences, publics and peoples. In the context of a critical discussion of deliberative approaches to politics, and with reference to the rhetorical tradition of thinking, I argue that political audiences are not necessarily disempowered when being spoken at. A performer must to some degree tailor their performance to the outlook and interests of the publics they come before, and that audience then finds itself in a position to judge what it sees. From this perspective a task for analysis is the identification and specification of the traditions and modes, forms and genres, trends and tendencies of public political performance – the grammars which make it possible and the opportunities for their creative and even transformative use.

Peoples are a problem

In Shakespeare's tragedy of *Coriolanus* a great warrior is exiled from Rome, sides with its enemies and dies without heroism at the hands of anonymous conspirators. The City, suffering terrible food shortages, is left weak and humiliated. In assigning responsibility for this critics of the play have pointed to the scheming and mendacity of the tribunes, the venality of the plebeians and to politics itself – such a hopelessly compromising activity that none can participate without losing honour and integrity (see George 2004). Yet something else is also central to the action of the play and to the decisions that set in motion its terrible events: stage-fright.

Martius (the hero of war with the Volscians) refuses to perform the role of 'Coriolanus, Hero of War with the Volscians'. He expects to be spared from the ritual that confirms high office in front of the people (and to avoid wearing the ceremonial 'gown of humility'). Sicinius, a tribune, insists: 'Sir, the people / Must have their voices; neither will they bate / One jot of ceremony'; Menenius, Martius's friend, urges him: 'fit you to the custom and / Take to you, as your predecessors have / Your honour with your form'. Nevertheless, in the face of both public demand and the obligations of tradition, Coriolanus still complains 'it is a part / That I shall blush in acting' (Act II, scene ii).

It is not only lack of willing that holds him back. Menenius explains that Martius is also incapable:

> Consider this: he has been bred i' the wars
> Since he could draw a sword, and is ill school'd
> In bolted language; meal and bran together
> He throws without distinction ...
>
> (Act III, scene i)

Perhaps it is this lack of skill that causes Martius to dislike so the occasions at which he must speak (and to despise the plebs who require it of him): 'I cannot bring / My tongue to such a pace' (Act II, scene iii) he explains, and when forced to perform cannot refrain from insulting his audience. With the leader unable to play the role assigned to him the people cannot play theirs; the polis falls into crisis and politics gives way to war.

In telling this story Shakespeare put into dramatic form some things that should be taken very seriously by both political scientists and political theorists. First of these is the observation that a certain sort of public performance is a fundamental element of the societal art of politics. Contrary to the assumptions of conspiracy theorists, power doesn't hide itself away and conduct its business in private. It appears in public dressed in the appropriate costume (ermine robes, military fatigues, finely tailored suit) and saying the appropriate words. These rituals are often of relatively recent invention (Hobsbawm and Ranger 1992) but they are far from superficial phenomena. This takes us to the second thing *Coriolanus* brings before the eyes. Such spectacles are usually taken to be indicative of the vanity of the powerful (their desire or need to be seen) and a way in which they subject us (forcing us to admire them, to genuflect to their glory). We imagine an audience required to attend and applaud an endless parade of tanks and troops, or one whipped into a xenophobic frenzy by finery, pomp and the rhythm of words. But in the performances Martius disdains – and this is the reason he disdains them – the people, far from being manipulated, are the manipulators. In them Martius is *required* to adapt himself to the people, to speak to *their* woes, to submit his person and his wounded body to *their* appraisal.

In actual politics (as opposed to Shakespeare's fictionalisation) there are many and varied examples of such a phenomenon – some of them rather like that portrayed in *Coriolanus*. The anthropologist Meyer Fortes, writing in the 1960s and reflecting on rituals of political office, offered the example of Ashanti rites of succession. On assuming the position of King, Fortes explained, the candidate appears 'before his people, he swears fidelity to them and is admonished by his senior councillors to remember, among other things, that he may never act without their advice and must rule with justice and impartiality' (Fortes 1962: 59). In the United Kingdom there are many similar examples: the 'investiture' of new members of the House of Lords; royal coronations; the annual opening of Parliament; commemorations of those killed in war. These rituals all involve (amongst other things) the uttering of a generic form of words. As in *Coriolanus*, an office holder is required to speak in public to an audience which can then pass judgement upon them.

In a 1948 study of political organisation among Native Americans, Robert Lowie records a number of examples including this from Curt Nimuendaju reporting on the Sherente:

> On many evenings ... I saw the chief assemble the village ... stepping in front of the semicircle he would impressively and vividly harangue the crowd for possibly an hour. Usually he circumstantially explained the half-forgotten ceremonial of some festival ... there followed a lengthy admonition ... to preserve ancient usage. In conclusion he would urge all to live in peace and harmony.
>
> (Cited in Lowie 1948: 16)

What the chief says is not of any immediate practical import; he issues no instruction, no call to arms and he addresses no particular pressing matter. He delivers an 'epideictic' address – a demonstrative and ritualised celebration that adheres to an implicit generic template. The structure of power relations within such a ritual is more complicated than it first appears to be. Formally, the dominant character, the chief is not acting autonomously; he is doing what tradition or habit compel. Furthermore, as anyone who speaks at a wedding or a prize-giving should know, public and ceremonial speech must communicate not what the speaker wants to say but what the audience expects and needs to hear. In order to remain as the chief who gives these speeches the chief has to say things the others won't mind hearing. That is why Pierre Clastres has argued that in societies such as that of the Native Americans speaking is not a right of power but a duty. 'Indian societies do not recognise the chief's right to speak because he is the chief', Clastres wrote, 'they require that the man destined to be chief prove his command over words. Speech is an imperative obligation for the chief. The tribe demands to hear him: a silent chief is no longer a chief' (1990: 153). For Clastres, 'The whole political philosophy of primitive society can be glimpsed in the obligation of the chief to be a man of speech' (1990: 153). The chief is *confined* to the domain of speech, within which he *owes* talk to the group as a condition of his being chief.

Echoes of this can still be heard in, for instance, the 'Speech from the Throne' in which the British monarch, opening a new session of Parliament, is required to conform to ritual and deliver an address written by others about what they will do with a power the Crown can longer exercise. Indeed, in contemporary democratic societies – despite the development of 'rational-legal' procedures and 'contractual' obligations regarding the successful delivery of 'public services' – the legitimacy of office still rests in part on the correct execution of ritualised speech moments. These are patterned occasions when a political leader (a general, a head of state or another office holder) delivers a generic address that is attended to by a particular audience. In the United States such speech moments are clearly institutionalised: the inauguration speech; the annual State of the Union address; party convention speeches (see Campbell and Jamieson 1990). In British politics similar set-piece speech performances pepper the political calendar from party conferences to necessary press appearances (see Finlayson and Martin 2008). During elections there are a variety of staged if unpredictable encounters with the public, victory and concession speeches, and as of 2010 there are leaders' debates. At the heart of British politics is the House of Commons in which ritualised divisions of time, symbolic props and rules specifying the locations and movements of individuals (Schechner 2003) make possible a variety of competitive performances between practitioners of a highly stylised form of speech. The House is a theatre for performances that are both histrionic and also agonistic (Crewe 2010; Waylen 2010).

All of these speech-rituals assign roles to participants, test or demonstrate the competence or authority of political actors and serve to affirm party, ideological or national identifications. They mark out boundaries of inclusion and exclusion, creating 'a sense of ordered histories of institutions, appropriate modes of behaviour legitimised by performance and recognition over time' (Rai 2010: 293). They are also opportunities for audiences to assess arguments, policies and character. Fitness to rule may be demonstrated through the delivery of a demonstrative epideictic speech that reaffirms the traditional ways of doing things – but unfitness may also be revealed and political actors exposed to the hostility, or indifference, of their audience.

The latter is something we see in *Coriolanus*. The theme may not always be in the foreground but the play is an effective dramatisation of the potential power of the people. This has certainly affected its critics. Many in the nineteenth century (perhaps aware of the demands of a restless 'mass') easily and happily condemned the plebeians' 'ungovernable licence and malignant ribaldry' (Drake quoted in George 2004: 10). Writing in the 1960s an altogether more liberal critic felt that *Coriolanus* was asking the same question as that which had recently and famously been posed by John F. Kennedy in *Profiles in Courage*: 'What is the role of the man of principle in politics? Can he act, involve himself in the world, and retain his honor? Can he uncompromisingly stand by his principles and yet be a force in the world?' (Rabkin 1966: 204). Rabkin sympathised with Martius's feeling that the populace is 'concerned only with what it can get for itself', desirous only of a leader 'willing and able to tailor himself' to them.

One might think that a starving populace is quite sensible to be concerned with getting things for itself, or that a free people is wise to try and contain its leaders (especially those skilled in the art of killing). Rabkin (who, to be fair, briefly notes that Coriolanus's refusal to bend is 'every bit as destructive' as the venality of the plebeians) writes: 'The citizens know it is a game they are asking Coriolanus to play, but his willingness to play the game would tell them that he is their man.' He then asks 'Do we really want Coriolanus to play the game?' The expected answer is clearly 'no' (1966: 208). Yet the play also poses a question which is the very opposite of that asked by Rabkin and Kennedy: do 'the people' have a place in politics? Can they be a force in the world? And for some the horror of the play is that the answer it gives to this question is clearly 'yes'. One of the things that public political performances can do – and which Shakespeare dramatises – is enable individuals to become, for a time, 'a people' and to take up a (quite possibly contentious) relationship not only with their leaders but also with their City and with themselves.

From critical reason to rhetorical performance

That 'the people' are a problem is hardly a feeling confined to drama critics. Indeed, one might say that it is this problem (or, more precisely, the constitution of this as a problem) that gave birth (and continues to give birth) to political philosophy. If the question which animates political philosophy is 'who should rule?' then it is also 'who should be ruled?' Platonic political theory is motivated by hostility to the proposition that the people can and should have a say in political affairs – they are the object of rule, not its subject. And for this reason Plato's political philosophy is concerned not only to prove the qualification of the philosophers to be kings but also the disqualification of the people from such office. Here, effort is not primarily directed at showing that various kinds of individuals lack the capacity to be a ruler but that *en masse* 'a people' cannot rule. Plato dislikes democracy's noisy audiences 'shouting or hammering their disapproval and approval – grossly exaggerated, in either case – of the things that are said and done' (1987: *Republic* 287). This is quite the opposite of the situation required for proper philosophical conversation. Patient dialectical exchange, the slow and arduous climb of concepts from the darkness of the cave to the clarity of light, best takes place between an older teacher and a younger pupil, away from the bustling city – and without an audience.

We find something similar in contemporary theories of political deliberation which take their inspiration from the Kantian ideal of an enlightened public, freeing itself from its immaturity and employing public reason to regulate itself and its rulers. Kant explains in his famous essay addressing the question of enlightenment that he is concerned with the freedom 'to make public use of one's reason in all matters'. This means, he clarifies, 'that use which anyone may make of it as a man of learning addressing the entire *reading* public' (my emphasis). Kant's public is not gathered in a town square or civic hall where it might act as one. It is a public of isolable (and perhaps isolated) individuals united by their consumption of something new – printed literary journals and periodicals (see Laursen 1986; Habermas 1989). This new medium enabled individuals to communicate their thinking publicly, and others to reflect upon it, even as everyone remained private.

The thinking these private enlightened individuals were to do was above all 'critical' in nature. The task of criticism in Kantian thought is that of 'determining and judging what is lawful in reason in general'; it is the 'court of justice for all controversies of pure reason' without which 'reason is as it were in the state of nature, and it cannot make its assertions and claims valid or secure except through war' (*Critique of Pure Reason*, A751–2). Like Plato, Kant does not care for the noise of the demos in the public square. He wants to clear it of polemicists, dogmatists and civic humanists (see Garsten 2006). And this way of thinking about publics and peoples has given rise to a tradition which, when it looks at the public sphere, sees untidiness – somewhere full of ill-made claims, unjustified assertions and badly schooled audiences. It wants to unclutter the public sphere so as to enable free individuals to commune with the General Will. The wager of deliberative political theory is that, if the right procedures can be found and put in place, then the universal rules implicit in our conduct as rational individuals will manifest themselves and govern our decision-making which can then, finally, be sure of its own justice. In a sense, then, the Kantian approach isn't really about deliberation. It is about engendering a situation in which (unhindered by the corruptions of public performance) what would always have been the right answer is able to appear.

This has given rise to a very particular way of conceiving of the problem of 'the people' in politics, and especially in democracy. Deliberative political theory thinks in terms of a number of separate 'objects': a speaker or orator of some kind, an audience and a text. The orator may not be a single figure – it may be an institution or medium of communication, an expert, a politician, another citizen or some other public figure; similarly the audience may be imagined as composed of everybody in a polity or some part of it, a literal or imagined community; the 'text' may be the articulation of a specific proposal or counter-proposal, an argument of some kind, or it may be conceived of as communication in the abstract. With these three elements in play the task of the political theorist is to arrange them in the right way so as to ensure the right outcome – to line them up so that none is in charge over the others, none can dominate and in combination they will sound harmonious. Very often this involves subtracting other elements – the mass media, venal demagogues, an uneducated people and so on.

For example, deliberative theorist Simone Chambers has proposed a distinction between two kinds of public communication: 'deliberative' and 'plebiscitary' rhetoric. The latter Chambers finds to be a 'pathology' of large-scale democracies. It consists of 'speech that is concerned first and foremost with gaining support for a proposition and only secondarily with the merits of the arguments or persuasion for that matter' (2009: 337). Such language is not so much rabble rousing as 'strategic'. Chambers associates it with contemporary campaign techniques (opinion polling to identify the median voter, psychological research to establish 'trigger' words and powerful 'framing' devices). Where deliberative rhetoric 'engages citizens' practical judgment', treating them as capable deliberators, plebiscitary rhetoric 'seeks to attract voters and as such treats its audience as a means to power' (2009: 337). Instead of being properly dialogical it is monological.

Like Plato, Chambers is worried by 'the size and unruliness of the mass public' which replaces mutual deliberation with asymmetrical and mediated communication (2009: 339). 'In democracies, where the sheer numbers of supporters is an important factor', she writes, 'plebiscitary rhetoric is always a threat to deliberative ideals' (2009: 337). To redress this imbalance she advocates an increase in opportunities for citizen-to-citizen encounters of a 'semi-Socratic' kind – smaller, back-and-forth exchanges freed from the pressures of a mass audience. These, she believes, can make citizens more capable, better able to evaluate oratory and experienced in the 'skepticism, self-confidence, and knowledgeable judgment' that are required of them (2009: 341). For Chambers, then, the problem of the people in politics is addressed by breaking up large publics so that individuals can experience something which makes them better. At the same time public communication must take a complementary form. The end results will be more just and rational societies. I suggest, however, it will also be the end of 'the people'.

Chambers and other deliberative theorists are not wrong to be concerned with the ways in which contemporary political performances are forced into moulds manufactured by strategy consultants or confined to speech genres defined by cable news channels. But she and they start from a misconception of the situations in and through which political communication and rhetoric take place. Deliberativists tend to write as if in politics one seeks to convince an opponent. A more common scenario is that one tries to beat an opponent in front of an audience. In an election one is not trying to win the votes of the other parties but to win from them the votes of the electorate. In a formal debate the efforts of the proposers of the motion to make a better case than their opponents are judged not by the opponents but by the audience before them. This, presumably, is exactly what some deliberative theorists would like to expunge from the polis. But in abolishing it one would abolish the audience also. And that, I suggest, would be a problem. For in such disputations, while orators may not engage in explicit dialogue with either their opponents or the audience, it is not the case that they are merely engaging in a monologue. Public talk is always polyphonic and in such situations something altogether more complicated is happening.

Rather than think of speaker, topic and audience as isolated elements awaiting their correct organisation by the political philosopher I would like to propose that we conceive of them as parts of one thing: a performance. A performance certainly includes those elements and they are clearly identifiable. But they exist only as things in relation to each other. A person on a platform reciting talking points in three part lists is not (yet) an orator and a crowd standing around in a the square is not (yet) an audience. These cannot come together without a 'text' – something to argue about and a form or genre that enables the parties to recognise that this is what they are doing. The performance is not only what happens on the stage. It is the entire occasion, a specific arrangement of all the elements within it. In so constituting the performance as the object of analysis we are not, I think, removing it from its context. The relations inside the performance – including those between speakers, audiences and texts – remain a concern. Also of importance is the relationship of the performance to other performances of the same sort (and of which it may be one iteration) and also performances of different kinds (for deliberation is not the only show in town).

Viewed in this way such performances are 'rhetorical situations' (Bitzer 1999) – combinations of people, events and problems which may be changed in some way by performative discursive acts. Prior relations between speaker, audience and the topic, dispute or issue at hand comprise a history that bequeaths a ready-made vocabulary, perhaps a genre of speech; a more general staging organises the subjects and objects of rhetorical action. That organisation of speech affects speakers just as it affects audiences.

Plato wanted rulers to learn virtue and wisdom and then apply it to the polis. The rhetoricians wager that through learning to perform in civic life one might become good at living it. As Isocrates, the great teacher of rhetoric, declared:

> I consider that the kind of art which can implant honesty and justice in depraved natures has never existed and does not exist, and that people who profess that power will grow weary and cease from their vain pretensions before such an education is ever found. But I do hold that people can become better and worthier if they conceive an ambition to speak well, if they become possessed of the desire to be able to persuade their hearers.
> (Isocrates 1980: *Antidosis* 272–6)

And for this reason, where Plato opposed imitative performance – learning 'the sort of thing … that a man would say, and a woman would say, and a slave and a free man, a subject and a ruler – the suitable thing for each' (*Ion* 504b) – the rhetorical tradition has embraced it.

The classical teachers of rhetoric had their students learn great speeches and invent examples of the kind of speech one might find in this or that situation, not so as to confine them to convention but so as to provide them with resources on which to draw when seeking to act within or upon concrete situations (Haskins 2000). In learning them one learned the contours and folds of civic space. For Isocrates, as Ekaterina Haskins puts it, 'by identifying with what fictional and historical characters say and do, a student grasps the repertoire of social roles and the range of situations more fully than does a person who receives lessons in moral philosophy without "living" its principles' (2000: 21). Similarly Cicero's ideal orator is not simply one who 'on any matter whatever can speak with fullness and variety' (*De Oratore* 1. 13. 59) but one whose eloquence is rooted in philosophy *and* in an understanding of the history, tradition and laws of the community to which they speak. They must be a person of the city, familiar with people's attitudes, customs and ways of communicating – one who masters 'everything that is relevant to the practices of citizens and the ways humans behave: all that is connected with normal life, the functioning of the State, our social order, as well as the way people usually think, human nature and character' (*De Oratore* 1. 11. 48). To learn to perform as a political actor is also to learn about the community and thus to become tied into it. That can, of course, generate only a politics of conservation dedicated to celebrating, maintaining and policing the borders of the community – of who is in it and of what can be thought and said within its world. But what one learns through imitative performance is the multifarious modes and means through which persons in action may create and employ meaning – the 'grammars' of public communication; a thick and nuanced grasp of a particular culture, community and context. And, just as grammar is a means and mechanism for policing the limits of a language, it is also a tool for making it say new things. The ability to understand and interpret the ways and means of a particular polity is a necessary skill for any who want to change it.

A mirror for peoples

As we have seen, deliberative theories are worried by audiences – by a public acting as a collective rather than as a series of individuals. Thus deliberative procedures not only constrain speakers – they also school audiences, drawing them into the correct use of the criteria of judgement. Rhetorical performances also, potentially, provide a kind of schooling for audiences – but in a very different way. To see why we have to understand a little more about how rhetoric works, and about what it is that a rhetorician is performing.

For Aristotle the most essential aspect of rhetoric was not emotion or figurative language but enthymemes. These are not – as is sometimes thought – inadequate, false or truncated forms of reasoning. The enthymeme is that kind of logical argument which draws on 'notions possessed by everybody' (Aristotle 350 BCE: *Rhetoric* 1355a). Note here that Aristotle says 'everybody' and not 'anybody'. He does not mean for a rhetorician to rely on just any opinion but on 'those accepted by our judges or by those whose authority they recognize' (Aristotle 350 BCE: *Rhetoric* 1395b). Lines of argument emerge from the interaction between the one advancing an argument with those to whom it is addressed.

Bitzer (1959) explains enthymemes in terms of the ways in which they form and use argumentative premises. In scientific, analytical, reasoning premises are laid down by a speaker ('Let x = 10'). In dialectical reasoning (such as that exemplified in Socratic dialogue) they are asked for and must be agreed to. In rhetorical enthymemes, Bitzer argues, 'the speaker does not *lay down* his premises but lets his audience supply them out of its stock of opinion and knowledge' (Bitzer 1959: 187). Where dialectic involves a direct question and answer, between participants in rhetoric there is an implied question and answer: 'enthymemes occur only when speaker and audience jointly produce them', and they unite speaker and audience in a process in which 'Owing to the skill of the speaker, the audience itself helps construct the proofs by which it is persuaded' (1959: 188). From this perspective rhetorical activity invokes a hermeneutic circle in which an interpretation of an audience by a speaker generates premises which are in turn interpreted by that audience, recognised (or not), and responded to (or not). As the contemporary rhetorical theorist Thomas Farrell expresses it, rhetoric involves the implementation of practical wisdom 'through the complementary participation of someone else: namely the rhetorical audience' (Farrell 1993: 73), and because appeals to that audience must be adapted to what that community already thinks – to its extant values and principles – through rhetoric 'the norms and conventions of a culture find themselves employed as premises of both recognition and inference' put to the test and collectively practised (Farrell 1993: 76).

What the rhetor attempts to perform, then, is a 'fusion of horizons' between what an audience already thinks in general and what it thinks it ought to think about some particular issue, exigency or action. This fusion is 'demonstrated' through performance. The enthymematic appeal to reason is combined with the appeal to 'ethos' – the character of the speaker, a performance aiming at 'identification'. This involves speaking in a style and tone congruent with the demands or expectations of the audience, employing emotive force in decorous ways (Burke 1969). Such identification, the 'emotional connection of audience with actor and text' may create 'the conditions for projecting cultural meaning from performance to audience' (Alexander 2006: 55). As Turner put it (cited by Alexander) 'realisation of character can be achieved only by "taking for granted the culturally defined roles supposedly played by that character: father, businessman, friend, lover, fiancé, trade union leader, farmer, poet"' (Alexander 2006: 58).

Placing such performances into the context of the fractured, dynamic and complex social orders of modernity (in which 'all that is solid melts into air') Jeffrey Alexander argues, contrary to the deliberativists, that the development of the modern public sphere has not involved the creation of a structured forum for considered debate but rather, 'the rise of a public stage, a symbolic forum in which actors have increasing freedom to create and to project performances of their reasons, dramas tailored to audiences whose voices have become more legitimate references in political conflicts' (2006: 51). Such performances do not automatically possess the aura of authenticity attendant on rituals in traditional society and actors must work to win legitimacy 'as authoritative interpreters of social texts', transforming 'interest conflicts' into persuasive, symbolic performances through which they present themselves as grand protagonists and 'exemplifications of sacred religious and secular texts' (2006: 52). The public political actor is performing the enthymeme – drawing on a repertoire of references and roles, a social imaginary, and presenting it back to the people in the context of a specific claim in the present. What the audience judges, then, is – in a specific but also literal sense – itself.

A popular and influential genre of political writing in the medieval and renaissance periods was the so-called 'mirror for princes'. Advice books often dedicated to a particular ruler, these sought to present (through the rearticulation of common moralisms and maxims as well as principles of governance) an image of an ideal prince in which an actual prince might come to see himself. A democratic community is not a prince – but it certainly can become tyrannical over a part or even over the whole of itself; it too needs a mirror. It must be able to manifest and look upon itself so that it might judge itself. Plato's quite proper concern was that the demos would be entranced by the vision of itself offered by the orators – and theirs, he thought, must always be a false and flattering mirror put before a sluggish and passive people.

In contrast to this, Jacques Rancière argues that looking is itself an action. At theatrical performances, 'The spectator ... observes, selects, compares, interprets. She links what she sees to a host of other things that she has seen on other stages, in other kinds of place. She composes her own poem with elements of the poem before her. She participates in the performance by refashioning it in her own way' (Rancière 2009: 13). Similarly, Alexander argues that 'audiences of social and theatrical dramas judge quality comparatively. Scripts, whether written or attributed, are compared to the great and convincing plots of earlier times' (2006: 76). Audiences actively interpret what is before them – they may affirm that a performance takes place in the time-honoured fashion, that it remains contained within the generic expectations; they may reject such repetition in favour of modification and rearticulation. Furthermore, if what they see is a rhetorical contest, a topic argued *in utramque partem* or on both sides of the question, they can then compare the rival versions played out directly before them. In all these cases an audience may make a judgement of the political actors *and* of the scripts they perform, the social repertoires that they employ and which come from and belong to that public. Many things *can* go wrong with this process – but Plato's view that it *must* go wrong and the deliberativists' conviction that it *must* corrupt seem to me unwarranted. There is no single way in which that people must be and the genius of democratic practice is that, rather than presume a consensus upon which the polis may be built, it accepts that there are always a number of possibilities for how a people may be. In seeing those possibilities performed and put into contention with one another, and in judging this performance of its own possibilities, a people brings itself into being.

Conclusion

I have argued that, when examining those moments where political actors perform in front of people, we should see the entire occasion as the performance and not confine our attention to the things which happen on the stage. Here, the analysts' role is not that of legislators or referees, those who set the rules or those who ensure compliance with them. 'Criticism' is instead analogous to the role of art or theatre critic and involves judgements not of the legality of the 'moves' made in a performance but of its overall form and quality. It may also involve explicating the nature and context of the performance – the derivation of its practice, the ways in which it conforms to or departs from established styles and scenarios. It may mean seeking out new and overlooked kinds of performance happening away from the main stage. Above all it means trying to explore the relationship between a particular performance and the polis from which it derives and to which it contributes. A definitive feature of any political or societal regime is how it organises (or fails to organise) such speaking and arguing and there are urgent questions to ask about how new systems of communication affect not only individuals' freedom of speech and governments' monitoring of it but also the capacities of publics to show themselves to themselves and to exercise collective as well as individual judgement.

Not all performances are good. That there are many terrible plays is not to be doubted but it would be precipitate to conclude that we should abolish the theatre. Similarly, that demagogues can manufacture and madden publics is not a justification for abandoning the latter. The answer to fear-mongering shock-jocks lies in the formation of new stages and the cultivation of new performers for new publics. Those stages may be virtual platforms or traditional legislative arenas, in Zucotti Park or outside St Paul's Cathedral. Politics is an endless 'materialisation' of peoples, a series of performances which take place 'in the gap between a place where the demos exists and a place where it does not, where there are only populations, individuals, employers and employees, heads of household and spouses, and so on ... performing this relationship, which means first setting it up as theatre, inventing the argument, in the double logical and dramatic sense of the term' (Rancière 1999: 88; as translated in Hallward 2006: 111).

The 'subject' of contemporary democracy is 'the people'. It is on their authority – their 'popular sovereignty' that governments are founded and it is in their name and for their interests that states act. If what happens on the public stage is understood as the creation and transmission of 'meaning' of some kind then something meaningful is also being created by the audiences which do or don't pay attention, or that go off and create a new stage somewhere else. Yet – as we all know – this 'people' is a fiction. 'The people' is not a natural or given category, the territory over which it claims authority is not fixed and contestation over who is included within it (the propertyless, women, those with a minority religion or none) is an evident fact of political history. Who the people are, what they are like – their virtues and vices, capacities and character – are open questions constantly answered by political actors of all kinds. Thus – peculiarly – 'the people' – the 'subject' of democracy – is also its object and a focal point of political action. This is why Ernesto Laclau claims that 'the political operation par excellence is always going to be the construction of a people' (2005: 153). Political movements try to name the people and show how they alone can speak for them.

This is a paradox of politics. The people, which makes a polity possible, on which the city is founded, is itself made possible by the polity which gives it form and order. Often in political theory and political practice this paradox is 'resolved' by appeal to a law external to the people such as a natural or divine law, or a necessary *a priori* presupposition that, as a condition of possibility for the people, might also be a source of a regulative principle which can govern it. It is also solved through assertions about 'tradition' – the historical representation of something 'innate' within a people – and, as we know all too well, through the violent imposition of one definition of the people. Exploring this paradox the political theorist Bonnie Honig urges us to embrace it so as to avoid too easy, too quick and too sharp a resolution into an either/or. She wants us to accept and exploit the ambiguity of the people, thus enabling 'a politics, in which plural and contending parties make claims in the name of public goods, seek support from various constituencies, and the legitimacy of outcomes is always contestable' (2007: 14). The chicken/egg problem of the foundations or sources of political order forces us, she writes, to begin democratic politics *in media res* (2007: 2–3). What we find in the middle of things, I suggest, is a variety of historical political practices – performances which may have the potential for a people to 'see' itself, to catch itself in the act of creating itself and reflect upon that act so that it might create itself anew – becoming democratic.

8 Street arts, radical democratic citizenship and a grammar of storytelling

Susan C. Haedicke

'Politics and art, like forms of knowledge, construct "fictions," that is to say *material* rearrangements of signs and images, relationships between what is seen and what is said, between what is done and what can be done', claims Jacques Rancière (2004: 39; emphasis in original). These 'fictions' link the knowledges created by politics[1] and art through their narrative practices that reconfigure what is seen, heard and understood about the contemporary world. The word 'fiction' used in this way signifies a strategy rather than a genre; it 'means far more than the constructing of an imaginary world. ... It is not a term that designates the imaginary as opposed to the real; it involves the re-framing of the "real"' (Rancière 2010: 141). Fictions are particular to what Rancière calls the 'aesthetic regime of the arts'. Temporally associated with modernity, the aesthetic regime offers a contrast to the other two regimes in Western art: the 'ethical regime of images' that focuses on the authenticity (or 'truth content') of the images and how they are to be used and the 'representative regime' that identifies what is appropriate for artistic representation and how it should be represented (mimesis). The aesthetic regime breaks from these strictures and disengages the arts from rigid rules of subject matter and form. It breaks down 'the mimetic barrier that distinguished ways of doing and making affiliated with art from other ways of doing and making' (Rancière 2004: 23), and in so doing, it not only establishes a connection between the art work and the social world, but significantly it also democratises art in that art becomes the domain of everyone. Fiction, as redefined within the aesthetic regime, is a strategy to alter perception and understanding and to expose the invisible; it 'is a way of changing existing modes of sensory presentations and forms of enunciation; of varying frames, scales and rhythms; and of building new relationships between reality and appearance' (Rancière 2010: 141).

Rancière's *re-vision* of the word 'fiction' enables him to claim an equivalence between the logics of construction of narrative elements in politics and art as well as in history and stories. Playing with the word *histoire* that, in French, means both *history* and *story*, Rancière proposes that:

> writing history and writing stories come under the same regime of truth. This has nothing whatsoever to do with a thesis on the reality or unreality of things. On the contrary, it is clear that a model for the fabrication of stories is linked to a certain idea of history as common destiny, with the idea of

those who 'make history', and that this interpenetration of the logic of facts and the logic of stories is specific to an age when anyone and everyone is considered to be participating in the task of 'making' history. Thus, it is not a matter of claiming that 'History' is only made up of stories that we tell ourselves, but simply that the 'logic of stories' and the ability to act as historical agents go together.

(Rancière 2004: 38–9)

If both history and stories construct meanings and 'produce effects in reality' (Rancière 2004: 39), then following Rancière's logic, it is possible to assert that politics and art are linked through a grammar of storytelling, a grammar of narration of the *histoire*, as the narrators rewrite the visible, the sayable and the thinkable into political and artistic narratives or 'fictions' that propose innovative and often controversial interpretations of events and ideas and create provocative images.[2] For Rancière, 'art and politics each define a form of dissensus, a dissensual re-configuration of the common experience of the sensible' (Rancière 2010: 140). Dissensus, he claims, is 'not a conflict of interests, opinions or values; it is a division inserted in "common sense": a dispute over what is given and about the frame within which we see something as given' (Rancière 2010: 69). A grammar of storytelling relies on dissensual principles and practices that reconfigure the status quo by troubling a sense of commonality or consensus with alternate voices inventing new ways of seeing, hearing and thinking and that suggest inventive strategies to alter what can be said or done about those perceptions and experiences. A grammar of storytelling disrupts a complacent stability by affecting a shift in the understanding of social space by transforming it 'into a space for the appearance of a subject: the people, the workers, the citizens' (Rancière 2010: 37). A grammar of storytelling shared by art and politics constructs dissensual 'fictions' that challenge and debate the social experience with claims of freedom and equality for all: hallmarks of democracy. A grammar of storytelling whether in art or politics transforms abstract ideas about freedom, equality and citizenship into familiar actions performed by recognisable players trying to achieve certain ends: narratives that place ethico-political issues and conduct into a frame in which the listener can link new perceptions and concepts to what is already known and understood.

Many contemporary street artists seem to translate these ideas into performance forms that reconfigure social and performative space by encouraging the public to become the storytellers, to become active participants in the *histoire* in actual public spaces in a city. Here, the artists suggest a stimulus by constructing the beginnings of story events, but the resulting narratives, often contradictory or competing, are in the hands of the audience. These artworks develop a grammar of storytelling based on democratic principles to create an event that relies on the interplay of the occasion of performance, the social participation of a public in practices of dissensus and the overturning of a familiar public place to make something happen. The artists strive to create a democratic space superimposed on a recognisable physical public space in which the spectators may achieve a sense of agency as they become active co-creators in the artistic process.

108 *Susan C. Haedicke*

First performed in 2004, but still often seen at annual street theatre festivals throughout Europe, Compagnie Mouton de Vapeur's *Les Quiétils* entices the spectator into a participatory role so that the theatrical experience is an exchange or a kind of physical conversation between the spectator and the Quiétils, grotesque creatures who mingle with the crowd and take their cues from the public's reactions to them. Artists and audiences together create a world in which the spectator makes meaning from the experience of the actual embodied encounter. The Quiétils (written as a made-up word, but when spoken sounds like 'qui est-il' or 'who is it') are travellers from elsewhere. The website whimsically describes the Quiétil as 'a general term used for all small-bodied mammifers, closed within a bony or scaly double husk named carapace. ... The sounds emitted by this species are not perceptible to the human ear, only pass through the skin. A migrating species.'[3] The Quiétils cannot blend in with the crowd and become invisible since their ugly appearance and unusual behaviour embody otherness. The heads of the creatures' bumpy, stone-like 'naked' bodies are attached to the chest or belly of the actor who manipulates the creature from within. The puppeteer's actual head is hidden in the large pack the traveller carries on his hunched back (Figure 8.1). The Quiétils are outsiders trying to understand and appreciate this new world in which they find themselves, simultaneously fascinated and frightened by how the people who surround them react and interact with them. Thus the spectator 'writes' the narrative of Otherness that the creatures then play out as they journey through the city.

The Quiétils never speak, but the exchanges between the creatures and the public shift back and forth between intimate one-to-one interactions and group dialogues where the crowd's inevitable responses of affection or mockery guide the outsiders' attempts to fit in. Since the Quiétils are not aggressive, the audience can easily embrace them and 'teach' them how to 'fit in'. This process of assimilation is played out time and time again as members of the public instruct the Quiétils to throw litter in the trash bin, to sit properly, to use a camera or to buy some food. Sometimes, a spectator rewards them with a photograph as they learn the proper etiquette or welcomes them into the group as the creature and a member of the public touch hands, but another may laugh at the creatures when they are unable to do a simple task like step up onto a curb given their short legs and relative lack of mobility, mock their awkwardness or even poke them with sticks or try to trip them.

These contrasting narratives of acceptance and rejection of the outsider, played out in embodied exchanges, not only between spectators and Quiétils, but also among audience members themselves as they react to each others' behaviour, represent a form of public debate in actual public spaces.[4] This embodied form of deliberative democratic discourse allows for two subject positions: one as 'citizen' making decisions about the narratives on display, the other as observer of the 'body politic' as fellow citizens react and engage. Could that act of observation lead to further action at a later date?

Street art events such as *Les Quiétils* thus create a performative version, perhaps even a rehearsal, of 'radical democracy' that rejects consensus for conflict and antagonism.[5] Predating Rancière's analysis of dissensus, Ernesto Laclau

Figure 8.1 Mouton de Vapeur, *Les Quiétils* (courtesy of photographer Susan C. Haedicke).

and Chantal Mouffe in *Hegemony and Socialist Strategy: Towards a Radical Democratic Politics* argue that a society is not a functioning democracy when its public space delegitimises debate and seeks compromise and agreement. Democracy is a form of social practice that challenges homogeneity and universality with charges of authoritarianism and that promotes mobilisations and pluralisms outside a single unified narrative. This radical pluralist democracy, Mouffe writes later, promotes the 'creation of a vibrant "agonistic" public sphere of contestation where different hegemonic political projects can be confronted' (Mouffe 2005: 3).[6] Agonism, Mouffe claims, is 'a relation not between enemies but between "adversaries," adversaries being defined in a paradoxical way as "friendly enemies," that is persons who are friends because they share a common symbolic space but also enemies because they want to organize this common symbolic space in a different way' (Mouffe 2000: 13). The tension between these groups should not be silenced or even be 'a relation of *negotiation* but of *contamination* in the sense that ... each of them changes the identity of the other' (Mouffe 2000: 10). A radical (or dissensual) democracy or 'agonistic pluralism' establishes an arena that does not ignore or erase other voices, but rather places them in an adversarial position as differing but equally valid positions, and it seeks to 'harness [conflict] in a productive way' (Mouffe 2000: 9).

In Mouton de Vapeur's *Les Quiétils* and many other very different street arts interventions, such as Jeanne Simone's *Le Parfum des Pneus* and Royal de Luxe's *The Sultan's Elephant*, where the audience constructs contrasting stories through their bodily actions and reactions, the performative 'contamination' creates an arena for the practice of pluralist democratic politics with its diversity, conflicts and antagonisms, as well as its sense of community. Here, the spectator parallels Mouffe's radical democratic citizen who 'must be an active citizen, somebody who *acts* as a citizen, who conceives of herself as a participant in a collective undertaking' (Mouffe 1992: 4). For Mouffe, the construction of an ethico-political *citizen's* identity 'should be one of the important tasks of democratic politics' (Mouffe 1992: 225). She challenges both liberal definitions of citizenship that concentrate on individual liberty and rights and civic republican definitions that argue for political participation and the public good. The former, she contends, limits the idea of citizenship to a legal status whereas the latter's emphasis on the 'common good' diminishes pluralism and can result in totalitarianism.[7] For Mouffe, these alternative positions present a false dichotomy. She argues instead for an idea of radical democratic citizenship as 'an articulating principle that affects subject positions of the social agent ... while allowing for a plurality of specific allegiances and for the respect of individual liberty' (Mouffe 1992: 235). This radical democratic citizenship involves an awareness on the part of individuals of a sense of belonging, not necessarily to a nation-state, but to an idea of 'we', and whilst this *membership* offers rights, it also carries responsibilities to the workings of the whole. Thus citizenship is not passive, but demands some form of action and engagement (even if symbolic), and a grammar of storytelling in both politics and art provides a structure or set of rules with which to test, define and debate citizenship in a variety of settings that often represent points of tension in democratic life.

The artistic interventions of Mouton de Vapeur, Jeanne Simone and Royal de Luxe rely on a grammar of narrative practices that displace the boundaries between artistic activities and acts of radical democratic citizenship as the story events *frame* the public space and the everyday with art and shift the focus away from representational art-making where the artwork reflects or *represents* (and so is *about*) external events, situations or issues. The performances replace *about-ness* with an *event-ness* that encourages multiple, often contradictory, 'fictions' constructed by the audience. Thus these interventions encourage, even compel, spectators to reassess what they see and understand about the quotidian and thus rewrite their role in the social space. For Rancière and Mouffe, this dissensus is nearly synonymous with progressive change, and the artists endeavour to structure even their open-ended performance events to achieve that creative possibility. Although spontaneity and public debate are key elements of a grammar of storytelling in street arts, in these interventions that blur art and non-art in actual public spaces, the artists must stay alert and be prepared to shift directions or distract the audience and passers-by in order to defuse tensions that could catapult the theatrical event from its *location* in a liminal art/non-art space where actual actions remain framed by art, albeit in a tangible public space, into a genuine *political* disturbance, even a riot. The two arenas of art and politics, while linked by a grammar of storytelling, must not become one. Rancière cautions that if the boundaries between them become too porous, they are in danger of cancelling each other out. While art and politics share dynamic characteristics and practices of rupture, instability and transformation, they do not function in the same way: 'If there is such a thing as an "aesthetics of politics", it lies in the re-configuration of the distribution of the common through political processes of subjectivation. Correspondingly, if there is a politics of aesthetics, it lies in the practices and modes of visibility of art that re-configure the fabric of the sensory experience' (Rancière 2010: 140). *Political* rupture and transformation, for Rancière, lead to a freer and more democratic society that defends equality among its citizens and can test that 'fiction' in concrete public spaces. *Artistic* rupture, in contrast, introduces the democratic ideals into the art form itself, argues Rancière. The participatory practices of street arts performances, however, do not act like the completed artworks imagined by Rancière, but rather they establish a grammar of storytelling that bridges art and politics and blurs the boundaries between the ways their distinct ruptures function by creating a dynamic experiential rapport between the artwork and the audience in urban public spaces: an amalgamation of production, reception and place. Here *invention* does not work in opposition to *reality*; rather the *imaginary* reframes, reinterprets, confuses, subverts or challenges notions of the *real* as each performance relies on the particular spectator-participants with whom the performers engage and on how these co-creators interpret and respond to the story beginnings that they are given.

Like Mouton de Vapeur's *Les Quiétils*, Jeanne Simone's *Le Parfum des Pneus* (The Perfume of Tyres) also creates an artistic event that invites the public to construct the narrative, but here the artists offer encounters with narratives more ambiguous than those of the Quiétils. This piece aesthetically intervenes in a public space, but not through elaborate costumes highlighting the characters' incongruity with daily life. Instead, *Le Parfum des Pneus* begins invisibly as the two performers, Laure Terrier and Camille Perrin, enter the public space as ordinary city dwellers. As they begin to play with the city and passers-by however, the narrative of the social space and its expected behaviours starts to shift. Trained as a dancer and performing choreographically in the piece, Terrier says that the improvisational dance or contact improvisation used in *Le Parfum des Pneus* enables her to enter into 'discussion' with the bodies next to her: the non-dancing body, the spectator, the passer-by. Her moving body that establishes points of contact with strangers overturns expectation and gives permission for other bodies who just happen to be there to reinhabit the public space. As ordinary people participate in the collective art-making, they rewrite the social spaces and interpersonal encounters that take place there. Even though the creative experience is transitory, it empowers an individual to become a storyteller with what Terrier calls 'instantaneous scripting'. Here the grammar of storytelling is in the encounter.[8]

The intentional performance of everyday activities that is a key strategy of the piece slows down or exaggerates ordinary actions like looking in a shop window, reading a sign, crossing a street or navigating around a fellow walker. This 'fiction' uses these altered or 'studied' spatial practices to 'map' the *place* of the street, bus stop or other site of circulation as it makes visible a surprising solitude in a crowd and challenges that narrative of lack of human connection with one of unexpected

112 *Susan C. Haedicke*

and ephemeral encounters. For Terrier, the artistic director of the company, *place* is not just geographic location, but rather a blend of de Certeau's 'practiced place' where connection is established between physical site and corporeal perception and Grant Kester's 'community + conversation' artworks that begin as a dialogue and find their artistic practice in the interpersonal relations experienced during the event. The mapping of the public space through movements of the body in *Le Parfum des Pneus* constructs an alternative narrative focusing on human connection, and the passers-by, like radical democratic citizens, participate in a deliberative democratic dialogue about the viability of that narrative as they embrace, tolerate or reject it through their bodily responses.

Each performance is improvised in response to the reactions and participation of the spectators whose responses range from playing with the dancers or at least letting them use their physical presence as a source of inspiration for the dancers' movements to walking away, pushing the dancers or honking loudly and braking just in front of a dancer crawling slowly across the street. The actors prefer to perform unannounced and so, even in a festival setting, do not reveal the location of the performance until an hour before so most of the 'audience' are not expecting to see a show. This unsuspecting public is a key element in the transformation of the social space from a space of transit into a space of human connection. In one performance, the two performers waited at a crowded trolley stop. Gradually, with another passer-by waiting there, together they created a 'choreography' of waiting. When the trolley arrived, they waved goodbye to their co-creator (Figure 8.2).

Figure 8.2 Jeanne Simone, *Le Parfum des Pneus* (courtesy of photographer Susan C. Haedicke).

At another moment, the performers and the public created 'music' from the buildings and other objects on the street. Sometimes, they explore the physical shape of ordinary urban objects like lamp posts, bicycle racks, benches and cars or imagine alternate functions for street barricades or rubbish bins. While these activities may not sound very exciting, it is thrilling to participate in the subversion of a busy commercial space as it transforms into a performance space where dissensual urban narratives of interpersonal connection and play are created and acted out. The sense of danger as drivers become angry while they wait through yet another red light or as passers-by bump into a dancer balanced on a ledge physically narrates the fragility of a radical democratic agonistic space. This participatory piece 'written' as a corporeal dialogue between performers and public seems to construct a performative form of Rancière's claim that the 'essential work of politics is the configuration of its own space. It is to make the world of its subjects and its operations seen. The essence of politics is the manifestation of dissensus as the presence of two worlds in one' (Rancière 2010: 37). Like politics as defined by Rancière, *Le Parfum des Pneus* superimposes a creative space of 'storytellers' and democratic citizens onto a space of transit by 're-figuring space, that is in what is to be done, to be seen and to be named in it' (Rancière 2010: 37).

The *Quiétils* and *Le Parfum des Pneus* each create a performative space that 'is also a doing, that does not pre-exist its doing ... [Its] space is practiced, a matrix of play, dynamic and iterative, its forms and shapes produced through the citational performance of self-other relations' (Rose 1999: 248). The passers-by who enter the performative space and choose to engage with the artists are not passive spectators of a theatrical event, but rather co-creators. They do not receive a fully formed performance; on the contrary, they help write its contrasting narratives with the actions and reactions performed by their bodies. These radical democratic citizen-spectators entertain new possibilities and begin to develop a critical awareness of the socio-political issues raised in and by the performing space. The radical pedagogy of Paulo Freire offers a key to understanding the political significance of developing a critical awareness of seemingly normative or natural aspects of social life. He insists that humans are unique among animals because they can construct history and culture as well as being shaped by them. It is the understanding of this agency to comprehend the world as it is *and* to intervene and alter its construction and its future that can lead to freedom. That liberation, Freire argues, is achieved through dialogue and problem-posing education where teacher and student bring different but equally important skills to solve the problem.

Like Freire, Rancière asserts that

> intellectual emancipation is the verification of the equality of intelligence. ... The distance the ignoramus has to cover is not the gulf between her ignorance and the schoolmaster's knowledge. It is simply the path from what she already knows to what she does not yet know, but which she can learn just as she has learnt the rest; which she can learn not in order to occupy the position of scholar, but so as better to practise the art of translating, of putting her

experience into words and her words to the test; of translating her intellectual adventures for others and counter-translating the translations of their own adventures which they present to her.

(Rancière 2009: 10–11)

For Rancière, this student parallels the 'emancipated spectator' who develops his or her *own* critical awareness and understanding of the performance. The artwork, Rancière argues, remains separate from the spectator and the artist but links the two: what he calls 'a third thing' (Rancière 2009: 14). It is through this 'third thing', offered by one and *translated* by the other but belonging to neither, that intellectual emancipation is achieved. A spectator does not become emancipated through participation in the performance, but through what Rancière calls 'a redistribution of places' (Rancière 2009: 15). A spectator achieves emancipation or critical awareness by translating the 'third thing' into his or her own experience, by linking it to what he or she already knows and, through that association, creating new knowledge. 'It is in this power of associating and disassociating that the emancipation of the spectator consists … Being a spectator is not some passive condition that we should transform into activity. It is our normal situation' (Rancière 2009: 17). For Rancière, an individual learns and acts by linking new ideas and experiences to what is already known.[9]

While the notion of 'emancipated spectator' offers a way to understand the potential for efficacy of art, Rancière limits its usefulness by defining *art* as a completed artefact rather than an ongoing dialogue in an interactive intervention. The interventions by Mouton de Vapeur and Jeanne Simone create an audience of 'emancipated spectators' at the same time as they challenge Rancière's assumption of a completed 'third thing' by developing dynamic art/non-art events that are active encounters in the here and now. The interventions offer the co-creator/spectator starting points to new understandings and knowledge construction through dialogue and thus reveal a political potential for performance different from that of a book or a painting.

Rancière claimed that an 'emancipated community is a community of narrators and translators' (2009: 22), and that emancipated community is in my final example where the public not only translated the story events, but also rejected and rewrote the story presented to them by the artists. In May 2006, surprised Londoners discovered a large smoking rocket embedded in the broken tarmac at the end of Regent Street. This unadvertised event heralded the start of the large-scale durational performance of *The Sultan's Elephant*, created by Royal de Luxe, one of France's oldest street theatre companies.[10] The next day, the Girl (five and one-half metres tall) emerged from the rocket. As soon as her head with its aviator's cap and goggles appeared, her eyes blinked open and she looked over the hundreds of people below. The crowd let out a collective gasp as she came alive. Every now and then, the Girl would glance at the technicians getting her ready to walk in the streets. They would respond with a nod or a wave – simple but effective momentary exchanges that established her alive-ness. At the same time, in the Horse Guards Parade, the Sultan with his concubines and court entertainers emerged from a gazebo-like structure on the back of a huge mechanical elephant, over eleven metres tall and weighing 42 tons. They were ceremoniously welcomed to London by the Lord Mayor of Westminster accompanied by many school children.

The inevitable emotionally charged meeting between the two giant visitors took place a couple of hours later, and for the rest of the weekend, they toured the city, sometimes together, but sometimes going off in opposite directions. The Elephant plodded slowly through the ceremonial heart of the capital city, disrupting business as usual and drawing crowds of over one million people. He trumpeted loudly, flapped his huge ears and sucked water into his trunk to spray the crowds. The Girl also went sightseeing, sometimes walking, sometimes on a scooter, and even on the top of an open-top London double-decker bus. After three days touring London, she said goodbye to the Elephant as he tenderly touched her face with his trunk. She got back into her rocket, and a fire was ignited underneath. Once the flames burned away, the rocket was opened to reveal that she had disappeared.[11]

This large-scale performance intervention offered an event of extraordinary artistry and technical skills, but the intense emotional connection that the crowds felt toward the Elephant and the Girl did not come from the scenography alone. Nor did it come from the *official* story told day-by-day in a detailed account in the free newspaper available on site: a complicated narrative, written in the style of Jules Verne, about a mythical Sultan from the Indies who travels through time in a mechanical elephant to find the little girl who visits him in his sleep and so disrupts his ability to govern. The audience on the street experienced and understood a very different story for which the Sultan's search was a mere footnote, dwarfed figuratively and literally by the two enormous puppets. The story that drew the crowds was the love that developed between the Girl and the Elephant, between two oversized travellers from very different worlds who, nevertheless, bonded quite publicly across difference. The *mechanical* wooden elephant escaped the role of time machine and mobile abode for the Sultan and his court in which he was locked in the show's written narrative and, like Pygmalion's statue, came to life through the intense love of his creator, only here the creator was the public. The Elephant, not as a dwelling but as a living creature, was the one to develop a rapport with the Girl. Their incredibly life-like movements enabled the spectators to personify the machines so that they could *see* their facial expressions change and could care about the puppets as though they were living creatures. It is 'as though the soul of a living elephant has migrated into this wooden one' (Webb 2006: 8) wrote one spectator. The Elephant and the Girl both seemed to have what Joseph Roach has identified as *It*, 'that certain quality, easy to perceive, but hard to define, possessed by abnormally interesting people' (Roach 2007: 1). The audience, enamoured of the Elephant and the Girl, were not particularly interested in the shenanigans of the Sultan and his court: his harem of five scantily dressed concubines, court entertainers and wrestling strong men, navigators busily studying huge maps, servants and even a European explorer. Many of the spectators I spoke to thought these characters were decorative ornaments for the Elephant, much like his tapestries. The more the Elephant came to life, the more the Sultan and his court on the Elephant's back became puppets.

The spectators created a complex performance narrative in the meeting and deepening love between the Elephant and the Girl. The audience spoke quite openly about this scenario of an encounter of cultures as my frequent conversations over the three-day event indicated and the many testimonies posted online confirmed, and the media mentioned this aspect as an example of socially responsible, efficacious art. This scenario had an erotic aspect as well. In the initial meeting in the Horse Guard Parade, the Elephant used his long and flexible trunk to court the Girl, quite tentatively at first as he seemed to sniff the newcomer, but he soon wrapped his trunk around her. Each morning he bathed her with water sprayed from his trunk, and when they travelled together, the Girl perched on his trunk as it rose between her legs. 'Now that's some first date!' exclaimed a young girl, who was standing next to me, to her giggling companions; other spectators whistled loudly. Yet this very public love affair was never crude since both the Girl and the Elephant were real and not-real, alive and not-alive simultaneously, and this engaging existential ambiguity challenged natural categories and expanded their possibilities for public intimacy. The London audience of *The Sultan's Elephant*, like Rancière's 'emancipated spectator', participated actively in the construction of their own narrative of encounter and harmony across cultures, time periods and species. As a community of *interpreters* or *translators* of the event, the spectators created their own artwork, alongside that of Royal de Luxe.

The love affair across difference was not the only story that the public constructed however. *The Sultan's Elephant*, as performed in the ceremonial centre of London in public spaces that up to that point had been reserved for events of 'national importance' offered the public the chance to disrupt and intervene in that tradition and to 'rehearse' the role of active citizen in a radical democracy as they participated in socio-political constructions of the city. Even though these democratic practices may not have been *consciously* understood, they were *unconsciously* implanted and actually experienced in the bodies of the spectators in real public spaces. This was possible in part because the audiences of the *London* production of the French creation *translated* the show's site-specificity so that it satirised and critiqued Britain's colonial past, even though that was not the artists' original intention. In London, the subversion of a narrative of empire became apparent in the détournement of iconic architectural symbols of the British Empire. The Girl dwarfed Admiralty Arch when she filled the archway as she passed through, and the Elephant diminished the structure even further, both physically and metaphorically, since he was too large to fit through the openings. The National Gallery shrank as the Elephant stood in front of its entrance, and the lions around Nelson's Column looked like play toys for the Girl. The Horse Guards Parade transformed into the campsite for the two puppets who *banished* the Queen's horses. During the durational performance, the juxtaposition of these monuments and the giant puppets seemed to challenge the assumption of colonial power of the British Empire and perhaps even mock contemporary England's reading of the past. This rewriting of familiar London landmarks was a constant source of laughter in the crowds.

The detailed plot of *The Sultan's Elephant* was created by Royal de Luxe to mimic one of Jules Verne's faux-authentic travel accounts, but the enormous audience community in London created a narrative that was a parodic re-enactment of an official state visit by the Sultan and his court. This text began when a representative of official London, the Lord Mayor of Westminster, and *local natives* (children from twenty-seven primary and secondary schools) welcomed the Sultan and his court to London, not as theatre actors, but as a visiting head of state and his court. Or when, in front of the National Gallery, the Sultan and his entourage descended to street level to shake hands with and listen to speeches by Minister of Culture David Lang as well as the Deputy of London and the head of the Arts Council London. The fictional characters inserted themselves into the actual ceremonial and official life of London, and the city officials acted as participants in the theatrical event, just like the children who rode on the Girl's arms or the spectators who tempted the Elephant to spray them. These officials entered the fantasy of the performance as themselves in their official capacity to welcome visiting dignitaries, greeting the exoticised faux foreign delegation.

However, the parody of the state visit was most blatant in the procession of the Sultan, his court and his elephant along the Mall. This ceremonial processional route that runs the length of the Mall from the Horse Guards Parade to Buckingham Palace is traditionally reserved for events of national importance. It is intriguing, therefore, to think about the procession of the mechanical elephant with exaggerated exoticisations of subaltern peoples of the British Empire on his back either as an event of national importance or, conversely, as an event significant enough in terms of art, cultural tourism, or enhanced urban identity to change tradition. On the Mall, the Elephant bellowed, sprayed the police and other city officials with water and even stopped to pee gallons of malodorous liquid. Spectators were quick to comment on the Elephant's cheekiness in relieving himself so close to Buckingham Palace. The Elephant processed along the Mall with as much dignity as the Horse Guards,[12] but he would always turn up the narrow Marlborough Road before reaching the gates of Buckingham Palace. Navigation on this road was very difficult for such a huge creature, and rumours flew through the crowds that if the Elephant with the Sultan on his back as a visiting head of state (real or not) arrived at the gates, the Queen, who was in residence at the time, would be required to greet him – and that, she refused to do! Over the weekend, the rumour began to be repeated with more and more certainty.

The Elephant and the Girl walked slowly through the streets in the heart of London, but they did not walk alone. In spite of the enormous size and potential danger of the creatures, the public could get very close. The only barrier separating the giants and the spectators as they travelled together through the city was a red and white striped plastic ribbon carried in a v-shape in front of the puppets by local volunteers to create a fluid, flexible barrier rather than a fixed one that would have held the crowds rooted to one spot to watch a parade. With the constantly moving ribbon, spaces were open both ahead of and behind the Elephant and the Girl, and the many spectators took advantage of them to create a *people's procession* that hints at an ambiguity between utopian experience and site of resistance. Lyn Gardner of the *Guardian* recognised the *people's procession* as an effective form of 'an artistic occupation of the city and a reclamation of the streets for the people' (quoted in Webb 2006: 104). Gardner's somewhat confrontational words hint at the role of active spectator-citizens (both city officials and the general public), as much a part of the whole show as the processions of the giants. Here spectator-citizens changed their roles *from* anonymous rushing city dwellers reacting to, but not directing, situations around them *to* active citizens with enough personal agency and communal clout to determine how their city could work. City officials, law enforcement officers and others who gave permission and planned the event's logistical details also felt empowered by the event as they began to imagine using the city in very different ways.[13] This was not a parade viewed by static spectators, but a people's procession (with the people being city residents and visitors as well as city officials).

Walking in the middle of the streets with the Elephant and the Girl not only enabled the urban inhabitants to experience the appeal of accessible public spaces, but also to walk in the shoes of an active democratic citizen. While the engaged spectators may not have consciously associated their actions with active citizenship and establishment of a radical democracy, their small acts of resistance against urban rules and codes of behaviour on actual city streets and their altered perceptions of iconic landmarks implanted democratic practices in their bodies and created a 'rehearsal space' for the public to practise active citizenship. With *The Sultan's Elephant*, the agonistic space created by the parody of a narrative of the power of the British Empire provided an arena in which Londoners could become storytellers of the *historie* and critics of the ceremonial rituals of official visits by heads of state.

Whether such performance interventions are anything more than entertaining interludes is difficult to evaluate. Clearly the transition from aesthetic experience to participation in socio-political life is not guaranteed: 'There is no straight path from the viewing of a spectacle to an understanding of the state of the world, and none from intellectual awareness to political action' (Rancière 2010: 143). Rancière tackles the issue of efficacy by developing three models that correspond to his concept of the three regimes of art. The *ethical immediacy* model and the *representational mediation* model are lumped under what Rancière calls the 'pedagogical model of the efficacy of art' (Rancière 2010: 136). But Rancière rejects the cause-and-effect link between artistic engagement and political activism implied by these two models of efficacy and instead argues for an

> aesthetic rupture [that] arranges a paradoxical form of efficacy, one that relates to a disconnection between the production of artistic *savoir-faire* and social destination, between sensory forms, the significations that can be read on them and their possible effects. Let us call it the efficacy of *dissensus*, which is not a designation of conflict as such, but is a specific type thereof, a conflict between *sense* and *sense*. Dissensus is a conflict between

a sensory presentation and a way of making sense of it, or between several sensory regimes and/or 'bodies'.

(Rancière 2010: 139)

It is this kind of 'conflict' that audiences experience in the performances by Mouton de Vapeur, Jeanne Simone and Royal de Luxe in the dialogue between an imaginative situation and an actual one. This efficacy of dissensus initiates a reconfiguration of the expected logic of social life, and in so doing effects social change, even if very small, by introducing another kind of social practice, giving individuals a wider repertory of democratic modes of citizenship.

Each of these projects engages the public with embodied narratives of democratic citizenship. The spectator-storytellers seem to follow a model similar to crowdsourcing or Open Source: 'buzzwords now and they are all about the virtues of non-hierarchical and participatory decision making' (Polletta 2013: 40). Here the physical response by one spectator initiates or inspires a further development of the story by others who add details through their actions. These performance interventions, performative forms of radical democracy, overturn the notion that spectators may be objective or 'disinterested' observers and, through their provocations, seem to grant permission to the public to do what they would not normally do in a public space and to break their routines. The radical democratic spectator-citizens thus enter public debate with their bodies in actual public spaces but within a protected frame of art. They construct 'fictions' that challenge and reconfigure what is seen, heard and understood about citizenship, politics, democracy, freedom, equality, self-determination *and* art. These acts of dissensus in the liminal space of imagination-actuality (unreality of theatre and reality of street) usually occur through physical statements made by the body and blur the distinctions between speech and action. The spectator-citizen thus participates in democracy by intervening in public deliberative discourses, sometimes unconsciously, through storytelling in bodily statements that are then remembered by the body. 'The politics of works of art', explains Rancière, 'plays itself out in the way in which modes of narration or new forms of visibility established by the artistic practices enter into politics' own field of aesthetic possibilities' (Rancière 2004: 65).

Notes

1 For Rancière, politics is synonymous with democracy since it is characterised by '"liberty" of the people' and resistance to domination. 'Democracy is not a political regime in the sense that it forms one of the possible constitutions which define the ways in which people assemble under a common authority. Democracy is the very institution of politics itself – of its subject and the form of its relationship' (2010: 32). Democratic political activity occurs when individuals challenge the political order and assume a self-aware subject position. The task of democratic action must be to disrupt the accepted connection between perception and meaning: 'Politics, before all else, is an intervention in the visible and sayable' (Rancière 2010: 37), and so it necessarily opposes the status quo and supports the rights of the powerless to become political subjects: radical democratic citizens.

120 Susan C. Haedicke

2 Sociologist Francesca Polletta argues that the story is a powerful political tool because people process stories differently than other forms of informational messages. Rather than analysing and evaluating the message or, on the contrary, absorbing it indirectly, 'we immerse ourselves in the story, striving to experience vicariously the events and emotions of the protagonist's experience' (2008: 27). Here, the story evokes a visceral response in which individuals engage with the story in the context of their own personal experiences. And, drawing on recent research, Polletta insists that 'this experience of immersion or "transportation" can lead to lasting changes of opinion' (2008: 27) and thus have a significant impact on social change. See also Polletta and Lee (2006).
3 Photographs, video clips and descriptive text (in French) are available on the Mouton de Vapeur websites.
4 See Parkinson (2012), where he argues for the necessity of physical public space for the *performance* of democracy.
5 See Janelle Reinelt's discussion of performance as a possible 'worksite for democracy and citizenship' in 'Performance at the Crossroads of Citizenship' (Chapter 3 in this volume).
6 Mouffe writes: 'To be sure, I am not the only one to use that term and they [sic] are currently a variety of "agonistic" theorists. However they generally envisage the political as a space of freedom and deliberation, while for me it is a space of conflict and antagonism. This is what differentiates my agonistic perspective from the one defended by William Connolly, Bonnig Honig or James Tully' (2005: 131, footnote 9).
7 Drawing on the ideas of Claude Lefort, Mouffe claims that modern society is 'characterized by the absence of a substantive common good' (1992: 229). Lefort, in 'The Question of Democracy', claims that with the 'democratic revolution', democracy's site of power was transferred from an external and identifiable source (the monarch) to 'the people', a vague and unstable location that meant that power did not belong to any one individual, but to the 'public'. For Lefort, democracy did not constitute a new form of government control that was now in the hands of the people. Instead, democracy represented a changed form of society built on uncertainty over the identity and role of 'the people'. The 'people' did not represent a fixed entity, but rather a potential constantly on the cusp of transformation. The notion of an uncertain democratic power determined by an enigmatic *public* shook the stability of monarchical rule. And that uncertainty, in turn, caused debate about the source of democratic power: what Lefort calls the 'question of democracy'. This question identifies the dilemma at the heart of democracy: power is located in the people, but 'the locus of power is an empty place ... This phenomenon implies an institutionalization of conflict' (1988: 17).
8 A description of *Le Parfum des Pneus* can be found at <http://www.2r2c.coop/societaires/index.php?le_num_rub=11> and a short video clip at <http://www.dailymotion.com/video/xhvwti_arts-de-la-rue-cie-jeanne-simone-le-parfum-des-pneus_creation>.
9 See also Polletta's analysis of storytelling in politics where she argues that the power of the story comes from the public's ability to relate it to familiar stories (Polletta 2008: 28).
10 For a more detailed analysis of this production, see Haedicke (2013: ch. 3).
11 Photographs and a documentary video are available at <http://www.artichoke.uk.com/events/the_sultans_elephant>.
12 There is an evocative photograph of the Horse Guards, in their official capacity, riding their horses to the Changing of the Guard at Buckingham Palace, but looking as though they are leading the huge Elephant behind them to an official welcome. It can be found in the gallery of photographs for Saturday, 6 May 2006 at <www.thesultanselephant.com>.
13 It is not an exaggeration to say that London's Cultural Olympiad (2012) was greatly influenced by *The Sultan's Elephant*.

9 Tahrir Square, EC4M

The Occupy movement and the dramaturgy of public order

Sophie Nield

In the autumn of 2011, a new form of protest began to be performed around the globe. It did not communicate a coherent 'message', nor did it initiate any widespread disorder. It did not pronounce its duration and politely go home after an acceptable period, nor did it summarise its demands in the form of easily readable and recognisable symbols. It came, it stayed and it said little. Whether this new tactic was a success or a failure is hard to judge, since it announced no terms through which it could be evaluated. But by holding public space over time – significant time, in some instances – the Occupy movement began to expose fault lines and flaws in the ways in which we think we understand protest and public disorder.

This chapter will unpick both the symbolic and material practices of conventional protest by proposing that they run the risk of recuperation into dominant modes of political expression. I think that, to an extent, Occupy made a space for a new kind of reading of political protest, one based in ideas of a doubled, theatrical appearance, and a dramaturgy of public order. Occupy itself was not, of course, the whole story. It was not, even, the alternative, for we cannot all live on the steps of St Paul's or in Zuccotti Park. But I think it pointed to a new set of questions for the ways in which we read symbolic political work. Once the question is no longer simply one of order versus disorder – the phalanx versus the swarm, the army versus the clown – a realigned grammar of public protest may reveal much about regimes of appearance: about presence, representation and visuality; about how to be invisible in plain sight; about which bodies signify, how and when, and, finally, about the condition of political subjecthood itself.

Occupy everywhere

The Occupy movement is generally acknowledged to have begun in September 2011, in response to a suggestion from the Canadian activist network Adbusters that Wall Street be occupied. The movement was also inspired by the sit-ins and popular occupations which had taken place in Cairo's Tahrir Square and elsewhere during the so-called Arab Spring of 2011, and those staged by the 'Indignados' of Madrid the same year. At its height, in late 2011, upwards of a thousand individual occupations were under way. The first was Occupy Wall

Street, and though most Occupys took the title of their own location – Occupy Oakland, for example, or Occupy London Stock Exchange (LSX) – the Wall Street title came to stand as a general term for the entire movement and, in a sense, operated as a spatial metonym; an idea to which I will return shortly.

Since 2011, there has been a burgeoning literature responding to and interpreting the phenomenon of Occupy, as the significance of the movement has been addressed by critics, academics and journalists (see Chomsky 2012; Taylor *et al.* 2011; Schrager Lang and Lang/Levitsky 2012). The question of spatiality became immediately significant, as commentators proposed that the occupations 'opened a space' for, variously, challenges to the dominance of the City of London and to Wall Street, and, in the case of Occupy LSX, staged some of the inherent contradictions in ownership, management of and access to public and private space (Klein 2011; Mirzoeff 2012). A second key concern of these early debates about the Occupy movement was the question of what, precisely, the protesters wanted: when they would issue their demands and what those demands might be. In October 2011, UK newspaper columnist Simon Jenkins commented in the *Guardian* that 'street protest against capitalism appears to have nowhere to go. The rioters of Athens and Madrid, the marchers of Milan and Frankfurt, the squatters of London and New York can grab a headline and illustrate a story, but then what? With no leaders, no policies, no programme beyond opposition to the status quo … it becomes mere scenery' (Jenkins 2011). Here of course Jenkins uses a familiar theatrical metaphor to dismiss Occupy's use of space as something artificial and two-dimensional: he calls it 'scenery'. Interestingly, he is clearly using this description explicitly to account for the supposed meaninglessness of the protest, as though in a scenic space nothing could truly signify, and until the movement cohered around a series of concrete demands, expressed through an appropriate and recognisable grammar of protest, its motives would remain obscure. In this chapter I want to unpick some of these assumed dynamics of space and signification in order to propose that it was precisely Occupy's manipulation of theatrical strategies and vocabularies which produced it as a potentially radical event.

Powers of various kinds have tended to express themselves through symbolic and theatrical means: from the national flag to carefully coordinated rhetorics of remembrance; from monarchical or presidential pomp to spectacular march-pasts and parades. It seems to me that this deployment of a politics of legibility – or legibility of politics – has led to an insistence that protest appear as an equally legible manifestation of 'demands', to be enacted through the public presence of the claim-makers, and expressed through increasingly symbolic or spectacular means. Furthermore, as I will explore, once protest has been limited to these 'acceptable' parameters, it becomes increasingly possible for authority to regulate protest by simply reducing access to public space and impeding the capacity of anyone to stage any claim in the accepted format. The HMIC[1] report into the policing of the G20 protests in 2009 allowed that protest activity can include 'demonstrations, assemblies, rallies, marches, parades, processions, pickets and strikes, leaflet drops', though the assumptions being made about the cathartic scope of such actions is clear: 'protests are an important safety valve for strongly held views' (HMIC 2009). As Eric Hobsbawm has noted, '(P)ublic revolts, riots and marches were institutionalised, that is to say, reduced to demonstrations, increasingly by prior negotiation with the police' (Hobsbawm 2007: 144). While Occupy of course manifested itself in public space in the form of camps and so on, I want to explore some of the ways in which this 'presence' is brought into tension with the insistence of the dominant powers that the theatrics of protests be expressed through a similar grammatical idiom as the performances of power. Might Occupy have proposed another, potentially more radical, mode of 'being there'?

The movement was, of course, already playing its own deliberately spatial politics; not only through the literal occupation of physical space, but also through the naming and invocation of other global sites of resistance. For many, the lodestone was Tahrir Square, whose name appeared on a perfectly reproduced Westminster Council street sign in the autumn of 2011: Tahrir Square EC4M, City of London. Naturally, many critics were swift to point out that the problems faced by occupiers – and citizens – in the West were not the same as those confronted by the people in Syria, Tunisia or Tahrir Square. The practice of parallel naming is, in fact, becoming an increasingly common tactic in symbolic protest, from the individual who claims that 'We are all [insert name here]' to this more specifically spatial application of Tahrir as metonym. Such literal generalisations, however, can easily give the impression that protesters are oversimplifying complex political situations in ways that are perhaps less than helpful. Occupy seemed, through its many spokespersons and interpreters, to be staging an overarching, if unspecific, critique of a global capitalism which has efficiently delivered into the hands of the 'one per cent' such a massively disproportionate amount of the available resources. Adjacent issues, such as transparency and accountability in financial and social management, the co-dependence of government institutions and big business, and (particularly in the US) the rights of the corporation as 'person' all loosely circulated around this generalised sense of disenfranchisement and disempowerment among 'ordinary' people.

The naming of spaces became first of all a performative act of solidarity, expressed within familiar registers of symbolic protest. When the Tahrir occupants sent a message of solidarity back to Occupy Wall Street, this made visible the fact of a global movement, but more significantly, reiterated the existing abstraction and substitution of the metonym for the 'thing' itself (Gabbatt and Shenker 2011). For of course, 'Wall Street' already operates as a sign. In common parlance, it is the shorthand term for the whole of the US economic system, in the same way that 'the City' serves as similar shorthand in the UK. When, in 2011, critics asked why Occupy LSX was bothering to occupy the London Stock Exchange, which since the economic downturn has been a small and primarily electronic operation, they were missing the point. The City is already everywhere: it is already a global imaginary; it is already symbolic.

Unsurprisingly, by early 2012, the slogan of the movement was 'Occupy everywhere'. Occupy the world: take it back from a rapacious form of capitalism that is not only secretive and corrupt, but which has taken as many forms of public space as possible, privatised them and sold them back to the people as spaces of consumption merely disguised as a public sphere. Despite this forceful *cri de guerre*, in the course of the spring of 2012 most of the actual camps were dismantled. Various legal processes of eviction took their course, and occupiers were removed from their locations by police, bailiffs and other security personnel. By 2013, the movement had become a globally dispersed set of interest groups, organising mainly around questions of debt and financial regulation, and the reactivation of the commons.

Significant critiques of Occupy have since emerged, particularly from the (sympathetic) left. David Harvey, in his 2012 *Rebel Cities*, outlines broad reservations with the idea of political horizontality, proposed as a radical alternative mode of social organisation by elements of the Occupy movement, and certainly enacted in the internal management of many of the individual camps. 'How can radical decentralisation – surely a worthwhile objective – work without constituting some higher-order hierarchical authority?' he asks.

> Much of the radical left – particularly of an anarchist and autonomist persuasion – has no answer to this problem. State intervention (to say nothing of state enforcement and policing) are unacceptable, and the legitimacy of bourgeois constitutionality is generally denied. Instead there is the vague and naive hope that social groups who have organised their relations to their local commons satisfactorily will do the right thing.
>
> (Harvey 2012: 84)

There are a number of immediate resonances with this critique, in particular with observations made in late 2011 about hierarchies of ethnicity and gender which appeared to be emerging in the internal dynamics of some of the Occupys. A number of reports circulated at that time detailed the issues faced by women, people of colour and other disenfranchised groups in getting their voices heard on the ground at the camps (McVeigh 2011). Furthermore, this kind of small-scale localism cannot, as Harvey argues, be expanded as a viable mode of living for a global population: he notes that these are 'visions of radical democracy and the governance of the commons, that can work for small groups but are impossible to operationalise at the scale of a metropolitan region, let alone for the seven billion people who now inhabit planet earth' (Harvey 2012: 125). In practical terms, it seems to me, this point certainly resonates with a more general critique of edge-dwelling as a resistant tactic, as, arguably, this kind of resistance relies on the very system it wants to counter for the 'spare' food and goods on which it exists. During an Occupy, a community is formed which, implicitly or explicitly, places itself in opposition to state or territorial governance while continuing to rely on the provisions of mainstream life in order to survive: roads, sanitation, infrastructure, donations from people who live and function within that mainstream and who are therefore able to offer free food, shelter and other material forms of support. The practice of direct democracy itself is also incredibly time-consuming. The schedules of Occupy LSX involved finance committees, general assemblies, cleaning rotas and staffing rotas for on-site universities and libraries.

At Occupy Wall Street there were many signs about acceptable and unacceptable behaviour, details of discussions and agreements with the local community, outreach committees and counselling provision. The days seemed to have a quiet, if not actively bureaucratic, tenor.

Yet these were lived spaces, and not just for the people who were camping there. More and more of the Occupy protesters, when asked, would explain that they were making the world in which they wanted to live by living in it; a world in which decisions were made collectively (albeit very slowly) and in which property was shared and equally distributed. As one participant commented, 'it is exciting that people ... have claimed a public space as both a symbol of distress, and a practical means of organising' (Schrager Lang and Lang Levitsky 2012: 13). This statement seems to me to capture something of the double-function of Occupy, which I think is what created it as a potentially radical form of protest; one which could not easily be recuperated into dominant patterns of meaning-making, and part of whose efficacy was the material staging of its relationship with its own symbolic work. The next section of this chapter will examine this proposal in more detail.

Prosceniums of protest: representation, presence, appearance

I argue that the theatrical events which powers of various kinds produce tend towards the abstract and the spectacular. The rhetorics and grammatical tropes of symbolic power are broadly familiar: sweeping parades of military and monarchical spectacle; flags, uniforms, massed displays of weapons and armies organised as spectacle; the distant motorcades of presidential display. All serve to summarise ideological and political positions in order that they be easily legible as the vocabularies of power. Often, they produce, and are produced by, a parallel, physical space: the broad processional avenue or immortal vista; the vast parade ground; the palace or castle, against which the ordinary person is positioned as spectator, participant or outsider.

I have written elsewhere of the operation of this kind of power, but it is worth rehearsing again in this context the important insight of French philosopher Henri Lefebvre, in his analysis of monumental spatialities and the sleight of hand which they practise upon their spectators. He notes, 'the reading of a space that has been manufactured with readability in mind amounts to ... a sort of "pure" and illusory transparency. It is hardly surprising that one seems to be contemplating the product of coherent activity and ... the emergence of a discourse that is persuasive only because it is coherent' (Nield 2006a, 2013; Lefebvre 1991: 313). In other words, part of the work of this kind of event is to erase contradiction and, with it, some of the potentialities for resistance that might come if power is perceived as somehow fractured and faulty. The illusion of coherence, order and right works to overlay provisionality, doubt and fragility. 'Reading' a space which has been thus organised, stage-managed and designed precisely in order to be read becomes redundant as a means of critique.

What is more, argues Lefebvre, by deploying its ability to spectacularise social relations, dominant space attempts to reabsorb the resistant by forcing its forms of expression into power's own grammatical structures, which thus become the only 'acceptable' form of symbolic political speech. He notes that 'appropriation, which ... ought to be symbolisable, ought, that is, to give rise to symbols that present it, that render it present – finds itself signified in this space and hence rendered illusory' (Lefebvre 1991: 310). In other words, as I will argue here, the ways in which protest is policed and regulated actively encourage it to form itself into these 'appropriate' rhetorical structures. Protesters are invited to 'make their point', to 'get their message across'; in other words, to translate what might otherwise manifest as civil disorder or violence into a discursive and legible statement of views. Opposition becomes in this way the 'representation' of opposition – expressing itself through a set of symbolic vocabularies permitted and legitimised by power.

There are many instances of current public order management which, I think, serve to illustrate this, especially in the ways in which the forces of authority continually seek to draw what we might term prosceniums around protest. The way the story usually goes is that protest (of whatever kind) is appropriate – symbolic, theatrical – until it crosses a line and becomes violent, or 'real', at which point it is curtailed by 'real' police actions. This narrative, however, is problematic in two ways. First, it ignores the effects of policing upon the dynamics of a given protest. Sociologist David Waddington has argued persuasively that public disorder often follows (rather than precedes) the intervention of police using containment or restraining tactics, from the use of police horses during the Suez crisis, through the use of teargas in 1968, and the triggering of resistant action in the face of police containment during the anti-poll tax protests of the early 1990s and anti-capitalist protests of the early 2000s (see Waddington 1992). Secondly, it allows the production – the inscription – of that line to be seen as a move to limit or curtail the extent of 'theatricality', rather than appearing as a theatrical or dramaturgical gesture in and of itself.

Often the line is one that is literally performed by uniformed personnel, as the army, the police or security guards try to prevent protesters from moving out of one area and into another. The sense of an actual 'staging' – the direction, definition and control of what appears *in* symbolic space, and the determination of what counts *as* symbolic space – is even stronger when we consider some of the recent tactics of public order policing. Journalist Dan Hancox reported in November 2011 that a 10-foot high steel fence had been unfolded, in sections, out of the backs of specially equipped vans, and strung across Trafalgar Square. This occurred in the closing stages of a large public sector strike, which had seen an estimated 30,000 teachers, hospital workers and civil servants march through the centre of London. It turned out that two hundred of these portable fences, designed for managing the public in the wake of chemical, biological or radiological disasters, had been purchased by the Home Office in 2008. In November 2011, people were being dispersed in Trafalgar Square through small exits in the barrier. They were, however, only allowed to pass through once they had discarded all the outward signs of their dissent; their placards, badges, posters and banners. 'Here is your state of exception, already in place,' noted Hancox. 'Steel cordons which were purchased to deal with the unthinkable, to deal with a nuclear holocaust or an, erm, zombie apocalypse, are now being used to prevent middle-aged teachers from strolling into Trafalgar Square, because they're carrying a political placard' (Hancox 2011).

This act of walling produced the 'sterile' area which is so frequently invoked now in discourses surrounding public order policing and the management of security. The metaphor of disease and pollution is of course a provocative one, but I will concentrate here on the ways in which I think these lines are functioning as prosceniums. They make distinction between the space of the protest, in which symbolic, representational and gestural acts function as a legitimate mode of meaning-making, and the space of the onlooker and the non-participant, in which they don't. A person who props a placard against a steel barrier, removes a badge or a silly costume and walks to the other side has not, of course, altered their actual political position. But it is no longer legible; no longer available to be read. They have moved 'off-stage'. And this, as Hancox notes, is walling as stratagem; capitalism slicing space up into utterly contemporary forms of enclosure with all its 'insistent performativity. Walls are often not particularly effective,' he writes. 'If anything, they can serve as important theatrical devices' (Hancox 2011).

This tactic is of course an exemplification of the capacity of power to regulate the access of protesters to areas of public space; to limit their capacity to stage their claims within what have become the accepted and acceptable (by which of course I mean licensed and lawful) modes of spectacular political discourse. The physical wall described above, and more intangible versions of lines and boundaries, work to exclude protesters from the very spaces within which they can legitimately perform dissent. In recent years, so-called 'illegal' demonstrations have run the risk of being subjected to the tactic of public order policing known officially as 'containment', and informally as 'kettling'. (By 'illegal' demonstrations I mean both those which have been called without the necessary permissions, and also those which may have had permissions granted, but are argued to have breached the terms of that permission by, for example, staging a sit-down, or going off-route.) 'Kettling' is a manoeuvre through which a group of people will be surrounded by police (very often in riot gear) and prevented from leaving a designated space. In the UK, the first 'kettles' were deployed against the anti-globalisation movement of the late 1990s and early 2000s. The official rationale is that containment restrains a crowd until any potential threat of disorder has dissipated, steam has been let off and the heat has gone out of the situation. In practice, however, kettled protesters have reported being subject to police violence, being refused access to toilet facilities or water and not being allowed to leave in order to, say, collect young children from school. Indeed, kettling continues to be challenged as a legitimate public order tactic through the courts.

Although kettling would seem, on the surface, to be working in the opposite way from the 'wall', to the extent that protesters are trapped *on-*, rather than *off*-stage,

I think that a related theatrical gesture is still being made. Blogger Rory Rowan has noted,

> Although (kettling) may at first seem the grossest form of numbskull territorialisation, it is in-fact a more complex spatial strategy that works precisely within the same logic of concentration and spectacle as symbolic protest ... The aim here is to identify, isolate and arrest the 'trouble-makers' so that they are punished both by making an example of them and putting them off further engagement in protest.
>
> (Rowan 2010)

Rather than clearing the stage, the actions of the police simply change the performance. Protest activity, within this newly altered mise-en-scène, is recast and (literally) reframed as illegitimate, potentially violent disorder, which, as all can see, has required the intervention of police to restrain and control it. The demonstration (which is acceptably symbolic) is being prevented from turning into the riot (which operates outside the permissible grammars of resistance). In this way, the 'proscenium', or 'frame' which stages protest as legible and legitimate activity is reinscribed. Resistance is recuperated into the exchange of symbols, and positioned once more as a representational, discursive activity, making a 'point' rather than a material breach in the social fabric.

It is not surprising that so many oppositional movements have sought to counter this forced march into representation and discourse by positing a return to 'presence'; a fully lived, unalienated experience that could resist the abstraction and violence of social order under globalised capitalism. One thinks here of the experimentations of 1968 – particularly in the US, where the alliance of the anti-war and broader ecological and counter-cultural youth movements such as the Yippies proposed radical alternative modes of spatialisation and cultural practice. Much of the discussion around the series of student demonstrations which took place in the UK in 2011, and also of course around the Occupy movement more widely, involved comparisons with the social movements of the 1960s, asking how far these struggles either repeated or transcended those of earlier times. Certainly, the convergence of student activism, grassroots organisation and urban riots made a persuasive case for questions of public culture and politics being once again highly contested. It is also clear that Occupy is echoing the practices of historical resistant movements which used the placing of the human body into public space – and present danger – as a means of challenging state power. The hunger striker, the political suicide, the person who places their physical self on, and even over, the line is working with the same kind of doubling of discourses, as physical presence is made to speak symbolically. Perhaps, then, the intransigence of the Occupy movement – its resistance to producing messages and manifestos, its sheer stubborn silent claiming of space – might be read as doubly subversive, and offer new perspectives on the relationship of symbolic and material protest actions.

Radical shifts have occurred in global spatialisation since Lefebvre made his proposals and it goes without saying that the practices of capital, global dispersals of wealth and poverty, and the work of class throw up historically specific challenges. Of particular interest and concern here are the shifts that have gathered around the so-called 'war on terror', and the impact which it has had on the security networks which are so often now invoked to regulate and prohibit protest activity. In addition to the stage management of protest activity through spatial manipulation discussed above, a second key concern in contemporary activism is the increasing restriction on the very right to protest. It is not simply a matter of the appropriate, or permitted vocabulary of protest being contested, thus affecting how that activity will be 'read'. It is increasingly a question of what is going to be allowed to appear in public space at all.

The management of protest in public is no longer simply being handled at the scene through strategies of public order policing, nor retrospectively through the judicial system. Increasingly, pre-emptive restriction and anticipatory security are being deployed to restrict protest, and further regulate what are, and are not, acceptable resistant practices.

In the run-up to the wedding of Prince William and Catherine Middleton, which took place in London on 29 April 2011, the *Guardian* newspaper reported that fifty-two pre-emptive arrests of protesters had taken place under public order legislation. Thirteen people were stopped at Charing Cross station, adjacent to Trafalgar Square, carrying anti-monarchy slogans and climbing equipment. Three people in zombie make-up (one wearing a t-shirt that read 'Marry me instead!') were stopped in a Starbucks on Oxford Street on 'suspicion of planning a breach of the peace'. Four people, including the activist Chris Knight, were arrested the evening before the event, as they planned a piece of street theatre in which an effigy of Prince Andrew was going to be beheaded on a fake guillotine (Batty 2011; Booth *et al.* 2011; Attewill 2011).

Before the London Olympic Games of 2012, a pre-emptive anti-social behaviour order was given to activist Simon Moore, who had protested against the building of an Olympic venue on Leyton Marsh (Walker 2012). Mr Moore was banned from going near the Olympics, but, interestingly, was also ordered to stay away from events organised for the Queen's Diamond Jubilee, the trooping of the colour and the State Opening of Parliament. What is particularly significant about the order against Mr Moore is the elision of the Olympics (against which he was actually protesting) with a number of other state or national ceremonies. The implication cannot help but be that, if he opposed the Olympics, Mr Moore would in all likelihood oppose those other, unrelated, ceremonies. This gives insight into the ways in which ostensibly disparate events seem to have become interchangeable theatres of power; part of the same articulation of nation, society, identity. This elision not only strategically diminishes the specificity of any critique or protest; it allows them to be dismissed as 'opposition for its own sake', undertaken by people who are simply 'refuseniks', 'rentamob', 'just after a ruck with the police'.

So how should protest speak when it is not allowed to speak; what language could be available, when acts of both speaking and not speaking are consistently regulated, restricted and stage-managed? Might the doubled performance of

Occupy – simultaneously acting *as* representation and *through* presence – offer a new mode for resistance? Might it enable a form of appearance not immediately recuperable into vocabularies of power; not immediately containable into permitted grammars and discourses of opposition?

Slavoj Žižek and Gary Younge, both in the *Guardian*, began to argue just this: that actually the occupation is its own demand and its own statement. Žižek, in particular, certainly recognised that a programme must begin to emerge, posing Lenin's question, 'what is to be done?' Yet he made clear his view that the moment for such an articulation had not yet come, adding, 'what one should resist at this stage is precisely such a quick translation of the energy of the protest into a set of concrete pragmatic demands ... what one should always bear in mind is that any debate here and now necessarily remains a debate on enemy turf; time is needed to deploy the new content. All we say now can be taken from us – everything except our silence' (Žižek 2011; Younge 2011).

The theatrical double in the public sphere

Judith Butler addressed Occupy and the spaces which it constituted, drawing particularly upon Hannah Arendt's proposal of the public sphere as 'space of appearance', in which we, the people, are required to appear to each other literally, in the flesh, in our bodies, in order to appear to each other as political subjects (see Butler 2011). Arendt argues that the polis, understood as the spaces-between-people, precedes its institutions. The people do not simply move into a space that is already there. Rather, appearance in the public sphere precedes representation, and it is the actions of the people which constitute the public sphere (see Arendt 1958).

What I want to do in the final section of this chapter is expand (Butler's reading of) Arendt's 'space of appearance', from one in which people are simply available to be seen by each other, to one explicitly framed and understood through the idea of theatrical doubling. As I have noted elsewhere, in theatre, the question of who exactly is present – actor, performer, character; material body or representational figure – carries precisely the sense of ambivalence that I think is reproduced in the experience of the political subject (Nield 2006b). Theatrical 'appearance' requires a figure to operate simultaneously in two registers: their material, physical, 'present' form, and as the figure which they imitate, represent or, more broadly, 'stand in for'. I think that Occupy produced a very particular form of protest. It functioned neither exclusively as alternative space of 'presence' (though that was part of its discourse), nor entirely as temporary space of symbolic representation, running the risks of recuperation into the dramaturgies of power. Rather, it performed private life in public space, and, simultaneously, functioned as symbol. It translated itself into a representation of what it actually was.

To illustrate what I mean by this idea, I will turn briefly to the staging of anonymity. Masking oneself at a protest is in part a practical measure to avoid identification: the tactical masking of the so-called 'black bloc' for example. A strong source of inspiration, certainly at the height of the anti-globalisation movement, was the Zapatista movement of south Mexico, led by Subcommandante Marcos (whose real identity is speculated about, but not known, as he always appeared masked in public). The EZLN (Zapatista Army of National Liberation) emerged from Chiapas in southern Mexico on 1 January 1994, at the exact moment of the institution of the NAFTA agreement, and their practice illustrates an important point about the counter-intuitiveness of masking and the implications for a politics of (in)visibility.

Calling themselves 'sin rostro' (the 'faceless') the Zapatistas, men and women alike, all wore face masks, stating that, 'with our faces exposed we are invisible. We cover our faces in order to be seen' (Balive 2011). The point being made here is about the invisibility of the poor, the working class, the peasant, the indigenous person with no access to spaces of speech and representation. They are invisible to the structures of representation, in both political and visual terms. They must literally costume themselves *as* the invisible in order to be seen; conceal themselves in order to become perceptible within the mechanisms of appearance. In this way, they become doubled as theatrical figures: they translate themselves into representations of what they actually are.

During Occupy, people slept, camped, negotiated bathroom privileges with local cafes and businesses, cooked, sat and lived domestic lives in the street. Occupy took the private body and made it speak as itself in public space. This is not to say that the body has not been made to speak symbolically in protest before: this is a long-standing trope in the dramaturgy of dissent after all. Diana Taylor's study of the public performances of the Mothers of the Disappeared in Plaza de Mayo in Argentina from the late 1970s onwards illustrates exactly such a deployment of personal experience as symbol – what she calls 'the Mothers' performance of motherhood' (Cohen-Cruz 1998: 79). It is also clear that it is precisely this doubling – this translation of the private self into public 'message' – which reciprocally protects the Mothers as they stage their claims. Taylor notes: 'Only by being visible could they stay alive in a society in which opposition was annihilated by the military' (Cohen-Cruz 1998: 78).

I want to close this chapter by proposing that the invocation of theatrical appearance calls to mind the necessities of political appearance: that one must take one's place in order to be able to speak; that one must appear to others in order to make claims in the public sphere. To stage one's own body in the street is to claim the right to be present in the street: a symbolic and material gesture in one. The public sphere exists for the regulation of private bodies as they are constituted as political subjects. Occupy became the metonymy for the crisis: it enacted what it demanded. To return to the comment of the occupier cited above, 'it is exciting that people … have claimed a public space as both a symbol of distress, and a practical means of organising' (Schrager Lang and Lang Levitsky 2012: 13).

In her discussion of the performative and the political, part of a series of conversations undertaken with Judith Butler, Athina Athanasiou invokes the idea of being 'beside oneself' in the public street. She is referring here to 'affect', to the condition of being 'taken out, given over, moved and moving' (Butler and Athanasiou 2013: 177). I think that this expression also says something about the condition of the doubled theatrical figure in protest; present as a material body which lives, sleeps and eats in the temporary space of the occupied camp; representing itself simultaneously as political subject and claim-maker. In Occupy, this doubling, this 'speaking for itself', appeared to expand into a set of very interesting consequences. First of all, the sustained refusal of the broader movement to make a coherent statement out of itself essentially reversed the usual function of symbolic theatrical gestures. Instead of summarising a political position into the form of symbol (action, flag, emblem, ceremony) the very refusal to articulate caused it to return onto ideological and other structures of power an exposing gaze which revealed something of their inner structures and contradictions. Depending on their locations, existing connections and the particular local difficulties and battles which they entered into, Occupys engaged, variously, the workings of the Corporation of London, debates over public and private property, the secrecy within which capital is managed, complicity between money and government, the federalisation of municipal policing in the US and relationships with organised labour and the union movement.

Athina Athanasiou speaks of 'a condition of corporeal standing in public – in the urban street. It is the ordinary and rather un-dramatic practice of standing, rather than a miraculously extraordinary disruption, that actualises here the living register of the event ... It is such a corporeal and affective disposition of stasis that derails, if only temporarily, normative presuppositions about what may come into being as publicly intelligible and sensible in existing politics' (Butler and Athanasiou 2013: 100). Bodies, which were holding open these contradictions in space and over time – not the half a day of a demonstration, but over long weeks or months – caused dichotomies to become apparent; drove a wedge between the components of symbolic behaviour and revealed them as masks for abstraction. As Harvey notes, 'Spreading from city to city, the tactics of Occupy Wall Street are to take a central public space, a park or a square, close to where many of the levers of power are centred, and, by putting human bodies in that place, to convert public space into political commons – a place for open discussion and debate over what that power is doing and how best to oppose its reach' (Harvey 2012: 161).

And it is this, finally, which perhaps opens the claim of Occupy to really 'occupy everywhere': not as a real camp or an actual occupation necessarily, but as a set of possible questions and renegotiations of the ways in which the commons, the public sphere and the conditions of political subjecthood have come to be enacted. Occupy took pieces of symbolic ground and staged real life. In doing this, it made citizens visible as political subjects. It was in many ways flawed, incoherent and less than specific about either its critique or its demands. Yet it opened up a space for reinterpreting the grammatical structures of public protest and public order, at least as they have consolidated in Western culture. As one participant of Occupy observed, 'we already occupy everything, so how can we "occupy everything"?'. What matters is the minimal difference, the shift in perspective that the injunction to occupy effects. We have to occupy in a different mode, assert our being there in and for itself, for the common, not the few ... We occupy everything because it is already ours in common' (Taylor *et al.* 2011: 92).

Note

1 Her Majesty's Inspectorate of Constabulary (HMIC) independently assesses police forces and policing across activity from neighbourhood teams to serious crime and the fight against terrorism.

10 Temporality, politics and performance

Missing, displaced, disappeared

Jenny Edkins

> Politics makes visible that which had no reason to be seen, it lodges one world into another
>
> (Jacques Rancière (2001: Thesis 8))

Performance is sometimes thought of as transitory – here one minute and gone the next – 'performance's only life is in the present', as Peggy Phelan puts it (1993: 146). She continues: 'Performance's being, like the ontology of subjectivity proposed here, becomes itself through disappearance' (1993: 146). Once it has taken place, once the action has appeared, it disappears without trace – or appears to. What has happened has gone – almost as if it had never happened. Traces, arguably, remain: a performance can be documented, repeated, remembered. But nevertheless, Phelan insists, 'the disappearance of the object is fundamental to performance; it rehearses and repeats the disappearance of the subject who longs always to be remembered' (1993: 147). Performance can also be seen as an essentially 'embodied praxis', and a focus on performance, for Diana Taylor, allows us to decentre written forms of knowledge, the objective and the non-expressive, and to see 'scenarios that do not reduce gestures and embodied practices to narrative description' (2003: 16, 17). For Phelan too, 'performance implicates the real through the presence of living bodies' (1993: 148). Embodiment implies agency and action: as Mike Pearson notes 'performance [has been adopted] in the social sciences as a synonym for human agency – as a trope of the transitive, as people doing things' (2006: 3).

Where someone disappears in a different circumstance – not the performance artist at the end of a show, but someone missing as a result of war, conflict, displacement or human rights abuses, or just because they have chosen to walk out – what has happened does not seem possible. Their relatives and friends can make no sense of it. People do not just disappear: here one minute and gone the next. Traces may remain – photographs, personal belongings – but the sudden absence shatters understanding. Unanswerable questions pose themselves. Were they indeed ever properly here? Did they exist at all? Did the family just imagine them? Could they really be properly gone? Will they not just walk in again one fine day? In these cases of what we might call, simplistically perhaps, real-life disappearances, presence is questioned and notions of time and place thrown into chaos. The questions of appearance and disappearance, the presence and absence of the embodied being that are central to attempts to say what performance is all about, are raised on another stage.

This chapter examines disappearances: real disappearances, disappearances of real, live, embodied people, not the disappearance of the bodies or the presence that could be said to constitute performance. Phelan's characterisation of performance can be and is disputed, and 'performance carries the possibility of challenge, even self-challenge, within it' (Taylor 2003: 15). Nevertheless, thorny and contested questions of appearance and disappearance, presence and absence, personhood and action that seem to be central to a discipline called performance studies are central to the interests of this chapter too. I do not want to suggest that the real world, whatever that might be, is the purview of international politics: my discipline, if I have one. Rather I would follow Adrian Kear in emphasising 'the need to think through politics and performance as modes and practices of aesthetic thinking, and to think them together as modes and practices of aesthetic politics' (Edkins and Kear 2013: 8). My wager is that examining questions of missing persons can help in this venture.

When persons are missing, displaced or disappeared, what happens next reveals how contemporary politics thinks of, produces and administers the person, and how this is challenged by practices that insist on another notion of personhood (Edkins 2011). The chapter examines insights from a series of accounts of missing persons and the responses of the relatives seeking to trace them and find out what has happened, asking how these might shed light on personhood, or what Phelan calls an 'ontology of subjectivity' (1993: 146). Relatives' searches for missing persons and their protests against disappearances collide with the bureaucratic practices of political authorities that see persons as objects. The instrumentalisation of persons is contested and the reappearance of the irreplaceable person-as-such demanded. But, crucially, these accounts of missing persons also show that what is called for is not the reappearance of the person as fully present, which would be a repeat of the original objectification, but rather an accommodation of the person as missing: never fully known or fully present. These insights traverse performance and politics and demonstrate the intersection of questions and concerns that lie at the heart of these areas of scholarship and practice.

Performance, like a missing person, evades capture, disturbs categories and demands a new form of politics, a politics where persons as such, as they hover in the liminality between appearance and disappearance, count, rather than a politics of presence. A lot hangs on what we think politics might be. Like performance, which Richard Schechner's definition stretches beyond something on a stage with an audience to 'any action that is framed, enacted, presented, highlighted, or displayed', politics can be read beyond conventional ideas of governments, parliaments, democracy and elections (2013: 2). Like performance, extended in this way it risks becoming everything – or nothing. In this chapter, I attempt to avoid this trap by taking a particular notion of politics, one that has in the past been designated by the term *the political*. In this view, 'the political represents the moment of openness or undecidability, when a new social order is on the point of establishment, when its limits are being contested' (Edkins 1999: 126). However, I want to retain the term *politics* here. Jacques Rancière does this by inventing a new term for what is commonly called politics, or what takes place when the new order is institutionalised; he calls this *police*:

> Politics is generally seen as the set of procedures whereby the aggregation and consent of collectivities is achieved, the organization of powers, the distribution of places and roles, and the systems for legitimizing this distribution. I propose to give this system of distribution and legitimation another name. I propose to call it *the police* [and] to reserve the term *politics* for an extremely determined activity antagonistic to policing: whatever breaks with the tangible configuration whereby parties and parts or lack of them are defined. ... Political activity is whatever shifts a body from the place assigned to it or changes a place's destination. It makes visible what had no business being seen, and makes heard a discourse where once there was only place for noise.
>
> (1999: 28–30)

It is interesting to note here that if performance were 'any action that is framed, enacted, presented, highlighted, or displayed' then it would be part of a police order (Schechner 2013: 2). If an action is already *visible as an action*, then it is not a political activity. The insistence on an activity that 'draws attention to that which is barely discernible' (Pearson 2006: 9) or that brings 'disciplines that had previously been kept separate into direct contact' (Taylor 2003: 16) is necessary for performance (or performance studies) to be political. Politics, for Rancière, involves an intervention in the distribution of the sensible, a disturbing of the way action, for example, is seen as separated from inaction, or presence from absence. Performance, configured as an artistic practice, can be highly political: 'Artistic practices are "ways of doing and making" that intervene in the general distribution of ways of doing and making as well as in the relationships they maintain to modes of being and forms of visibility' (2004: 13).

The bringing together of grammars of performance and politics enacted in this volume can also be political, in Rancière's terms, intervening in and potentially reconfiguring the disciplinary/police order. In the conversation between performance and politics that Adrian Kear, Mike Pearson and I have been developing in Aberystwyth since 2007, we have been concerned not so much with developing shared grammars, but rather building on a shared theoretical orientation, shared points of focus and shared approaches to research forms or genres of output (Edkins and Kear 2013). Our work rejects a framework that sees certain forms of theatre as political or certain forms of traditional politics as a performance to explore connections at a deeper level – to do with the expanded views of both politics and performance that I have attempted to articulate above. But we live with a certain acceptance of misunderstanding. Many synergies cannot be pinned down, or perhaps should not be pinned down. We would I think agree that 'we do not understand each other – and recognise that each effort in that direction needs to work against notions of easy access, decipherability, and translatability' (Taylor 2003: 15).

It is in this spirit that this chapter offers a discussion of missing persons. I do not translate my terminology into what I might think would be a performance studies vocabulary. Nevertheless, I hope that performance studies scholars will find that this account of the actions of relatives and families of missing people has something of interest to offer in relation to their concerns with disappearance/appearance, absence/presence, temporality and politics. I begin by setting out what drew me to this topic in the first place, and how working on it in the archives was particularly moving. I then select three instances to examine in more detail: first, the display of missing posters after 9/11 in Manhattan and the delayed identification of those killed in the London bombings of 2005; second, the methods of tracing families of displaced persons in the aftermath of the Second World War; and finally, the protests of the Madres against the disappearances in Argentina.

The *one* counts

> History rounds off skeletons to zero.
> A thousand and one is still only a thousand
> That *one* seems never to have existed
>
> (Wisława Szymborska 1998: 42)

My fascination with the question of missing persons and the responses to them seemed to begin with the aftermath of 9/11: the events in Manhattan after the collapse of the twin towers of the World Trade Center. The posters that appeared on the walls and shop fronts, and that remained in place for years afterwards, seemed incredibly moving. The same posters appeared in Bloomsbury in London after the bombings in July 2005, though in London they were removed as bodies were identified. However, what caught my attention in this case – and prompted my anger – was something different: the delay in the identification process and the callousness of the authorities in the face of the distraught relatives of missing people.

The responses to those searching for missing relatives reveal an objectification and instrumentalisation of persons that typifies contemporary forms of political community, where community is seen to be made up of the addition of pre-existing individuals with common interests or identities: forms of community that have been analysed in terms of Foucault's notion of biopolitics, Agamben's sovereign power, or Rancière's police order (Foucault 2010; Agamben 1998; Rancière 1999). Different notions of community are conceivable: an inoperative community, a coming community or an unavowable community, for example (Nancy 1991, 2000; Agamben 1993; Blanchot 2006; Santner 2006). To explore these questions of personhood and political community further, I widened my study of responses to missing, displaced or disappeared people and protests against objectification beyond the aftermath of 9/11 and the 7/7 bombings. I found many of the same concerns emerging in the case of displaced persons after the Second World War in Europe, where the scale of the problem and the difficulties of establishing tracing services was much greater, with some 40 million people on the move. I looked at the efforts put into tracing those people missing in action, where who owned the body of a soldier (and the information about it) is brought sharply into question. And, interestingly, in the case of Argentina's disappeared, I found activists who had refused what comfort of 'closure' might come from identification of remains in favour of continuing political action.

In amongst all these missing people are those who disappear voluntarily: who walk out on their families, sometimes temporarily, sometimes never to return. In all these instances, it seemed to be particular people, often women, who fought against the indifference of the authorities and played a role in changing how missing people and their families are conceived of and dealt with. The question of missing people seems to command an immediate response from friends and neighbours and a widespread fascination; it turns out that many have some direct but hidden personal experience of someone going missing in their own family or background. Although people do not just disappear – although it seems impossible – it nevertheless seems to happen with surprising frequency and in unexpected circumstances, and, moreover, it seems to reverberate with some deep sense of how even people we think we know – ourselves even – are in some sense unknowable or 'missing'.

Towards the end of my work in the archives of Second World War I came across an account of a train crash. On 30 May 1945 a transport of displaced persons halted outside Rheda station in Germany was hit by another train. Four people were killed and several injured. Of those killed one was identified, three were not. Their bodies were taken to hospital, to be buried later, and their belongings turned over to the local mayor for safekeeping. Forms were completed giving personal details, very similar to those collected after an accident or disaster to this day, and photographs of the faces of the unidentified people taken. The reverse of the photographs gives basic details of the unknown person – their height and other physical characteristics. Fingerprints are preserved and, finally, pinned carefully to other specially designed cards, small pieces of fabric, each about an inch square, snipped from each item of clothing the person wore. I found it extraordinarily moving that hidden deep in the archive – held nowadays in the UN in New York, thousands of miles from where the accident occurred – were these little pieces of material, small fragments that remained of these lives lost, preserved in case, out there in the world, maybe there was someone for whom these fragments would have significance: remains embedded in the ongoing, never-ending present of the archive.

Most moving of all, though, was the fact that amidst all the chaos of 40 million people on the move, millions more killed or murdered in cold blood – people objectified, racialised, murdered in their masses – someone had taken the trouble to make this record of three unidentified persons ... persons who mattered only to those who knew them: three persons among 40 million. I was reminded of the poem by Wisława Szymborska, *Starvation camp near Jaslo*. She writes of how history is indifferent to the singular person: 'That *one* seems never to have existed' (1998: 42). But in this New York archive, that *one* counts – on the assumption that someone, somewhere, sometime, may be looking for them.

I return to the period after the Second World War shortly, but first I want to say something very briefly about two other instances I looked at: missing persons in Manhattan in 2001 and London in 2005.

Missing: Manhattan and London

> We all lost you all, and mourn together. We are not sightseers.
> (Mariette, WTC viewing platform, 26 January 2002)

In an archaic form of appeal, missing posters in their thousands appeared on the streets on Manhattan after the fall of the twin towers. The posters juxtaposed snapshots of innocent personal moments with physical details: height, build, scars, tattoos – and appealed for information, not only details of the person's whereabouts, but the story of what might have happened to them. As Mark Wigley puts it, 'when the façades came down the faces of the invisible occupants who were lost came up, filling the vertical surfaces of the city in pasted photocopies' (2002: 82–3). Those who had been concealed behind the plate glass of corporate architecture were suddenly made visible: the absent rendered stunningly present.

The people in the posters had been objectified and instrumentalised not only as victims by the hijackers but as heroes by the federal government, and, already, before the event, as workers by the architects and corporations of the World Trade Center. In a relatively short time after the events, order had been reimposed, the site cleared for rebuilding and forensic identification procedures put in place at vast expense. The time of the state was re-established: a linear time of national heroism, security and revenge. But the missing posters were left up for many years afterwards – long after it became clear the missing would not be found. These posters, it seemed to me, were not just memorials to missing people, though they were that too of course. They seemed to me like a collective scream, a protest against the way people had been treated, a demand to hold open the temporality of trauma and a demand for a different politics. What the posters said was that these were ordinary people. They were not anonymous workers or heroes, but our neighbours: people who went to work one morning and were overtaken by disaster. Just like people anywhere. They had been in some sense already missing, objectified. As the bare life of the city-state, they had been hidden behind the façades of the buildings, but they were now exposed to view and claimed as important. The posters protested that concealment and claimed a place for those pictured, and people like them elsewhere, in the realm of visibility – as subjects, each *one* hugely significant to friends and family.

In the London bombings of 2005 there were posters again – though in this case they were not allowed to remain in place for long. What was most striking was the heartless treatment of the relatives – those who reported people missing. People affected by the bombings were objectified and instrumentalised, not once but several times. First, of course, as victims: the bombers didn't care who they were, any people would have done. Second, when the emergency became apparent, those caught up in the bombings were treated as objects to be governed: systems and procedures, and health and safety protocols were put before speed of rescue. Then in the immediate aftermath of the bombings, the victims and their relatives were treated as suspects by the police: officers combed through CCTV images of everyone's journeys that morning, searched their belongings for any useful evidence and took DNA material for analysis, all without any meaningful communication of information about the person's whereabouts to their relatives. Finally, disaster victim identification or DVI protocols kicked in: a form asking for detailed 'ante-mortem' information had to be completed: questions covering a dozen pages delved into a missing person's appearance – height, weight, shape of nose, surgical procedures, etc.; their belongings – had they been wearing a watch? Jewellery? The whole was a process of one-way data collection: those phoning the missing persons help line were asked endless questions but given no information in return, and liaison officers were appointed to extract information for the police investigation, not to help families in their search.

The anguish of the relatives was expressed movingly by Marie Fatayi-Williams, whose son Anthony had been caught up in the bus explosion in Tavistock Square. Five days after the explosion she made an impromptu speech on the street as close as she could get to the site of the explosion. Holding up his photograph, she said:

> This is Anthony, Anthony Fatayi-Williams, 26 years old, he's missing and we fear that he was in the bus explosion ... on Thursday. We don't know. We do know from the witnesses that he left the Northern line in Euston. We know he made a call to his office at Amec at 9.41 from the NW1 area to say he could not make [it] by the tube but he would find alternative means to work. Since then he has not made any contact with any single person. ... This is now the fifth day, five days on, and we are waiting to know what happened to him. ... I am proud of him, I am still very proud of him but I need to now where he is, I need to know what happened to him. I grieve, I am sad, I am distraught, I am destroyed. ... Where is he, someone tell me, where is he?
> (Fatayi-Williams 2005)

It is likely that the police had known Anthony's fate for a number of days by then, but that they had chosen not to reveal any information to the family. People were told to go home and wait. Difficulties with identification were not the problem as they had been in New York. Rather it was, as a report by the London Assembly later described it, a lack of consideration:

> Procedures tend to focus too much on incidents rather than individuals, and on processes rather than people. Emergency plans tend to cater for the needs

of the emergency and other responding services, rather than explicitly addressing the needs and priorities of the people involved.
(Greater London Authority 2006: §1.15, 9)

This form of objectification, the treatment of persons as nothing but objects of administration and not subjects with needs – dead bodies in all but name – is what the posters in Manhattan were protesting. The time of the state – the linear, procedural time of process and organisation, history, heroes and nations – collides with trauma time – the suspended, deferred time of absent presence for the relative left in an agony of not knowing. Marie Fatayi-Williams's story is suspended in the present tense, 'a present which is not a transition, but in which time takes a stand and has come to a standstill' (Benjamin 2006: 396): 'Where is he, someone tell me, where is he?' is her cry.

Displaced: post-war Europe

> When you move from this cave to that rubble pile, be sure to give us your change of address.
> (Kathryn Hulme 1960: 122)

None of this is new. In the aftermath of the Second World War in Europe, we find a similar clash between the standstill of trauma time, which blasts open 'the continuum of history' and the homogeneous linear time of forms of objectification, which miss the person in their concern for administration and order, and which are contested by organisations acting on behalf of families (Benjamin 2006: 396). A graphic representation of how this worked is found in a flow chart in the UK National Archives at Kew (SHAEF 1945). This flow chart shows how displaced persons – referred to as 'DPs' – were processed in the so-called assembly centres or refugee camps of the United Nations, which at that point comprised just the wartime Allies. Before anything else, those arriving at the camp were deloused – sprayed with DDT – and checked medically. They were then registered and categorised: only displaced persons of Allied nations were entitled to help; enemy nationals were not. The arrangement of the camps was very much by nationality, and the priority of the camp authorities was repatriation: displaced persons were to be sent back as soon as possible to their countries of origin, whether they wanted to return or not – and of course, given the changed cartography of Europe, many did not. But in the end, as the flow chart shows, they emerge as objects ready for what is described on the chart as 'disposal'.

Many of the displaced protested – ultimately leaving the camps to fend for themselves or to flee possible repatriation. Many were more concerned with locating family members and, in the absence of any help from the authorities, they would travel from camp to camp in their search. Some of those working in the camps were sympathetic and attempted to help those searching, and contest the objectification too. Kathryn Hulme writes of the impact of her first day in Wildflecken camp:

> Never again would I be able to look on a refugee mass, even in pictures, and see it collectively, as a homogeneous stream of unfortunate humanity that could be handled with the impersonal science of the engineer who does not ever think of drops of water when he is controlling a flood. Human data would be added to the years of days following that first one, but each new individual encounter would repeat the misery in a slightly different form so that you could never lump it together in convenient categories and dispose of these in one sweeping group decision. The 'DP problem' was an easy generality that you had accepted until you met that problem in the grassroots and saw that it had as many faces as there were people composing it.
>
> (1960: 8–9)

She was sympathetic to those who sought permission to leave to search for relatives. She tells us of one boy who had already found his mother in one camp and his sister and brother in another, and now came to ask for permission to go and look for his father, 'whom somebody had said that somebody had seen wandering about in the ruins of Munich'. She continues, 'He was certain he could find his father as he had found the other members of his family scattered like leaves over the map of Germany' (Hulme 1960: 10).

Although a priority for the people themselves, tracing services were not important in the view of the military or embryonic civilian authorities. Camp volunteers had been trained in methods of setting up tracing bureaux, but no information was forthcoming to help. They were reduced to exchanging lists between camps (Wilson 1947: 52–3). A difference of priorities was evident here, as in other instances of missing people. The military authorities issued 'stand still orders', requiring people to remain in place so as not to impede military movements, or to gather in camps, rather than foraging for themselves in the countryside in a disorganised manner. Categorisation was all important so that they could proceed with repatriation, and the focus, as in London, was on process, not people. The voluntary organisations were insistent on the importance of setting up tracing services that could respond to enquiries by actively engaging in searching, and that would deal with enquirers of all nationalities. They would focus on people not process – though their procedures, honed through long years of experience, were much more effective than the hastily put together methods adopted by new agencies set up by the military.

The military planning in 1944, with its insistence on gathering people in camps to prevent unorganised trekking and speed repatriation provoked a furious response from the director of the Foreign Relations Department at the British Red Cross, Miss S. J. Warner. She wrote to a high-ranking officer at the War Office Civil Affairs section expressing her concern at 'the lack of any system in the territories in Germany occupied by the United Nations for enquiries from relatives and friends of the many thousands not only of displaced persons but of German nationals with whom it is desired to get in touch'. At that stage the Red

Cross had thousands of enquiries waiting to be dispatched, as well as hundreds that had already been sent to the military authorities but to which there had been no reply. 'We also', she added, 'have hundreds of patient enquirers who come in daily or who write to us and to whom we have to reply that there is no way of assisting them' (Warner 1945). What infuriated her more than anything was that the Red Cross was expert at tracing, and the authorities refused to make use of that experience. And what is more, the Red Cross was taking the blame for a failure it had no control to prevent.

The amateurish approach the military finally put in place fell apart in any case. Proceeding in its usual way through procedure and category, the attempt was inevitably flawed: missing persons disturb categorisation. A memorandum issued in 1945 on 'General instructions for all officers engaged in tracing and search' was divided into sections, depending whether the search was for living persons, children, deceased persons, or missing persons. It lacks any indication as to how one is supposed to know before commencing the search whether the person being sought is living or dead. At another point, a section heading announces that it is concerned with establishing the fate of those persons who cannot be found, which seems to present difficulties too. The various attempts to bring missing people within a bureaucratic framework reminds me of the 'Chinese encyclopaedia' that Foucault refers to at the beginning of *The Order of Things*, where animals are categorised into '(a) belonging to the emperor, (b) embalmed, (c) tame, (d) sucking pigs, (e) sirens, (f) fabulous, (g) stray dogs, (h) included in the present classification, (i) frenzied, (j) innumerable, (k) drawn with a very fine camelhair brush, (l) et cetera, (m) having just broken the water pitcher, (n) that from a long way off look like flies' (1970: p. xv).

This is a heterotopia. It disturbs. It makes us see the impossibility of thinking like that. In the same way, missing people disturb. They show up the way the administrative categories of a police order do not hold: a missing person cannot be identified in the abstract. You cannot tell that someone is missing by looking at them. A person is only ever missing in relation, when they are missed by someone else.

Disappeared: Argentina

> this is my daughter,
> she still hasn't come home
> She hasn't come home in ten years.
> But this is her photograph.
> Isn't it true that she's very pretty?
>
> (Marjorie Agosin, in Weschler 2006: 8)

I want to move on finally and very briefly to the case of the disappeared in Argentina. The protests of the relatives of the disappeared are well known, particularly those of the Madres and their regular encircling of the Plaza de Mayo. On a particular day every week, they gather in this square in the administrative and symbolic heart of Buenos Aires, take out their trademark white headscarves and walk in silence around the phallic monument at the square's centre. In the beginning, they took the authoritarian government at its word: reminding it of its claimed respect for human rights, they went to every official office they could think of asking for information about their missing children. Their slogan – *aparicion con vida*, or 'you took them away alive, we want them back alive' – led to their labelling as madwomen. Eventually the authoritarian military regime fell, and a democratic regime took its place. At that point, trials of those responsible for the disappearances were not common, though a few did take place, and the Madres continued their protests and their demand for justice.

Later, exhumations of the remains of the disappeared began. The disappeared were made to appear, not as live political subjects but as dead bodies, identified by forensic archaeologists. While some relatives were thankful to have confirmation of the fate of their sons and daughters, for others it was not enough for the authorities to return a bag of bones and claim that that was the end of it. This group broke away from the other Madres and refused to allow their relatives to be exhumed and identified. They refused the certainty on offer. Instead, they carried on with their protests under the slogan *aparicion con vida*. They insisted that identification without justice was not what they wanted. The names of the murderers were known, but they were not being held responsible. But more than that, the justice they demanded was not just the trials of those responsible for disappearance. They demanded the return and the recovery of their children as fully political beings, not just bare life (Agamben 1998). Their politics had led to their disappearances, and they should not be made to reappear without acknowledgement of the political struggle for which they had died.

This refusal led to continued visibility – and continuation of the political struggle for a broader justice. Refusing identification, refusing to lay missing persons to rest, maintained the trauma as visible and the demand for political inclusion alive.

The loss of missing people is an ambiguous loss – those missing or disappeared are neither living nor dead – and this form of loss is particularly difficult to live with (Boss 1999). However, there is another, more profound sense in which there is ambiguousness. Eric Stener Carlson in his book *I Remember Julia* recounts how he spoke to people who knew one of the disappeared, whom he calls Julia (1996). The book gives their thoughts and memories of her, but somehow these don't add up: they don't come together into a coherent single person. The person remains missing, despite all these memories. Carlson asks 'are these stories merely echoes sounding against the dark wall of memory, a few scattered glimpses, and then nothingness?' His response is that, 'as with any personality, full of contradictions and complexities, Julia cannot be seen in her entirety' (1996: 181). Who she was is untraceable, the memories do not cohere. Perhaps there is no 'entirety' anyway: perhaps persons are not whole or complete, but fragments in any case, like the fragments for forensic identification: the person as such is missing.

We are used to thinking of the identity of a person as made up of a series of characteristics, or of a series of roles that they play – as teacher, consumer, politician, etc.

But this is to think in terms of *what* someone is, not *who* they are. The *what* is to some extent something that can be replaced – we can find someone else to teach if a particular teacher is not there, someone else to do the shopping. But the *who* is what is lost and what is absolutely irreplaceable when someone goes missing. It is not just that there is *no one* there, but that that particular unique being, that particular *someone*, is not there. And this is why missing people disturb administrative classifications, as we have seen. Perhaps, as Adriana Cavarero tells us, 'the reality of the self is necessarily intermittent and fragmentary', so that the story of a person like Julia 'does not have at its centre a compact and coherent identity' (2000: 63). The person as such, the *who*, does not exist independently in any case, but only in relation, and it is this relationality that missingness brings to light. Cavarero again: 'the ontological status of the *who* – as exposed, relational, altruistic – is totally *external*' (2000: 89). The *who* does not possess 'a mysterious interiority' that can be assembled forensically, out of fragments (2000: 89). The *who* is not something inside the person, some identity a person themselves might possess, but external, something that exists only in and through relationality. We are not first of all independent individual beings, who then form collectivities; rather, we are primarily relational beings, who, given our contemporary social and political framing, have come to think of ourselves as separate.

Conclusion

> Political being-together is a being-between: between identities, between worlds.
> (Jacques Rancière 1999: 137)

We have seen two interwoven forms of politics taking place in the struggle that surrounds missing, displaced and disappeared people: two types of politics that produce two different views of the person. First, we have *a politics that misses the person*, a politics of objectification and reduction to data: a biopolitics, a police order. Second, we have *a politics of the person as missing*, a politics that recognises that persons are never fully known, never separate: a politics of the 'who' not the 'what'.

This second form, a politics of the person as missing, is a politics that disturbs, that inserts one world into another, and maybe even one that makes Rancière's police orders of whatever sort unstable if not impossible. This second form of politics is what I call a politics of the person-as-such, which is a politics of the person as unknowable and unknown, a person embedded in relations of unknowingness or in political being-together, which perhaps shares something with theatrical being-together also. In that sense we are all missing persons.

The upshot of course is that people do not, in fact, disappear: it is indeed impossible. As Ariel Dorfman says, 'when they tell you / that I am / completely absolutely definitely / dead / don't believe them / don't believe them / don't believe them' (2002: 25). There are always remnants, remains, traces – in family members, in objects, in writings, in fragments of bone, in memories. But if people are not separate individuals to begin with, but connected beings – connected not just with each other but with the rest of the animate and inanimate world – then things change. When a node of those connections is broken – when someone goes missing – we work hard to repair what has been lost, to reinstate the intensity of connection we had before. But the loss is one of degree, not absolute. As Judith Butler puts it, loss 'furnishes a sense of political community of a complex order ... bringing to the fore the relational ties that have implications for theorizing fundamental dependency and ethical responsibility' (2004: 22). These ties of which we are composed extend not just to our immediate circle but beyond, and indefinitely so, both in time and space, making a nonsense of any attempt at categorisation or delimitation. It is not just missing people that disturb.

If people do not just disappear, then where does this leave our thinking about performance? Can a performance be here one minute and gone the next if minutes do not follow each other in the straightforward linear fashion this implies? If interconnectedness means that no thing – not just no person, if person implies what we call a human being – ever disappears as such, what can it mean to say, as Phelan does, that 'performance's only life is in the present' (1993: 146)? If theatre is 'the locus of appearance *par excellence*' and 'appearance matters, and matters as the very "stuff" that provides the species "theatre and performance" with its substance, specificity and specialness', where does that leave disappearance – and not just any disappearance, but the disappearance of a person-as-such (Kear 2008a: 1)? If performance is an 'embodied praxis' how does that relate to the absent presence of a missing person, someone who remains present in the life of their family despite their bodily absence (Taylor 2003: 16)?

These questions cannot be addressed fully here, of course. But there is a risk, in making a connection between a person's disappearance 'in real life' and disappearance or appearance 'on stage', of seeing the appearance of an irreplaceable person-as-such – someone with particular connections with other particular persons-as-such – as similar to the appearance of someone on stage. Although a stage set-up invites appearance – as audience we are led to expect an actor to appear – it does not involve a missing person. Similarly, when a politician or another figure appears 'in public' they generally fulfil a role or take up a place prescribed from them in the existing police order. As we have noted, a missing person is only missing in relation, only missing when they are missed by someone else, and missed as a *who* and not a *what*: not missed because of the function they fulfil – what they do – but because of who they are. Although an empty stage demands the appearance of an actor – in other words there is a relationality of sorts there, the relation between stage and spectator, actor and audience – the absent actor is absent only as cipher: any person walking on stage can be the one we are waiting for, indeed any one at all walking on stage at that moment will appear as an actor by virtue of the staging. The search for a missing person succeeds when one particular person and that person alone appears: no other person will do, no one else can take their place.

In his discussion of Phil Collins's photographic portrait, *abbas amini*, Adrian Kear points out that a political appearance – the disruption of Rancière's distribution of the sensible – is not the same as the appearance of the person as object, as name-bearer (2008b: 20). Like Julia in Carlson's work, in this image asylum seeker Abbas Amini, who sewed his lips, eyes and ears in an act of protest, 'remains secreted, veiled, closed to view in the work that bares both his name and face: remaindered from representation even as his appearance marks its interruption'. Here it is the artistic work that presents appearance to us as a political intervention in regimes of visibility: it give us an absent presence – perhaps like the absent presence of the missing person. This thought is suggestive of ways of thinking the politics of personhood-as-such: as soon as that politics becomes a demand for naming, recognition, presence, visibility, identification or exhumation, as it did in Argentina, for example, it risks entering into the existing police order, rather than challenging it. A politics of the person as missing has to remain a demand on behalf of, or, as Véronique Pin-Fat and I have suggested elsewhere, an assumption of, bare life as such (2005). The initial protests of the Madres or the missing posters in New York City were, arguably, precisely that, as were the arguments of the Red Cross or the London Assembly report. These were examples of a demand that the person appear as such, in all its missingness, not as the object of administration or governance.

11 Performance and politics

Ceremony and ritual in Parliament[1]

Shirin M. Rai

Introduction

This article explores the performance of ceremony and ritual as a frame through which to examine political institutions such as parliaments. It examines some issues of definition – what are the key distinguishing features of ceremony and ritual? It then sketches the sociology and the sociopathy of ceremony and ritual – how do they mark tradition and modernity and what exclusions and terms of inclusion do they help stabilise? Finally, it examines the framing of power relations through the performance of ceremony and rituals and suggests, following and extending Hobsbawm and Ranger (1992), that ceremony and rituals are always gendered and often 'invented traditions' that are critical to stabilising and reproducing the power of institutions. The argument here is that ceremony and ritual are constitutive of and constituted by dominant social relations and that through their performance they both sediment as well as disturb the circulation of power. In conclusion, the article suggests that while 'new institutionalist' perspectives are an important step towards uncovering the various relational ties between formal and informal power, the study of political institutions would benefit from examining the performance of ceremony and rituals not simply as historical backdrops but as operative frames of power in public life.

Studying parliaments

Despite continuing and, some would say, growing attacks on parliamentary institutions as weak and ineffective, corrupt and out of touch (Pennings 2000; Kapur and Mehta 2006; Barkan 2008; Hudson and Tsekpo 2009), they continue to be important to the politics of states. Parliaments make laws and develop public norms and also legitimise political systems. For citizens in parliamentary systems, state openings, debates, no-confidence motions or resignation speeches all make for grand theatre. Parliaments are also symbolic institutions – of the national state and its political system: in the context of India, for example, Nehru referred to the 'majesty of parliament' (Kapur and Mehta 2006: p. iii) and called the Indian parliament a 'temple of democracy'.[2] Often parliaments are housed in grand buildings that symbolise the power of these institutions (Puwar 2010), as well as that of the nation, or its aspirations towards some democratic norms and ideals. Staged in these buildings, ceremonies and rituals become markers of recognition of us as 'national' subjects or of the distance between ordinary citizens and political elites. Parliaments are often presented as undifferentiated institutions, although they are historically marked with deep divisions of class, race, gender, (dis)ability and sexuality. In most cases parliaments remain privileged spaces dominated by men from the upper classes, castes or dominant religions, regions and races – for example, men constitute 83 per cent of membership of parliaments worldwide. This privilege finds shape, colour and voice in parliamentary ceremony and ritual, as through their performance they make visible links with the past, renew a sense of identity of 'the nation' as well as the nation-state and construct/reproduce/perform historical privilege.

Parliaments are representative institutions but are also representative of a particular phase of modern capitalism. In the second and third waves of democratisation, explicit links are made between representative democracy and efficient and contemporary capitalism. Market preference and political preference come together in the exercise of economic and political power of individual citizens as consumers of economic and political goods. Parliaments, therefore, are critically embedded in the political economy of modern state systems and create spectacles of, as well as represent, a particular set of structures-in-dominance. This representation is often legitimised in ways that do not explicitly make the links between political economy and political institutions. Rather, parliamentary institutions seek to legitimise their representative characteristics through invoking historical and nationalist aspirations of the modern nation-state in tandem. While this provides a powerful framework of legitimacy, this also creates tensions in the functioning of parliament, leading to a fractured identity of the institution. These tensions are often visible in ways in which the performance of ceremony seems to synthesise the historical and everyday rituals of contemporary politics, while at the same time revealing gaps between this synthesis and the ever changing political landscape.

Studies of parliaments have largely focused on the functions that parliaments perform – deliberative, legislative, legitimising and symbolic. Parliamentary studies as a subfield has also developed different typologies of legislative institutions. And socialisation of parliamentarians has been an important focus of research as scholars have sought to explain why legislators behave the way they do (Mughan et al. 1997). This has been examined from functionalist, behaviouralist perspectives, from the perspective of role theory (Saalfeld and Müller 1997) as well as rational choice theory (Strøm 1997). Although these perspectives have contributed enormously to the debates on parliaments, increasingly the insights they have developed have been folded into the broadening field of new institutionalism, which sees institutions 'not simply [as] equilibrium contracts among self-seeking, calculating individual actors or arenas for contending social forces. They are collections of structures, rules and standard operating procedures that have a partly autonomous role in political life' (March and Olson 1984; see also Franceschet 2010; Waylen 2010; Celis and Wauter 2010). There has also been some interest in

Figure 11.1 Parliament of South Africa (courtesy of photographer Rachel Johnson).

the ways in which architecture and space shape parliamentary business (Goodsell 1988; Dovey 1999; Puwar 2010) and some interest in the performance of political rhetoric in parliaments (Finlayson 2007; Ilie 2003). Political anthropologists have turned their gaze to legislative institutions to explain how cultures of deliberations affect the functioning of parliaments (Crewe and Muller 2006; Crewe 2007). The argument here is that abstract concepts such as nation and democracy can only be understood through symbolic means, and the performance of rituals is a way of participating in the nation or in democratic processes (Crewe 2010).

Ceremony and ritual are understood variously – some translate ceremony and ritual as norms and rules, while others are careful to distinguish the formality of ceremony from the more informal, everyday unselfconscious performance of ritual; some focus on the disciplinary aspects of ceremony and ritual, others on the power of disruption of these; some explicitly address gendered inequalities that sediment through ceremony and rituals, while others address this issue indirectly by showing how the performance or disruption of ceremony and ritual demarcates the spaces of gendered participation (Rai 2010). These different approaches also reflect different disciplinary frameworks – new/historical institutionalism, political anthropology (Crewe 2007), sociology (Puwar 2010), poststructuralism (Rai 2010; Spary 2010). However, here I hope to contribute to the further opening up of parliamentary studies through bringing the performance of ceremony and ritual into focus when analysing parliaments, through which we also open up a new way of thinking about institutional power. The following sections review

Performance and politics 151

Figure 11.2 Parliament of India (courtesy of photographer Carole Spary).

the literature on ceremony and ritual in the context of political institutions and the study of power.

Defining ceremony and ritual – framing social relations

Studying ceremony and ritual in politics challenges the utilitarian and rational choice understanding of political scope, decision-making and policy-outcomes. It highlights the role of emotion, sentiment and affect in politics and helps us understand how everyday rituals and ceremonial performances hold disparate interests, histories and visions of the future together against all odds, while at the same time embodying the possibilities of evolutionary, transgressive and disruptive change. As Kertzer suggests, 'To understand the political process, then, it is necessary to understand how the symbolic enters into politics, how political actors consciously and unconsciously manipulate symbols, and how this symbolic dimension relates to the material bases of political power' (1988: 2–3). In other words, I would argue that performance mediates structures and agency; while actors perform ceremony and ritual, they do not do so in a vacuum – social relations embed them as cultural histories, political economy and institutional norms. These social relations fundamentally affect performance, which in turn re-presents these social relations to culturally produced 'subjects capable of "hearing"' such utterances (Brassett and Clarke 2012: 4). However, social relations are mediated through performance – understood, imbibed, interpreted, made visible, resisted or, alternatively, taken for granted, as read.

It can be argued that ceremony and ritual in parliament are deployed both to awe and to put beyond contestation the everyday workings of institutions and in

Figure 11.3 Westminster security, UK Parliament (courtesy of photographer Faith Armitage).

so doing secure the dominant social relations that obtain within it. It can also be argued that through ceremony and ritual provide the glue that binds – individuals to each other, to the social forms within which they perform and to commonly held ideals and ideas that cohere within societies and polities. This is not to make ceremony and ritual functional to the study of power but to articulate the delicate and often overlooked interlacing between spectacle and power – power is performed. Following Agamben (2007), one could ask the question 'Why does power need glory?' and suggest that the answer might be that glory blinds those who investigate power with all its embellished attachments to the powerful,[3] while at the same time, the performance of power often produces the affect of ceremony and ritual. The majesty of power, thus delineated through ceremony and ritual materially and discursively, structures the possibilities of opposition. This is important because governmental power is, to use Agamben's phrase, vicarious – it is constructed and reproduced, in part, through ceremony/ritual through which new meanings of power are inscribed. Routinisation, socialisation and ritualisation do not here mean powerlessness or meaninglessness; on the contrary through these processes power becomes invisible, sedimented, 'commonsensical' and part of our way of thinking about ourselves as well as those who govern us. In parliaments, rules and norms become in/visible through ceremony and ritual – mirroring dominant social relations on the one hand and on the other, almost through a sleight of hand, making them disappear from view. It is this quality perhaps – of combining hyper-visibility with invisibility – that makes it so important to study ceremony and ritual in parliamentary politics. In the next section I examine some definitional issues related to ceremony and rituals in politics.

For our purposes here, ceremony means an activity that is infused with ritual significance, performed on a special occasion, while ritual means the prescribed order of performing ceremonial acts; I thus distinguish the hyper-visibility of ceremony and routinisation of ritualised performance. I also distinguish between formal (ceremonial) power and informal (ritualised) power. Ceremony can be described as providing the solemnity, formality and grandeur (gravitas) to rituals, which are more often seen as the performance of everyday routines, behaviours and activities that reproduce and reinvent power. Ritual can be seen as 'action wrapped in a web of symbolism' (Kertzer 1988: 9). Where scholars do not distinguish between the two, we see the common features of ceremony and ritual: repetition; acting or performance, which suggests contrivance and not spontaneity, stylisation such that 'actions and symbols used are extra-ordinary themselves, or ordinary ones are invested with special meanings, setting them apart from others; order as a dominant mode, through precise and organised (sometime exaggeratedly so) events; evocative style of staging events to produce a sense of belonging, and a collective dimension which has a social meaning' (Moore and Myerhoff 1977: 7–8). Kertzer also emphasises the dramatic character of ritual wherein 'people participate in ... dramas and thus see themselves as playing certain roles [which] ... provokes an emotional response' (1988: 11).

However, much of this literature does not focus on the specifically gendered aspects of ceremony and ritual – the performative masculinities and femininities that are at the centre of these, which as Butler (1990) has argued, are needed not only to shore up our political institutions, cultural discourses but also as constitutive elements of gendered social hierarchies. Codes of dress, speech and deportment, modes of participative actions, norms and behaviours all provide clues to the social hierarchies that are played out in politics and political institutions. The roles that women and men play dramatise the political moment, the discursive power as well as the gendered social order operative in specific historical contexts, and in doing so reveal for us underlying social tensions which point to the palimpsestic nature of political institutions.

Ceremony and ritual can thus be analysed at two different levels: first, institutionally, as the casting of spectacles through which the formal-juridical power of the state is operationalised through the in/formal technologies of legitimation. Here we can view both the formal power of the state and the agentic and capillary power of interpretation (Foucault 1977). These interpretations are mediated by both particularistic identities and universalistic rhetoric. Second, we can analyse ceremony and ritual at the level of performance, where bodies perform in space and time – as men, women, able and less able, black or white – leaving traces which mark exclusions and inclusions (Coole 2007). This affect then enables or disables their ability to represent – their constituents, their identities and themselves. In so doing it also structures the possibilities of destabilisation of power.

However, ceremony and ritual do not just happen – they are performed, on a stage, with actors in place, rehearsals to hone the performance the actors, anticipation of audience response immediately and over a longer period of time. Alexander has outlined a cultural pragmatics of social performance that underlines not its materiality but its performance; he focuses on the travel from ritual to performance and back again – from 'de-fusion' to 're-fusion' of performative elements that make for stories that are convincing and therefore powerful and fundamentally believable (2006). My argument is different – it is that the materiality of performance allows us to reflect upon its power; that by disaggregating the various elements of performance we can assess how political actors – individual and institutional – harness material bodies, rituals and ceremonies, sounds and voices with great effort and labour to generate a political syntax that is both accepted and challenged by different audiences; that the interactions between performance and its reception generate politics. So, the performance of ceremony and ritual are constitutive of their mode of production and reception. The smoother the performance the easier it might be for ceremony and ritual to 'stand in' for ideas and ideologies that they represent and for the social relations that embed them, and for the social cohesion or *dissensus* they generate.

Sociology and sociopathy of ceremony and ritual

Durkheim (2001) suggested that social coherence was achieved through a common recognition and translation of ritual to create order in society. There was also, however, the presumption of the sacred in this order – ritual was by definition attached to religion's boundedness, providing *legitimate* cohesion. When ritual is repeated over time, as individuals are taught and identify with key rituals, they recognise each other as co-participants and become a community. The participation in ritual then defines society, as well as makes recognition of those 'of the society' possible. Goffman adapted Durkheim's framework to suggest that in contemporary society, 'What remains are brief rituals one individual performs for and to another ... interpersonal rituals' (1971: 63). However, for Goffman, this performance does not take place through autonomous acts. Rather, through invoking 'framing' as a device, he asserts that individuals *negotiate* their way in performance of rituals *arriving* at the socially embedded frame, not creating it: 'Organizational premises are involved, and these are something cognition somehow arrives at, not something cognition creates or generates' (1974: 274). Further, in *Gender Advertisements*, he points out that institutionalised practices 'do not so much allow for the expression of natural differences between the sexes as for the production of that difference itself' (1977: 324); gender matters. Goffman also outlines what he calls 'situational proprieties', which include 'culturally learned practical knowledge' that allows individuals to 'fit in', 'be good' and 'not make a scene' (1963: 11) as well as 'enabling conventions' (1983: 5) that frame common expectations against which interactions are judged.

For Durkheim, rituals were seen as 'traditionalising' mechanisms through which societies cohered, while for Goffman individual interaction is the performative mode of contemporary societies. Durkheim then is a good starting point for us here in that he asks the fundamental question about why we need to study ritual and gives us an answer about coherence of societies[4] to which ritual is moot, but ultimately he reproduces the 'orientalist' substructures of power in the distinctions that he seeks to draw between traditional and modern societies through his study of ritual. As we will see below, these traditionalising mechanisms continue to be produced ('invented) by modern states in order to create markers of belonging and recognition among citizens of nation-states. Goffman, on the other hand, suggests that all contemporary societies work through individual interaction which is socially defined, organised, sanctioned and ordered.

Invoking and critiquing Durkheim

Neo-Durkheimian scholars emphasise that individual identities of citizens find collective shape through witnessing and/or participating in rituals (Shils and Young 1953). In this tradition, where political rituals provide the integrative glue for societies, there were important studies of the Coronation (Warner 1959), the Investiture of the Prince of Wales (Blumler 1971) and Memorial Days, such as Veterans' Day (Warner 1959). While this body of scholarship was not centrally concerned with whether rituals needed religious roots, they were conscious that selective borrowing from religious rituals created powerful symbols of national solidarity which could be mobilised for attainment of national goals (Verba 1965 in Lukes 1975: 295). The neo-Durkheimian scholarship thus provides a normative functionalist account of rituals, which Lukes (1975) criticises on the following counts: first, that this scholarship assumes normative consensus, where there might be interpretive disagreement; second, and following from this, that rituals can be better analysed if we see them as contributing to the manufacturing of consent, where alternative value systems are not available (298; also see Lane 1984) rather than reinforcing shared values.[5] Third, Lukes takes issue with the neo-Durkheimians on account of the particular rituals that they analyse – largely integrative rather than oppositional – to make their case. In so doing they overlook how rituals, Orange marches in Northern Ireland for example, can also be performed to underline the dominance of the dominant political values and can therefore exacerbate conflict rather than improve social relations between opposing groups (Lukes 1975: 300), even while reinforcing solidarity among the dominant groups.

Rather than giving rituals an integrative and uncritical role in society, Lukes posits persuasively that political rituals play, as Durkheim argued, 'a cognitive role, rendering intelligible society and social relationships, serving to organise people's knowledge of the past and present and their capacity to imagine the future ... though placing it [as Durkheim did not] within a class-structured, conflictual and pluralistic model of society' (Lukes 1975: 301). Through such an analysis, Lukes is also able to raise different questions about the actors involved and the power exercised. Which social groups have the power to prescribe performances and specify the rules which govern them? 'In the interests of which social groups does the acceptance of these ways of seeing operate? And what forms of social relationship and activity are in consequence ignored as of less or no significance?' (Lukes 1975: 302). However, while Lukes outlines what role cognitive – rather than normative functionalist – political rituals play in our understanding political systems, and elaborates on what study of particular rituals might reveal about specific political contexts, he tells us almost nothing about the sedimented and reflective power of political ritual – of how power is reflected as well as challenged in and through political ritual. This is curious because of Lukes's interests in political power and its circulation. While implicit in the questions that he poses, gendered modes of power do not make an appearance in Lukes's work. Unlike Goffman, he doesn't make an explicit analysis of gendered power – invoking instead gendered scholarship in his argument with Foucault (Lukes 2005: 99–107). He also does not have much to say about *how* we might research political rituals. What theoretical and methodological frameworks might be useful to understand political power through researching political ritual? In the end, both Durkheim and Lukes view ritual as having a function, a purpose in social and political life – unlike poststructuralist explanations outlined below, they do not reflect upon the meanings attached to rituals in everyday life as individuals relate to each other and to the communities of which they are part.

Ceremony and ritual as 'invented traditions'

In their provocative book, *The Invention of Tradition* Hobsbawm and Ranger (1992) develop an important insight which fundamentally challenges the Durkheimian understanding of ceremony and ritual, which is that while some traditions evolve and adapt over time to become part of our social and historical map, others (and in particular in the context of nationalism) are invented through interventions by political and social elites.[6] According to Anderson, nationalism allowed the secular transformation of fatality into continuity – something that only religious discourses had articulated before the rationalising thrust of Enlightenment (1991: 10–11). As continuity demanded reproduction of future national generations, of national/cultural values and stability of social forms, as well as the reproduction of the national populations, and as both class and gender disturbed the stability of the new social relations that were normalised through nationalist political discourses and later through post-colonial constitutional and legal mechanisms, invented traditions became an important glue to hold the nation together. These invented traditions are given a historical foundation through the use of 'ancient materials ... by borrowing from the well-supplied warehouses of official ritual, symbolism and moral exhortations' (1983: 6) just as they are from placing them within the folds of literary and bureaucratic writings which are the products of colonial invasions, rule and framing (Said 1978).

This argument cuts away at the Durkheimian understanding of tradition vs. modern – that which is solid (tradition) melts into air when we see its invented and contingent (modern) character.

Thus, the study of the invention of tradition is clearly visible in the colonial and post-colonial contexts where national state formation needs the imaginaries of history. As nationalism, following Benedict Anderson (1991), can be seen to be imagined, ceremony and ritual provide the fixed points of recognition of that imaginary. If nationalism creates the Other it does so in part through the ritualisation of public life, through the evocation of music, art, colour and texts, through ceremonials of the everyday as well as that of dramatic events, and in so doing 'traditionalising' new as well as old modes of being (Virmani 2008). Nationalism creates and is reproduced through myths about the origin of peoples and nations, and the sanctification of their gendered political norms. Nationalism, in creating the Other also creates danger – and it demands unity, order and ceremonial to achieve its goals of stability of imagination, of territory and of recognition. Ceremony and ritual tend to close off possible alternative frames of meaning, which at the same time remain challenged from the danger within – of indeterminacy, of plurality, of spontaneity and of opposition or even rejection (Moore and Myerhoff 1977: 17–19). 'Since ritual is a good form for conveying a message as if it were unquestionable, it often is used to communicate those very things which are most in doubt' (ibid. 24). Gender relations in particular are grist to this mill of stabilisation – appropriate behaviour, issues of access to public spaces, gendered roles which are sanctified through norms of social interaction, containment of challenges to the social status quo, are all part of the landscape of nations and nation-building (Chatterjee 1993; Sangari and Ved 1990; Rai 2002). There is the affect of stability in a situation of inherent instability; there is an assumption of consensus in the context of alternative imaginaries; there is formality and repetition in the face of informal circulations of power and spontaneous eruptions of dissent. In this framework, ceremony and ritual generate a 'common [gendered] knowledge' (Crewe and Muller 2006: 9) and a gendered vocabulary of power, which then influence perfomativity through recognition, repetition and ritualisation. Performance of ceremony and rituals also creates symbolic knowledge, which is special to the context and therefore requires 'learning' by those wishing to use or interpret it – often this knowledge is implicit rather than explicit, layered in the levels of meaning to one or more symbols, which might be read singly or together, able to make connections between the past and the present and allow expression of or 'discipline' powerful emotions and relationships within secular, institutional contexts (Crewe and Muller 2006: 13).

However, it is worth noting that while ceremony and ritual are a gendered spectacle, which militate against indeterminacy through sedimentation of constructed norms and identities, they are also internally fragile and need repeated shoring up because of the challenges that new actors bring to the stage. The reflection of power in ceremony and ritual, while seemingly constant over time, is constantly shifting – like disturbances in a pond, ripples of disorder roll out through the performance of these but are also quickly contained, with the pond reverting to its fragile stillness in the moment. Political performances have the potential to generate a frisson, which has sometimes real and long-lasting results and at other times, it fizzles out quickly, without ensuing change. Thus, while performance can consolidate power, because 'performances precipitate degrees of liminality, they are [also] capable of transforming social relations' (Alexander 2006: 13). Turner has defined liminality as a 'threshold' between these two different existential planes: 'a realm of pure possibility whence novel configurations of ideas and relations may arise' (1970: 97). As the traces of power in the performance of ceremony and ritual become discernible to those bystanders, disruption becomes a possibility. Such disruption by its very nature is not predictable and takes different forms, which can be highly creative and carry within them the potential of opening up new political spaces, vocabularies and discourses which challenge the dominant modes of power. Those who are 'space invaders' (Massey 1994; Puwar 2004) in parliaments, for example, are potential conspirators challenging the circulation of power within institutions – women MPs who make public the racism, sexism and homophobia operative in parliaments (Hill and Revill 2008).

Performing belonging and citizenship

Thus far, we have examined the definitions of ceremony and ritual and reflected upon their cognitive and normative functions, which have underlined their necessity for social coherence, marking of political transitions and their securing of power relations as well as their internal fragility, even if this means inventing traditions where none existed or imbuing old traditions with new meanings. Ceremony and ritual are also critical for marking the boundaries of inclusion and exclusion – suggesting citizenship through performance. Ceremony and ritual at times disguise or even conceal what is present – conflict, political differences, social tensions, disruptive moments – by creating a sense of ordered histories of institutions, appropriate modes of behaviour legitimised by performance and recognition over time; they help reify politics. While at times conflict over values that is depicted in and through ceremony and ritual can be a means of mutual recognition, a sense of exclusion from it can also be generated for those witnessing it, which can lead to alienation. As I have noted above, recognition, inclusion and exclusion all take gendered forms and in so doing reproduce the gendered hierarchies that are ritualistically performed. Young focuses on three aspects of ceremony that signal to these imagined communities that we call nation-states those who are members as well as to those who are not. Belonging is, Young argues, underlined through different modes of public recognition – *greeting* or public acknowledgement which fosters trust between those involved; *rhetoric*, which allows the speaker to bring specific points to public attention and 'situating speakers and audience in relation to one another'; and *narrative*, which could empower the marginalised to bring their experiences to bear upon public debate.[7] Without these being performed and participated in – making or receiving greetings for example or speaking as well as listening, being spoken and listened to – internal exclusions can easily take root in even formally equal settings. We therefore need to understand how ceremony and ritual are preserved, performed and presented in all societies in order to maintain social cohesion and how they leach across time and space, despite challenges, reforms and ruptures, to give new meanings and recognition as societies evolve.

The markers of belonging are embodied – in bodies that can be distinguished in terms of their sex/gender and race, as well as in bodies that are more difficult to distinguish on grounds of class and sexuality. The social relations of a nation-state demand a frame within which to stabilise their form. Feminist work has always seen social relations to be gendered. In her book *Gender Trouble* Butler argued that gendered power is a fiction that needs to be sustained in the domain of political economy through social performitivity. Through the enactment of dominant gender roles we recognise, circulate and reproduce the meanings of masculinity and femininity and thus perpetuate gendered social hierarchies. In Butler's work we find how these social relations, mediated through gender and sexuality, are enacted and performed and in so doing perpetuate gendered social hierarchies constituting and constitutive of political institutions and their workings. While she does not explore the nature of ceremony and ritual, through an engagement with her ideas on gendered performativity we can begin to make linkages between everyday and structural power.

Witnessing performance

If ceremony and ritual is performance, the question arises, who witnesses this and whether that tells us something about the nature of performance, the power play involved as well as the possibilities and limits of the spectacle? Lukes formulates this in the following terms: 'that if power is to be effective, those subject to it must be rendered susceptible to its effects' (2005: 91). Foucault, however, wrote that power is tolerable only on condition that it masks a substantial part of itself. Its success is proportional to its ability to hide its own mechanisms (1977: 86). Ceremony and ritual, as noted above, perform on two levels – by their hypervisibility they enthral those who 'must be rendered susceptible' and by obscuring dominance through theatricality, ritualisation and routinisation they mask the mechanisms through which dominance is exercised.

Reception theory posits that a text needs a reader; a performance, a spectator; and art, a viewer; and that those who receive also interpret, but within boundaries of imagination set by the text, performance or art. If this is so, then the neglect or ignoring of the narrative can be seen not as something fixed, as presented by the author, performer or artist but as an act that is mobile, stretched and challenged and struggled over. As Saward has noted: 'representative claims only work, or even exist, if "audiences" acknowledge them in some way' (2006: 303). To ignore the message, to turn one's back on it, to walk past it without stopping to look, to speak over it, can be a subversive act of 'reading'. The audience of ceremony and ritual, both internal and external, is then rendered susceptible, either by suggesting that what is performed is what politics is or by suggesting that the performance is of no consequence and therefore neither is the politics that it represents. Further, Baumann brings to our attention a different approach to audience, which suggests that rituals are addressed as much to 'members' – those who belong to nations and its institutions – as to 'Others' (1992: 99).

The presumption of an audience or spectators is built into the 'invented' performance of ritual. Thus, the audience doesn't need to be present in the space where ceremony and ritual is performed to have an affect on the performance. The audience that is outside of the space is assumed to be witnessing the performance as much as those who are present – through media, news reports and word of mouth. As Kershaw notes, '[M]ediatisation [is] a crucial process in dispersing performance throughout culture' (2003: 227).

Conclusion

In a parliamentary institution, where each individual formally carries equal legitimate power – having been elected by individual citizens in free and fair elections – how do political agendas get represented? How is individual competition within parliament organised, played out in an effective way? What modes of working are normalised such that MPs self-discipline, are able to cooperate as well as compete and the public is able to view parliament as a functioning, worthwhile organisation, reflective of democratic practice? And does ceremony and ritual help in the self-regulation of political institutions such that they might function efficiently and effectively? The new institutionalist framework, diverse though it is – rational choice, historical or sociological institutionalism – has insisted upon viewing institutions as having an 'inner life', with its own logic, norms and rules that determine its actions, making these institutions 'actors' in their own right, displaying an internal coherence. Thus, March and Olson argue that 'This new institutionalism emphasises the relative autonomy of political institutions, possibilities for inefficiency in history, and the importance of symbolic action to an understanding of politics' (1984: 734).

However, while all the different strands of new institutionalism focus on aspects of how institutions need to gain internal stability (structuring choice, framing choice and normalising or socialising choice-makers) in order to function efficiently, they do not pay enough attention to how this internal coherence comes about in the everyday life of institutions. In this chapter I have argued that the micro-practices of power observed in the performance of ceremony and ritual in parliament form the substance of state authority as well as challenges to it and the casting of political spectacles is both the effect of that power and constitutive of it. As I have argued elsewhere, a focus on performance and/in politics 'reveal[s] the historical arch (Corrigan and Sayer 1985) that connects deep political and discursive power to its immediate performance; that certain discourses, performances and representations find greater resonance, reception and recognition than others, depending upon the dominant ideas of historical time. The performance then becomes part of a repertoire with a long history of social relations' (Spary and Rai 2013).

In this chapter we have seen that parliament brings into focus performance and politics rather well because, compared to other governance institutions, it is more visibly performative. Parliaments are not only authorised to represent, they also somehow claim to collectively mirror the society and nation at large. They not only make laws and hold the executive accountable, but also make a 'representative claim' (Saward 2010, 2006) – to represent different constituencies, identity groups and interests. If this claim is seen as valid – through the shaping of parliamentary membership by regular, free and fair election, or through the quality of debate, for example – then the parliament and indeed the country is seen to be democratic; if not, then democracy as practised is held in doubt. But claims are 'made' through both formal and informal, ritualised and ceremonial modes of performance. The theatricality of parliaments makes it easier for us to bring into focus the importance of the performance of ceremony and ritual. We are able to distinguish a grammar of both politics and of performance through the ceremony and ritual that is enacted institutionally and through individual practices. In the enactment and its reception of ceremony and ritual we can trace threads of key concepts such as representation, legitimacy and authenticity of parliamentary institutions. If we take parliamentary debate to be a ritual of democratic representation, governed by rules and norms such as a heightened sense of prestige and formality with respect to space, speech, dress, movement and gesture, then we can judge how the enactment of debate and deliberation provides us with political clues about how to read not only parliament as a political institution but also democratic politics itself.

Notes

1 A version of this chapter was first published in the volume *Ceremony and Ritual in Parliament* (Routledge). My thanks to the publishers for allowing me to publish it here, with minor changes. My thanks also to Diana Coole, Emma Crewe and Joni Lovenduski for insightful comments on the first draft. Shortcomings are all, of course, mine.
2 It is interesting that both words – majesty and temple – invoke sacrality, which is central to ceremonial moments and the performance of ritual.
3 Agamben, following Foucault, makes the point that 'this is an incredibly sophisticated fiction, this subtle economy of power according to which god in order to govern absolutely must act as if the creatures were governing themselves'; ibid.
4 The concern with coherence is of course also linked to the Marxist study of ideology and/as hegemony that is the set of ideas subscribed to by the dominant social classes and which is underpinned by the power of the state (Gramsci 1971) as well as the of the political economy of the ownership of the media and the 'manufacturing' of consent (Herman and Chomsky 2002).
5 An important insight here is that value consensus is not only insufficient as an explanation for social integration, it is also not necessary.
6 See Virmani 2008, on the invention of the Indian flag and the struggles around this invention.
7 Young (2000: 53).

12 Bringing the audience back in

Kenya's Truth, Justice and Reconciliation Commission and the efficacy of public hearings

Gabrielle Lynch

In the literature on transitional justice mechanisms, most notably international criminal courts and truth and reconciliation commissions (TRCs), attention is increasingly given to the language and structures, or grammar, of performance. The reason is two-fold. First, these processes are clearly performed in that they are stage-managed, loosely scripted, involve different actors and interlocutors, and have targeted audiences. Second, and more importantly, understandings of their likely impact are increasingly tied to the efficacy of their performance in contributing to tangible change through the interaction of audience and performer. The common idea is that, in a time of transition, broad reforms – such as new legislation, a constitution or institutions – require a performance or enactment of change to become effective (Cole 2010: p. xi). More specifically, transitional justice mechanisms are valued, at least in part, because of their ability to embody transition and thus for their role in helping to shape popular perceptions of the state and associated political regime, *and* for their potential role in the public articulation, acceptance and internalisation of new shared narratives and ideals, such as forgiveness, reconciliation, accountability, tolerance, human rights and national unity, and thus for their contribution to nation-building.

In this way, international criminal courts have been presented as 'spectacles of legality' that render crimes and 'the sweeping neutral authority of the rule of law' visible to affected and international audiences (Lawrence Douglas cited in Cole 2010: 1), and which, 'when effective as public spectacle, stimulate public discussion in ways that foster the liberal values of toleration, moderation, and civil respect' (Osiel 2000: 2). The force of public apologies are similarly linked to 'their *ritual convention* and their *ritual form*', which, when successful as 'arousing and collective emotional activities, manage to exert power on the affective level' (Horelt 2012: 348 and 367).

For TRCs, recognition of their performed character and the significance of their dramaturgical nature is reflected in the substantial resources dedicated to, and academic focus on public hearings. Early truth commissions did not hold public hearings and were largely fact-finding bodies that 'sought to make leaders morally and politically accountable, to expose abuses that had been obscured by a miasma of lies, and to acknowledge the stories of individuals whose own realities had been denied' (Shaw 2007: 190). In contrast, TRCs, 'of which South Africa's was the most influential in shaping an internationally compelling template for healing, redemption and closure', are rooted in the idea that public truth-telling 'operates simultaneously on personal and national levels' (ibid.) – with the performance of public hearings, rather than a final report, presented as making the strongest impression on people's imagination and memories (Sanders 2007: 4). As one well-known South African journalist summarised: 'There were Truth Commissions before ... But those commissions were about the result, the final report. Our Truth Commission was not about the final report, but about the *telling of the story*' (De Preez in Orr 2000: p. ii, emphasis added).

The South African TRC is the best known of all truth commissions – forty have been convened around the world between 1974 and 2009 (Hayner 2011: p. xiv). It is also the most discussed in academic texts, novels, films and plays (Hutchison 2013), and became known to people 'largely through its hearings' (Cole 2010: 4). For those involved in the South African TRC, these sessions were a 'performance of memory, loss and grief' (Ross 2003: 15) that was intricately tied to a grammar of performance *and* vocabulary of healing. The TRC thus presented itself as not only seeking to uncover and establish factual truths, which would then be published in a final report, but as also offering a public stage for truth-telling, which would be cathartic for individual witnesses by providing them with a forum to share their personal or narrative truths – many of whom attested 'to the fact that they had found relief, and experienced healing, just through the process of telling their story' (Tutu 1999: 127). In addition, public truth-telling was meant to contribute to national healing through an interactive process of speaking and listening that enjoined performers and audiences in an articulation of new shared memories or social truth, *and* in the performance of a new nation that rejected the abuses of the past or the 'beginning of an acceptance of accountability and a commitment that what we had experienced must never happen again' (Boraine 2000: 8).

The idea of the South African hearings as a performance staged for full dramatic impact to embody and cultivate a new notion of South African-ness, or way of being South African, is captured by the Commission's deputy chairman, Alex Boraine, who writes of how with the first hearing:

> At last the curtain was raised; the drama which was to unfold ... had witnessed its first scene ... The ritual, which was what the public hearings were, which promised truth, healing, and reconciliation to a deeply divided and traumatised people, began with a story. This was the secret of the Commission – no stern-faced officials sitting in a private chamber, but at a stage, a handful of black and white men and women listening to stories of horror, of deep sorrow, amazing fortitude, and heroism. The audience was there too, and a much wider audience watched and listened through television and radio. It was a ritual, deeply needed to cleanse a nation. It was a drama.
> (2000: 98–9)

The idea that this drama embodied a new human rights conscious nation, whilst also contributing to new national(ist) narratives, is in turn summarised by Charmaine McEachern who emphasised how the apartheid state could organise and institute apparatuses that tortured and killed in the certain knowledge that this would be kept concealed ... Here lies the fundamental paradigm shift at the moral and political core of the TRC as a media event; in *its* terms such state power was illegitimate and unlawful and previously immune officers of the state were to be held accountable, at the very least at the level of explaining their part in the apartheid system of domination. As such it clearly signalled a break with the past, even as the past was its focus. This break both authorised claims about the 'newness' of the nation and set in motion the re-interpretation of history.

(2002: 41)

Given this understanding of TRC hearings, audiences become central to analyses of the Commission's efficacy. All performances require an audience, but for political performances the individuals and groups who constitute the relevant audience(s) is often unclear (Spary and Rai 2013). For the South African TRC, however, the critical audiences were the Commission staff, who had to manage the hearings, deal with victims and perpetrators, and write a final report and offer recommendations, *and* a broader public – both in terms of those physically present and those who engaged with the process through broader media coverage and public debate (Hutchison 2013: 36). The engagement of South Africa's citizenry was important at two levels. First, for testimony to prove cathartic, there have to be 'sympathetic witnesses' (Minow 1998: 70) – the idea being that 'knowing that one's tears are seen may grant a sense of acknowledgement that makes grief less lonely and terrifying' (ibid. 68). Second, and more importantly, if hearings are to work according to the myth of the South African ideal-type, a large secondary audience has to be struck by public testimony and react to it in ways that contribute to increased empathy, to a perception that the hearings are performing a new kind of state *and* to a process of remembering and forgetting that can help forge a new and shared understanding of a nation's past and future trajectory. In South Africa, the idea was ultimately that 'through telling these stories the "master narrative" of colonial and apartheid South Africa was undermined, contradicted, and replaced by the story of struggle, suffering, and the "miracle story" of transition to democracy' (de Gruchy 2002: 23). For public hearings to be successful, therefore, they must lead to a particular kind of transformative interaction between performers and an immediate and remote audience.

This methodological approach means that the mass media serve 'as both essential actors in the TRC drama, as well as the stage on which much of the drama [is] performed' (Krabill 2001: 568), since the 'oft-mentioned role of forging a common national history of the apartheid era would be impossible without the mass media's ability to disseminate the work of the TRC' (ibid.). Indeed, for a TRC to help shape 'collective consciousness' – and thus provide 'a moment of common experience' that compels people 'to discuss a common issue' in ways that represent 'the beginnings of a common if contentious understanding of the past' (ibid. 569, 570 and 571) – hearings must become a 'media event'. More specifically, routine broadcasting must be interrupted, pre-planned events outside of the media must be aired live, they must be 'presented with reverence and ceremony' and enthrall 'very large audiences' (ibid. 569). This occurred in the South African context as 'radio, television and the press worked to mediatise [the TRC] ... so constructing it as an extended media event' (McEachern 2002: 33) – a feat that no other TRC has managed.

Unsurprisingly, given such lofty aims, the practical efficacy of bearing witness through a TRC has prompted significant debate. Critics highlight, for example, how difficult it may be to admit pain and attest to particular harms (Ross 2003: 127); how speaking can lead to a retraumatisation, or even revictimisation of witnesses (Hamber 1999; Krog 1999: 112); and of how people may feel alienated and used as they lose control of the circulation, interpretation and political appropriation of 'their' story (Ross 2003). Much attention has also been given to how voices can be rendered ineffective if 'no-one listens' (Borneman 2002: 295), with any temporary cathartic effect diminished if the rule of law and social justice are not promoted and authoritarian practices and structural inequalities not tackled (Chapman and Ball 2001; Mamdani 2002; Hamber 1997; Stanley 2001; Wilson 2001). Finally, political motivations behind public truth-telling can manipulate the message relayed and its impact and detract from more appropriate or pressing developments. For example, a truth commission can simply be used as a political ploy to dampen criticism through an appearance of 'doing something' (McCargo 2010). It can also stand as a 'theatre of power' that provides an opportunity for the state to try and construct a particular historical narrative (cf. Ashforth 1990). This can help 'create a shared sense of the past, which *can* facilitate the negotiations for a better future' (Hutchison 2013: 81) *or*, alternatively – or indeed simultaneously – lead to a 'new silencing' and 'partial appropriation of what was said by a national discourse' (Bozzoli 1998: 193) that legitimates a new nation-building project to the neglect of more popularly accepted justice mechanisms (Wilson 2001).

While such debates are important, disproportionate attention to the South African example – where TRC hearings were generally well attended and, more importantly, were widely covered by local and international media (Cole 2010; Krabill 2001; Krog 1999; McEachern 2002) – has detracted from prior questions about whether such public forums ever enjoy an engaged audience in the first place. This is important since, for many of the TRC's successors, the impact of public hearings has been limited – not only by initial mandates, political manipulations and so forth – but by the failure of hearings to perform 'newness' or to create 'new' national(ist) narratives, and by extremely limited public interest. Thus analysts of the Sierra Leonean TRC talk of how 'testimony was delivered in a rather detached and clinical way' (Kelsall 2005: 368), with many doing so in 'the hope that this would give them access to economic assistance' (Shaw 2007: 184) – rather than as a means of individual and national catharsis – leading to small and often fairly bored immediate audiences and to limited media coverage and public debate. Consequently, the Sierra Leonean hearings failed to become a media event, to provide a powerful performance of a new nation, or to bring about new national(ist) discourses or imaginaries.

166 *Gabrielle Lynch*

This chapter addresses the importance of – and potential obstacles to – audience engagement by looking at Kenya's Truth, Justice and Reconciliation Commission (TJRC), which sat from 2009 to 2013, but is little known outside of Kenya and poorly understood within Kenya. The analysis draws upon extensive fieldwork conducted in Kenya between 2011 and 2013, which includes interviews with TJRC staff, journalists, civil society activists, witnesses and members of the public, and participant observation of public hearings, women's forums and adversely mentioned persons hearings in Upper Eastern, Western, Rift Valley and Nairobi. However, due to the sensitivity of the subject matter, limited use is made of direct quotes, while interviewees are anonymised and the interview or hearing location is sometimes also omitted.

The analysis starts with an overview of the TJRC, then turns to the staging of public hearings and key reasons for low levels of public engagement, and, finally, provides some thoughts on the need for hearings to be seen to be legitimate, exciting and politically relevant for them to prompt the kind of audience engagement that could even begin to contribute to the transformative process encapsulated in the myth of the South African model. The implication is that, to be politically successful, processes that depend on the efficacy of their theatrical performances must give greater consideration, first, to ensuring a large, engaged and receptive audience, since, without such an audience, there is no interactive dimension between performer and audience and the significance of the *public* nature of hearings or similar performative processes gets lost. The presence of an audience then raises secondary questions about the actual impact of particular performances and immediate and long-term affective responses, which lie beyond the scope of this particular contribution.

Kenya's Truth, Justice and Reconciliation Commission

> [H]ealing is a process ... [the] final goal is acceptance of our diversity, its challenges and complexities for survival of Kenya as a nation.
> (Presiding Chair during the closing ceremony of public hearings in Busia, Western Kenya, July 2011)

The idea for a Kenyan TJRC was initially raised following general elections in December 2002 in which Mwai Kibaki and the National Rainbow Coalition (NaRC) beat Uhuru Kenyatta (President Daniel arap Moi's chosen successor) and the Kenya African National Union (KANU). This momentous event, which saw the peaceful transfer of power from President Moi (after twenty-four years at State House and forty-seven years in the legislature) and displacement of KANU (the ruling party since independence), prompted a moment of great celebration and hope. Indeed, in early 2003, a Gallup opinion poll rated Kenyans as the most optimistic people in the world (Branch and Cheeseman 2005: 325), and it was during this 'honeymoon period' that President Kibaki appointed a Task Force on the Establishment of a TJRC, which recommended that a Commission be established and outlined an appropriate institutional architecture (Bosire and Lynch 2014).

However, Kibaki ignored the Task Force's recommendation, and a TJRC was not established until after the post-election crisis of 2007/8, which saw over 1,000 people killed and almost 700,000 displaced in two months of unprecedented violence (Lynch 2009: 604). The TJRC that was established in the wake of this crisis was mandated to investigate a much wider range of injustices and abuses – from acts of state repression and irregular land acquisition to perceptions of economic marginalisation and causes of political violence and ethnic tension – from the time of the country's independence in December 1963 to the end of the post-election crisis in February 2008. In addition, the TJRC was tasked with promoting peace, justice, national unity, healing and reconciliation among the people of Kenya – an extensive mandate, which reflected a general consensus that, while the post-election crisis was triggered by claims of a stolen election, it was fuelled by much more deep-seated problems and grievances (Bosire and Lynch 2014).

The TJRC was established by an Act of Parliament in December 2008, commissioners were appointed in August 2009 and the Commission started a two-year mandate in early November 2009. However, in August 2011, the Commission was awarded a six-month extension and – after successful applications for two further extensions – eventually submitted a final report on 3 May 2013. The Commission was headed by a chair (Bethuel Kiplagat), supported by a vice-chair (initially Ms Betty Murungi), three international commissioners (Ronald Slye (American), Berhanu Dinka (Ethiopian) and Gertrude Chawatama (Zambian)) and four national commissioners (Tecla Wanjala, Tom Ojienda, Margaret Shava and Ahmed Sheikh Farah). Then, when Murungi resigned in April 2010 in protest of Kiplagat's refusal to step aside, Wanjala became deputy chair and, from November 2010 to January 2012, the acting chair as well.

In terms of its main activities, the TJRC hired and trained statement takers across the country to collect statements and memoranda, and a civic education team conducted stakeholders meetings across the country. An investigations team looked into potential 'window cases' with final cases for public hearings selected by the Commission's legal team. Public hearings, in camera hearings and women's forums were then held across the country; adversely mentioned peoples hearings were held in western Kenya and Nairobi and a series of institutional and thematic hearings in Nairobi. The research team was responsible for leading the writing up of the final report and was assisted by consultants hired to write reports on a number of key issues including militias, ethnic conflict, minority groups and the previous commission of inquiry reports.

At a technical level, the Commission can boast significant achievements (Bosire and Lynch 2014). The team 'collected the largest number of statements of any truth commission in history ... over 40,000' (TJRC 2013: p. iii); held a series of hearings at which 'a hunger, a desire, even a demand for the injustices of the past to be addressed' was powerfully expressed (ibid.); and produced a final report that runs to over 2,000 pages and provides a detailed overview of historical injustices as well as recommendations for constitutional and institutional reform, further investigations, prosecutions, lustration and reparations. Moreover, the final report was relatively well received – including by many of its critics who saw the report, and specifically its recommendations, as a way to lobby the government for full implementation of the new constitution, further institutional reforms and punitive and reparative justice for past wrongs (Bosire and Lynch 2014).

However, despite such achievements and future potential, during its lifespan, the Commission was generally regarded as having been a failure and a waste of state resources. This negative assessment stemmed, in large part, from a belief that few of the Commission's recommendations would ever be implemented. This perception gained credence from the credibility crisis that overshadowed the Commission's life (discussed below), but also from Kenya's long history of commissions of inquiry, which have produced lengthy reports but whose recommendations have largely been ignored. Unfortunately, events to date suggest that people were right to be sceptical. Thus, while the TJRC Act sought to increase the likelihood of implementation by including the requirement of an implementation committee and submission of biannual implementation reports by the Minister of Justice to parliament with reasons for any areas of non-implementation – as of July 2014 – parliament is yet to debate the report. Instead, the National Assembly has passed an amendment to the Act, which empowers MPs to alter the report and thus more easily ignore its recommendations (Lynch 2014b; *Saturday Nation* 2013).

However, negative assessments also stemmed from an idea of what a TRC *should* look like – a perception that is heavily informed by the myth of the South African model where truth-telling is believed to have been characterised by emotional public hearings that brought victims and perpetrators together, facilitated individual and national catharsis and captured the public imagination in ways that helped shape new national narratives. The next section discusses the TJRCs public hearings in more detail, with attention given to levels of public awareness, apathy and scepticism; and implications for the efficacy of such public performances.

TJRCs public hearings and their audiences

> TJRC is a truth-telling institution. [It provides a] platform for injustices to be *aired, heard and reported* nation-wide to facilitate justice, national reconciliation, healing and the restoration of dignity and peace.
> (Presiding Chair's closing remarks at public hearings in Western Kenya, July 2011; emphasis added)

> He says he's an old man and happy to tell everything and happy to say it in public, but there's no one here so it's as good as in camera!
> (Member of the TJRC staff at an adversely mentioned persons hearing in Western Kenya, July 2011)

For TJRC staff, public hearings – in addition to publishing a final report and making recommendations – were central to how they believed that they would meet their mandate. This understanding is reflected in the time and resources dedicated to public hearings. Thus, despite an initially short time frame and limited finances, between April 2011 and March 2012, the Commission opted to hold regional hearings – public, in camera and women's forums – in thirty-five locations, alongside adversely mentioned people's hearings (which were generally conducted in Nairobi with the exception of two days in Bungoma in western Kenya) and a series of thematic and institutional hearings in Nairobi. This is significant since, while the TJRC Act required that the Commission have hearings and that they be public, unless there were good reasons to hold them in camera, no direction was given as to how many hearings should be held and where (Kenya 2008).

The importance attached to hearings was also expressed in the TJRC's final report, which notes how:

> The written word, no matter how poetic, cannot convey accurately the passion with which people demanded to tell their stories and the integrity and dignity with which they related their experiences. It cannot convey the silence, the tears, and the emotions that engulfed the [venues] ... It can neither convey the tears that were shed before this Commission nor the tears that were shed by the Commission's staff and Commissioners ... So while this Report is the final product of this Commission ... we know that the work of the Commission is also written in the hearts and souls of each and every person who interacted with the Commission: the statement takers and statement givers; victims, adversely mentioned persons, and those who reside simultaneously in both categories; witnesses who testified in public, and those who testified in camera; those employed by the Commission, and those who took on the task of monitoring and reporting on the work of the Commission; and finally, the millions of others who may have viewed a news story, or read an opinion piece, or seen the Commission's truck with our logo, Tusirudie Tena! [We should not go back there again! Or Never Again!] blazoned on its side.
> (TJRC 2013: pp. iii–iv)

But how were these performances conducted?

In terms of venues, public hearings were held in a variety of buildings from municipal council rooms, teacher training sites and agricultural college buildings to church halls and churches. However, in contrast to the South African TRC where venues constituted 'reclaimed spaces that had been denied to black South Africans under apartheid' (Hutchison 2013: 29) – and thus directly contributed to a performance of transition – in Kenya, hearings were often tucked away in non-symbolic spaces, which reinforced a burgeoning idea that the TJRC was just another commission of inquiry. Hearings were also inadequately signposted. One example was Nairobi, where hearings were mainly held at the NHIF building – a shopping mall and office block outside of the Central Business District where one had to go up an escalator and a flight of stairs before finding a small sign to the TJRC's 'public hearings'. Together with poorly advertised hearing schedules, last-minute changes to dates and venues, and a website that was often out of date, poor signposting meant that it was difficult to know where and when hearings would be held even if one read the national newspapers, had reliable internet access and purposively kept an ear out for information about the Commission.

In terms of stage management, the usual format was for commissioners to sit at the front of the room on a small platform on large black padded chairs behind a long table. Sign language interpreters were then situated in front and slightly to the left or right. Down on the floor, and to one side, was a table for the witness, the leader of evidence (who was to guide the witness and ask questions), the hearing clerk (who swore in witnesses and processed any documents submitted) and a member of the special support unit or a trained counsellor (who was there to comfort witnesses if and when necessary). The decision to place witnesses on the floor below the Commissioner's differed from the South African TRC where, while, at the first hearings,

> commissioners were arrayed on stage before the audience while the witness sat at the front of the house, back to the audience, facing the commissioners. This spatial arrangement changed fairly quickly in the TRC process, for organizers felt it did not accurately symbolize what the commission was about. The new format placed witnesses on the stage adjacent to the commissioners, both seated at tables angled slightly toward each other. This arrangement enabled both the commissioners and the witness to face outward toward the house, making clear who the real audience was for the TRC and for the testimony given before the commission.
>
> (Cole 2010: 93)

In contrast, when I asked TJRC staff about their choice of seating arrangements, which placed witnesses on a lower level, and at a 45 degree angle to the commissioners and the public gallery, they reassured me that this was what Kenyans expected from such an official body and that they were following protocol. However, this decision to use familiar staging meant that the hearings were marked by a sense of 'once-againness' (cf. Taylor 2003: 32), rather than of transition and change, which reinforced a perception that the TJRC was just going to be another commission of inquiry.

Next to the witness table a second table was usually situated in the middle of the room facing the commissioners with transcription recording equipment and any international observers or 'important visitors'. People situated at this table were provided with headphones and could choose whether to listen to the proceedings in English or Kiswahili. This was where I sat, and other observers (over the course of hearings that I attended) included commissioners from two other state commissions – the National Cohesion and Integration Commission (NCIC) and the Kenya National Commission of Human Rights (KNCHR) – representatives from the KHRC, International Commission of Jurists-Kenya Section (ICJ-Kenya), the German Embassy, German development agency (GiZ) and United Nations Development Programme (UNDP). The latter two constituted the principal external donors of the process. During closing ceremonies in each location, this table was also occupied by local dignitaries including provincial administrators and elders who – together with politicians – tended to be absent from the rest of the proceedings unless giving testimony.

The translators' booth was usually situated at the opposite side of the room from the witness table, where TJRC staff ensured – whether the witness was speaking in English, Kiswahili, or a local vernacular – that testimony was available in English and Kiswahili and that, if necessary, any questions posed by the leader of evidence or commissioner were translated into the appropriate language. English translation was vital as none of the three international commissioners spoke Kiswahili, and at least one international commissioner had to attend every public hearing according to the Commission's own hearing rules. Kiswahili translation was also required as, with the exception of some hearings in Nairobi, this was the language in which testimony was relayed to the general public through loud speakers.

Venues also had a dedicated 'media area', which was usually next to the translators so that cameras could zoom in on both witnesses and commissioners. I never came across international media at the hearings I attended (with the exception of a documentary-maker at a hearing in Nairobi), and the presence of local and national media varied – this dedicated area sometimes home to no one but the Commission's own video-man. Media attendance varied between but also within locations as journalists often left as soon as they had secured their story. The fact that witnesses waited in the venue for their turn to speak, meant that many were conscious that their story would not receive the media coverage enjoyed by some of the preceding speakers.

Finally, behind the 'witness' and 'observer' tables sat the general public – usually on plastic chairs – who listened to proceedings in Kiswahili. The fact that the 'VIP table' usually divided this audience from the rest of the proceedings reinforced the sense of a two-tier audience. First, there was the commissioners, media and VIPs who could choose what language to listen to the proceedings in and who could clearly see the witnesses and their expressions and bearing. Second, was the general public who were offered no such choice and who could hear the witness, or at least a translation of their testimony, but could often not see them. The exception was those instances – such as some hearings in Nairobi and Kisumu – where proceedings were also captured on a big screen. Such differences in oral and visual experiences, not only made it harder for the general public to stay focused on proceedings (as revealed in ad hoc conversations and interviews), but also suggested that, as an audience, they were less important, which did little to counter perceptions that the hearings were, in effect, a familiar performance, rather than an enactment of transition and the beginning of a new national consciousness.

Audience size varied significantly between locations, with hundreds of people at hearings in Kuria and Kisii, as compared to a handful of people at the second day of public hearings in Bungoma. Public attendance tended to drop off during the hearings in any one location and was especially poor when hearings went on after sunset. For example, according to one observer, there were about 500 people present for the initial launch of the TJRC hearings, which took place in Garissa in northern Kenya in April 2011, but this reduced to just over 100 for the start of the actual hearings in Garissa and to about 20 by the time that local hearings concluded. This decrease in audience size reflected the hearings' shortcomings as an engaging performance, but also raised important questions about who the witnesses were talking to. Were they simply talking to commission staff so as to inform the final report? And, if so, why did large sums of money need to be spent on holding the hearings in public? Or, were they supposed to be talking to the nation? In which case, surely their testimony was rendered ineffective in the face of a limited local audience and media coverage. Unfortunately, the Commission often seemed unclear as to who the relevant audiences were. Thus, on the one hand, staff and commissioners often spoke of the importance of witness testimony for catharsis, for increasing public awareness and for fostering debate, but often seemed unfazed by instances where there were no media and only a handful of citizens in attendance – the regional coordinator on one such occasion simply quipping that the TJRC had 'no quorum'.

In terms of protocol, or the scripting of public hearings, sessions began with the national anthem and commission prayer, which was read out by the regional coordinator, while people were asked to stand up when commissioners entered or left the room. Sessions ended with an ad hoc prayer by a selected member of the public. Witnesses were sworn in – either by swearing on the Bible or the Koran – whereupon they then read out, summarised or were led through their statement or memorandum by the leader of evidence. They were then asked questions by the leader of evidence and commissioners, which tended to be for clarification or additional information, and as a way for commissioners to offer empathy and promises of assistance or commitment, rather than as a means of cross-examination. On the first day of public hearings in any one location this process often lasted for several hours, which led to an increasingly tight programme that negatively impacted on levels of concentration, as the audience was either offered an abundance or scarcity of information. In camera hearings apparently followed a similar structure but without the presence of media, observers or members of the general public.

Witnesses were selected by the Commission's legal team as 'window cases' – or as people whose statement or memorandum was deemed to be representative of the common issues or problems faced or experienced by different communities in any given area. Due to the temporal and thematic scope of the commission's mandate and limited time available, about half of the witnesses who appeared were people deemed to be knowledgeable of local histories and specific problems and, as a result, were often divorced from the abuses and injustices discussed, which tended to then be relayed in a fairly matter of fact way. This was in stark contrast to the testimony of first-hand victims who often offered less useful 'factual' truths, but relayed more effective 'personal' or 'narrative' truths. Significantly, the overarching and context-setting memoranda were often scheduled first – an ordering of events that rendered it even less likely that hearings would capture people's imagination and may have contributed to a falling off in audience size. This shortcoming was reinforced by the fact that testimonies tended to jump from one issue to another – with one witness, for example, talking about post-election violence, the next about historical land injustices and the next about problems facing disabled residents. This was problematic since, while it ensured that the Commission covered different aspects of its mandate, it meant that the hearings lacked an overarching narrative, which affected attendance in any one area. It also limited debate outside of the hearings, which then had further repercussions for levels of public interest and media engagement, as a negative cycle of disinterest, disengagement and limited coverage set in.

In addition to public and in camera hearings, women's hearings were also held in each location. These women-only events were far less formal and often highly emotional. Female commissioners, or, in their absence, the CEO and/or the head of special support, sat at the front of the room, but were not seated up on a platform and sometimes the room had to be rearranged from public hearings the day before. In addition, while the women were asked to stand when the commissioners entered and left the room, proceedings started with an ad hoc prayer and songs and dancing in which the female staff (including the commissioners) were full participants. It was also not uncommon for female commissioners to come from behind their table to personally console women who succumbed to tears when telling their story. The logic behind these hearings was, according to TJRC staff, that fewer women had written statements and submitted memorandum than men and, when they did so, often talked in general terms or about male relatives, rather than about their experiences 'as women'. However, given that the decision to hold women's hearings seems to have been made fairly early on in the Commission's lifespan, this approach may stem, at least in part, from predications of limited women's engagement based on the South African experience where relatively few women gave testimony and those that did tended to concentrate on the abuses suffered by sons and husbands rather than those inflicted on their own bodies (Goldblatt and Meintjes 1997; Ross 2003).

The regional coordinator organised these hearings – or, if the coordinator was a man, his female deputy – with the help of female statement takers from the area, and the format varied. Thus, in some areas, for example in Bungoma and Busia in western Kenya, a number of women were pre-selected to speak on the basis that they were known to be able to speak to issues specific to particular groups or communities, for example, as widows or internally displaced people. These women were then followed by an 'open mic' session, while in other locations, such as Kapsokwony in Mt Elgon, the whole meeting was 'open' with women simply asked to raise their hand if they wished to speak. At all of the women's hearings I attended, the number of people who wished to speak increased as the session progressed, with half a day always proving too short.

These sessions often proved more emotional and powerful than their public counterparts. In part, this was due to the 'open mic' approach, since you never knew what to expect and were left with an impression of scale, as often every woman in the room seemed to have a story, and an increasingly heart-wrenching story, that they wanted to tell. Moreover, women were unprepared for the emotions that might be unleashed and it was not uncommon for those who spoke, or were listening, to cry and even break down. In turn, the pain and trauma was much more palpable and one was left with a much stronger impression of trauma *and* catharsis. However, while these sessions left a strong impression upon those who attended – including the commissioners, commission staff, members of the public and myself – they were often not covered by the media and any male journalists who arrived were turned away at the door. This raised questions regarding their efficacy. For example, at the women's hearings in Bungoma, the final 'witness' was led from the room sobbing after sharing a story of brutal rape, which prompted a lone female voice to sing amidst the silence of others in attendance. The next day, one commissioner described how she had just wandered around in the afternoon as the hearings had been too much; and she thought it would be good if women could talk before men, as the men should know how much the women suffer. Yet the immediate audience for these hearings was limited and purely female. Thus, while 'over 1,000 women attended the women's hearings across the country, with an average of 60 women in each hearing' (TJRC 2013: p. xvii) this falls far short of a national audience, given a national population of around 40 million. In addition, there was a negligible audience outside of the physical venue given limited levels of media coverage. As a result, women tended to be talking to a small group of other women from their area, rather than to their fellow Kenyans more broadly.

Hearings for adversely mentioned persons (AMPs) took place after public, women's and in camera hearings – although 'after' could be the next day or several months later. When these hearings were held in Nairobi, they were held in an auditorium at the NHIF building or at the Kenyatta International Conference Centre (KICC) downtown. Both locations are relatively formal and attracted the national press and a number of local and international observers. Hearings for AMPs followed a common format whereby a selection of people who had been adversely mentioned in people's statements were summoned to appear before the Commission, where – if they decided to appear – they read out a statement or were led through their testimony by the leader of evidence and were then 'cross-examined' by the leader of evidence and commissioners. However, while some of these hearings attracted a fairly sizeable audience and some media coverage, the level of engagement was still relatively limited, especially when compared to the South Africa example. In part, this was because media coverage tended to focus on the mere attendance of AMPs with any shock value limited by the fact that no AMP admitted to any wrongdoing and, instead, usually 'did not know', 'could not remember' or suggested that responsibility 'lay elsewhere' – either up or down the chain of command. There was thus relatively little to report or discuss.

Finally, thematic hearings were held in Nairobi where experts presented memoranda and answered questions on issues such as children, people living with disabilities, ethnic tension and violence, and torture. These general overviews – while potentially useful for establishing 'factual' truths – tended to enjoy fairly limited audiences and media coverage and, as a result, initiated almost no public debate.

Indeed, TJRC hearings failed to attract sizeable immediate audiences *or* to become a media event. Hearings were usually not aired live on either the TV or radio, stories rarely made it on to the evening news or to the front pages of the national newspapers and there was limited discussion on national and local radio. Instead, coverage of proceedings was usually limited to short articles towards the middle of the newspaper, while local media only tended to cover hearings in their particular area. The TJRC did have a small communications team who, among other things, produced occasional inserts for the national newspapers and helped produce short shows for TV. However, the fact that the latter were aired at different times on different TV stations during the course of only some of the public hearings minimised their public impact. The TJRC also had a social media presence; however, the fact that a total of 1,420 tweets had been posted by December 2013 – with the Commission enjoying only 687 followers – suggests that its impact was negligible. This poor communications record is due to a number of different factors. This includes the broader political context (discussed below) and problems with scripting and stage management (discussed above), but also a poor communications strategy, and a number of commission staff bemoaned the fact that this aspect of the TJRC's work was headed by a former news anchor rather than by a more experienced communications officer.

Coverage that was given to TJRC hearings also failed to foster a sense of excitement about the process or to kick-start a broader debate, and thus failed to trigger a reinforcing cycle of interest, discussion and coverage. For example, one of the only public hearings I attended that became 'front-page news' involved the testimony of Bernard Ndege in Kisumu who escaped from a house that was set on fire in Naivasha during the post-election violence in which eleven members of his family along with eight others were burnt alive. Ndege's story is well known in Kenya and the combination of his emotional narrative and physical appearance, which is marked by patches of pink skin, ensured that his testimony was widely reported. However, subsequent questions about whether Ndege's appearance is the result of burns, as is often assumed (including during the commissioners' questioning), or of a skin problem resulting from stress, detracted from the power of his testimony and reinforced the idea of a troubled and problematic process that did little to foster clear moral narratives. This was in contrast to the South African TRC where a number of defining moments – such as the wail of a victim's mother on the second day of the human rights hearings and subsequent re-enactment of a torture technique by a white security official on a former black victim – helped to capture the public imagination and fed into a context where these sessions could become an extended media event. In contrast, public hearings in Kenya received little attention, and – to make matters worse – the majority of media coverage that the TJRC did receive focused on problems with the process, most notably the chairman issue discussed below, which served to further undermine public excitement and reinforce a growing sense of 'once-againness'. Moreover, the focus on problems and challenges was particularly pronounced when it came to opinion pieces written by prominent civil society activists in the leading dailies, which enjoy wide readership and sometimes prompt public debate.

This impression that TJRC hearings enjoyed limited public engagement was supported by informal discussions with people in towns while the hearings were ongoing and in interviews and discussions with people during the course of the Commission's life. Comments typically described the TJRC in the following terms: the TJRC is a 'non-starter' (interview with Kalenjin peace activist, Eldoret, 3 March 2011; interview with Kikuyu peace activist, Nakuru, 7 March 2011); people 'have well founded fears that its time will lapse before it even gets off the ground' (civil society activist, Nairobi, 21 March 2011); the process is 'doomed' (civil society activist, Nairobi, 28 April 2011); if there is 'anything that I've not followed well it's the TJRC' (Kikuyu clergyman, Murunga, 6 May 2011); and there has been a 'lack of sensitization and ... people don't understand the commission' (participant in TJRC civic education meeting, Molo, 21 July 2011). Such impressions and comments are also supported by local opinion polls. For example, in a survey conducted in June 2011, 52 per cent of Kenyans said they were aware of the TJRC, but 45 per cent did not know that it existed, while 2 per cent said that they 'did not know' if they were aware of the TJRC or not, and 1 per cent chose not to respond (KNDR, June 2011: 10). Moreover, if anything, levels of awareness seemed to have declined over time. Thus, in an opinion poll conducted by Ipsos Synovate in June 2013 – just a month after the report's release – only 33 per cent knew of 'a commission that recently submitted its report to the President, accompanied by the controversy over a section of the Land chapter', which could only have been the TJRC, and which was one of the critical stories that had received significant media coverage. Moreover, of those who could identify the TJRC only 16 per cent had 'a lot' of confidence that the Report's recommendations would be implemented, 40 per cent 'some', 37 per cent 'none at all' and 6 per cent were 'not sure' (<www.ipsos.co.ke/home/index.php/downloads>). How can one explain such limited engagement and confidence beyond the problems of stage management and scripting outlined above, and what are the implications for ensuring more effective performative processes in future?

Bad theatre, ignorance, apathy and pessimism: explaining the TJRC's limited audience

> [T]he TJRC has lacked gravitas from its inception and has therefore not had much impact as hoped...The TJRC Commissioners and staff have worked hard, considering the financial and capacity constraints that encumbered the commission from the start. However, persistent lack of support from civil society, discomfort with its methodology, and inadequate media coverage of the hearings means the commission has continued to perform below its optimum potential.
> (KNDR, October 2011: 63)

> I would be surprised if people know what [the TJRC] is, it's mandate, or even if people turn up.
> (Interview with retired senior civil servant from Western Kenya, Nairobi, 2 May 2011)

Bringing the audience back in 177

Limited media coverage of and public engagement with the TJRCs public hearings stem from a number of different issues that relate both to the broader context in which the Commission was working and to the Commission's internal wranglings and dynamics. This section does not seek to provide an exhaustive account of these issues, but instead provides a broad overview to contextualise conclusions regarding the need for processes that seek to shape public debate to pay greater attention to the presence of an engaged and receptive audience – which depends in large part on the efficacy of their theatrical performance to do so.

Kenya has had many commissions of inquiry, which have documented the country's violent and unjust past; however, commission recommendations have usually been ignored (Africog 2008: 19). As a result, commissions of inquiry are increasingly seen as 'conduits for [the] cover-up and entrenchment of the culture of impunity' (KHRC 2011: 3), rather than as a means for tackling injustice and spearheading reforms (Bosire and Lynch 2014). This creates a paradox whereby a history of human rights abuses and injustice led many people to think that Kenya needed a TJRC, but people's previous experience of commissions led them to be inherently suspicious of what such a process was likely to achieve. Ultimately, the idea that the TJRC was going to be like previous commissions of inquiry – in that it would write a detailed report that would then be relegated to dusty shelves – was reinforced from the outset by the fact that there had been no political transition (the TJRC was instead established following a disputed election that led the incumbent president to enter a power-sharing agreement with his opponent) and by a credibility crisis that revolved around the chairman, Ambassador Bethuel Kiplagat. A sense of 'once-againness' was then reinforced by the way in which public hearings were scripted and stage-managed.

The whole first year of the Commission's life was absorbed by the chairman issue, as civil society activists led calls for Kiplagat to resign and/or for the commission to be disbanded (Bosire and Lynch 2014). Opposition to Kiplagat stemmed from the fact that he was a Permanent Secretary (PS) in the Ministry for Foreign Affairs at the time that the then Minister, Robert Ouko, was murdered; he was named in a presidential commission of inquiry into land grabbing – popularly known as the Ndungu Report – as someone who benefited from irregular land allocations under President Moi; and, as the PS for Foreign Affairs, had attended a meeting in Wajir in February 1984 at which some say a decision was made to round up all the Degodia men in the area for interrogation. This decision led to the infamous Wagalla massacre when an unknown number of men died whilst in detention at Wagalla airstrip in northern Kenya. Given this background, critics argued that Kiplagat should be summoned before the Commission and that his appointment was a deliberate attempt by government officials to undermine the process from the outset (Bosire and Lynch 2014).

Civil society pressure for Kiplagat to resign or for the Commission to be disbanded was then reinforced by other voices. This included a press statement by ten former truth commissioners – led by the unrivalled moral voice of Archbishop Desmond Tutu, the former chair of the South African TRC – in which they noted how 'truth commissions must enjoy the confidence of the public to succeed.

Since objective grounds of a reasonable apprehension of bias on the part of Ambassador Kiplagat exist in the minds of the public, he is duty bound to resign for the greater good of the commission and country' (24 February 2010).[1] With time, opposition to Kiplagat's leadership also grew within the Commission and, in April 2010, the deputy chair resigned in protest. This was critical since, within Kenya, it was only Kiplagat and Murungi who were widely known, which meant that the Commission not only lacked a moral voice, but also a recognised one. This stood in contrast to South Africa where President Nelson Mandela 'set the example of the great reconciler' and Archbishop Desmond Tutu was viewed by many 'as the perfect person to [lead] ... the process of national healing and reconciliation, given his Christian compassion and moral stature as an activist bishop' (Graybill 2002: 11 and 27). As one Kenyan peace activist summarised, the 'image of success [has] to do with a number of things including the nature of the transition ... and then hav[ing] iconic figures that can inspire people – we don't have that' (interview, Nairobi, 17 March 2011).

To add to this crisis, a perception emerged among Kiplagat's own Kalenjin community that the reason people were 'fighting him' was because of his ethnic identity and that it was 'only a Kalenjin chairman who will issue a balanced report on historical injustices in the Rift Valley' (interview with Kalenjin elder, Eldoret, 2 March 2011). The campaign against the chairman was perceived as part of a broader process whereby the Kalenjin, who constitute about 11 per cent of the Kenyan population, were 'being vilified as monsters, as people who caused [the post-election violence of 2007/8]' (interview with Kalenjin academic, Eldoret, 5 March 2011).

This credibility crisis paralysed the commission for the first year of its initial two-year mandate. It also led to a loss of public confidence and fuelled a negative reinforcing cycle whereby this saga – together with associated questions regarding the suitability of several of the other commissioners, sections of the TJRC Act and, as time went on, the quality of the TJRC's work – prompted many civil society organisations and donors to walk away from the Commission and allowed the government to step back from a process that had initially been pushed by civil society activists and foreign mediators. This was vital as it meant that, even when Kiplagat stepped aside to pave the way for a special tribunal from November 2010 to January 2012, most civil society organisations remained critical of the TJRC and either rejected it outright or vacillated between disengagement and strategic and partial engagement that helped reinforce an overwhelmingly negative image of the Commission among the general public (Bosire and Lynch 2014). This lack of interest then discouraged the country's profit-making media houses from paying the Commission much attention, ensuring that the TJRC never enjoyed the 'Extensive media interest and coverage [which, in the case of South Africa, had] brought this ritual event ... into people's homes and thus made it part of their routine world' (McEachern 2002: 26).

However, one cannot fully understand the strength of opposition to Kiplagat's appointment – or the failure of the TJRC to become a media event and public dismissal of its work – without considering the push for those deemed most responsible for the post-election violence of 2007/8 to be held criminally accountable. To summarise, the Commission of Inquiry into Post-Election Violence, or Waki Commission, recommended that a Special Tribunal be established to try those most responsible. However, following parliament's failure to legislate for such a body, the International Criminal Court (ICC) was invited, in July 2009, to conduct investigations. In December 2010, the Office of the Prosecutor (OTP) announced the names of six Kenyans under investigation; charges were confirmed against four individuals in January 2012 – two of whom, Uhuru Kenyatta and William Ruto, went on to win the presidential election in March 2013. Amidst these developments, the cabinet released a statement on 30 July 2009 saying that it would address the perpetrators of the post-election violence, in part, through a strengthened TJRC – the popular interpretation being that the Commission would be used as a substitute for accountability and punitive justice (Bosire and Lynch 2014). As one civil society activist noted, the idea that the government would extend the mandate of the TJRC 'sowed the seed that it might be used to whitewash post-election crimes', which further eroded public confidence in the Commission and its ability to meet its mandate (interview with civil society activist, Nairobi, 3 May 2011).

Developments at the ICC also impacted on the TJRC's work in other ways. First, there was some confusion at the local level about the relationship and difference between the two bodies, which was exacerbated by limited civic education and the similarities between the TJRC statement and ICC victim registration forms. Thus, while interviewees who had heard of these bodies knew that the ICC was an international court that was investigating prominent Kenyans for their alleged role in the post-election violence, and that the TJRC was a government commission of inquiry, many did not know that the TJRC's mandate extended beyond the post-election violence and were sometimes unsure about whether information collected by the latter would be shared with, or be used to support, proceedings at the ICC. Second, and more importantly for the interaction of performer and audience, the ICC completely upstaged the TJRC as any development, or hint of a development – at least during the Commission's lifespan – absorbed the focus of local, national and international print, TV and radio media. Thus, while the TJRC was denigrated as just another commission of inquiry, the relative novelty and potential impact of the ICC – which saw leading politicians fly to and from The Hague to sit in a court with legal representatives and stern judges, and then get elected to run the country – meant that its international character and unpredictability rendered it a relevant process that could have significant ramifications for the country's future and was thus something 'worth watching'. For the Court's supporters, the process seemed capable – at least for much of the lifespan of the TJRC hearings – of providing the kind of justice that would be impossible within Kenya. For the ICC's opponents, the Court was feared for its potential to remove popular leaders from the local political stage, and became central to debates surrounding the country's 2013 election (Lynch 2014a).

The ICC was not the only development that distracted attention away from TJRC hearings. The Commission was also upstaged by: a successful referendum on a new constitution in 2010; a subsequent array of institutional reforms; and electioneering around the 2013 elections. The process was complicated by the emergence of a pervasive 'peace narrative', which urged all Kenyans to remain peaceful during the 2013 elections (Cheeseman *et al.* 2014), but which also became interwoven with the revival of an old peace-versus-justice debate to the detriment of a truth-telling process that could recommend further investigations, prosecutions and lustrations, among other things. As one interviewee noted: 'the TJRC is going to unearth and create even more problems ... as Christians we preach to forget past sins' (interview with Kikuyu clergyman, Murunga, 6 May 2011).

This array of challenges was then interwoven with problems that stemmed from the Commission's own limited capacity, which, for example, led to poor advertising of hearings and signing of venues, and limited communication of changes to hearing schedules. The level of popular mobilisation also depended on the work of those employed at the local level, with a number of people frustrated, for example, with the regional coordinator in one part of the country who did not seem to mind that there were public hearings with 'no public' and just sat 'with his feet up reading the paper ... while people are testifying!' (interview with TJRC staff member, 2011).

Finally, when people did attend the hearings – both members of the public and journalists – the performance staged often failed to enthrall, causing the hearing attendances to fall off with each subsequent day in any location. The reasons are multiple but include an extensive mandate and short time frame that led to an over-reliance on memoranda by community spokesmen who were often divorced from the abuses discussed; the fact that the perpetrators' voices ended up being absent from the truths told; and lack of an overarching moral narrative as witness testimonies could shift from the post-election violence of 2007/8 to land disputes or the marginalisation of local minorities in the course of any one hearing. As one commissioner noted in a discussion, [s]he was often not clear what the point of the hearings was, which affected media and public interest. In his/her opinion, the Commission needed to be more strategic about the issues heard so that the hearings could be a more effective 'drama', which required greater consideration being given to 'what our story ... is'. Somewhat ironically, one of the problems they cited was that the Commission was spending so much time in the field conducting public hearings that they did not have time to take stock (conversation with one of the TJRC commissioners during public hearings in Bungoma, July 2011).

Conclusions: the need to take audience seriously

According to Eric Brahm, 'the degree to which [a truth] commission's findings are accessible by the public seems more crucial' for its impact than whether the hearings are public or not (2007: 31). However, while this may be true for the impact of a final report, and the likelihood that a government implements its recommendations – given that 'the more open the process is, the more costly the signal is likely to be' of non-implementation (ibid.) – this is not true for the impact of hearings. Instead, truth commissions opt to hold hearings because testimony is meant to help establish 'factual truths' that can then feed into a final report and recommendations, but TRCs opt to hold these hearings in *public* because the process of telling and listening – or the interaction between performers and audiences – is believed to be able to contribute to personal and national healing by providing a forum for personal narratives to be shared, for a new state to be enacted and 'social' truths to be aired and, with luck, officially acknowledged and publicly internalised. The publicness of these hearings thus becomes central to their efficacy as a transformative mechanism that can be cathartic for witnesses and help foster a sense of transition and new national consciousness.

As a result, the grammar of performance is essential for any analysis or evaluation of TRCs. First, there needs to be an audience that listens to personal narratives for the purposes of catharsis, that watches the hearings' enactment of 'new-ness' and that engages with the overarching social narratives in ways that produce a 'new' understanding of a country's past and future trajectory. However, as the case of the Kenyan TJRC reveals, the presence of an audience that closely follows public hearings is not given. Of central importance in this regard is the extent to which hearings enjoy substantive media coverage. However, for hearings to become a 'media event' that can stimulate public debate as envisaged by the myth of the South African model, routine broadcasting must be interrupted for live coverage of pre-planned events that are characterised by pomp and circumstance and enthrall the general public (Krabill 2001: 569). This means that, on the one hand, a TRC has to provide 'good theatre' – it has to captivate, excite and stimulate. On the other hand, it also has to conduct its work in an environment where its performances are interpreted as 'good theatre' and as something 'worth watching' by a broader public.

This did not happen in the Kenyan context where TJRC hearings were characterised by small immediate audiences, limited media coverage, negligible public debate and low levels of public awareness and expectation. The process therefore lacked the kind of engaged and receptive public that is essential for a transformative interaction between performers and an audience(s) that could potentially lead to catharsis, a sense of a new state and national consciousness as envisaged by the South African model.

The implication is that much greater attention needs to be given to whether an engaged and receptive audience is following such performances – an analysis that points to the importance of a commission's communications strategy, advertising and media coverage, but also of popular interpretations of what such a process will likely achieve, and thus to the importance of broader political contexts, the credibility of key actors and the effectiveness of scripting and stage management. Thus, while public hearings are clearly pre-planned outside of the media and can be aired live – and TRC staff can ensure that they are performed with sufficient pomp and circumstance – it is far more challenging, and largely context dependent, whether or not hearings will draw in an audience in a way that encourages profit-oriented private media houses to interrupt routine broadcasting and ensure the continuous live coverage that is associated with public debate and production of new shared values and national narratives.

However, even if citizens are present and engaged, this does not ensure that public hearings will achieve their goals, and it is not obvious that the interaction of performers and audiences would have been transformative in the Kenyan context even if public hearings had attracted large immediate audiences and become an extended media event. Instead, presence and engagement simply raises secondary questions about the efficacy of performances and immediate and long-term affective responses. For example, do witnesses find their interactions with audiences – from the commissioners and public gallery to the broader public – cathartic? Or does their experience leave them feeling newly traumatised and victimised? Do the hearings embody the idea of transition and perform a new kind of state, or are they interpreted as familiar performances that foster a sense of 'once-againness'? Is an overarching narrative produced that is popularly accepted and which contributes to healing and reconciliation, or does public debate simply reveal the level of division and even promote further conflict?

The presence of an audience is thus just a first step, but it is an important one, since, as Ron Krabill argues in the context of South Africa: 'People may vehemently disagree about whether the TRC process has affected the country positively or negatively, but they are talking about it. While this clearly does not lead to reconciliation in and of itself, it does represent the beginnings of a common if contentious understanding of the past' (2001: 571). In contrast, while the Kenyan TJRC may have a role to play as a fact-finding body that has published a report with an array of recommendations, the point of holding its hearings in *public* was largely lost.

Note

1 Available to download from <http://blog.marsgroupkenya.org/2010/02/25/desmond-tutu-and-other-international-justice-figures-call-on-ambassador-bethuel-kiplagat-kenyan-tjrc-chair-to-step-down>.

13 Betrayal and what follows

Rituals of repentance, healing and anger in response to the church sexual abuse scandal in Ireland

Joshua Edelman

This chapter looks at an arena of social conflict in early twenty-first-century Ireland that straddles the boundaries between religion and politics, and four performances that seek to address that conflict in one way or another. In so doing, it tries to examine questions of the limits of political legitimacy and how performance can help in its assertion. With this case study, I want to suggest that it is not just in its claims to represent the public or its will that political assertions share grammatical links with performance. These links also appear when the question of authority's legitimacy is raised. Traditionally in Ireland, religion has had an important role in the performative assertion of legitimate authority, even (or especially) when that legitimacy is not linked to a democratic mandate. But can this practice continue to function in the contemporary post-secular world? When religion's own authority is undermined, who or what can step in to reassert it? The grammar of this balancing act between religion and political authority is not so much dialectical as performative. This case study will help us better understand the workings of that performative grammar and, in particular, the agonistic relationship between church and state that has traditionally been central to it. That agonism can change and develop, but its ongoing presence, I argue, does much of the social work of asserting solidarity.

Recently, a number of political theorists have turned to religious discourse to make sense of the nature and the practice of political authority in the post-secular world. Giorgio Agamben (2011), for instance, has turned to the early church understandings of political authority to supplement his earlier reading of Carl Schmitt in *Homo Sacer* (Agamben 1998). By differentiating and explaining the relationship between divine sovereignty and princely governmentality, he helps to explain how the display of authority interacts with the exercise of it. For the present project, however, I am more drawn to Jürgen Habermas's investigation of the appropriate role of religion in the post-secular state – not as an intellectual model, as in Agamben, but as a potent if dangerous social force.

Habermas's larger project is the establishment of a sound philosophical grounding for the ongoing work of constitutional, democratic European politics. Since the publication of his influential *Structural Transformation of the Public Sphere* (1962) he has put forward the idea of the consent – or at least dialogue – achieved in the discursive public sphere as the shape that grounding will take. But the difficulty is that Habermas's ideal public sphere does not allow all manners of discourse within it. In order to maintain its democratic and egalitarian character, Habermas argues for the rigorous exclusion of any arguments which depend on sectarian theological claims – that is, any which are not equally acceptable to those of all faiths or none. Some critics have noted that this public sphere – which Habermas traces back to the coffeehouses of Elizabethan England – was not in fact as purely egalitarian as Habermas implies. Its inhabitants were largely white, male and middle-class, and the form of reasoning that grew in them may have been marked by this background. Political actors have other means of constructing arguments available to them, even if it is this (originally male, bourgeois) form that much contemporary political philosophy has marked as an appropriately disinterested rationality.

Perhaps because of these limitations, Habermas has noted that the overt impersonal justifications that the public sphere can offer are simply not enough to sustain contemporary political life. They may suffice for making personal moral choices, but in themselves, arguments based on a strictly impersonal rationality cannot address the key problem of a diverse, contemporary democracy: the breakdown of solidarity (Habermas 2010: 76). In an echo of Adorno via Johan Baptist Metz, Habermas talks about 'an awareness of what is missing' – how philosophy used to be able to offer that sense of solidarity, but can no longer. Part of Habermas's project is thus intellectual archaeology, an attempt to exhume solidarity-building ideas from the common intellectual heritage that Western philosophy shares with the great world religions. This 'assimilation of unexhausted contents' will, he hopes, help democratic debate fill the role of social cohesion that religion used to satisfy (Habermas 2010: 80).

However, this act of digging is also problematic for Habermas, because the public sphere that undergirds political practice is grounded in a form of Kantian reasoning that excludes religious claims as insufficiently universal. And so Habermas has a difficult task: to establish some rules for 'translation' – the means by which religious arguments can to be rephrased into non-sectarian terms that respect diversity, and also the deference that religious reasoning must show to the scientific process as fallible but authoritative over matters appropriate to it. Habermas is searching for ways that religious and secular reasoning can speak *with* one another, without erasing the fundamental differences between religious and secular worldviews or modes of reasoning. American critic Stanley Fish (1999: 69–70) argues that Habermas falls at this hurdle, failing to respect the fundamental otherness of religious reasoning and its fundamental untranslatability into secular discourse. Even if Habermas does not share Fish's view that this is an insurmountable obstacle, he does not seem too optimistic about the possibility of finding adequate solidarity through this mode of translation. However, he sees no other tools with which to work.

This is where the political power of performance can present itself as a grammatical alternative that is distinct from – and thus points out the non-universalism of – the rational discussion of the coffeehouse. Habermas is, of course, a philosopher in the Kantian tradition. He conceives of the social work of religion in the terms of philosophy: as the making of propositional arguments, even if ones grounded in a form of reasoning foreign to the formal abstract logic of the Kantian tradition. And so the question of what can be allowed into the public sphere becomes a question of which arguments are valid, helpful or so on. But what if this is simply not the way religion operates? The logic of performance might be other than the propositional logic of philosophical argument; if the social solidarity religion offers is achieved through performative means, we have no need to articulate or translate the arguments it makes in order to describe, or make use of, its effectiveness.

Back in 1974, the anthropologist of religion Maurice Bloch coined a phrase that has become something of a mantra in the study of ritual: 'you cannot argue with a song' (Bloch 1974: 71). Bloch was not arguing that a song cannot advocate for and encourage ideas or positions that ought to be scrutinized. Rather, the medium is just too limited; there is simply no space within most songs for argumentative engagement.[1] That may mean that songs – by which, of course, Bloch meant dances, rituals and formalized performances of all sorts – are able to produce a sort of group identity, camaraderie and solidarity that are in an important sense 'unspeakable'. Charles Taylor (2011) has recently argued that post-secular society needs a recognizable concept of its collective identity in order to function; if that act of collective self-definition is grounded in definitions that make use of particularistic rather than universalistic reasoning – and Taylor proposes no universalistic basis for self-definition – then so be it. Perhaps this is the work that songs can do. But this also means there is no guarantee that the work done by these songs will be fair, healthy or democratic. There may be something totalitarian in a song that is particularly insidious *because* it is not susceptible to argument by a democratic public. This is Habermas's problem – how do you evoke an anti-egalitarian solidarity without giving in to the dangers of particularism? He hopes the common intellectual history of philosophy and the great religions will keep him from danger. I am not so sure.

In this context, I turn to my case study. Over the last decade and a half, the sex abuse scandal in the Catholic Church has taken a huge toll on the church's image amongst both its members and the rest of the world. Perhaps nowhere on earth has that scandal been as fiery as in the Republic of Ireland, where the church has for decades been the most important institution in the nation, with more influence and arguably more power than the state itself. For most of the Republic's history, the church had near-exclusive responsibility for the education and social welfare of Irish citizens, and it occupied a wide and powerful role in the civic life of the country. This is not a matter of a few paedophilic priests. It is, rather, an issue of an institution that has, for half a century, facilitated, justified and covered up decades of rape and torture of Irish children, particularly the most poor and vulnerable, in significant numbers.

The effect of this scandal has been so large as to exceed the bounds of criminal law to become a challenge to the legitimacy of political authority in Irish society. It touches on that unspoken and unspeakable ecclesial underpinning to the Republic, forcing Irishmen and women to re-examine basic assumptions about the nature and character of their social authorities; more specifically, the depth of just how fallible and untrustworthy they can be. Many of us have come to terms with a distrust of politicians, but extending this distrust to the church, and to such a hideous crime, is far more socially confounding. The anthropologist Victor Turner, looking ethnographically at different societies around the world, described such crises of authority as 'social dramas' (Turner 1974: 32–45). Like the deaths of kings, these were moments when cracks appeared in the underpinning structures of social authority. Turner noted that these dramas were essentially built on agonistic narratives and that they could end either with a reassertion of the social structure (with whatever modifications were necessary) or with its rupture. Very often, Turner found, ritual performance was the tool used to do that social work of reasserting or rupturing.

That is the case for the performances that this chapter will examine. They made use of both ritual traditions and performative innovations to do the work of healing – or at least reconfiguring – the relationships between society, church and state in Ireland, as well as between the republican humanist political philosophy of the Irish state and the nationalist, Catholic justification that sits just below the surface.

None of the four central performances that I will look at here consciously framed themselves as artworks. This is not to say that the Dublin theatre and art community did not respond to this crisis: it did, and continues to do so, in compelling and creative ways. Three of the most celebrated performances deserve a mention here. *The Blue Boy*, devised by Feidlim Cannon and Gary Keegan for their company, Brokentalkers, uses personal memory, multimedia, recorded interviews and masks to depict the experience of abuse at the so-called industrial schools. Gerald Mannix Flynn's *James X* uses a much simpler, personal testimonial approach to present his own story of abuse. And Louise Lowe's *Laundry*, staged by her company ANU Productions for the Dublin Theatre Festival in 2011, brought audience members into the site of the Magdalene Laundries, which acted as asylums, prisons and slave-labour houses for Irish women who had run afoul of social codes or contemporary sexual mores. Dublin's last Magdalene Laundry operated until 1996. In the performance, audience members walked through the space and had a series of one-to-one conversations with the inmates, eventually being given personal responsibility to help one escape.[2] All three of these productions were acclaimed and made an important contribution to the public debate on the crisis. But on the whole, their goal was aesthetic: they aimed to communicate a meaning to or provoke an emotional reaction in the spectator. They did not, as the performances I discuss below do, attempt to *intervene* directly in that crisis. In Austinian terms, this is the difference between a locutionary function and an illocutionary one. These three aesthetic performances were an important part of the public discussion surrounding the crisis, but the four I will discuss here attempted to change the facts *of* that crisis. Without denying the political potential of art, I see this distinction between aesthetic comment and illocutionary intervention as a useful one to maintain.

Two of the performances I analyse here took place in Dublin, one in Rome and one in London. Each, in its own way, was a ritual of healing. Two involved the church asking forgiveness for its past actions, so that its relationship to its members could be repaired, and two sought to re-establish the church's authority on different terms. Each was a necessary and proper response to the crisis, though none was wholly successful in its work. I hope that putting the four next to one another will clarify the performative struggle for the legitimation of authority in a society where church and state are as deeply imbricated as Ireland. While Ireland may be a strong case, it is far from unique: if Habermas's or Agamben's insights are as general as they claim, then the struggle between democratic and ecclesial authority at play in these performances can find its analogue in democratic societies far beyond Irish shores and is indeed one element in the grammar of politics and performance.

The breaking of a relationship as a result of misdeeds and the need to repair that relationship through forgiveness is, of course, a canonical story in Catholic doctrine: it is the situation in which we all find ourselves after the fall. The ritual performance the church has developed to fulfil that need for repair is confession, or, more formally, the Sacrament of Penance and Reconciliation. Confession is a performative means by which *individuals* can rid themselves of their sins and reconcile their relationship to God. In my first example, the church used a performative model of confession to devise a means of reconciling the church's relationship to the world.

As part of the 2000 Jubilee Year, Pope John Paul II conducted an extraordinary mass at St Peter's Basilica in Rome on 12 March, the First Sunday of Lent. Called the 'Day of Pardon', it was quite a simple service, but one that the Vatican hierarchy was unusually keen to establish as a liturgical innovation. It was a ritualized attempt by the church to admit its own faults, seek reconciliation from God and, in so doing, assert a new relationship between itself and the rest of the world.[3] The church had not attempted anything of its kind before, particularly in its effort to assert such a clean break with its own past. After a homily offered by the Pope imploring his flock to 'forgive and ask forgiveness', a succession of seven cardinals came forward to call on the church to confess past sins committed by its members and in its name. This litany of seven included sins in general, sins committed 'in the service of truth', sins of Christian disunity, sins against the Jewish people, sins allied with colonialism and missionary exploitation, sins against women and sins 'in relation to the fundamental rights of the person'. These cardinals were chosen to represent those parts of the church which, historically, were most involved with the issue for which they were asking pardon. The confession of sins in service of truth, for instance, was recited by the prefect of the office which, during the Counter-Reformation, led the Inquisition. (That prefect, interestingly, was Joseph Cardinal Ratzinger, later to become Pope Benedict XVI.) After each confession, the Pope, on behalf of the church, addressed his prayer for forgiveness to God, a Kyrie Eleison was sung in call and response and a lamp was lit. At the conclusion of these prayers, the Pope embraced the crucifix, according to the liturgy, 'as a sign of penance and veneration'. The tone of the ritual, as in much official Vatican liturgy, was thick with historical and intellectual reference, stately, sincere and formal.

As was intended, this small performance reverberated widely. Echoes of it sounded in formal responses from other religious groups, such as the United Methodists and the Israeli Chief Rabbinate. It also became a template for (and authorization of) others within the Catholic Church who sought a liturgical means of repenting for the church's past sins, both those of prior centuries and those much closer to home. It was also seen as a personal victory for John Paul II in his effort to repair the church's relationship with its non-Catholic neighbours, especially Protestants and Jews. Its use of all the church's trappings of institutional authority – the Pope's personal presence, the participation of high-level members of the Roman curia, the setting in St Peter's – made it appear that this was not John Paul personally but the church *as a body* which was seeking penance and reconciliation. That was new and provocative. Danielle Celermajer, in her study of national apologies, looks at the ritual as an effort to express 'the social nature of sin and repentance', which amounted to quite a radical move in the context of the privatization of the idea of sin and repentance in Catholic thought that she traces back at least to the sixteenth-century Council of Trent (Celermajer 2009: 139). Many of those who supported the 'Day of Pardon' saw it as an important move towards humbleness and reconciliation and one that invited response and dialogue from others.

However, not all of these reverberations were positive. Many critics thought the language used in the performance was too general. The lack of specific mention of the Holocaust, for instance, was upsetting to many Jews with whom John Paul II had been in dialogue, and others noted that while the sin of abortion was singled out for specific mention, no such specificity was offered for the 'sins against the dignity of women'. Others saw the service as mere words, even hypocritical ones, since they were not backed up by any new or meaningful action. More conservative voices objected to what they saw as a dangerous weakening of the Vatican's spiritual authority: as one of the church's key roles in the world is to facilitate the forgiveness of sin, an admission that the church herself is sinful might undermine her ability to perform that sacrament. They would have preferred a reiteration of the church's function as an evangelical teacher, bringing the light of the Gospel to the people of the world.

Some critics made more serious objections to the formal act being performed by this ritual. They relate to its initial development out of the sacrament of confession and the ways in which the Day of Pardon liturgy diverged from, or failed to fit within, that model. There were two major problems: who was speaking and who was being addressed. At the level of the speaker, it is clear in individual confession who is speaking: the individual Catholic person who has committed sins. But whether or not the church, as a body, can commit sins is somewhat thorny theologically. This new liturgy deliberately side-stepped this question by referring only to the sins of 'men of the Church' or 'Christians' or 'them'. By putting some distance between the institution of the church and those members of it who have sinned, the liturgy preserved the possibility of an unstained church, even if it has sinful members. This was a hotly debated issue at the time, and some Catholic theologians, such as Hans Küng, would have preferred a confession of sins that were genuinely *of* the church. Jeremy Bergen (2011: 127) describes the liturgy that was eventually adopted as 'deny[ing] the concept of collective guilt', but connects this to a traditional issue of collective guilt that John Paul had worked very hard to rebut: the collective guilt of the Jewish people for the death of Jesus.

While the issue of who was confessing was problematic, the question of *to whom* they were confessing was even more difficult. A confession of sin is not an apology, and the liturgy pointedly never used that word. Instead, it was an *acknowledgement* of past sins, a prayer *on behalf of* those who had been wronged by the church's actions and a request *to God* to forgive the church for its actions. The wronged parties themselves, as mere mortals, cannot grant forgiveness. The official explanation of the service stated that the Pope's confession of sins was 'addressed to God', but 'made before men' (Vatican 2000c). The human audience was formally acknowledged, but it was not the addressee. That audience – which, recall, is the very society with which the church hopes to heal its relationship – had no formal role in this Day of Pardon. Nothing was asked of it and its voices were not included.

This, of course, did not sit well with victims groups. Secrecy and silencing have played a key role facilitating the church's cover-up of sex abuse, and the absence of victims from this Day of Pardon seemed to be a continuation of that act of silencing. As this mass has served as the template for most other Catholic services of repentance or healing, including those in Ireland (such as Scallon 2011), they, too, seem to privilege the church's position over that of abuse victims and thus fail to do the necessary work of social reconciliation. Survivors of sexual abuse and their families tend to be particularly suspicious and dismissive of these ritual confessions. When I asked a representative of SNAP, the Survivors Network of those Abused by Priests, about such rituals, his response was clear:

> Speaking only for myself I place no value in the words of church officials. Both personally and [in] my work with dozens of survivors, I have found all church officials [to be] insincere, duplicitous and manipulative if not lying frauds ... I acknowledge that there are a few people who look to the church for atonement but I don't know any ... Until the church officials acknowledge full complicity in their cover-ups ... any other demonstration of 'atonement' is cruelly manipulative.
>
> (Lennon 2012)

Here, Lennon is equating the Catholic Church with its hierarchy. Theologically speaking, that is a mistake. While the hierarchy may be its most visible manifestation, the church consists of the community of believers. The hierarchy exists to serve and guide that community; it cannot wholly define it, no matter how much it may try. And so, here certainly are survivors who seek out healing and atonement in the context of rituals which we need to recognize as part of the church's work, even if they are quite particular rituals which take pains to marginalize the hierarchy.

My second example is a similar performance from the group MACSAS (Minister and Clergy Sexual Abuse Survivors). The group was founded by Margaret Kennedy, who has led it for over fifteen years. Both Catholic and Protestant clergy abuse survivors can join MACSAS, but its members are predominantly Catholic women, many with Irish roots. What differentiates MACSAS from other survivors organizations such as SNAP is that, as part of offering support and fellowship to its members, it has developed its own set of ritual performances to offer healing, support and community. These rituals take place either on private retreats amongst group members, or in ordinary churches as supplements to their regular weekly worship. The patterns and language of these liturgies have been developed collectively by MACSAS members over the years to reassert the relationship between themselves and their church in a way that speaks to their condition and is seen as a just and appropriate rebalancing of power between the church, victims and the state (MACSAS 2012; Kennedy 2012).

As liturgical innovations, these services deserve more attention than I can give them here.[4] I will limit myself to a single case: the 'Service of Remembrance and Proclamation' held 26 November 2011 at St Giles-in-the-Fields, a small Anglican church in London's West End traditionally known as the 'Poets' Church'. As noted on the service sheet, it was held 'as a part of a compensation agreement with the Diocese of London'. Though Archdeacon William Jacob served as rector, the service was typical of MACSAS's rituals. The liturgy was assembled and guided entirely by survivors; Dr Jacob read what had been written for him. Rather than the stately formality of the Roman Day of Pardon, the congregation was raucous and participatory; there was not just group singing but shouting, clapping and stomping of feet.

I want to highlight three aspects of that ritual that demonstrate the ways it modelled – and thus, sought to create – a new and reconfigured relationship between personal, ecclesial and civil authority. The first is an emphasis on the community of survivors collectively sharing their personal stories, which is the basis of much of MACSAS's work. While not all MACSAS members are comfortable sharing stories in public, the group placed a great value on the courage of those who are. The liturgy at St Giles was structured wholly around Dr Kennedy's story of rape, survival and overcoming, including her history with MACSAS and her Ph.D. work on clerical sexual exploitation of adult women. The prayers and litanies that framed this story both emphasized the participants as survivors becoming legitimate, speaking subjects against the backdrop of a church that had tried to silence them, and used a call-and-response form that drew attention to the collective nature of that emergence:

> Survivor: We were not supposed to talk
> All: We were meant to be silent
> Survivor: We were meant to keep it a secret
> All: But now we are talking
> Survivor: We were not supposed to be angry
> All: But now we are raging

Survivor: We were not allowed to cry
All: Now we are weeping.

(Kennedy 2011: 6)

In this prayer, the survivors are speaking protagonists, and the antagonist is the expectations imposed on them by church authorities and others. By focusing on the voice of the survivor, and by placing the act of sharing stories at the heart of this ritual, this service took up a very different subject position than the Roman example. The service did not involve survivors addressing the church, as much political advocacy on behalf of survivors tends to do. Rather, in this performance, survivors addressed God in their own voice, but more frequently, they addressed one another, often in the second and third person plural. The performative assertion of the community of survivors as a speaking subject is a supremely political act. In itself, this assertion marks a major part of the new political reality which this performance aims to create.

Second, these narratives were performed in as participatory a manner as possible, within a much less hierarchical form than other church rituals. This may be due to these performances' origins in retreats run by MACSAS and its predecessor, Christian Survivors of Sexual Abuse (CSSA). One technique that MACSAS often uses is the participatory visual aid, which Kennedy explained was particularly useful. Generally, each person is given a small paper shape – at St Giles, these were 'peace birds' – on which they are invited to make their contribution (what they fear, pray for, feel or something similar), all of which are then brought together into a single image and transformed in this act of sharing. One service asked attendees to write their fears on teardrops, which were then placed on a large poster in which they, together, watered flowers. In another service, attendees wrote their emotions onto white bricks, which were then built into a wall that was knocked down over the course of the service. For similar reasons, there is a great deal of communal hymn singing: simple, anthemic hymns that reinforce the intended emotional message and build bonds of group solidarity. A modified version of 'The Servant Song', by late-twentieth-century Methodist New Zealander Richard Gillard is especially popular, with its emphasis on struggle and solidarity: 'We are pilgrims on a journey / we are travellers on the Road; / We are here to help each other / walk the mile and bear the Load.'

Third, the metanarrative into which the St Giles service fits remains a firmly Christian one. The liturgy speaks of God and Christ; it included a reading from Romans 8; and in fact, the wording of Kennedy's prayers was not wholly different than John Paul's. While both were Christian services, they took as their models different sacramental narratives. Rather than the narrative of a relationship broken through sin and healed through confession and forgiveness – which is a story told from the sinner's perspective – MACSAS's service offers as its key narrative the coming together of the whole community of believers in their particularity for worship and celebration. If the Roman Day of Pardon was modelled on confession, the St Giles service was modelled on the Eucharist. I think we do MACSAS an injustice if we regard their work as post-Christian or anti-Christian.

There is anger here about the sins of church officials, certainly, but there is no desire to separate from the church. In fact, the political work of this performance is the opposite: it is not a declaration of independence, but a (just and loving) demand for a deserved place around the Lord's Table.

MACSAS's performances, though astute politically and effective in giving survivors a voice to address the acute and specific trauma they face, have rarely if ever attracted much attention in the wider community. The larger social trauma created by the sexual abuse scandal is not really something MACNAS's work addresses. There are a number of reasons for that. MACSAS necessarily tailors its work to the relatively small community of survivors and their closest allies. For the sake of its supportive character, such communities need to be guarded as safe, semi-private spaces. It is reasonable that the press and the public do not wish to intrude, and as a consequence, such services are less well known. There is another issue, however. If we recognize the crisis of social authority to be profound and serious, we are more likely to put credence in a performance that seeks to address it using modes of performance that, through formal ritualization, match what we have been taught to recognize as profound and serious. The Pope and seven cardinals in full regalia (all men, of course) appear to meet that criteria. A group of middle-aged women sharing stories, doing crafts together and literally singing 'Kumbaya' do not, however much authority we *wish* they had or how much authority they *deserve*. One of Catherine Bell's arguments regarding ritualization (echoing those of Bloch decades earlier) is that its use of authorized and formalized clothing, actions, movements and words is part of how we come to recognize ritual actions as supra-mundane and thus deserving of our attention (Bell 1997: 139–50). MACSAS's rituals make use of none of these markers of formality and authority.[5] These performances, though effective, simply are not structured to be recognized as 'serious' rituals.

My third example draws the first two together. Could a ritual be devised that combines the visible seriousness of the Roman Day of Pardon, but avoids its philosophical problems? Could one make a performance that revolves around the voices of survivors, as in MACSAS's work, but gains greater social resonance through formal ritualization? If such a performance were possible, I would argue that it would look something like the extraordinary Liturgy of Lament and Repentance held in Dublin in February of 2011, at St Mary's Pro Cathedral, Dublin, and led by Dublin Archbishop Diarmuid Martin and apostolic visitor Cardinal Sean O'Malley, the Archbishop of Boston (Archdiocese of Dublin 2011a). This was a formal worship service in Dublin's largest Catholic Cathedral, and the liturgy was written by the two archbishops in consultation with survivors' groups. Unlike the Day of Pardon, victims of sexual abuse spoke first and often of their own experience. When the archbishops spoke, they said what they ought to say: both explicitly admitted the church's sin and asked forgiveness on their own behalf and on behalf of the church, not only of God but also of the survivors themselves. They acknowledged the survivors' experience and that there was little they could say in the face of it. They explicitly said that they did not expect forgiveness to be wholly granted on that day and acknowledged that this was the beginning of a long healing process. But the service nevertheless marked a break between a sinful church that had refused to listen and a more humble one that sought forgiveness.

The correct words, though, were not enough. Because of the mistrust that had accumulated, the church had lost its authority to make persuasive arguments. The performance created was designed to circumvent discursive logic and make an affective case for a new relationship between the church hierarchy and the Irish public. This ritual used a number of performative means to make this case affectively persuasive without articulating an argument for it; I will highlight three here.

First, the service made excellent use of silence and stillness to model the church's humility and desire to listen. In the opening moment, the two archbishops prostrated themselves before an empty altar, where they lay on the floor in complete silence for nearly a minute before the choir began to sing. This is not a posture we expect to see an archbishop assume. Opening the service with this act of self-abasement by two authority figures visibly and affectively demonstrated the more humble political role into which the church sought to place itself (without, of course, making any actual promise of a changed church policy to which it would be committed). It also set a more equal tone for what followed, which was less a church call for repentance, as in Rome, and more a dialogue between church authorities and abuse survivors. Archbishop Martin gave a homily on silence, addressed directly to abuse victims in the second person. He asked that an archbishop not preside over this liturgy, but instead that it be presided over by the silent Cross. He spoke about his inability to accomplish the forgiveness he wished with his own words, concluding: 'I, as Archbishop of Dublin and as Diarmuid Martin, stand here in this silence and I ask forgiveness of God and I ask for the first steps of forgiveness from of [sic] all the survivors of abuse' (Archdiocese of Dublin 2011b: para. 9). While it is not quite true that Martin did not preside over the service, this remains an extraordinarily passive role for the church as an institution to adopt.

Second, if one of the church's difficulties was the hierarchy's inability to speak with authority, the service consciously incorporated a number of different voices to emphasize that the desire to heal was not the church's alone. As I have mentioned, survivors themselves composed the liturgy alongside the archbishops, and the church's public willingness to listen to their testimony and experiences was central to what the ritual was designed to demonstrate. At least one survivor, however, came up to the altar uninvited to tell his story. He wore jeans, carried a rucksack and had a far less polished manner than the other speakers; this intervention was clearly not scripted. Archbishop Martin, however, stood back and allowed him to continue, and he received substantial applause when he finished. The liturgy also included lengthy readings from the Murphy and Ryan Reports, the Irish government's *civil* investigations into sexual abuse in the Dublin Archdiocese and at Catholic residential schools, as well. The texts, which were unequivocal and much harsher than the archbishops' own words, were read from the choir with amplification such that the speaker was not visible to those assembled. This disembodiment in the cathedral setting gave the text substantial authority, and, as these much-discussed reports were certainly recognized by most attendees, it was a case of a civil document being used to bolster the effect and power of a religious rite.

Thirdly, the service used the ritual of footwashing. This moment of the service was the most memorable to those in attendance and provoked considerable tears. In an echo of Jesus's gesture of humbling himself before his disciples at the Last Supper – and also echoing a traditional Catholic practice of Maundy Thursday – the two archbishops washed the feet of six abuse survivors who had been invited to the altar. The survivors sat on elevated chairs and the archbishops remained at the level of their feet. This took place in silence. Some of the survivors held hands. Again, the symbolism was legible, traditional and powerful; it drew potency from its grounding in known Catholic symbolism, even if the meaning of the gesture was particular to this ritual. Footwashing, or 'Pedivaldium', has been described as the 'sacrament that almost made it' into the canon (Macchia 1997: 239; see also Thomas 2004). Karl Barth noted that, in the Gospel of John, the rest of the Last Supper does not appear and the scene of footwashing takes its place, emphasizing Jesus's role as servant (Barth 1961: 3. 476). Frank Macchia (1997: 247) considers footwashing as an antidote to the oversacramentalism of the church and that its continuing use 'implies that holiness must be understood in solidarity with the poor and oppressed'. While the theological details of footwashing may not have been known to all those in attendance, its humble, anti-authoritarian and Christian references still resonated.

The 'footwashing service', as it was generally known, was the subject of a great deal of discussion around Ireland and, unlike the Roman Day of Pardon, the response was generally positive. While for many, the service was still too little, too late, it was a performance with clear and understood intentions, similar to those of the promised Dublin memorial that is to be built to victims of clerical child abuse. I do think this performance was able to articulate a relationship between the church hierarchy and survivors that was satisfying for some part of the public, which knows it will never see an Irish archbishop charged with a crime. Sadly, this goodwill was short-lived. Following further reports on sexual abuse in the Archdiocese and the complicity of the hierarchy, charges of hypocrisy immediately arose again. Jill Dolan describes the potential that performative forms have to model the feeling of utopia as 'ephemeral but powerful' (Dolan 2005: 63). That seems to have been the case here; despite its potency, the affect of solidarity the service offered was not robust or permanent enough to overshadow the stream of revelations.

Even in the short term, though, members of the Irish public welcomed this performance. Some of the least welcoming were survivors themselves. A small number of them picketed in front of the Pro Cathedral during the service. Those who did allow themselves to have their feet washed were quite conflicted and were seen as collaborators and sellouts by other members of the survivors' community.[6] But again, consider the political work that the performance aimed to achieve. The church sought to restore its claim to social authority and this required it to actively, publicly, sincerely and openly acknowledge its sins and seek forgiveness from those who had been abused by it. This is the case whether the survivors welcome such a move or not; for the social drama to play out, their participation is required, but their consent is not. It might be that this service performed the relationship that the Irish people would like the church to have to the survivors, regardless of what the survivors themselves would wish.

Thus for some, the only spiritually satisfying performance was my final example, which was not a church service at all. In July 2011, a devastating report on child abuse in the Cork area diocese of Cloyne and the Vatican's efforts to keep information about this abuse away from civil authorities was published. That month, the Taoiseach (prime minister), Enda Kenny, gave a speech in the Irish Parliament in which he declared that 'the historical relationship between church and state in Ireland could not be the same again'. The speech, which did not shy away from terms like 'rape', 'torture' and 'betrayal', was the most defiant any Irish government had ever been towards the Vatican.

> This is not Rome. Nor is it industrial school or Magdalene Ireland, where the swish of a soutane, smothered conscience and humanity and the swing of a thurible ruled the Irish Catholic world This is the Republic of Ireland in 2011. It is a republic of laws, of rights and responsibilities; of proper civic order; where the delinquency and arrogance of a particular version, of a particular kind of 'morality', will no longer be tolerated or ignored.
>
> (Dáil Éireann 2011: 520)

These words struck a nerve. The speech was reprinted in full on the front page of the next day's *Irish Times* and received extensive coverage in the media and online. Though it was a simple parliamentary speech, the image of a politician defying the Vatican was hugely popular. It is worth noting that this was, in fact, a performance and not a meaningful act of governance. As a parliamentary speech, it was not made in support of any substantial piece of legislation. No policies were changed, no diplomats were expelled and no bishops were arrested. Certainly, this was a political act, but I see no reason to treat it as any more or less of one than the other performances this chapter has described. The difference was only the authorization of the actor: the elected political authority of government was able to exercise a form of sovereignty (in Agamben's terms) that archbishops, survivors and popes could not.

A few months later, Ireland closed its embassy in the Vatican. The explanation that this was simply a cost-cutting measure, while perhaps true, was believed by almost no one. While some disagreed with the decision, for many survivors, this was exactly the spiritual boost that they had sought. This was not a meaningful diplomatic change; Ireland's diplomatic affairs at the Vatican can easily be handled through its Italian embassy, also in Rome. Rather, this was a ritual of dissociation which, like all effective solutions to social dramas, served to inscribe a new and more stable social order on Irish society.

Interestingly, this was an appeal to the justice, power and strength of the *state*, not to a concept of solidarity that transcends democratic politics. From this final example, we might even conclude that Habermas's 'what is missing' may, in fact, be able to be found *within* the democratic political order itself, at least in those cases where the assertion of the common rights of humanity can be assimilated into a zealous patriotism for the republic. In the presence of a villain church, a state may temporarily play spiritual saviour. This is not sustainable in the long run. However, from these attempts to build justice in response to this crisis, one can see a few ways in which these performances address social crises by filling civic needs with religious imagery and religious needs with civic language.

Religious and democratic authority necessarily exist in an unstable tension in the post-secular society. The distinction between the ultimate sovereignty of religion and the governing authority of the polis is both essential to and an impediment for the modern constitutional state. The necessary blurring that this tension demands is one that performance is well equipped to accomplish. This has certainly been the case for the recent crisis of legitimacy in the Irish state.

However, I would suggest that we understand this case not as a specifically Irish problem, nor as one particular to nations with a history of strong religious identification. Around the world, recent decades have seen both a growth in religious tensions as secularism fades and an increasing scepticism that the formal mechanisms of democratic elections can ensure a genuinely democratic form of government. When crises come, as they did in Ireland, the legitimacy of authority needs to be re-established and a variety of performative means can be used to do so. I would suggest that the greater lesson to be drawn from this case is that such performances seem to function more effectively when they are agonistic. The traditional agon in post-Enlightenment political theory has been between church and state, and this remains an active and necessary form of legitimation in many parts of the world. But the pattern of forgiveness and healing suggests that a different agon is possible: that between the (flawed) past and the (corrected) future. In Ireland, the church sought to perform this agon to relegitimize itself after the abuse crisis, using its past sinful character as antagonist to the humble, listening church of the present. Grammatically, that agon holds much promise as non-revolutionary means of renewing authority But should it fail, the traditional agonistic relationship between church and state remains present, potent and performable to affectively assert a solidarity that impersonal reason alone cannot manage.

Notes

1 More technically, Bloch (1974) argues that rituals as a genre make use of highly formalized, limited and thus impoverished forms of communication, in terms of language, gesture and all other communicative forms. There is thus effectively no 'meaning' in the act of performing a ritual; if meaning is based on the ability to choose between one semantic option and another, and ritual is designed to formalize all communicative acts and thus minimize the choice available, there is no choice and thus no meaning. Ritual songs, because they 'almost completely predict the linguistic journey that the singer undertakes', are necessarily in a situation where 'no argument can be communicated' (ibid. 71). Such communication has 'no propositional force. It has only illocutionary force'

(ibid. 76). Interestingly, Bloch sees this emphasis on persuasion over argumentation as characteristic of religion *as opposed to* politics. The latter, he argues, needs more supple tools that can address contingent reality, while the former has no such need. While I find Bloch's reasoning helpful, as this chapter will show, I do not think the line between *Realpolitik* and impractical religion can be drawn so neatly.

2 In addition to Lisa Fitzpatrick's Chapter 5 in this volume on *Laundry*, see also Singleton (2013).
3 For more on the service, see Bergen (2011: ch. 4). The Vatican also created a website for the service (Vatican 2000a), which includes the service text (Vatican 2000b).
4 I discuss the liturgical work of MACSAS and its predecessor, Christian Survivors of Sexual Abuse, more fully in Edelman (2014).
5 Bell's larger discussion requires her to distinguish between 'formalism' and 'traditionalism'; my argument here refers to both.
6 I draw this fact from personal discussions with survivors in Ireland which, for reasons of confidentiality, I cannot cite more fully here.

14 Closet grammars of intentional deception

The logic of lies, state security and homosexual panic in cold war politics

James M. Harding

On the performative logic of lies and the politics of the right to know: an introduction to intelligence, espionage and state secrets

If such a thing as a grammar of truth existed, one would be hard pressed to find a more basic principle for that grammar than the bold assertion made by Nietzsche's Zarathustra when he proclaims, 'Whoever is unable to lie does not know what truth is'.[1] The funny thing about lying, however, is that unlike telling the truth, lying – by most definitions of the term – is marked by a much more complex level of intentionality than is normally associated with most forms of telling the truth. Indeed, the philosopher David Simpson not only defines lying as an act of deliberate untruthfulness and of 'intentional deception', but he emphasizes that lying is something that we 'do [...] to someone' (1992: 624–5).[2] Every liar, Simpson argues furthermore, 'assumes the possibility of [falsely] representing some state of affairs and of presenting him or herself as believing that representation' (634). There is an undeniable aura of performance hovering about this kind of assumption and self-presentation, and hence hovering about lying itself. Not only does the assumption cited by Simpson require the kind of self-reflexivity that performance studies scholars have long associated with performance as a concept; inasmuch as lying is something one does 'to someone', the presentation of one's self as 'believing that representation' is a unique kind of performance because it also works on an audience or public that ultimately does not remain unaffected by the lie done to them.

The liar performs, but so too does the lie itself. The lie performs its effects on the liar's audience, and inasmuch as lies have currency and influence in the public sphere, they always possess a political undercurrent as well. In short, lying is as transactional as it is performative, and it is thus located at the intersection of performance and politics.

Rather than focusing on the intersection of performance and politics, however, most philosophical discussions of lying address the broader issues of ethics and morality that are part of the baggage that accompanies even the very attempt to define what constitutes a lie as such. Typical in this regard are reflections on the fundamental principles – the grammar, as it were – of the act of lying: reflections, for example, on whether 'a false statement [made] with the intent to deceive others' (Carson 2006: 286) is always wrong regardless of context and circumstance or, conversely, whether there are instances when such statements are nonetheless ethically and morally permissible and thus do not actually constitute 'genuine cases of lying' (287). In his reflections on morality, ethics and 'The Definition of Lying', for example, Thomas Carson notes that 'the most well-known version' of this latter approach argues that 'a necessary condition of one's lying is that the person to whom one's statement is directed has a right to know the truth, so that speaking falsely to someone who has no right to know the truth cannot be a lie' (ibid.). If there is a sense of performance accompanying the telling of lies more generally, so too is there an underlying grammar of performance to be found in the classic ethical distinction that Carson cites between immoral and morally justifiable uses of false statements and intentional deception. But it is a grammar that is less scripted than improvizational and that is less prescriptive than descriptive.

In some respects, that grammar corresponds roughly with Noam Chomsky's famous distinction between the surface and deep structures of discourse. Like Chomsky's rather quixotic quest for a universal grammar (a quest that he ultimately abandoned), philosophers too have struggled to find the moral and ethical bedrock buried in the deep structures beneath the surface of expressions consciously formulated with the intent to deceive – buried, that is, beneath false statements that on the surface would seem, if detected, to be lies, but that, following the rule of the 'right to know', may not be lies at all. While philosophers may debate the deep structures of this later distinction, the reasons for citing it as a point of departure for this chapter are multiple. First of all, regardless of whether 'speaking falsely to someone who has no right to know the truth' does or does not constitute a 'genuine case of lying', it still involves a self-reflexive presentation of fabrication as fact. It is still a performance. And second, it is the kind of performance that is woven into the very fabric of modern notions of the state, of the politics of state secrecy and, most important of all, of the consciously deceptive practices of state-sanctioned espionage and intelligence gathering. Morally and ethically contested though 'intentional deception' may be, its use in both private and public social interactions comprises one of the crucial intersections of performance and politics, and hence is the focus of this chapter.

In the affairs of the state, the tension between the 'right to know' and the calculated diversions of 'intentional deception' – not only against those who do not have the 'right to know' but also by those who, in the name of one state, want to know what another state chooses to classify, secure and hide – obviously involves much more than the telling of an individual lie. What I want to suggest here, though, is that the logic of the lie – with all of its moral and ethical ambiguity – makes up the underlying grammar of state security and intelligence gathering. I am less concerned here with the cumulative individual lies that facilitate what Eva Horn has described as 'the very essence of state security' (2011: 107) than I am with a more general sense of praxis and with a mode of performance – fictions and fabrications constructed and performed on a grand scale – that echo in an expansive and resonant way Simpson's basic notion that an individual lie is something that we 'do [...] to someone'.

Broadly conceived, Simpson's precept is the foundational grammar of a very special and problematic mode of the performance of politics: the politics of security and intelligence. Indeed, its structural traces are hard to miss in serious reflections on the ethical consequences of intelligence gathering. Writing specifically on the question of the ethics of intelligence collection, for example, Ross Bellaby argues:

> Intelligence collection can [...] violate an individual's autonomy when it uses deception or manipulation. Using 'unofficial covers' [...] whereby an intelligence officer receives a new identity to allow access to areas and people otherwise out of reach, involves extensive levels of deception and manipulation. However, by intentionally providing another individual with false information, the intelligence officer is distorting the individual's view of reality and therefore forcing the individual into decisions based on the officer's terms rather than his own reasons and wishes.
>
> (2012: 106)

It is Bellaby's contention that the rules are fairly clear about who is a 'legitimate target' for such strategies of 'deception or manipulation'. Just as a soldier is bound by international law to distinguish between actual combatants and civilians, so too are members of the intelligence community bound, according to Bellaby, to target their own kind. Only those who have consented to 'participate in the world of national security', he maintains, count as legitimate targets for the 'deception and manipulations' that are the stock and trade – the cloak and dagger – of intelligence work (115).[3] And yet history reminds us time and again that this is not the case. Beneath the surface-level clarity of Bellaby's argument the deep structural and historical realities of state security and intelligence are murky, and their distinctions between legitimate and unacceptable targets have always been provisional at best.

In this chapter I want to suggest that historically the political performances of those deep structural realities – the grammar of security and intelligence – have played out against the backdrop of competing notions of the right to know, the desire to know and the right to keep secrets or maintain privacy. I would suggest furthermore that those performances are torn between two centres of political tension. First of all, there is, on the one hand, the formidable tension that exists in Western democracies between the state's legitimate need for security, secrecy and intelligence and its democratic obligations, on the other hand, to transparency, oversight and the rule of law. Second, so too is there the significant tension that exists between an individual's legitimate expectation or right to personal privacy and the state's presumptive right to violate privacy in the name of security regardless whether an individual does or does not belong to the world of national security operatives. On the surface of things, these two centres of tension are not necessarily in conflict. There are, as Horn notes in an echo of a long line of political philosophers, 'clandestine means for achieving laudable goals' (2011: 113). But further beneath the surface in the deep structures of what we might call the dark secrecy of state (in)securities the two have a long history of clashing. Following the logic of the lie – the grammar of surface and deep structures – the laudability of the goals mentioned by Horn may or may not justify the means, and, as she herself notes, the sanctioned use of state secrecy may cloak a downward spiral that crosses 'the boundary [... separating a] government's rational rules' from 'its vices' (ibid.). Echoing the seventeenth-century political philosopher Arnold Clapmarius, Horn notes that 'the "secure and secret privileges of maintaining power"' ought not to be confused with 'the misdeeds and infamies of power' (ibid.). Be that as it may, in the centuries that have followed Clapmarius, the former has consistently provided opportunity and cover for the latter.

Examples from the history of espionage repeatedly confirm this latter assertion, but among those examples few have been taken up as publicly or with such revealing self-reflexivity as has the history of the Austrian intelligence officer and double agent Colonel Alfred Redl, not only by the intelligence community itself but also by the theatrical community as well: by those who swear by politics and those who swear by performance. Indeed, Redl's own personal history provides a classic case study in the clash between state secrecy and personal privacy that I am suggesting is foundational to the grammar of politics and performance within the realms of intelligence and espionage. But it is not merely Redl's personal history in and of itself that provides the most revealing insight into that grammar. It is how Redl's personal history has been used to deceive and manipulate the public, how on the surface of things it has been brandished in the name of national security to justify bigoted goals and presented in the name of the US government's 'rational rules' to sustain 'its vices' – how, in short, it has been adapted to the logic of the lie – that makes Redl's personal history and legacy of interest here.

Political deception, passing secrets and the closet: the many performances of Colonel Alfred Redl

As a historical figure, Colonel Alfred Redl has been through many performances. A career officer of humble origins, Redl performed well enough to rise quickly through the ranks of the Austrian Army around the turn of the twentieth century. His performance at the academy was equally impressive. He graduated from the Lemberg Cadet School in 1878, and by 1900 he had become 'an officer in General Baron von Giesel's Kundschaftsstelle, [which was] Austria's counterintelligence corp'. In the KS, he excelled as well. He became head of counterintelligence in Vienna, modernizing its techniques of surveillance, interrogation and intelligence gathering. After breaking an alleged spy ring, he was promoted in 1907 'to the rank of major and named [...] director of espionage for Austria'. With his new assignment, he left Vienna for Prague where he became a colonel and had direct communications with 'the chief of staff for [... Austria's] Eighth Army' until he committed suicide in 1913 (Hearn 2006: 364–6). Those familiar with the history of Redl know the reason for his suicide. Beneath the brilliant performances of a seemingly stellar career, Redl was involved in an altogether different performance, leading a double life ultimately discovered by an intelligence officer to whom Redl, ironically, had taught the very techniques of counterintelligence that ultimately led to his own downfall.

For over a decade Redl had sold vital Austrian military secrets first to the Russians, then to the French and the Italians, and finally to anyone who was willing to buy them. Even his early renown for having broken the spy ring was an instance of cunning political performance. When, for example, the Austrian Foreign Office learned that the Russians had somehow obtained documents outlining Austria's contingency war plans – documents that Redl, in fact, had provided the Russians – Redl was given the assignment to find the traitor. So in an act of profound cynicism, the Russians decided to sell out some of their own agents in order to protect someone whom they considered to be more valuable. They gave Redl the names of some low-level spies in Austria whom Redl subsequently had arrested and framed for the espionage that he himself had done. In a very literal sense, this was the kind of lie that one does 'to someone'.

This staged arrest and framing of other low-level players was clearly only the opening act, but a decade later, when Redl was finally apprehended, the scope of his treasonous performances – the scope of his breach of the 'right to know' rules – was never revealed because it was never learned. As an apparent point of honour, his fellow Austrian officers followed the ritualized codes of their own profession and gave him the opportunity to kill himself before he was interrogated. Such ritualized practices are a mode of performance in their own right, but precisely what kind of performance surrounded Redl's suicide is difficult to say. In her essay on the 'Logics of Political Secrecy', Horn reminds us that 'secrecy has its own rules and limits, rules of caution, rational foresight, and strategic shrewdness' (2011: 113). What remains unclear in the historical record of Redl's suicide is whether the rules of secrecy were in play in the suicide itself: whether in the deep structure of a ritualized suicide, the codes of military honour were exploited so that Redl would be unable to implicate potential co-conspirators during the brutal interrogation that would have preceded his inevitable subsequent execution. This is the kind of performance that is the stuff of speculation, conspiracy theories and grand lies. Shrouded in secrecy, it is also the stock and trade of high stakes politics performing in the shadowy realms of intelligence communities.

Whatever the circumstances of Redl's suicide, the amount of material that he passed on to the Russians and others was substantial enough to have made him one of the most infamous figures in the history of espionage. But it was not the sheer quantity of material that Redl sold to Austria's enemies and rivals that has given him enduring notoriety. Rather it was the much more personal level of intentional deception that was a necessary part of his private daily life. Added to the deceptive manipulations and performances of espionage, counter-espionage and political betrayal, Redl was involved in a much deeper and personal mode of performance, one that has been at the centre of controversy for more than three-quarters of a century and that bridges the politics of secrecy and the rules of the 'right to know' with those of a cautiously guarded sense of personal privacy. Beneath Redl's uniform, a queer man was passing in a profoundly homophobic political organization. This was no easy performance in a institution like the Austrian military intelligence corps at the beginning of the twentieth century, and I would suggest that the weight of the bias against homosexuality with which Redl had to contend was strong enough to carry over into the written histories about him, but more about that momentarily.

Those histories tell us as much about the performative logic of state secrecy and its politics as they do about Redl himself. With regard to secrecy in general, it is worth recalling that in his essay 'To Do Justice to Freud', Derrida argues that 'the secret of the secret' is that it is an 'art and technique' (1994: 246) and that secrets are not so much kept as they are used for 'effect'. Indeed, their value resides in what Derrida calls 'the secrecy effect' (1994: 245), an effect that Derrida likens to magic and that is achieved by knowing how to make others 'suppose knowledge and believe in the secret' (246). There is clearly a performative sleight of hand in all of this: a substitution of knowledge and fact with an assertion whose veracity cannot be challenged or subjected to scrutiny by the many because its status is privileged, classified and accessible only to an elect few.

Secrets – particularly state secrets – are what individuals are required to accept more often than they are what individuals are allowed to share and know, even when secrets have a profound effect on the individual lives of the many or of an unprivileged minority. It is this powerful aspect of a secret, namely its effect, that ultimately challenges Eva Horn's notion that 'fiction is actually the only (or at least the most lucid) way to speak, as it were, "openly" about the precise nature of political secrecy without falling into the trap of the secrecy effect' (2011: 118). By contrast, I would suggest that it is hard to see how fiction – which by definition is a self-acknowledged fabrication – can contend with the force of an assertion whose veracity is beyond challenge or scrutiny and whose tangible political power can literally destroy people's lives. The secret is less like fiction than it is like the lie. Indeed, the secret is something, like the lie, that one does to someone. And the secret does things as well. Like the lie, it is performative.

Following the rules of the 'right to know', Redl was certainly doing something to others in the secrecy that he maintained not only about his sexual identity but also about his partial Jewish heritage as well. In an obvious sense, this was largely a defensive maneuver to keep others from doing something bigoted and discriminatory against him. That is the logic of passing. But if the performative aspects of secrecy – 'the secrecy effect' – are true on an individual level, as is the case with Redl's passing, they are also true on a grander scale with regard to the politics of state secrecy. Some indication of that grand-scale 'secrecy effect' is evident in the impact that the intelligence community has had in propagating a specific historical narrative about Redl's acts as a double agent.

Based in large part on the privileged authority of narratives provided by the intelligence community itself, historical accounts tend toward a one-sided explanation of Redl's decision to turn. The general argument, as we will see momentarily, is that Redl betrayed his country because the Russians photographed him with a male lover and were thus able to blackmail him into passing state secrets. Yet this narrative is simplistic enough to be misleading, and that is in fact what makes it interesting. It is not merely that the large sums of money that Redl received from the Russians as well as from others like the French and Italians complicate the blackmail narrative and leave a great degree of uncertainty about whether Redl was blackmailed or motivated by financial gain. Misleading though it may be, the blackmail narrative has enjoyed a powerful enough cultural and political resonance that if one is to speak of Alfred Redl's many performances, it is as important to consider how his history has performed politically as it is to consider the politics of his own performances.

Ultimately, the question of how Redl's history has performed politically is about deep structure – where the telling of his tale has less to do with Redl himself than with the political interests of those who, beneath the surface, have bent his history to serve their own agendas. These bent historical narratives are not simple lies, but they do follow the performative logic of lies. Indeed, the force of these narratives – how they actually perform – derives in large part from the fact that they have occurred at sites that sanction 'intentional deception', and also from the fact that the telling of these deceptive narratives has played out against the backdrop of competing notions of the 'right to know'. Here the question of performance is not so much about accuracy or the bending of the facts pertaining to Redl's history as it is about the multi-layered politics of security and privacy. It is about how the constructed narratives of Redl's history regulate access to a privileged, secret and altogether different body of knowledge and praxis.

Much of that regulation is the product of using Redl's manipulated history to perform diversionary tactics – a strategy that ironically turns the bent historical narrative of Redl into a prime example of the very praxis that it is intended to conceal and protect. So to speak of how Redl's history has performed politically is to speak of how the conscious manipulation of his historical narrative has functioned as a kind of political ruse: a stratagem of forwarding one narrative that is controversial enough to divert political attention from activities and practices that might not stand the test of public scrutiny. When such stratagems become visible, it tends to result from a disconnect between the manipulated appropriation of Redl's history and the context in which that appropriation occurred, and this brings us to two mid-century appropriations of Redl's narrative. In both instances, politics and performance converged in forums and formats where 'the secrecy effect' was on full display.

The first appropriation surfaced at an unlikely site. Far removed from the cultural and historical contexts of the Austro-Hungarian Empire, a manipulated version of Redl's history found its way, of all places, into the halls of the United States Congress. There performance and politics have a long history of converging in carefully staged congressional hearings, but few moments have matched the theatrics in the hearings associated with the communist witch-hunts of McCarthyism. In 1950, an offshoot of those same hearings began when the Senate

Committee on Expenditures in Executive Departments commissioned a subcommittee to investigate the presence of homosexuals in the government and the security risks that their employment supposedly entailed. Behind the scenes, the intelligence community was deeply invested in the outcome of the hearings associated with that investigation. That investment became readily apparent when the head of the CIA gave testimony that suddenly made the case of Alfred Redl the centrepiece of those hearings, since the version of Redl's history that he presented conveniently confirmed the committee's governing assumption that homosexuals were susceptible to blackmail and hence a risk to state security. Indeed, the skewed CIA testimony provided the only 'documented' evidence confirming this assumption.

Perhaps with the privilege of historical hindsight – the kind of hindsight that still has visions of Secretary of State Colin Powell presenting doctored evidence before the UN Security Council in 2003 in order to rationalize the pending war with Iraq – the image of the CIA colluding with a Senate subcommittee and presenting false historical narratives in 1950 may seem a bit quaint. But beyond the simple blurring of politics and performance, this collusion marks a key transformation in the public sphere. One might cite the collusion as a moment when the prerogatives of state security eclipsed democratic demands for transparency and oversight. Perhaps a more accurate characterization, I would suggest, would be to describe the collusion as a moment when the intelligence community usurped a system of checks and balances, effectively turning that system into a public theatre not for debating or exploring, but for obscuring its own unspecified interests. 'This', Horn notes, 'is what secrecy is all about': keeping 'compromising information locked away not only from public scrutiny but from government scrutiny as well' (2011: 116). As will become apparent momentarily, in 1950 that 'compromising information' had little to do with sexual orientation but the public's interest in issues of sexual orientation had a lot to do with keeping genuinely compromising information locked away.

The second appropriation may seem as far removed from the halls of the US Congress as it was from the security apparatus of the Austro-Hungarian Empire. But perhaps London's Royal Court Theatre was a less unlikely site for a manipulated narrative of Redl's history. There in June of 1965 John Osborne's play *A Patriot for Me* premiered.[4] The production of Osborne's play, which took provocative artistic license with Redl's history, followed a trajectory that stood in marked contrast to the congressional hearings in the US a decade and a half earlier. If the US Congress was intent on forcing homosexuals out of the closet so as to oust them from government service, the British government was intent on forcing Osborne's play and its complex portrayal of Redl back into the closet – intent, that is, on forcing the open portrayal of illicit sexualities and clandestine affairs of the state out of public debate and back into the realms of secrecy where traditionally they belonged.

The British government has a long history of looking unfavorably on any discussions of intelligence services that might reflect badly on Her Majesty's own Services, particularly satirical ones like that found in Osborne's play. But the reaction against *A Patriot for Me* was an especially conservative one. Whereas the US government took liberty to invade the privacy of government employees, the British government took action, ostensibly in the name of public safety, and forced the Royal Court to make a clear distinction in their production between those who had a 'right to know' what went on in Osborne's play from those who didn't. Indeed, the Lord Chamberlain required the Royal Court temporarily to disband as a public theatre and reincorporate as a private club in order to proceed with their intended production of *A Patriot for Me*.

If the earlier congressional hearings in the US marked the performance of politics, the Royal Court Theatre production of *A Patriot for Me* in the UK marked the politics of performance, and the Lord Chamberlain himself became a *de facto* performer in that production. Although they came from opposite ends of this performance–politics chiasmus, the congressional hearings of 1950 and the production of Osborne's play at the Royal Court Theatre in 1965 nonetheless converged in important ways. First of all, both are arguably linked through the tactics of diversion: the use of transgressive sexuality to distract public attention away from the actual activities of intelligence services, not only to keep those activities 'exempt from public control and debate', but also to maintain the security of what Horn calls 'a discretionary space for actions that do not have to be accounted for, that will not have to stand the trial of legitimization [and] that will not have to be justified – since ideally, they will never be known or discussed' (2011: 108). In no uncertain terms, that 'discretionary space' is the deep structural space linking the diversionary tactics of the US congressional hearings in 1950 with those surrounding the Royal Court Theatre production of *A Patriot for Me* in 1965.

As a 'space for actions', so too is that discretionary space a space of performance, and, as an admittedly clandestine space, it is also a space that bears an uneasy resemblance to the closet. Arguably, there could hardly be a more appropriate metaphor than the closet for characterizing the 'discretionary spaces' and clandestine affairs of the state, and, in this respect, it is perhaps not a matter of coincidence that the question of closeted sexual identities functioned so readily as a diversionary substitute for an intelligence community seeking to avoid accountability or having 'to stand the trial of legitimization'. For if the closet is nothing else, it is a discretionary space much in tune with the logics of state secrecy, of 'intentional deception' and of lying. All of these mark the discretionary space that Horn cites as a space where the parameters of conventional meaning are contested, and inasmuch as state secrecy and intelligence in the twentieth century was primarily a 'man's game', there is an important echo here of Eve Kosofsky Sedgwick's classic assertion in *Epistemology of the Closet* that 'the most crucial sites for the contestation of meaning in twentieth-century Western culture are [...] quite indelibly marked with the historical specificity of homosocial/homosexual definition' (2008: 73). One can call it homosexual panic or whatever one likes, the cadre of men running intelligence communities have always been afraid that someone is going to discover their dirty little secrets.

Insecurities of the state and the deceptive public hearings: the politics of restaging Redl

In fact, the appropriateness of using 'the closet' to characterize the secret affairs of the state – particularly in the 1950s when the case of Alfred Redl made its way onto the stage of US Senate hearings – is only strengthened by a closer consideration of the role that the narrative of his history performed in the larger context of what scholars call 'the lavender scare' (i.e. the fear that homosexuals posed a threat to national security). In his book *The Lavender Scare*, which documents the persecution of gays and lesbians in the US federal government during the cold war, David Johnson presents a compelling case, for example, that both in the government and in the mainstream press during the McCarthy era the term 'security risk' was a coded expression of homosexual panic. Not only was it a euphemistic avoidance of the terms 'homosexual' and 'sexual pervert', Johnson argues, but it was also a terse packaged judgment of gays who were sometimes also referred to in the press as 'men of unconventional morality' whose habits, according to the government and the press, made 'them especially vulnerable to blackmail' (2004: 6). The irony of this coded euphemism is that, even beyond McCarthyism, the 'fear that homosexuals posed a threat to national security and needed to be systematically removed from the federal government' (or, say, the military) has always been based largely on assumption and bigoted conjecture. As Johnson emphatically notes, there is no evidence that any 'gay American was ever blackmailed into revealing state secrets' (2004: 9–10). Hence Alfred Redl's rather bizarre entrance into the annals of US Senate history.

Early in 1950, the lavender scare was pervasive enough that Senator Clyde Hoey, who was the chair of the Committee on Expenditures in Executive Departments and who also chaired the rather astonishingly named 'Subcommittee on Employment of Homosexuals and Other Sex Perverts in Government' began hearings that investigated the extent to which homosexuals posed a clear risk to state security. At the behest of President Truman's office, this subcommittee sought testimony confirming the assumption that homosexuals posed clear security risks because the performance pressures of having to pass in a heterosexual society supposedly left them weak and vulnerable. Without any sense of the implicit indictment of all clandestine operatives working under cover or of the consequent irony in their claims, military intelligence officers fell in line with the President's directive and dutifully testified that homosexuals 'were highstrung and neurotic from leading double lives', and hence were vulnerable to being blackmailed into spying against their own country (Herek 1990: 1036). Equally blind to the ironic double standard of this kind of testimony, Hoey's committee accepted it on faith yet struggled to find evidence in support of the homophobic generalizations that they had heard and presumably agreed with. Since no evidence from past or recent US history could be found to support the committee's assumptions or the conjecture by military intelligence officers, the newly appointed Director of the CIA, Admiral Roscoe Hillenkoetter, came to the rescue.

Hillenkoetter gave a command performance before the committee and became their star witness when he presented a carefully manipulated account of the case of Colonel Alfred Redl. Not only did Hillenkoetter neglect to tell the committee that Redl received lucrative compensation for the information that he supplied, but, as David Johnson has noted, Hillenkoetter also fabricated information to enhance his argument. He made up a story about the Russians first discovering Redl's sexual identity, then supplying him with a young 'newsboy' and finally bursting in on the two of them in a hotel room while they were 'engaged "in an act of perversion"' (Johnson 2004: 108). It was a sensational lie that performed an instrumental role in the subsequent persecution of gays and lesbians in the 1950s. Lies are, after all, what one does to someone. This creative intervention – a stellar performance by almost any measure – may not have been worthy of an Oscar but it might have earned Hillenkoetter a charge of perjury had it not been for his privileged status as the keeper of state secrets.[5] Still, it is not the lying *per se* that is significant here. It is particulars of the lie, the singling out of the homosexual community, which had all the markings of a political ploy.

Some sense of the significance of those particulars arguably can be found by returning momentarily to the politics of lying, or, more simply put, to political lying. In a rather spirited albeit problematic defence of political lying, Glen Newly suggests, for example, that citizens in a democratic society are likely to suspend their expectations of openness and transparency and 'explicitly condone the government's use of dissimulation from time to time where this secure[s], or [... is] thought likely to secure, public benefits such as national security or economic stability' (1997: 108). But the legitimacy of political lying, so Newly argues, also extends beyond this general willingness to suspend the expectation of openness and transparency in government. In some instances, he argues, 'citizens' even 'have the right to be lied to' (1997: 109) because it is only through lies that 'policy' that they are in favor of can be 'implemented' (111). Bizarre though this line of reasoning may be, it actually provides a guideline for understanding Hillenkoetter's performance in the Senate hearing.

Draped in dissimulations, Hillenkoetter's testimony was in this respect a performance that killed many birds with a single stone. First of all, homosexuals were more of a threat to the biases of conventional mainstream morality than to national security, but lies suggesting that they threatened the latter helped to ensure that policy openly supporting heteronormative values would be implemented. So too were lies suggesting that homosexuals were a national security threat sensational and scandalous enough to distract public attention from more dubious activities done in the late 1940s and early 1950s in the name of national security – activities, for example, like granting immunity and ultimately offering affiliation with the CIA to former Nazi intelligence officers like Reinhard Geheln and the members of his WWII German intelligence network.[6] Hiring ex-Nazis was the kind of sordid affair best left unaddressed in public. Finally, there was that lie of omission: Hillenkoetter conveniently forgetting to mention the substantial amount of money that Redl received for betraying his country's secrets. Subtle but decisive, this was perhaps the most significant moment of intentional deception in Hillenkotter's testimony. For the implication that Redl had been motivated by the profit motive to betray his country not only suggested that every agent was a potential security risk. The profit motive as such was also one of the core ideological values that the CIA set out to defend in its cold war battles with the Soviets. To suggest that the profit motive or even corruption was more of a threat to national security than queers or commies was a bit of a problem, particularly since there was ample evidence to support such a claim. When all was said and done, no one seems to have cared that Hillenkoetter neglected to share this uncomfortable bit of information, or, for that matter, that at multiple levels Hillenkoetter committed perjury. Amid the homosexual panic that hovered about the subcommittee, he was given a pass. Numerous gays and lesbians working for the government were forced out of the closet, vilified and, despite their loyal service to their country, shown the door.

Redl at the Royal Court

When *A Patriot for Me* premiered at the Royal Court Theatre fifteen years after Hillenkoetter's public testimony in the US, the British government had not yet officially acknowledged the existence of MI6 and would not do so for another thirty years. Its existence was, of course, an open secret, and at one level that open secret fueled 'the secrecy effect'. But in the UK, there were obviously things that one did not speak about in public. In the mid-1960s, intelligence and buggery figured high on the list, and, on the face of things, the Lord Chamberlain's decision to deny the Royal Court Theatre a licence for public performances of *A Patriot for Me* in 1965 was tantamount to punishment for the theatre's lack of discretion in both respects: punishment for its willingness to speak openly about matters deemed unsuitable for public discussion or debate. Arguably, that decision reinforced a wide cultural expansion of the notion of the discretionary spaces that Eva Horn specifically links to matters of state security and that is premised upon the idea that actions which are not known or discussed need not be accounted for. As is the case with matters of state security, such spaces, when extended through culture and society, tend to be positioned precariously between 'rational rules' and 'vices' – or more precisely stated, between a prescription for civil order and a recipe for corruption and abuse. So too are a Lord Chamberlain's decisions about the privilege to show or to see – like the setting of the rules for the 'right to know' – a regulation of the flow of knowledge or ideas that ostensibly protects the public's interest but that in its deeper structures potentially shores up the political prerogatives of a small ruling elite.

If such potential was at play in 1965, one could do far worse than to place the Lord Chamberlain's decision to deny the Royal Court Theatre a licence for public performances of *A Patriot for Me* against the backdrop of the actual political events that not only were unfolding around the Royal Court Theatre's show but that were also subtly related the very issues that Osborne's play exposed to biting critical scrutiny. The most prominent among those issues were critical reflections on the susceptibility of the discretionary spaces of state secrecy to corruption and a recasting of the issue of blackmail within a larger struggle over the state's ability to manipulate others through the use of threats. Whether a desire to dampen public debate of these issues was behind the Lord Chamberlain's decision is difficult to ascertain. But if there was no direct connection, the coincidental correspondence between the concerns addressed by Osborne and the political events unfolding around the premier of *A Patriot for Me*, suggest, at the very least, that when the Lord Chamberlain did not grant the licence to the Royal Court Theatre, he was working within a mindset that was very much in line with that of the intelligence community and Members of Parliament.

With regard to state secrecy, historical hindsight reminds us not only of how controlled actual public debate about the intelligence community could be in the UK but also of how close to home *A Patriot for Me* actually was to the major political issues that the intelligence community was addressing in the mid-1960s. For example, in the year directly prior to the Royal Court Theatre production, a major event occurred within the intelligence community that bore just enough resemblance to the rough plot of Osborne's play that it would have easily invited disquieting comparisons if either had been granted a full and transparent public vetting. That event was a closing chapter in the long embarrassing history of the Cambridge Five. In 1964, Anthony Blunt, the Surveyor of the Queen's Pictures and a former member of MI6, confessed to being a spy for the Soviets and to being the fourth man in the Cambridge spy ring that had profoundly compromised British intelligence in the early defining years of the cold war. Rather than revealing yet another embarrassing failure of the British intelligence service to the public (after the earlier defections of Donald MacLean and Guy Burgess in the 1950s and, more recently, Kim Philby in 1963), the intelligence community responded by classifying Blunt's confession as a state secret, which it remained for the next fifteen years. Indeed, Blunt was granted immunity from prosecution in exchange for his confession. Like Redl, Blunt had close ties with the Russians, gave up lower level agents to protect himself, was openly homosexual and his espionage was not the result of blackmail. It was no small embarrassment that Blunt was also a distant cousin of the Queen, and this apparently afforded him exemptions that Redl himself did not have. But they were the kind of exemptions – indeed, the kind of social privilege and entitlement – that were not far removed from the focus of the criticism that Osborne articulated through his creative manipulation of Redl's history.

The Blunt affair was conducted within the discretionary spaces of state secrecy and did not become common knowledge until Margret Thatcher publicly outed Blunt in Parliament in 1979 – something that shrewdly put Thatcher just ahead of and hence distanced her from a forthcoming outing of Blunt in the press that was accompanied by understandable accusations of a cover-up. So while the Blunt affair looms in the background of the Lord Chamberlain's decision in 1964, it is doubtful that he was responding directly to it in his decision to deny a public licence to the Royal Court Theatre. But inasmuch as any cover-up – and cover-ups follow the darker side of the rules of 'the right to know' – is intended to protect someone's interests, the cover-up of the Blunt affair and the Lord

Chamberlain's rejection of the Royal Court Theatre's request for a licence for public performances of *A Patriot for Me* had a lot in common. Both conveniently thwarted a public debate that not only questioned the integrity of the intelligence community in general but also of its willingness to lend its services to the personal interests of a ruling elite in particular.

If the Blunt affair was too closely guarded a secret to impact the Lord Chamberlain's office directly, there was certainly correspondence to be found between his decision not to grant the Royal Court Theatre a public licence for producing Osborne's play and the subtly manipulated debates about blackmail and homosexuality that were unfolding in the halls of Parliament just as Osborne's play was moving toward production. Not only do those debates add an important contextual nuance to the Lord Chamberlain's decision, but, more importantly, the underlying logic of those debates exploited a deep structural contradiction in the popular conception of the threat posed by blackmail. That conception, which was premised upon a false binary between blackmail and security – the kind of binary that was also central to hearings conducted in the US Senate fifteen years earlier – helped to create a profoundly dishonest diversion from a more basic struggle over the control of the political power of threats: the power, that is, to keep secrets, to cover up, or to use intentional deception not so much to protect individual or national interests but rather to coerce individuals to act and perform in specific ways and in accordance with specific agendas.

Where those agendas cater to the interests of an elect few, corruption is likely afoot. This, at least, is one of the crucial implications of *A Patriot for Me*. Beneath the surface of the question of whether *A Patriot for Me* was suitable for a public performance or was the racy stuff that belonged in a private club, I would thus suggest, a far more significant power struggle was underway, one spearheaded by politicians in Parliament who had much to lose if cultural events like the Royal Court Theatre's production of *A Patriot for Me* drew popular attention to and ultimately against the subtle self-serving undercurrents of their legislative strategies. In this respect, the Lord Chamberlain's decision to force the Royal Court to reincorporate as a private club helped to deflect attention from a struggle over the performative logic of secrecy, blackmail and the control of threats – a struggle in the deeper structures of which the distinctions between the three began to fade.

Evidence of that struggle was not difficult to find. In the same year that *A Patriot for Me* was forced into a private club, legislation was taking shape that aimed at decriminalizing homosexual acts between two consenting males ostensibly in order to curtail the threat of blackmail. Introducing the legislation that would ultimately become the Sexual Offences Act 1967, Leo Abse justified the proposed change in existing laws against homosexuality by arguing that 'blackmail is the ambience which wraps itself around the existing law'.[7] But rather than actually moving toward the more open and tolerant society it seemed to embrace, the 1967 Act's primary effects were: first of all, the neutralization of the threat that blackmail posed to the political and performative power of 'the secrecy effect' in the hands of the state; and second, the creation of a loophole from prosecution primarily for homosexuals of high social and economic standing. Unfortunately, there is not enough space in this essay to go into the particulars of the Act. But in simplest terms, the Act was as much, perhaps even more, about class and privilege as it was about homosexuality, and, more than anything else, such realms of privilege, entitlement and immunity were the focus of Osborne's most bitter criticism in *A Patriot for Me*, and nowhere was that criticism on greater display that in what is arguably the drama's most infamous and celebrated scene.

The ostentatiousness that Osborne's drama required in performance and Osborne's biting critique of the discretionary spaces of the ruling elite both culminated in the infamous drag queen ball at the opening scene of Act 2 where, with the exception of a woman who has been snuck into the ball as a joke, Redl is the only person not dressed in drag. Amid an ocean of drag queens, Redl stands alone in his military uniform. What makes this image of a uniformed Redl so powerful is that the queens at the ball come primarily from the Austrian ruling classes: lords, barons, counts and their hangers-on – from those, that is, who are protected by their social status or by some sort of temporary patronage; from those, in short, whom Redl might see but does not observe in an official capacity. While Redl's uniform – like the uniform of the CIA's Admiral Roscoe Hillenkoetter – is a visual reminder to everyone present that Redl, as the head of intelligence, moves within the spaces of discretion that are empowered by secrecy and lies and that enable him to do things to others, he is at the ball not to gather intelligence, but to pursue the social and political connections that will enhance his standing and power, and this means turning a deliberate blind eye to the transgressive behaviour of the powerful while demonstrating his authority over those without social standing. This is readily apparent when Redl impresses the ball's host Baron von Epp by brutally assaulting one of the hangers-on, an overly effeminate and indiscreet young queer. As Redl takes his leave and the young drag queen lies writhing in pain on the ground, the Baron tells the young man: 'You silly boy! I knew you shouldn't have flirted with Colonel Redl. He's a dangerous man' (Osborne 1966: 76). But what makes Redl dangerous and a threat is not his homosexuality or the susceptibility to blackmail that is often ascribed to him. It is rather his willingness to carry the authority of his office into his private social interactions: his willingness to use the discretionary spaces of state secrecy and to bend the rules of the 'right to know' for those of high standing and for his own personal advantage. It is his willingness to use the impunity that comes with his office as a cover for brutalizing those beneath him, for putting them in their place and for advancing his own position at their expense.

Beneath all of the ostentatiousness and flaunting, *A Patriot for Me* ultimately is less about homosexuality opening the door to blackmail than it is about the corrupt use of the providence of threats, the discretionary spaces of state secrecy and the logic of lies for one's own personal gain. In this respect, *A Patriot for Me* does not contrast the threat of blackmail with the state's 'rational rules' or its exclusive claim to the providence of threats for the legitimate purposes of governance but rather likens it to the state's 'vices', its 'misdeeds' and 'infamies' (Horn 2011: 113), all of which have to do with the ways in which the mechanisms of power perform when – as is the case with matters of state secrecy, the province of threats, or even the logic of lies – they are left unchecked.

The invisible government

The strength of Osborne's critique notwithstanding, the infamous drag queen ball ironically brings us back to Admiral Hillenkoetter's 1950 testimony before the US Senate 'Subcommittee on Employment of Homosexuals and Other Sex Perverts in Government'. Although substantial differences would seem to place Osborne and Hillenkoetter at opposite ends of the political spectrum, the two actually share an uneasy alliance in the way that their bent and distorted histories of Redl lend credence to Sedgwick's classic argument that 'the nominative category of "the homosexual" [… has endured] not […] because of its meaningfulness to those whom it defines but because of its indispensableness to those who define themselves against it' (2008: 83). In the case of *A Patriot for Me* that moment of definition comes not with fine but with broad brushed strokes that blur the boundaries between decadence and homosexuality in a portrayal that equates the self-serving vices of a ruling class with a stereotypical, effeminate image of homosexuality. If the intent here was to find an image that would cast corruption in a negative light, the implicit effect was also to disparage homosexuality as a form of corruption and decadence. Although this kind of rhetoric is more subtle than suggesting outright that homosexuals are a threat to national security because they are subject to blackmail, it is not that far removed from the more subtle aspects of Admiral Hillenkoetter's testimony fifteen years earlier: namely, his attempt to define the intelligence community in opposition to what, in a moment of profoundly disingenuous irony, he also portrayed as a corrupt and conspiratorial tendency among homosexuals.

The irony in Hillenkoetter's assertion resided in the fact that he attempted to deflect attention from the conspiratorial predilections of the intelligence community itself by attributing such tendencies to homosexuals as a fundamental character trait. His testimony suggested that, beyond their supposed susceptibility to blackmail, gays and lesbians are self-serving and cannot be trusted because their first bonds of loyalty will always be to the homosexual community. Arguing that they prefer to advance their own kind, Hillenkoetter concluded that homosexuals are thus dangerous because they create a *de facto* 'government within a government' (Johnson 2004: 112). For anyone with even a general sense of history, the notion that a 'government within a government' is something that we ought to fear is hardly an outrageous idea. But this moment of calculated, intentional deception was just a little too close to home. Removed from the bigotry of homophobia and seen from an historical perspective, the idea of 'a government within a government' is more applicable to America's intelligence and espionage apparatus than to its gay or lesbian communities.

Back in 1964, David Wise and Thomas Ross made the case for this same argument in the classic critique of the intelligence community that they developed in *The Invisible Government*. Indeed, Wise and Ross opened their book with the statement: 'There are two governments in the United States today. One is visible. The other is invisible', and I would suggest that this distinction between visibility and invisibility is simply a variation of the surface and deep level structures that I have posited throughout this chapter: a distinction that in this case only exists because of the performative logic of intentional deception. The invisible government, Wise and Ross argue, 'is the interlocking, hidden machinery that carries out the policies of the United States in the Cold War'. It 'gathers intelligence, conducts espionage, and plans and executes secret operations all over the globe' (1964: 5). The invisible government is, in short, that entity of security and intelligence that occupies the space of discretion and the providence of threats where the right to know, intentional deception and the logic of lies have full, unchecked reign.

Though it utilizes the CIA, FBI and the National Security Council, the invisible government lies beyond the reach of the bodies that provide oversight of those organizations. The invisible government, they noted, is run 'by a small directorate, the name of which' – and this is worth highlighting – Wise and Ross said, 'is only whispered' (ibid.). In fact, the invisible government has sustained its invisibility by repeatedly changing its name and structure. Wise and Ross cite its earliest names: the 'Special Group' and the '54/12 Group', but in the same year that they published their book, the 'Special Group' became the '303 Committee' and the '40 Committee'. Since then, it has been named the 'Operation Advisory Committee', 'NSC Special Coordination Committee', the 'National Security Planning Group' and the 'Special Intelligence Office', but whatever name or structure it assumes, Wise and Ross's questions still resonate: 'How many Americans have ever heard of the "Special Group"? [...] The name of this group, even its existence, is unknown outside the innermost circle of the Invisible Government' (ibid.).

In light of such elusive invisibility, there is no shortage of irony in Hillenkoetter's rhetorical sleight of hand when testifying about Alfred Redl, homosexuals and security risks. Sounding the alarm that homosexuals had a dangerous predilection for secrecy and conspiracy was little more than a cynical strategy that Hillenkoetter used to protect the same predilection for himself and his kind. And who are his kind? They are those for whom deception, duplicity and calculated betrayal are deemed necessary evils – the stock, trade and means justified by an end vaguely defined and inscrutable because it falls under the privileged category of national security: a category we might dare to call a self-perpetuating and tightly guarded closet ... locked tight with the serpentine logic of the lie.

All this, of course, begs the question, whose kind was Alfred Redl? One possible answer might be found in the fact that his suicide resulted not from being outed as a queer but as a double agent. But what of his queerness, and of the need as a gay man to pass undetected, to dwell within the closet and live by codes of secrecy, discretion and the right to know – all 'in order to avoid harassment, persecution, discrimination and physical violence'? (Herek 1990: 1041). Implicitly embracing 'the rules of the right to know', Gregory Herek has argued that such necessities were never really explored by Hoey's subcommittee, and he suggests, furthermore, that the need to pass undetected in an anti-gay heterosexual society, while blatantly unjust, has potentially given homosexuals strategies for survival that would make them adept at the kind of discretion and secrecy required by honourable government service. Perhaps. But strategies for survival that are cultivated by the experience of injustice and by an absence of civil rights, I would suggest, are of a fundamentally different moral and ethical order than the ends-justifying-the-means logic that the intelligence community historically has used to rationalize its 'necessary evils'. The question here is not whether one is susceptible to blackmail. It is whether one is willing to blackmail, rationalize it in the name of state security, and thus, following the logic of lies, call it something else. The question here is not whether one leads a calculated life of secret discretion as a strategy to avoid persecution because one is queer but whether one leads a life of secret discretion in order to avoid the structures of democratic oversight in whose name one ostensibly acts.

In 1964, a year before John Osborne's play *A Patriot for Me* opened at the Royal Court Theatre after having initially been denied a licence for public performance from the Lord Chamberlain, David Wise and Thomas Ross told their readers that the motivation for writing their book was a firm belief that 'even in a time of Cold War, the United States Government must rest, in the words of the Declaration of Independence, on "the consent of the governed"'. Theirs was a call for transparency, for oversight and for checks and balances. Wise and Ross argued furthermore that 'there can be no meaningful consent where those who are governed do not know to what they are consenting' (ibid.). As a point of contrast, the Lord Chamberlain's censoring of Osborne's play seems a petty gesture, but it does leave the many performances of Alfred Redl at a crossroads. Following the multiple levels of the right to know, one may ask at what point will the queer Redl be able to come safely out of the closet and live without fear? Similarly, one may also ask, at what point will the intelligence officer Redl be forced out of the discretionary spaces of state security that allow him to generate fear in others for his own personal advantage and do so without impunity?

Notes

1 Nietzsche (1987: 402).
2 It was from Simpson's use of a longer passage from *Thus Spoke Zarathustra* that I was reminded of the short quote with which I begin my discussion. Simpson included that quote in the larger passage that he cites and uses as an epigraph.
3 One example of the general consensus among scholars of state security regarding legitimate targets is evident in the fact that Bellaby bases his own argument on the work of Tony Pfaff and Jeffery Tiel and their essay 'The Ethics of Espionage' (2004).
4 *A Patriot for Me* has spawned subsequent modifications of Redl's history as well, having been adapted in the mid-1980s by the film director István Szabó for the film *Oberst Redl* (1985), which stared Klaus Maria Brandauer.
5 Of course, Hillenkoetter himself was a bit of an odd bird, as became apparent a decade later. In 1960, when he was no longer Director of Central Intelligence but was now a member of the Board of Directors of the National Investigations Committee on Aerial Phenomena, he achieved enduring fame by writing a letter to Congress, which was later

reported in the *New York Times*. In that letter, according to the *Times*, Hillenkoetter stated that 'behind the scenes, high-ranking Air Force officers are soberly concerned about the UFO's' and that 'through official secrecy and [public] ridicule, many citizens are led to believe the unknown flying objects are nonsense', and he charged that 'to hide the facts, the Air Force has silenced its personnel'. See: 'Air Force Order on "Saucers" Cited', *New York Times*, Feb. 27, 1960.

6 See, for example, Tim Weiner, *Legacy of Ashes: The History of the CIA* (2008) for a more detailed discussion of Gehlen and the Gehlen Organization.

7 Cited in Peter Alldridge (1993: 374).

15 Afterword

Sovereign and critical grammars

Michael Saward

According to the late ethnomethodologist Harold Garfinkel (1967: 11), all modes of social expression and practical action are 'contingent ongoing accomplishments of organized artful practices of everyday life'. The structures and actions of political life are no exception. As accomplishments, they are regular and predictable in many ways but never inevitable, never structurally determined beyond the actions, motives and understandings of participating and observing individuals. To use the key concept of this volume, grammars of politics – sets of 'recognizable rules or codifications that facilitate communication' (Rai and Reinelt (this volume): 2) – are critical to the ongoing accomplishments of political life, be they the maintenance of particular orders or structures, or the disruption, displacement or alteration of those orders or structures. Those grammars are performed, or are deeply implicated in performances which can sustain or produce distinctive social and political orders (or their effective disruption). Performances constitute politics, deploying grammars (rules, codifications) to sustain familiar political understandings and to generate new ones. I shall refer to the phenomenon within which such grammars are enacted as 'performative politics', a phrase intended to draw attention to both the theatrical and productive (or constitutive) elements of performance in and of politics. Performative politics combines the theatrical *with* the productive: it is rehearsed or repeated citational action designed to draw, or with the effect of drawing, special attention to the alleged existence and character of entities such as nation-states.

This Afterword looks back over the rich array of grammars described or revealed in the preceding chapters. One volume cannot, of course, claim to offer a full or systematic account of such grammars. Further, as the Editors' Introduction notes, grammars of performative politics shift and change, and expand and contract in their scope and importance. Nonetheless, the diversity and cross-disciplinary character of the chapters brings to light a fascinating set of grammars of politics and performance, and prompts critical questions about the relations between politics and performance. In this chapter I aim to map the grammars which emerge, before stepping back to ask key questions about the achievements of performance in and of politics: (1) What do different grammars of politics and performance constitute, focusing on the subject, objects and audiences of politics; (2) What do they seek to make perceptible, temporally, spatially and otherwise? (3) What role do such grammars play in the attempt to generate political legitimacy? And (4) in what ways do different grammars, fuelled by widely varied motives and intentions, overlap, borrow and even mirror each other?

Sovereign and critical grammars

I begin with a two-part picture of the grammars of performative politics which is, admittedly, over-simplified; I do so in order to anchor more effectively subsequent discussion which renders a more multi-sided and nuanced picture. *Sovereign grammars* are those which are deployed in the performative politics of the state or other established and constituted authorities. *Critical grammars* are those which are deployed in the performative politics of actors who question, criticise or seek to transform the foundations, dominant understandings of sovereign or authoritative structures.

As revealed across the chapters in this volume, sovereign grammars play strongly towards the general and the homogeneous, a large-scale (often national) sense of oneness or commonality of attachment or belonging. Ritual and ceremony play key roles – from elements of parliamentary procedure to national anthems – and carefully controlled (and often consistently repeated) spaces, scripts and settings are used. Sovereign grammars also include modes of deflection of attention away from the sorts of questionable actions that might be justified by 'raisons d'état'.

Critical grammars, on the other hand, tend to particularise citizens and others, as individuals and/or as members of distinct subgroups (e.g. as 'indigenous people' or other minorities), and to do so in ways that lend them an often problematic or challenging specificity. They tend to the more temporary and to the more spontaneous. The use of spaces is less predictable, and while often loaded with symbolic meaning may include demonstrations, protests and occupations of spaces. Sometimes the use of space will assert a political dimension about place or people where the latter are not normally identified or thought of as political. An assertion of presence, often an unsanctioned presence, can be crucial, not least as one way of asserting an uncharacteristic or unusual visibility of a people or a claim. Asserting the significance of particular spaces, identities and claims can also be an assertion that new or different publics are being formed, or exist, which need to be taken into account politically.

What do grammars constitute?

A key sovereign objective of performative politics seeks to constitute the citizen body as one. This effect is often achieved or sought through repeated deployment of appropriate grammars. The success of political performances depends, as Derrida points out, on successful 'citation' or 'iteration' of cultural codes or signs (1988: 15–17). Failure is a 'necessary possibility' (Derrida 1988: 15); performatives must, in other words, draw on cultural resources with their own instabilities, conflicts and weaknesses – iterability 'is at once the condition and the limit of mastery' (Derrida 1988: 107). The provisional success of a performative gains authority 'through the repetition or citation of a prior and authoritative set of practices' (Butler 1997: 51).

The care with which public authority is variously staged and scripted through sovereign performances (Parkinson) has an encompassing element, designed to be visible and to reach all parts of the polity and all citizens of the polity in a common manner. This is a double process of constituting subjects and objects; through staging and scripting, the state (subject) is made to stand for the people (object) in a process of political and/as aesthetic representation, and at the same time citizens are made to stand for the state, or to bear or symbolise state authority through citizenship. Sovereignty works through a grammar of a single unified narrative of state and citizen, as subject and object (Haedicke); there is only one 'we' (Nield). There is an ideal-typical citizen characteristic and outlook, one which confirms and conforms to a singular and to some degree homogenised picture – idealised 'should be' images and personas are offered to citizens as mirrors for their own characters (Weber). (This is not to deny that, in states which have clear – however thin – liberal and democratic elements, there is a surface acceptance or celebration of differentiation or diversity *and* the deeper assertion of a common and homogenised citizen-character, as Weber's critique of the US post-September 11 public service campaign makes clear).

Both ceremony and ritual in different forms are closely linked sovereign grammars. A key feature of sovereign rituals is their depersonalised character; rituals partake of participant status and the significance of transitions and contexts, and not the specific personalities involved in them. For example, ritual often involves 'correct execution of ritualised speech moments' involving generic forms of words (Finlayson). As such, their tenor as performative grammars is to apply (in principle equally) to all, thereby reinforcing a common sense of we-ness. Rituals may reassert authority, possibly in an outwardly reconfigured form, in times of tension or crisis (Lynch, Edelman), may dignify parliamentary procedures (Rai) and may act as a grammar of unanswerable emotive force (Edelman).

In short, sovereign grammars of performative politics (seek to) constitute a unity out of potential, and even acknowledged, diversity – a unity of citizen character types, of destiny, of belonging, of permanent authority and its locus. In doing these things, such grammars also seek to constitute an audience out of citizen subjects-objects, an appreciative, accepting and inclusive set of observers or recipients of sovereign performances, who even in the more passive mode as an audience will act upon recognition of the performed authority.

What do critical grammars constitute?

On the evidence of the preceding chapters, critical grammars of performative politics seek to constitute an array of subjects and objects. They may assert the active, potentially awkward or non-cooperative citizen against the more passive subject-citizen noted in the previous section (Reinelt). They may constitute new notions of publics or 'counterpublics' (Reinelt, Nield), and in that way also constitute 'the alternative'. In this way, alternative 'we's' are offered or claimed. The subjects making up these alternative collectives may be characterised more strongly as agents, with distinctive capacities which derive from their assertion and not from one or other form of sovereign grant. They may likewise assert particular citizen identities, drawing upon and potentially subverting sovereign image-making as they do so (Weber's alternative takes on 'I am an American' reverse the sovereign 'out of many, one', to assert 'out of one, many). They may assert the importance of situated and lived experience against abstract and idealised sovereign conceptions of appropriate experience, and in so doing highlight vulnerabilities that are glossed over in dominant characterisations of citizens as both subjects and objects (Fitzpatrick). In short, critical grammars are often put to work in the assertion of (a) agentic unpredictability, (b) unacknowledged or overlooked capacity for independent questioning, thinking and action, and (c) issues and tensions arising from particular perspectives and lived experiences which pose a direct challenge to homogenising, 'flattening' sovereign discourses of citizenly attributes and the terms of belonging.

Sovereign grammars of visibility, time and space

Political visibility, like other political phenomena, is an accomplishment. Sometimes political invisibility is an accomplishment too. In other words, these are intended or unintended achievements of practices, many of which are performances. What is seen (or perceived), and where and when, partakes of grammars of performative politics. Sovereign grammars favour the 'legislative chamber', the 'conference room' and the 'committee room', literally perhaps, and metaphorically too as spaces of predictability, order and enforced procedure. Grammars using such specific spaces emphasise visible control as well as exhibiting a certain regime of visibility in the form of a stable hierarchy of visibility and significance of places. Secrecy and diversion of attention may seem to be the opposite of such controlled modes of visibility, but as Harding points out there is a 'secrecy effect' which can add to a diffuse sense of sovereign knowingness and power. The regularity of sovereign visible performances – such as ceremonies which by their nature are highly visible – in appropriate spaces and at appropriate times (or intervals) further reinforces interpretations of place as mattering, or if invisible as not mattering (Nield). These sovereign grammars are crucial to the sustaining of sovereign authority; as Finlayson notes, in modernity (even if 'all that is solid melts into air' is exaggerated) authorities have to work hard and continuously to establish authoritative interpretations of space and time as rightly dominant.

Critical grammars of visibility, time and space

Critical grammars of visibility, time and space appear to offer a sharp contrast to sovereign grammars. The accomplishment of visibility in time and space is often one of assertion against the current of sovereign grammars which normalise and regularise the times and spaces of political assertion. This was sharply the case, for example, in the use of theatre to reclaim a form of public sphere in besieged Sarajevo (Jestrovic). Visibility is more precarious, and potentially more ephemeral, in the form of demonstrations, protests and 'stunts' for example (Parkinson). Selective, targeted and creative use of varied media, such as asserting 'critical difference' through film (Weber), or using fiction to achieve visibility (Haedicke), may be crucial to the uncertain achievement of a measure of visibility. Grammars of appropriation and exposure – often targeting selectively elements or materials of sovereign grammars – may be crucial in such efforts (Weber), along with the closely related notion of 'manipulating theatrical strategies' (Nield).

The uses of space and place emerge as crucial elements in critical grammars, and crucial in particular to the achievement of political visibility. Naming and renaming spaces may be one key performative strategy (Nield), and likewise directly appropriating controversial spaces in order that they be seen and experienced in a new light (Fitzpatrick). Sometimes separate from and at other times aligned with such grammars is that of occupation; indeed, occupation as a grammar may make creative use of the symbolism of 'permanency' which accompanies sovereign grammars of the spaces of power, challenging the idea of temporary protest by at least mimicking the grammar of assumed continuing (rightful) presence. It is worth noting that the fact that critical grammars are often involved in the temporary rather than the permanent, or the temporary mimicking the permanent, does not imply that more sporadic, unpredictable or precarious critical grammars in action are somehow weaker in comparison. By regularising and normalising the spaces and times (and time-spans) of power, sovereign grammars leave themselves exposed in principle to creative and assertive acts which (suddenly, surprisingly, counter-intuitively) assert particular temporalities (see Edkins on the temporality of suffering and trauma) or a troubling significance of spaces such as the Irish laundries (Fitzpatrick).

Generating political legitimacy

Working in a broadly inductive way, I have sought to tease out some of the key grammars of performative politics which the chapters reveal, describe and appraise. The key questions guiding the identification of grammars have focused on those emerging from the varied analyses: the constitution of subjects, objects and audiences (in short, identities), and the performative deployments of, and challenges to, time, space and visibility. To locate grammars of performative politics in this way is to try to identify the strategies and effects of performances. But we can take this one further, important step. Visibility and identity (for example) are generated through performance, notwithstanding the multiplicity of intentions and motivations behind performance, and the fact that the intentionality of performance is not necessarily attached to the performers. That purpose can be captured in the desire or need to generate political legitimacy. Itself a complex concept and phenomenon, my focus here is on political legitimation as process and perception: the presence of legitimacy as an ongoing and always incomplete process (legitima*tion*), and as a matter of perceptions of participating and implicated actors rather than as an independently derived or extra-contextual standard. Taking the sovereign and critical grammars identified across the volume, what are their intended, hoped-for or potential products with respect to the generation of political legitimacy? (Note that I do not claim that legitimacy *is*, or *was*, produced in any particular case; rather, that we can identify some key effects of performative grammars which may act as legitimacy-generating factors.)

Legitimacy and sovereign grammars

We can identify a range of potentially legitimacy-producing factors arising from sovereign grammars. The generalisability or universality which sovereign grammars often perform – 'out of all, one' – may generate a sense or perception of *inclusion*. Inclusion, in turn, carries a suggestion of *equality* at a foundational level, even if a polity exhibits a range of formal and informal inequalities between citizens (and between citizens and other residents). The grammars of regularity and predictability may generate perceptions of *stability*, as well as of ready or ever-present and stable forms and loci of *authority*. A number of sovereign grammars partake of ritual and ceremony, in varied forms (from the spoken to the displayed). Such performances may generate perceptions of *dignity* and *significance*; performances that are repeated and granted importance by those who organise, lead or otherwise participate in them suggest or imply significance beyond the moment of performance itself, a capturing of some elusive but fundamental character of the polity which is worthy of recognition and acceptance (Rai). Ceremony can likewise contribute to a sense of *transcendence* of the particular (implying the presence of something like Rousseauian general will above and beyond particular wills). The unified sovereign narratives, the repeated performances of 'we, the people', underline such potential achievements by reiterating *commonality*. Performances of secrecy too imply authority, knowledge and power – the polity knows things, has access to things, some of them of such importance that it protects or hides them while showing that it does so (Harding).

Sovereign grammars may also generate ideal identities for conscious (or subconscious) emulation or absorption, reinforcing a sense that particularity is outweighed by selected images of what the people are, together, or what values and projects they can or should hold in common. These may be fictionalised experiences or characterisations, of course, but they are presented or performed as real reflections of pre-existing identities or attributes of citizens and leaders. Finally, the state can use such sovereign grammars to represent cleansing, renewal and change; they can perform a new or renewed political order, as in the example of truth and reconciliation commissions (Lynch).

Legitimacy and critical grammars

Oppositional or alternative political actors, deploying critical grammars, have different senses of legitimacy to generate through performance. In a range of important cases, they need to attempt to puncture sovereign grammars, to assert particularity and presence. Critical grammars may generate legitimacy by generating force, momentum and resonance through particularity and presence. The attempt to construct *counterpublics* is interesting in this context – 'publics' are resonant of important political actors, with claims that ought to be heard (Reinelt). We-ness is politically powerful, and critical grammars can generate powerful senses that there are alternative 'we's' to the sovereign, homogenised collective image (Haedicke; Nield). Such grammars may also generate a sense of the active and/or activist citizen, carrying a sense of *dynamism* and *conviction*. Non-sovereign *agency*, or the possibility and potential of agentic autonomy within or despite the blanket coverage of sovereign authority, may be generated. Related to this is the assertion of difference, which may appeal to observers as approaching a (subjective or inter-subjective) sense of *authenticity* through particularity and the recognition of difference (Weber). Indeed, one might reasonably summarise the contrast between sovereign and critical grammars with respect to legitimacy as one between performing authority, on the one hand, and performing authenticity, on the other.

Borrowed grammars and hidden opposites

Just as exceptions can prove a rule, so some of the most interesting aspects of grammars of politics and performance identify moments where the sovereign/critical distinction breaks down, or is hybridised in practice. It is no contradiction to say that, for example, the most effective deployment of the sovereign grammars identified above may be supported by the strategic use of the critical grammars; likewise, selective nods in the direction of sovereign grammars may be perceived as useful by the state's or government's critics as they seek to sustain or extend their visibility or a sense of the significance of their message. For example, the use of more personal, 'authentic' identities within grammars of sovereign authority is not at all unusual, especially in times of widespread disillusion with established political structures and leadership. Individual leaders are offered as real people, with public convictions that stem from their personal experiences or passions. It is often a fine line to tread, but such developments do not undermine the notion of more depersonalised sovereign grammars; rather, the account of the leader with the three-dimensional personality we are often given (always a selective account, to be sure) gains whatever salience or currency it can muster *by virtue of* its momentary and artful departure from permanent or background sovereign grammars.

Similarly, actors deploying critical grammars will at certain moments seek to 'borrow' from the arsenal of sovereign grammars, to gain (or so it is often hoped) a sense of persistent importance, transcendent significance, or authority that the distinctive particularity of their assertions might lack by their very nature. The generating and use of (e.g.) protest rituals may be one instance. A sense of collectivity – a different 'we' that may even be asserted as a direct challenge to characterisations of the sovereign 'we' – taps into an important element of sovereign grammars. Consider for example that the occupation of public buildings and running up national flags characterised anti-government, pro-Russian dissent in eastern Ukraine in 2014. Further examples may include the use of the slogan 'Not in our name' in the demonstrations against the invasion of Iraq in the United Kingdom, and the use of 'We are the 99%' in the discourse of Occupy (Nield).

The possibility – sometimes, politically, the necessity – of 'borrowing' alternative grammars of performative politics arises in part from a background sense of 'hidden opposites'. We need to exercise care in the analysis here, resisting any easy background functionalism which assumes a neat equal and opposite equation between a given set of sovereign grammars and a given set of critical grammars. Nonetheless, we can argue that (1) for any specific grammar of performative politics, (2) an opposite can be identified, construed or constructed, which can (3) be deployed strategically against that grammar. For example, a crucial sovereign claim is that of representing the (single, overarching) collectivity. A hidden opposite may be the silencing effect that can accompany representation: if for instance elected parliamentarians speak or stand for you, it is assumed that you do not need to (or are not ordinarily expected to) speak or stand for yourself, even if you think the elected officials are misrepresenting you. Similarly, if 'horizontality' is a spatial metaphor that forms part of some alternative social and political movements, notably in recent years Occupy, then sovereign authorities can and do assert the hidden opposite, verticality (e.g. 'the horizontal is fine, but how do you govern in the end without specialisation of tasks and functional and organised locations of collective decisional authority?'). Or consider for example planning and spontaneity, consensus and conflict, reinforcing and contesting accounts of the significance of place, and so on.

For a given political actor, individual or collective, selective borrowing and deploying the hidden (or, as the case may be, not so hidden) opposite may be understood as alternative strategies in ongoing political struggles.

Conclusion

Political scientists and political theorists have often made easy nods in the direction of theatricality and acting in politics. Playing off centuries-old prejudices – stemming from Plato, revived and refined by Rousseau (1960), and ironically reinforced by a key work in the contemporary concept of performativity, Austin's *How to Do Things with Words* (1975) – the presence of theatricality in politics was often summarily condemned as non-serious, or non-genuine. For all its diversity, the discipline of performance studies has a strong and laudable tradition of radical political comment. Arguably, political scientists and political theorists need to take performance in politics seriously, and performance studies scholars to take performance in mainstream politics seriously alongside radical or marginal actors and critiques. This is one core thread to arise from this volume. The grammars of performance and politics are complex modes through which performances are constructed and construed, and by which they may be rendered effective or ineffective. I have suggested that a distinction between sovereign grammars and critical grammars of performance and politics arises from the rich variety of cases and arguments presented in the volume – so long as we understand that political actors and political observers will and should disrupt such ready distinctions at important points in their activities. Users of sovereign grammars may focus above all on generating a sense of authority, and those of critical grammars a sense of authenticity. But each will also, in varied ways, look to strategic use of grammars that are meat and drink to its opponents and critics.

Embracing both mainstream and critical actors and performances, the chapters in this book illustrate the rich variety of performances in politics. At the same time, by developing the notion of grammars as rules or codifications that foster communication, the book provides a crucial focus for analysing the nature and impact of performative politics. We look forward to continuing theoretical development of the idea of grammars, not least how their status as 'rules' fosters both rigid and flexible modes of performative politics. Armed with these tools, future research may explore further particular grammars, and continue to trace the development of new and hybrid grammars, not least those enabled by new communication technologies. It may also usefully examine the uneasy 'dance' of sovereign and critical grammars – when, how, why and to what effect they contrast, overlap, or borrow from each other. In a highly performative world, continuing to generate new insights into performative politics is critical to our ability to grasp the changing nature of politics itself.

Bibliography

Abélès, Marc (2006) Parliament, politics and ritual. In Crewe, Emma, and Müller, Marion (eds), *Rituals in Parliaments: Political, Anthropological, and Historical Perspectives on Europe and the United States*. Frankfurt am Main: Peter Lang.

Ad Council (2004a) *I am an American (2001–Present)*, <http://www.adcouncil.org/default.aspx?id=141> [accessed Feb. 2014].

Ad Council (2004b) *I am an American (2001–Present)*, <http://www.aef.com/exhibits/social_responsibility/ad_council/2486> [accessed Feb. 2014].

Africog (African Centre for Open Governance) (2008) *Commissions of Inquiry in Kenya: Seekers of Truth or Safety Valves*. Nairobi: Africog.

Agamben, Giorgio (1993) *The Coming Community*. Tr. Hardt, Michael. Minneapolis, MN: University of Minnesota Press.

Agamben, Giorgio (1998) *Homo Sacer: Sovereign Power and Bare Life*. Tr. Heller-Roazen, Daniel. Stanford, CA: Stanford University Press.

Agamben, Giorgio (2000) *Means Without Ends*. Tr. Casarino, Cesare and Binetti, Vincenzo. Minneapolis, MN, and London: University of Minnesota Press.

Agamben, Giorgio (2007) *The Power and the Glory*. 11th B. N. Ganguli Memorial Lecture, Centre for the Study of Developing Societies. New Delhi, 11 Jan.

Agamben, Giorgio (2011) *The Kingdom and the Glory: For a Theological Genealogy of Economy and Government*. Tr. Chiesa, Lorenzo. Stanford, CA: Stanford University Press.

Ahmed, Sara (2000) *Strange Encounters: Embodied Others in Post-Coloniality*. London: Routledge.

Ahmed, Sara (2004) *The Cultural Politics of Emotion*, Edinburgh: Edinburgh University Press.

Alexander, Jeffrey C. (2006) Cultural pragmatics: Social performance between ritual and strategy. In: Alexander, Jeffrey C., Giesen, Bernhard, and Mast, Jason (eds), *Social Performance: Symbolic Action, Cultural Pragmatics and Ritual*. Cambridge: Cambridge University Press.

Alexander, Jeffrey C., Giesen, Bernhard, and Mast, Jason (eds.) (2006) *Social Performance: Symbolic Action, Cultural Pragmatics, and Ritual*. Cambridge: Cambridge University Press.

Alldridge, Peter (1993) Attempted murder of the soul: Blackmail, privacy and secrets. *Oxford Journal of Legal Studies*, 13(3), 368–87.

Alsultany, Evelyn (2007) Selling American diversity and Muslim American identity through nonprofit advertising post-9/11. *American Quarterly*. 59(3), 593–622.

Althusser, Louis (1971) Ideology and ideological state apparatuses (notes towards an investigation). In: *Lenin and Philosophy and Other Essays*. Tr. Brewster, Ben. New York: Monthly Review Press, 127–86.

Bibliography 227

Anderson, Benedict (1983) *Imagined Communities: Reflections on the Origin and Spread of Nationalism*. London: Verso.
Anderson, Benedict (1991 [1983]) *Imagined Communities: Reflections on the Origin and Spread of Nationalism*. Revised edn. London: Verso.
Andreas, Peter (2008) *Blue Helmets and Black Markets: The Business of Survival in the Siege of Sarajevo*. Ithaca, NY, and London: Cornell University Press.
Anu Productions (n.d.) <http://anuproductions.ie> [accessed Dec. 2012].
Appadurai, Arjun (1990) Disjuncture and difference in the global cultural economy. *Public Culture*, 2(2), 1–24.
Archdiocese of Dublin (2011a) Liturgy of lament and repentance, <http://www.dublindiocese.ie/content/liturgy-lament-and-repentance> [accessed Aug. 2014].
—— (2011b) '20/2/2011 Reflections from Liturgy and Lament and repentance, <http://www.dublindiocese.ie/content/2022011-reflections-liturgy-lament-and-repentance> [accessed Aug. 2014].
Arendt, Hannah (1958) *The Human Condition*. 2nd edn. Chicago, IL, and London: University of Chicago Press.
Aristotle (350 BCE) *Rhetoric*. Tr. W. Rhys Roberts. The Internet Classics Archive, <http://classics.mit.edu/Aristotle/rhetoric.html> [accessed May 2014].
Ashforth, Adam (1990) Reckoning schemes of legitimation: On commissions of inquiry as power/knowledge forms. *Journal of Historical Sociology*, 3(1), 1–22.
Ashley, Richard K (1989) Living on borderlines: Man, poststructuralism, and war. In: Der Derian, James, and Shapiro, Michael J. (eds), *International/Intertextual Relations: Postmodern Readings of World Politics*. Lexington, MA: Lexington Books, 259–321.
Attewill, Fred (2011) Anti-royalists banned from London protests. *Metro*, 26 April, <http://metro.co.uk/2011/04/26/anti-royalists-banned-from-london-royal-wedding-protests-653532> [accessed Aug. 2013].
Auslander, Philip (1999) *Liveness: Performance in a Mediatized Culture*. London and New York: Routledge.
Austin, J. L. (1975), *How to Do Things with Words*. 2nd edn. Ed. Urmson, J. O., and Sbisa, M. Oxford: Clarendon Press.
Backscheider, Paula (1993) *Spectacular Politics: Theatrical Power and Mass Culture in Early Modern England*. Baltimore, MD: Johns Hopkins University Press.
Balibar, Etienne (2003) *We, the People of Europe? Reflections on Transnational Citizenship*. Princeton, NJ: Princeton University Press.
Balive, Teo (2011) *The Mask of Anarchy*, 7 Nov., <http://territorialmasquerades.net/the-mask-of-%E2%80%98anarchy%E2%80%99> [accessed Aug. 2013].
Balme, Christopher B. (2008) *The Cambridge Introduction to Theatre Studies*. Cambridge: Cambridge University Press.
Barkan, Joel D. (2008) Why some legislatures develop and others do not: African legislatures and the 'third wave' of democratization. Enhancing the Effectiveness of Parliaments: Challenges and Opportunities, 934th Wilton Park Conference.
Barker, Rodney S. (2001) *Legitimating Identities: The Self-Presentations of Rulers and Subjects*. Cambridge: Cambridge University Press.
Barnes, Colin, and Oliver, Michael (1995) Disability rights: Rhetoric and reality in the UK. *Disability and Society*, 10(1), 111–16.
Barth, Karl (1961) *Church Dogmatics*, vol. 3. Edinburgh: T. & T. Clark.
Barthes, Roland (1995) *S/Z: An Essay*. Tr. Miller, Richard. New York: Hill & Wang.
Batty, David (2011) Royal wedding protest: Three anti-capitalist activists arrested. *Guardian*, 28 April, <http://www.theguardian.com/uk/2011/apr/28/royal-wedding-protest-three-arrested> [accessed Aug. 2013].

228 Bibliography

Baumann, Gerd (1992) Ritual implicates 'others': Rereading Durkheim in a plural society. In: Dde Coppet, Daniel (ed.), *Understanding Rituals*. London: Routledge.

BBC News (2011) State multiculturalism has failed, says David Cameron, 5 Feb., <http://www.bbc.co.uk/news/uk-politics-12371994> [accessed Jan. 2014].

Bell, Catherine (1992) *Ritual Theory, Ritual Practice*. New York: Oxford University Press.

Bell, Catherine (1997) *Ritual: Perspectives and Dimensions*. Oxford: Oxford University Press.

Bellaby, Ross (2012) What's the harm? The ethics of intelligence collection. *Intelligence and National Security*, 27(1), 93–117.

Benjamin, Walter (1969) The work of art in the age of mechanical reproduction. In: Arendt, Hannah (ed.), *Illuminations*. Tr. Zohn, Harry. New York: Schocken Books, 239–41.

Benjamin, Walter (1997) *One-Way Street and Other Writings*. Tr. Jephcott, Edmund, and Shorter, Kingsley. London: Verso.

Benjamin, Walter (2006) In: Eiland, Howard, and Jennings, Michael W. (eds), *Walter Benjamin: Selected Writings: 1938–1940*, vol. 4. Cambridge, MA, and London: Belknap Press of Harvard University Press.

Bergen, Jeremy (2011) *Ecclesial Repentance: The Churches Confront their Sinful Pasts*. Edinburgh: T. & T. Clark.

Berlant, Lauren (1991) *The Anatomy of National Fantasy*. Chicago, IL: University of Chicago Press.

Berlant, Lauren (1997) *The Queen of America Goes to Washington City: Essays on Sex and Citizenship*. Durham, NC: Duke University Press.

Berlant, Lauren (2008) *The Female Complaint: The Unfinished Business of Sentimentality in American Culture*. Durham, NC: Duke University Press.

Bevir, Mark, and Rhodes, R. A. W (2010) *The State as Cultural Practice*. Oxford: Oxford University Press.

Bhabha, Homi (1990) *Nation and Narration*. New York: Routledge.

Bhabha, Homi (2004) *The Location of Culture*. New York: Routledge.

Bial, Henry (2007) *The Performance Studies Reader*. 2nd edn. London and New York: Routledge.

Bitzer, Lloyd (1959 [2010]) Aristotle's enthymeme revisited. In: Rhetoric Enos, Richard Leo, and Agnew, Lois Peters (eds), *Landmarks Essay in Aristotelian*. London: Routledge, 179–91.

Bitzer, Lloyd (1999 [1968]) The rhetorical situation (reprinted). In: Lucaites, John L., et al. (eds), *Contemporary Rhetorical Theory*. London: Guilford Press, 217–26.

Blanchot, Maurice (2006) *The Unavowable Community*. Barrytown: Station Hill.

Blau, Herbert (1982) *Take up the Bodies: Theatre at the Vanishing Point*. Carbondale, IL: University of Illinois Press.

Bloch, Maurice (1974) Symbols, song, dance and features of articulation: Is religion an extreme form of traditional authority? *European Journal of Sociology*, 15(1), 54–81.

Bloom, Allan (1996) *Shakespeare's Politics*. Chicago, IL: University of Chicago Press.

Blumler, J. G., Brown, J. R., Ewbank, A. J., and Nossitter, T. J. (1971) Attitudes to the monarchy: Their structure and development during a ceremonial occasion. *Political Studies*, 19, 149–71.

Bohman, James (2007) *Democracy across Borders: From Demos to Demoi*. Cambridge, MA: MIT Press.

Boone, Pat (2008) <http://www.greenisthenewred.com/blog/pat-boone-warns-of-sexual-jihadists-and-homo-grown-terrorists/811> [accessed Feb. 2014].

Booth, Robert, Laville, Sandra, and Malik, Shiv (2011). Royal wedding: Police criticised for pre-emptive strikes against protestors. *Guardian*, 29 April, <http://www.theguardian.com/uk/2011/apr/29/royal-wedding-police-criticised-protesters> [accessed Aug. 2013].

Boraine, Alex (2000) *A Country Unmasked: Inside South Africa's Truth and Reconciliation Commission*. Oxford: Oxford University Press.

Borneman, John (2002) Reconciliation after ethnic cleansing: Listening, retribution, affiliation. *Public Culture*, 14(2), 281–304.

Bosire, Lydiah, and Lynch, Gabrielle (2014) Kenya's search for truth and justice: The role of civil society. *International Journal of Transitional Justice*.

Boss, Pauline (1999) *Ambiguous Loss: Learning to Live with Unresolved Grief*. Cambridge, MA: Harvard University Press.

Bourdieu, Pierre (1984) *Distinction: A Social Critique of the Judgement of Taste*. Tr. Nice, Richard. London: Routledge.

Bourdieu, Pierre (1991) *Language and Symbolic Power*. Cambridge, MA: Harvard University Press.

Bourdieu, Pierre (2001) *Masculine Domination*. Tr. Nice, Richard. Cambridge: Polity Press.

Bozzoli, Belinda (1998) Public ritual and private transition: The truth commission in Alexandra township, South Africa 1996. *African Studies*, 57(2), 167–95.

Brahm, Eric (2007) Uncovering the truth: Examining truth commission success and impact. *International Studies Perspectives*, 8(1), 16–35.

Branch, Daniel, and Cheeseman, Nic (2005) Briefing: Using opinion polls to evaluate Kenyan politics, March 2004–January 2005. *African Affairs*, 104(415), 325–36.

Brassett, James, and Clarke, Chris (2012) Performing the sub-prime crisis: Trauma and the financial event. *International Political Sociology*, 6(1), 4–20.

Brown, Wendy (2006) *Regulating Aversion: Tolerance in the Age of Identity and Empire*. Trenton, NJ: Princeton University Press.

Burke, Kenneth (1969) *A Grammar of Motives*. Berkeley, CA: University of California Press.

Bush, George W. (2001) Address to a Joint Session of Congress and the American People. *American Rhetorical*, 20 Sept., <http://edition.cnn.com/2001/US/09/20/gen.bush.transcript> [accessed Feb. 2014].

Butler, Judith (1990) *Gender Trouble*. London: Routledge.

Butler, Judith (1993) *Bodies that Matter: On the Discursive Limits of Sex*. New York and London: Routledge.

Butler, Judith (1997) *Excitable Speech: Politics of the Performative*. London and New York: Routledge.

Butler, Judith (2004) *Precarious Life: The Powers of Mourning and Violence*. New York: Verso.

Butler, Judith (2009) *Frames of War: When is Life Grievable?* London and New York: Verso.

Butler, Judith (2011) Bodies in alliance and the politics of the street. *European Institute for Progressive Cultural Policies*, <http://www.eipcp.net/transversal/1011/butler/en> [accessed Aug. 2013].

Butler, Judith, and Athanasiou, Athina (2013) *Dispossession: The Performative in the Political*. London: Polity Press.

Byers, Jack (1998) The privatization of downtown public space: The emerging grade-separated city in North America. *Journal of Planning Education and Research*, 17(3), 189–205.
Campbell, Karlyn Kohrs, and Jamieson, Kathleen Hall (1990) *Deeds Done in Words: Presidential Rhetoric and the Genres of Governance*. Chicago, IL: Chicago University Press.
Carlson, Eric Stener (1996) *I Remember Julia: Voices of the Disappeared*. Philadephia, PA: Temple University Press.
Carlson, Marvin (2003) *The Haunted Stage: The Theatre as Memory Machine*. Ann Arbor, MI: University of Michigan Press.
Carlson, Marvin (2004) *Performance: An Introduction*. 2nd edn. London and New York: Routledge.
Carney, Sean (2005) *Brecht and Critical Theory: Dialectics and Contemporary Aesthetics*. New York and London: Routledge.
Carson, Thomas L. (2006) The definition of lying. *Noûs*, 40(2), 284–306.
Causey, Matthew, and Walsh, Fintan (eds) (2013) *Performance, Identity, and the Neo-Political Subject*. New York and London: Routledge.
Cavarero, Adriana (2000) *Relating Narratives: Storytelling and Selfhood*. Tr. with an introduction by Kottman, Paul A. London: Routledge.
Celermajer, Danielle (2009) *The Sins of the Nation and the Ritual of Apologies*. Cambridge: Cambridge University Press.
Celis, Karen, and Wauter, Bram (2010) Pinning the butterfly: Women, blue collar and ethnic minority MPs vis-à-vis parliamentary norms and the parliamentary role of the group representative. In S. M. Rai (ed.), *Ceremony and Ritual in Parliament*. London: Routledge.
Chambers, Simone (1996) *Reasonable Democracy: Jürgen Habermas and the Politics of Discourse*. Ithaca, NY: Cornell University Press.
Chambers, Simone (2009) Rhetoric and the public sphere: Has deliberative democracy abandoned mass democracy. *Political Theory*, 37, 323–50.
Chan, Gaye, and Sharma, Nandita (2007) Good grief! Melancholic States Conference, Lancaster University, UK, 27–28 Sept.
Chapman, Audrey R., and Ball, Patrick (2001) The truth of truth commissions: Comparative lessons from Haiti, South Africa, and Guatemala. *Human Rights Quarterly*, 23(1), 1–43.
Chatterjee, Partha (1993) *The Nation and its Fragments: Colonial and Postcolonial Histories*. Princeton, NJ: Princeton University Press.
Cheeseman, Nic, Lynch, Gabrielle, and Willis, Justin (2014) Democracy and its discontents: The Kenyan elections of 2013. *Journal of Eastern African Studies*.
Cheng, Joseph Y. S. (ed) (2005) *The July 1 Protest Rally: Interpreting a Historic Event*. Hong Kong: City University of Hong Kong Press.
Chomsky, Noam (2012) *Occupy*. London: Penguin.
Chomsky, Noam, and Herman, Edward S. (1994), *Manufacturing Consent: The Political Economy of the Mass Media*. London: Vintage Books.
Cicero. *De Oratore*. <http://archive.org/stream/cicerodeoratore01ciceuoft/cicerodeoratore01ciceuoft_djvu.txt> [accessed May 2014].
Clastres, Pierre (1990 [1974]) *Society Against the State*. London: Zed Books.
Cohen, Bernard (1992) Representing authority in colonial India. In: Hobsbawm, Eric, and Ranger, Terence (eds), *The Invention of Tradition*. Cambridge: Cambridge University Press.

Cohen, Jean (1996) Democracy, difference, and the right of privacy. In: Benhabib, Seyla (ed.), *Democracy and Difference: Contesting the Boundaries of the Political*. Princeton, NJ: Princeton University Press, 187–217.

Cohen-Cruz, Jan (ed.) (1998) *Radical Street Performance: An International Anthology*. London and New York: Routledge.

Cohen-Cruz, Jan, and Schutzman, Mady (1993) *Playing Boal: Theatre, Therapy, Activism*. New York and London: Routledge.

Cole, Catherine M. (2010) *Performing South Africa's Truth Commission: Stages of Transition*. Bloomington, IN: Indiana University Press.

Coole, Diana (2007) Experiencing discourse: Corporeal communicators and the embodiment of power. *British Journal of Politics and International Relations*, 9(3), 413–33.

Coomaraswamy, Radhika (2005) Preface: Violence against women and 'crimes of honour'. In: Welchman, Lynn, and Hossain, Sara (eds), *Honour*. London: Zedbooks.

Corrigan, P., and Sayer, D. (1985). *The Great Arch: English State Formation as Cultural Revolution*. Oxford: Blackwell.

Crewe, Emma (2007) *Lords of Parliament: Manners, Rituals and Politics*. Manchester: Manchester University Press.

Crewe, Emma (2010) An anthropology of the House of Lords: Socialisation, relationships and rituals. *Journal of Legislative Studies*, 16(3), 313–24.

Crewe, Emma, and Muller, Marianne (eds) (2006) *Ritual in Parliament*. Frankfurt am Main: Peter Lang.

Cronin, Anne (2004) *Advertizing Myths: The Strange Half-Life of Images and Commodities*. London: Routledge.

Crouch, Tim (n.d.) <http://www.timcrouchtheatre.co.uk/shows/the-author/the-author> [accessed Jan. 2014].

Cullen-Owens, Rosemary (2005) *A Social History of Women in Ireland 1870–1970*. Dublin: Gill & Macmillan.

Dáil Éireann (2011) *Commission of Investigation Report in the Catholic Diocese of Cloyne: Motion*, 20 July, <http://debates.oireachtas.ie/dail/2011/07/20/00013.asp> [accessed Sept. 2013].

Davis, Oliver (ed.) (2013) *Rancière Now: Current Perspectives on Jacques Rancière*. Cambridge: Polity.

Debord, Guy (1999) *The Society of the Spectacle*. Tr. Nicholson-Smith, Donald. New York: Zone Books.

De Certeau, Michel (1988) *The Practice of Everyday Life*. Tr. Rendall, Steven. Berkeley, CA: University of California Press.

De Gruchy, John W. (2002) *Reconciliation: Restoring Justice*. London: SCM Press.

Della Porta, Donatella, and Reiter, Herbert (eds) (1998) *Policing Protest*. Minneapolis, MN: University of Minnesota Press.

Derrida, Jacques (1978) The theatre of cruelty and the closure of representation. *Writing and Difference*. Tr. Alan Bass. London: Routledge.

Derrida, Jacques (1988) *Limited Inc*. Evanston, IL: Northwestern University Press.

Derrida, Jacques (1994a) Nietzsche and the machine: Interview with Jacques Derrida by Richard Beardsworth. *Journal of Nietzsche Studies*, 26, 79–90.

Derrida, Jacques (1994b) 'To do justice to Freud': The history of madness in the age of psychoanalysis. *Critical Inquiry*, 20(2), 227–66.

Derrida, Jacques (1995) *The Gift of Death*. Tr. Wills, David. Chicago, IL: University of Chicago Press.

232 Bibliography

Derrida, Jacques (1996) *Archive Fever: A Freudian Impression.* Tr. Prenowitz, Eric. Chicago: University of Chicago Press.

Devane, R. S. (1924) The unmarried mother: Some legal aspects of the problem, I and II. *Irish Ecclesiastical Record*, 55–68 and 172–88.

Diklić, Davor (2004) *Teatar u ratnom Sarajevu 1992/1995.* Sarajevo: Biblioteka Manhattan.

Dolan, Jill (2005) *Utopia in Performance: Finding Hope at the Theater.* Ann Arbor, MI: University of Michigan Press.

Dollimore, Jonathan, and Sinfield, Alan (1985) *Political Shakespeare: Essays in Cultural Materialism.* Manchester: Manchester University Press.

Dorfman, Ariel (2002) *In Case of Fire in a Foreign Land: New and Collected Poems from Two Languages.* Tr. Grossman, Edith. Durham, NC: Duke University Press.

Dovey, Kim (1999) *Framing Places, Mediating Power in Built Form.* New York: Routledge.

Dovey, Kim (2001) Memory, democracy and urban space: Bangkok's 'Path to Democracy'. *Journal of Urban Design.* 6(3), 265–82.

Dryzek, John (2000) *Deliberative Democracy and Beyond: Liberals, Critics, Contestations.* Oxford: Oxford University Press.

Dryzek, John (2010) *Foundations and Frontiers of Deliberative Governance.* Oxford: Oxford University Press.

Dryzek, John, Downes, David, Hunold, Christian, Schlosberg, David, and Hernes, Hans-Kristian (2003) *Green States and Social Movements: Environmentalism in the United States, United Kingdom, Germany, and Norway.* Oxford: Oxford University Press.

Dunsire, Andrew (1973) Administrative doctrine and administrative change. *Public Administration Bulletin*, 15 (Dec.), 39–56.

Durkheim, Emile (2001) *The Elementary Forms of Religious Life.* Ed. Cladis, Mark F. Tr. Cosman, Carol. Oxford: Oxford University Press.

Edelman, Joshua (2014) Clerical betrayal and Christian affirmation. *Performance Research*, 19(2), 35–43.

Edelman, Murray (1988) *Constructing the Political Spectacle.* Chicago, IL: University of Chicago Press.

Edelman, Murray (1995) *From Art to Politics: How Artistic Creations Shape Political Conceptions.* Chicago, IL: University of Chicago Press.

Edkins, Jenny (1999) *Poststructuralism and International Relations.* Boulder, CO: Lynne Rienner.

Edkins, Jenny (2011) *Missing: Persons and Politics.* Ithaca, NY: Cornell University Press.

Edkins, Jenny, and Kear, Adrian (eds) (2013) *International Politics and Performance: Critical Aesthetics and Creative Practice.* London: Routledge.

Edkins, Jenny, and Pin-Fat, Véronique (2005) Through the wire: Relations of power and relations of violence. *Millennium: Journal of International Studies*, 34(1), 1–24.

Elstub, Stephen (2010) The third generation of deliberative democracy. *Political Studies Review*, 8(3), 291–307.

Emert, Toby, and Friedman, Ellie (2011) *'Come Closer': Critical Perspectives on Theatre of the Oppressed.* Amsterdam: Peter Lang.

Falasca-Zamponi, Simonetta (2000) *Fascist Spectacle: The Aesthetics of Power in Mussolini's Italy.* Berkeley, CA: University of California Press.

Farrell, Thomas (1993) *Norms of Rhetorical Culture.* New Haven, CT: Yale University Press.

Fatayi-Williams, Marie (2005) Straight from the heart: Speech given near Tavistock Square, London, Monday 11 July. *Guardian*, 13 July, <http://www.theguardian.com/uk/2005/jul/13/july7.uksecurity23> [accessed Feb. 2014].

Ferriter, Diarmuid (2004) *The Transformation of Modern Ireland 1900–2000*. London: Profile Books.
Ferriter, Diarmuid (2009) *Occasions of Sin: Sex and Society in Modern Ireland*. London: Profile Books.
Fine, J., Vine, J., and Donia, R. (1994) *Bosnia and Herzegovina: A Tradition Betrayed*. New York: Columbia University Press.
Finlayson, Alan. (2007) From beliefs to arguments: Interpretive methodology and rhetorical political analysis. *British Journal of Politics and International Relations*, 9, 545–63.
Finlayson, Alan (2012) Rhetoric and the political theory of ideologies. *Political Studies*, 60(4), 751–67.
Finlayson, Alan, and Martin, James (2008) 'It ain't what you say …': British political studies and the analysis of speech and rhetoric. *British Politics*, 3, 445–64.
Finnegan, Frances (2001) *Do Penance or Perish*. Dublin: Congrave Press.
Fischer, Frank, and Forester, John (1993) *The Argumentative Turn in Policy Analysis and Planning*. Durham, NC: Duke University Press.
Fish, Stanley (1999) Baroque multiculturalism. In: *The Trouble with Principle*. Cambridge, MA: Harvard University Press.
Fortes, Meyer (1962) Ritual and office in tribal society. In: Gluckman, Max (ed.), *Essays on the Ritual of Social Relations*. Manchester: Manchester University Press, 53–88.
Fortier, Anne-Marie (2008) *Multicultural Horizons: Diversity and the Limits of the Civil Nation*. London: Routledge.
Fortier, Anne-Marie (2010) Proximity by design? Affective citizenship and the management of unease. *Citizenship Studies*, 17(1), 17–30.
Foucault, Michel (1970) *The Order of Things: An Archaeology of the Human Sciences*. London: Tavistock/Routledge.
Foucault, Michel (1977) *Discipline and Punish: The Birth of the Prison*. Tr. Sheridan, Alan. London: Penguin.
Foucault, Michel (2010) *The Birth of Biopolitics: Lectures at the Collège de France, 1978–1979*. Tr. Burchell, Graham. London: Palgrave Macmillan.
Franceschet, Susan (2010) The gendered dimensions of rituals, rules and norms in the Chilean Congress. In S. M. Rai (ed.), *Ceremony and Ritual in Parliament*. London: Routledge, 394–407.
Fraser, Nancy (1992) Rethinking the public sphere: A contribution to the critique of actually existing democracy. In: Calhoun, Craig (ed.), *Habermas and the Public Sphere*. Cambridge, MA: MIT Press, 109–42.
Fraser, Nancy (1995) From redistribution to recognition? Dilemmas of justice in a 'postsocialist' age. *New Left Review*, 1/212 (July–Aug.), 68–93.
Fraser, Nancy (1997) Heterosexism, misrecognition and capitalism: A response to Judith Butler. *Social Text*, 52–3, 279–89.
Fraser, Nancy (2013) A triple movement? *New Left Review*, 81 (May–June), 140–9.
Freire, Paulo (1989) *Pedagogy of the Oppressed*. Tr. Ramos, Myra Bergman. New York: Continuum.
Freire, Paulo (1994) *Pedagogy of Hope: Reliving Pedagogy of the Oppressed*. Tr. Barr, Robert. New York: Continuum.
Freire, Paulo (1998) *Pedagogy of Freedom: Ethics, Democracy, and Civic Courage*. Tr. Clarke, Patrick. Lanham, MD: Rowman & Littlefield.
Fung, Archon (2003) Survey article: Recipes for public spheres. Eight institutional design choices and their consequences. *Journal of Political Philosophy*, 11(3), 338–67.

234 Bibliography

Gabbatt, Adam, and Shenker, Jack (2011). Tahrir Square protesters send message of solidarity to Occupy Wall Street. *Guardian*, 25 Oct., <http://www.theguardian.com/world/2011/oct/25/egyptian-protesters-occupy-wall-street> [accessed Aug. 2013].

Garaghy, M. (1923) *Idols of Modern Society*. Dublin: Irish Messenger.

Garfinkel, H. (1984 [1967]) *Studies in Ethnomethodology*. Cambridge: Polity Press.

Garsten, Bryan (2006) *Saving Persuasion: A Defence of Rhetoric and Judgement*. Cambridge, MA: Harvard University Press.

Geertz, Clifford (1980) *Negara: The Theatre State in Nineteenth-Century Bali*. Princeton, NJ: Princeton University Press.

George, David (2004) *Shakespeare Critical Tradition: Coriolanus*. Bristol: Thoemmes Continuum.

Gibson, Rachel, and Miskin, Sarah (2002) Australia deliberates? A critical analysis of the role of the media in deliberative polling. In: Warhurst, John, and Mackerras, Malcolm (eds), *Constitutional Politics: The Republic Referendum and the Future*. St Lucia: University of Queensland Press, 163–75.

Giles, Steve (1998) *Bertolt Brecht and Critical Theory: Marxism, Modernity and the Threepenny Lawsuit*. Amsterdam: Peter Lang.

Gilroy, Paul (2006) *Postcolonial Melancholia*. New York: Columbia University Press.

Glynn, Evelyn (2011). *Breaking the Rule of Silence*, 20–28 Oct., <http://www.magdalenelaundrylimerick.com> [accessed Dec. 2012].

Glynn, Joseph (1921) *The Unmarried Mother*, ser. 5, 18 (Nov.), 461–7.

Goffman, Erving (1963) *Behaviour in Public Places: Notes on the Social Organization of Gatherings*. New York: Free Press.

Goffman, Erving (1971) *Relations in Public: Microstudies of the Public Order*. New York: Basic Books.

Goffman, Erving (1974) *Frame Analysis: An Essay on the Organization of Experience*. Cambridge, MA: Harvard University Press.

Goffman, Erving (1977) The arrangement between the sexes. *Theory and Society*, 4, 301–32.

Goffman, Erving (1983) The interaction order. *American Sociological Review*, 48, 1–17.

Goldblatt, Beth, and Meintjes, Shelia (1997) Dealing with the aftermath: Sexual violence and the truth and reconciliation commission. *Agenda*, 36, 7–18.

Goldhill, Simon, and Osborne, Robin (1999) *Performance Culture and Athenian Democracy*. Cambridge: Cambridge University Press.

Golub, Spencer (1984) *Evreinov: Theatre of Paradox and Transformation*. Ann Arbor, MI: UMI Research Press.

Goodin, Robert (2005) Sequencing deliberative moments. *Acta Politica*, 40, 182–96.

Goodin, Robert (2008) *Innovating Democracy: Democratic Theory and Practice After the Deliberative Turn*. Oxford: Oxford University Press.

Goodin, Robert, and Dryzek, John (2006) Deliberative impacts: The macro-political uptake of mini-publics. *Politics and Society*, 34(2), 219–44.

Goodsell, C. (1988) The architecture of parliaments: Legislative houses and political culture. *British Journal of Political Science*, 18(3), 287–3.

Gorz, Andre (2004) Interview with André Gorz. *Multitudes*, 15, 209.

Gramsci, Antonio (1971) In: Hoare, Quintin, and Nowell-Smith, Geoffrey (eds), *Selections from the Prison Notebooks of Antonio Gamsci*. New York: International Publishers.

Graybill, Lyn S. (2002) *Truth and Reconciliation in South Africa: Miracle or Model?* London: Lynne Rienner.

Greater London Authority (2006) *Report of the 7th July Committee*. London.

Greenblatt, Stephen (1980) *Renaissance Self-Fashioning: From More to Shakespeare*. Chicago, IL: University of Chicago Press.

Guha-Thakurta, T. (1992) *The Making of a New Indian Art: Artists, Aesthetics and Nationalism in Bengal, c.1850–1920*. Cambridge: Cambridge University Press.
Habermas, Jürgen (1989 [1962]) *The Structural Transformation of the Public Sphere: An Inquiry into a Category of Bourgeois Society*. Cambridge, MA: MIT Press.
Habermas, Jurgen (2010) *An Awareness of What is Missing*. Cambridge: Polity.
Haedicke, Susan C (2013) *Contemporary Street Arts in Europe: Aesthetics and Politics*. Basingstoke: Palgrave Macmillan.
Hajer, Maarten (2005) Setting the stage: A dramaturgy of policy deliberation. *Administration and Society*, 36(6), 624–47.
Hajer, Maarten (2009) *Authoritative Governance: Policy-Making in the Age of Mediatization*. Oxford: Oxford University Press.
Hallward, Peter (2006) Staging equality: On Rancière's theatrocracy. *New Left Review*, 37, 109–30.
Hamber, Brandon (1997) Living with the legacy of impunity: Lessons for South Africa about truth, justice and crime in Brazil. *Latin American Report*, 13(2), 4–16.
Hamber, Brandon (1999) *The Burdens of Truth: An Evaluation of the Psychological Support Services and Initiatives Undertaken by the South African Truth and Reconciliation Commission*. Johannesburg: Centre for the Study of Violence and Reconciliation.
Hancox, Dan (2011) *Kettling 2.0: The Olympic State of Exception and TSG Action Figures*, 7 Dec., <http://dan-hancox.blogspot.co.uk/2011/12/kettling-20-olympic-state-of-exception.html> [accessed Aug. 2013].
Harrington, John, and Mitchell, Elizabeth (eds) (1999) *Politics and Performance in Contemporary Northern Ireland*. Amherst, MA: University of Massachusetts Press.
Harvey, David (2012) *Rebel Cities: From the Right to the City to the Urban Revolution*. London and New York: Verso.
Haskins, Ekaterina V. (2000) 'Mimesis' between poetics and rhetoric: Performance culture and civic education in Plato, Isocrates, and Aristotle. *Rhetoric Society Quarterly*. 30(3), 7–33.
Hayes Solicitors (n.d.) Courts asked to balance rights of mother and unborn child, <http://www.hayes-solicitors.ie> [accessed Dec. 2012].
Hayner, Priscilla (2011) *Unspeakable Truths: Transitional Justice and the Challenge of Truth Commissions*. 2nd edn. London and New York: Routledge.
Hearn, Chester G. (2006) *Spies and Espionage: A Directory*. San Diego, CA: Thunder Bay Press.
Hénaff, Marcel, and Strong, Tracy (eds) (2001) *Public Space and Democracy*. Minneapolis, MN: University of Minnesota Press.
Hendriks, Carolyn (2006) Integrated deliberation: Reconciling civil society's dual role in deliberative democracy. *Political Studies*, 54(3), 486–508.
Herek, Gregory (1990) Gay people and government security clearances: A social science perspective. *American Psychologist*, 45(9), 1035–42.
Her Majesty's Inspectorate of Constabulary (HMIC) (2009) *Adapting to Protest*, 5 July, <http://www.hmic.gov.uk/publication/adapting-to-protest> [accessed Jan. 2014].
Herman, Edward S., and Chomsky, Noam (2002) *Manufacturing Consent: The Political Economy of the Mass Media*. New York: Pantheon.
Hill, Amelia, and Revill, Jo (2008) Racism rife in Commons, says MP. *Observer*, 13 April, <www.guardian.co.uk/world/2008/apr/13/race.houseofcommons> [accessed Oct. 2009].
Hindson, Paul, and Gray, Tim (1988) *Burke's Dramatic Theory of Politics*. Aldershot: Avebury.

Hobsbawm, Eric (2007) *Globalisation, Democracy and Terrorism*. London: Little, Brown.
Hobsbawm, Eric, and Ranger, Terence (eds) (1992 [1983]) *The Invention of Tradition*. Cambridge: Cambridge University Press.
Honig, Bonnie (2007) Between decision and deliberation: Political paradox in democratic theory. *American Political Science Review*, 101(1), 1–17.
Hood, Christopher, and Jackson, Michael (1991) *Administrative Argument*. Aldershot: Dartmouth.
Horelt, Michel-André (2012) Performing reconciliation: A performance approach to the analysis of political apologies. In: Palmer, Nicola, Clark, Phil, and Granville, Danielle (eds), *Critical Perspectives in Transitional Justice*. Cambridge: Intersentia, 347–68.
Horn, Eva (2011) The logics of political secrecy. *Theory, Culture and Society*, 28(7–8), 103–22.
Howard, Jean E. (1994) *The Stage and Social Struggle in Early Modern England*. London and New York: Routledge.
Hudson, Alan, and Tsekpo, Anthony (2009) *Parliamentary Strengthening and the Paris Principles, Synthesis Report*. London: ODI and Parliamentary Centre.
Hulme, Kathryn (1960) *The Wild Place*. New York: Cardinal.
Humphries, Steve (director) (1998) *Sex in a Cold Climate*. Testimony Films [Motion Picture].
Hutchison, Yvette (2013) *South African Performance and Archives of Memory*. Manchester: Manchester University Press.
Ilie, Cornelia (2003) Discourse and metadiscourse in parliamentary debates. *Journal of Language*, 2(1), 71–92.
Isin, Engin F., and Wood, Patricia K. (1999) *Citizenship and Identity*. London: Sage Publications.
Isocrates (1980) Antidosis. In: Norlin, George (ed. and trans.), *Isocrates: Vol. II*. Cambridge: Harvard University Press.
Jenkins, Simon (2011) Occupy Wall Street? These protests are not Tahrir Square but scenery. *Guardian*, 20 Oct., <http://www.theguardian.com/commentisfree/2011/oct/20/occupy-wall-street-tahrir-scenery> [accessed Aug. 2013].
Johnson, Barbara (1980) *The Critical Difference: Essays in the Contemporary Rhetoric of Reading*. Baltimore, MD: Johns Hopkins University Press.
Johnson, David K. (2004) *The Lavender Scare*. Chicago, IL: University of Chicago Press.
Johnson, Rachel E., Armitage, Faith, and Spary, Carole (2014) Pageantry as politics: The state opening of parliaments. In: Rai, Shirin M., and Johnson, Rachel E. (eds), *Disciplining Representation: Ceremony and Ritual in Parliaments*. Basingstoke: Palgrave.
Kapur, Devesh, and Mehta, Pratap Bhanu (2006) The Indian Parliament as an Institution of accountability. *Democracy, Governance and Human Rights Programme*. Paper 23. Geneva: UNRISD.
Kateb, George (1981) The moral distinctiveness of representative democracy. *Ethics*. 91(3), 357–74.
Kear, Adrian (2008a) Editorial: On appearance. *Performance Research: A Journal of the Performing Arts*, 13(4), 1–3.
Kear, Adrian (2008b) Intensities of appearance. *Performance Research: A Journal of the Performing Arts*, 13(4), 16–24.
Keating, Sara (2009) What site specific really means (interview with Louise Lowe), <http://www.irishtheatremagazine.ie> [accessed Dec. 2012].
Keenan, Thomas (1997) *Fables of Responsibility: Aberrations and Predicaments in Ethics and Politics*. Stanford, CA: Stanford University Press.

Kelsall, Tim (2005) Truth, lies, ritual: Preliminary reflections on the truth and reconciliation commission in Sierra Leone. *Human Rights Quarterly*, 27(2), 361–91.
Kennedy, Dennis (1993) *Foreign Shakespeare: Contemporary Performance*. Cambridge: Cambridge University Press.
Kennedy, Margaret (2011) Service of remembrance and proclamation, <http://www.macsas.org/PDFs/News/remembrance_service/margaret_kennedy_service_sheet.pdf> [accessed Sept. 2013].
Kennedy, M. (2012) Personal interview with Joshua Edelman, Greystones, Ireland, 6 May.
Kenya, Republic of (2008) *The Truth Justice and Reconciliation Act, 2008*. Nairobi: Government Printers.
Kershaw, Baz (2003) Curiosity or contempt: On spectacle, the human, and activism. *Theatre Journal*, 55(4), 591–611.
Kertzer, David (1988) *Ritual, Politics and Power*. New Haven, CT: Yale University Press.
Kester, Grant H. (2004) *Conversation Pieces: Community + Communication in Modern Art*. Los Angeles, CA: University of California Press.
KHRC [Kenya Human Rights Commission] (2011) *Lest we Forget: The Faces of Impunity in Kenya*. Nairobi: KHRC.
Kingdon, John W. (1984) *Agendas, Alternatives and Public Policies*. Boston, MA: Little, Brown.
Klein, Naomi (2011) Occupy Wall Street: The most important thing in the world now. *The Nation*, 6 Oct., <http://www.thenation.com/article/163844/occupy-wall-street-most-important-thing-world-now#> [accessed Aug. 2013].
KNDR [Kenya National Dialogue and Reconciliation] (2011) *Annex 1: Kenya National Dialogue and Reconciliation Monitoring Project National Survey*. Dialogue Kenya, <http://www.dialoguekenya.org/Monitoring/%28June%202011%29%2010TH%20Review%20Report%20Annex%201.pdf> [accessed Feb. 2014].
KNDR [Kenya National Dialogue and Reconciliation] (2011) *Kenya National Dialogue and Reconciliation Monitoring Project 11th Review Report*. Dialogue Kenya, <http://www.dialoguekenya.org/Monitoring/%28October%202011%29%2011TH%20Review%20Report.pdf> [accessed Feb. 2014].
KNDR [Kenya National Dialogue and Reconciliation] (2012) *Kenya National Dialogue and Reconciliation Monitoring Project*. Dialogue Kenya, <http://www.dialoguekenya.org/Monitoring/%28March%202012%29%201ST%20Review%20Report.pdf> [accessed Feb. 2014].
Krabill, Ron (2001) Symbiosis: Mass media and the Truth and Reconciliation Commission of South Africa. *Media, Culture and Society*, 23(5), 567–85.
Krog, Antjie (1999) *Country of my Skull*. London: Vintage.
Kruger, Loren (2004) *Post-Imperial Brecht: Politics and Performance, East and South*. Cambridge: Cambridge University Press.
Laclau, Ernesto (2005) *On Populist Reason*. London: Verso.
Laclau, Ernesto, and Mouffe, Chantal (2001) *Hegemony and Socialist Strategy: Towards a Radical Democratic Politics*. 2nd edn. London and New York: Verso.
Lam, Wai-man (2004) *Understanding the Political Culture of Hong Kong: The Paradox of Activism and Depoliticization*. Armonk, NY, and London: M. E. Sharpe.
Lane, Christel (1984) *The Rites of Rulers: Ritual in Industrial Society – The Soviet Case*. Cambridge: Cambridge University Press.
Laursen, John Christian (1986) The subversive Kant: The vocabulary of 'public' and 'publicity'. *Political Theory*, 14(4), 584–603.

Leach, Edmund (1976) *Culture and Communication: The Logic by which Symbols are Connected.* Cambridge: Cambridge University Press.
Lefebvre, Henri (1991) *The Production of Space.* Tr. Smith, Donald Nicholson. Oxford and Cambridge, MA: Blackwell.
Lefort, Claude (1988) *Democracy and Political Theory.* Tr. Macey, David. Cambridge: Polity Press.
Lehmann, Hans-Thies (2006) *Postdramatic Theatre.* Tr. Jürs-Munby, Karen. London and New York: Routledge.
Lennon, T. (2012) [email] Message to: Edelman, J. 12 April.
Lewis, Gail (2004) Racialising culture is ordinary. In: Silva, E. B., and Bennett, T. (eds), *Contemporary Culture and Everyday Life.* Durham: Sociology Press.
Lister, Ruth (2003) *Citizenship: Feminist Perspectives.* 2nd edn. Basingstoke and New York: Palgrave Macmillan.
Litvin, Margaret (2011) *Hamlet's Arab Journey: Shakespeare's Prince and Nasser's Ghost.* Princeton, NJ: Princeton University Press.
Lofland, Lyn (1998) *The Public Realm: Exploring the City's Quintessential Social Territory.* New York: Aldine de Gruyter.
Lowie, Robert H (1948) Some aspects of political organization among the American Aborigines. *Journal of the Royal Anthropological Institute of Great Britain and Ireland,* 78(1–2), 11–24.
Lucey, Cornelius (1936) The problem of the woman worker. *Irish Ecclesiastical Record,* 449–67.
Luddy, Maria (2007) Sex and the SINGLE GIRL in 1920s and 1930s Ireland. *Irish Review.* 35, 79–91.
Lukes, Stephen (1975) Political ritual and social integration. *Sociology,* 9(2), 289–308.
Lukes, Stephen (2005) *Power: A Radical View.* 2nd edn. London: Palgrave Macmillan.
Lupton, Julia Reinhard (2011) *Thinking with Shakespeare: Essays in Politics and Life.* Chicago, IL: University of Chicago Press.
Lynch, Gabrielle (2009) Durable solution, help or hindrance? The failings and unintended implications of relief and recovery efforts for Kenya's post-election IDPs. *Review of African Political Economy.* 36(122), 604–10.
Lynch, Gabrielle (2014a) Electing the 'alliance of the accused': The success of the Jubilee Alliance in Kenya's Rift Valley Province. *Journal of Eastern African Studies,* 8(1): 93–114.
Lynch, Gabrielle (2014b) Silence over truth commission's report on injustices is baffling. *Saturday Nation,* Nairobi, 10 May.
McAuley, Gay (ed.) (2006) Remembering and forgetting: Place and performance in the memory process. *Unstable Ground: Performance and the Politics of Place.* Brussels: Peter Lang, 149–76.
McCafferty, Nell (1985) *A Woman to Blame: The Kerry Babies Case.* Dublin: Attic Press.
McCargo, Duncan (2010) Thailand's National Reconciliation Commission: A flawed response to the Southern Conflict. *Global Change, Peace and Security,* 22(1), 75–91.
McCarthy, J. (1940) A report on abortion. *Irish Ecclesiastical Record,* 337–53.
Macchia, Frank (1997) Is footwashing the neglected sacrament? *Pneuma,* 19(2), 239–49.
McEachern, Charmaine (2002) *Narratives of Nation Media, Memory and Representation in the Making of the New South Africa.* New York: Nova Science Publishers.
McInerney, M. A. (1921) The souper problem in Ireland. *Irish Ecclesiastical Record,* 140–66.

McKenzie, Jon (2001) *Perform or Else: From Discipline to Performance*. London and New York: Routledge.
MACSAS (2012) *About Us*, <http://www.macsas.org.uk/MACSAS%20About%20Us.html> [accessed: Sept. 2013].
McVeigh, Karen (2011) Occupy Wall Street's women struggle to make their voices heard. *Guardian*, 30 Nov., <http://www.theguardian.com/world/2011/nov/30/occupy-wall-street-women-voices> [accessed Aug. 2013].
Madanipour, Ali (2003) *Public and Private Spaces of the City*. London: Routledge.
Maira, Sunaina Marr (2010) *Missing: Youth, Citizenship, and Empire After 9/11*. Durham, NC: Duke University Press.
Malik, Kenan (2009) *From Fatwa to Jihad: The Rushdie Affair and its Legacy*. London: Atlantic.
Mamdani, Mahmood (2002) Amnesty or impunity? A preliminary critique of the Truth and Reconciliation Commission of South Africa. *Diacritics*, 32(3–4), 33–59.
Managhan, Tina (2008) Grieving dead soldiers, disavowing loss: Cindy Sheehan and the im/possibility of the American antiwar movement. Violence, Bodies, Selves workshop. Manchester, 23 March.
Mansbridge, Jane (1999) Everyday talk in the deliberative system. In: Macedo, Stephen (ed.), *Deliberative Politics: Essays on 'Democracy and Disagreement'*. New York: Oxford University Press, 211–239.
Mansbridge, Jane (2003) Rethinking representation. *American Political Science Review*, 97(4), 515–28.
March, James G., and Olson, Johan P (1984) The new institutionalism: Organisational factors in political life. *American Political Science Review*, 78(3), 734–49.
Marciniak, Katarzyna (2006) *Alienhood: Citizenship, Exile, and the Logic of Difference*. Minneapolis, MN: University of Minnesota Press.
Marquiez, Miguel, and Ferran, Lee (2011) Norway shooting suspect Anders Breivik: Attacks were 'price of their treason', ABC News, 25 July, <http://abcnews.go.com/Blotter/anders-breivik-hearing-closed-pulpit-alleged-shooter/story?id=14152129> [accessed Jan. 2014].
Martain, Diarmuid (2011) Reflections from liturgy of lament and repentance, <http://www.dublindiocese.ie/content/2022011-reflections-liturgy-lament-and-repentance> [accessed Sept. 2013].
Massey, Doreen (1994) *Space, Place and Gender*. Cambridge: Polity Press.
Mbembe, A. (1992) Provisional notes on the postcolony. *Africa: Journal of the International African Institute*, 62(1), 3–37.
Meaney, Gerardine (1991) *Sex and Nation: Women in Irish Culture and Politics*. Dublin: Attic Press.
Minow, Martha (1998) *Between Vengeance and Forgiveness: Facing History After Genocide and Mass Violence*. Boston, MA: Beacon Press.
Mirzoeff, Nicholas (2012) The many futures of Occupy. *Huffington Post*, 21 Sept., <http://www.huffingtonpost.com/nicholas-mirzoeff/the-many-futures-of-occup_b_1897204.html?utm_hp_ref=elections-2012> [accessed Aug. 2013].
Mitter, Partha (1995) Western orientalism and the construction of nationalist art in India. *Oxford Art Journal*, 18(1), 140–3.
Mitter, Partha (2007) *The Triumph of Modernism: India's Artists and the Avant-garde, 1922–47*. London: Reaktion Books.
Moore, Sally F., and Myerhoff, Barbara G (eds) (1977) Introduction: Secular ritual. Forms and meanings. *Secular Ritual*. Amsterdam: Van Gorcum.

240 Bibliography

Mouffe, Chantal (ed.) (1992) *Dimensions of Radical Democracy: Pluralism, Citizenship, Community*. London and New York: Verso.

Mouffe, Chantal (2000) *The Democratic Paradox*. London and New York: Verso.

Mouffe, Chantal (2005) *On the Political*. London and New York: Routledge.

Mouffe, Chantal (2007) Artistic activism and agonistic spaces. *Art and Research*. 1(2), 1–5.

Mouton de Vapeur (n.d.) Les Quiétils. *Mouton de Vapeur,* <http://moutondevapeur.com/?page_id=25> [accessed Jan. 2014].

Mouton de Vapeur (n.d.). Les Quiétils. *Artistic Dossier,* <http://moutondevapeur.com/wp-content/uploads/2012/06/quietils.pdf> [accessed Jan. 2014].

Mughan, Anthony, Box-Steffenschmeier, Janet, and Scully, Roger (1997) Mapping legislative socialisation. *European Journal of Political Research*, 32, 93–106.

Murray, Christopher (1997) *Twentieth Century Irish Drama: Mirror up to Nation*. Manchester: Manchester University Press.

Nagel, Joanne (1998) Masculinity and nationalism: Gender and sexuality in the making of nations. *Ethnic and Racial Studies*, 21(2), 242–69.

Nagel, Thomas (1995) Personal rights and public space. *Philosophy and Public Affairs*, 24(2), 83–107.

Nancy, Jean-Luc (1991) *The Inoperative Community*. Tr. Connor, Peter, Garbus, Lisa, Holland, Michael and Sawhney, Simona. Minneapolis, MN: Minnesota University Press.

Nancy, Jean-Luc (2000) *Being Singular Plural*. Tr. Richardson, Robert, and O'Byrne, Anne. Stanford, CA: Stanford University Press.

Newly, Glen (1997) Political lying: A defense. *Public Affairs Quarterly*, 11(2), 93–116.

Nield, Sophie (2006a) There is another world: Space, theatre and global anti-capitalism. In: Harvie, Jen, and Rebellato, Dan (eds), *Contemporary Theatre Review: Theatre and Globalisation*. London: Routledge, 51–61.

Nield, Sophie (2006b) On the border as theatrical space: Appearance, dis-location and the production of the refugee. In: Kelleher, Joe, and Ridout, Nicholas (eds), *Contemporary Theatres in Europe*. London: Routledge, 61–72.

Nield, Sophie (2013) Siting the people: Power, protest and public space. In: Tomkins, Joanne, and Birch, Anna (eds), *Performing Site-Specific Theatre*. Basingstoke: Palgrave Macmillan, 219–32.

Nietzsche, Friedrich (1987) *Thus Spoke Zarathustra*. In: Kaufman, Walter (ed.), *The Portable Nietzsche*. New York: Penguin Books, 103–439.

Oakeshott, Michael (1962) *Rationalism in Politics and Other Essays*. London: Basic Books.

Oliver, Kelly (2001) *Witnessing: Beyond Recognition*. Minneapolis, MN: University of Minnesota Press.

O'Neill, John (1998) Rhetoric, Science and Philosophy. *Philosophy of the Social Sciences*, 28(2), 205–25.

Ong, Aihwa (1999) *Flexible Citizenship: The Cultural Logics of Transnationality*. Durham, NC: Duke University Press.

Orgel, Stephen, and Keilen, Sean (eds) (1999) *Political Shakespeare*. New York: Garland.

Orr, Wendy (2000) *From Biko to Basson: Wendy Orr's Search for the Soul of South Africa as a Commissioner of the TRC*. Saxonwold, SA: Contra Press.

Osborne, John (1966) *A Patriot for Me*. London: Faber & Faber.

Osiel, Mark (2000) *Mass Atrocity, Collective Memory, and the Law*. New Brunswick, NJ: Transaction Publishers.

Owens, Patricia (2009) Reclaiming 'bare life'?: Against Agamben on refugees. *Journal of International Relations*, 23/24, 567–82.

Parenti, Christian (2003) *The Soft Cage: Surveillance in America from Slavery to the War on Terror*. New York: Basic Books.
Parker-Starbuck, Jennifer (2008) Pig bodies and vegetative states: Diagnosing the symptoms of a culture of excess. *Women and Performance: A Journal of Feminist Theory*, 18(2), 135.
Parkinson, John (2006) *Deliberating in the Real World: Problems of Legitimacy in Deliberative Democracy*. Oxford: Oxford University Press.
Parkinson, John (2007) The House of Lords: A deliberative democratic defence. *Political Quarterly*, 78(3), 374–81.
Parkinson, John (2009) Symbolic representation in public space: Capital cities, presence and memory. *Representation*, 45(1), 1–14.
Parkinson, John (2012) *Democracy and Public Space: The Physical Sites of Democratic Performance*. Oxford: Oxford University Press.
Parkinson, John, and Mansbridge, Jane (eds) (2012) *Deliberative Systems: Deliberative Democracy at the Large Scale*. Cambridge: Cambridge University Press.
Pavis, Patrice (1998) *Dictionary of the Theatre: Terms, Concepts, and Analysis*. Toronto: University of Toronto Press.
Pearson, Mike (2006) *'In Comes I': Performance, Memory and Landscape*. Exeter: University of Exeter Press.
Pennings, Paul (2000) Parliamentary control of the executive in 47 democracies. 28th Joint Sessions of Workshops of the European Consortium for Political Research, 14–19 April, <http://www.Essex.Ac.Uk/ECPR/Events/Jointsessions/Paperarchive/Copenhagen/Ws10/Pennings.PDF> [accessed Oct. 2009].
Pelias, Ronald, and Van Oosting, James (1987) A paradigm for performance studies. *Quarterly Journal of Speech*, 73, 219–31.
Pfaff, Tony, and Tiel, Jeffery (2004) The ethics of espionage. *Journal of Military Ethics*, 3(1), 1–15.
Phelan, Peggy (1993) *Unmarked: The Politics of Performance*. London: Routledge.
Plato (389 BCE) *Ion*. Tr. Benjamin Jowett, <http://classics.mit.edu/Plato/ion.html> [accessed May 2014].
Plato (1987) *The Republic*. Tr. Desmond Lee. London: Penguin.
Plato (1989) *Republic of Plato*. Tr. Allan Bloom. 2nd edn. New York: Basic Books.
Polletta, Francesca (2008) Storytelling in politics. *Contexts*, 7(4), 26–31.
Polletta, Francesca (2013) Participatory democracy in the new millennium. *Contemporary Sociology: A Journal of Reviews*, 42(1), 40–50.
Polletta, Francesca, and Lee, John (2006) Is telling stories good for democracy? Rhetoric in public deliberation after 9/11. *American Sociological Review*, 71(5), 699–723.
Potolsky, Matthew (2006) *Mimesis*. New York and London: Routledge.
Puwar, Nirmal (2004) *Space Invaders: Race, Gender and Bodies Out of Place*. Oxford: Berg.
Puwar, Nirmal (2010) The architexture of parliament: Flaneur as method. In: S. M. Rai (ed.), *Ceremony and Ritual in Parliament*. London: Routledge.
Rabkin, Norman (1966) The tragedy of politics. *Shakespeare Quarterly*, 17(3), 195–212.
Rae, Paul (2011) Pigs might fly: Dance in the time of swine flu. *Theatre Journal*, 63(3), 403–24.
Rai, Shirin M. (2002) *Gender and the Political Economy of Development*. Cambridge: Polity Press.
Rai, Shirin M. (2010) Analysing ceremony and ritual in parliament. *Journal of Legislative Studies*, 16(3), 284–97.
Rai, Shirin M. (2010) *Ceremony and Ritual in Parliament*. London: Routledge.

Bibliography

Rai, Shirin M. (2014) Political aesthetics of the nation: Interventions. *International Journal of Postcolonial Studies* (DOI: 10.1080/1369801X.2014.882147).

Rai, Shirin M. (2014) Political performance: A framework for analysing democratic politics. *Political Studies* (DOI: 10.1111/1467-9248.12154).

Rai, Shirin M., and Johnson, Rachel (eds) (2014) *Disciplining Representation: Ceremony and Ritual in Parliaments*. Basingstoke: Palgrave Macmillan.

Rancière, Jacques (1999) *Disagreement: Politics and Philosophy*. Tr. Rose, J. Minneapolis, MN: University of Minnesota Press.

Rancière, Jacques (2001) Ten theses on politics. *Theory and Event*, 5(3), 1–16.

Rancière, Jacques (2004) *The Politics of Aesthetics: The Distribution of the Sensible*. Tr. Rockhill, Gabriel. London: Continuum.

Rancière, Jacques (2009) *The Emancipated Spectator*. Tr. Elliott, Gregory. London: Verso.

Rancière, Jacques (2010) *Dissensus: On Politics and Aesthetics*. Tr. Corcoran, Steven. London and New York: Continuum.

Rapaport, Amos (1982) *The Meaning of the Built Environment*. Beverly Hills, CA: Sage.

Read, Alan (2008) *Theatre, Intimacy and Engagement: The Last Human Venue*. Basingstoke: Palgrave Macmillan.

Rebellato, Dan (2009) *Theatre and Globalization*. Basingstoke: Palgrave Macmillan.

Rehfeld, Andrew (2009) Representation rethought: On trustees, delegates, and gyroscopes in the study of political representation and democracy. *American Political Science Review*, 103(2), 214–30.

Reinelt, Janelle (2006) Towards a poetics of theatre and public events: The case of Stephen Lawrence. *TDR: The Drama Review*, 50(3), 69–87.

Reinelt, Janelle (2011) Rethinking the public sphere for a global age. *Performance Research*, 16(2), 16–27.

Reinelt, Janelle (2012) Performance at the crossroads of citizenship. *Journal of Performing Arts Theory*, 19, 6–15 in Serbian; 98–107 in English.

Reinelt, Janelle, and Hewitt, Gerald (2011) *The Political Theatre of David Edgar: Negotiation and Retrieval*. Cambridge: Cambridge University Press.

Reinelt, Janelle, and Roach, Joseph (eds) (1992) *Critical Theory and Performance*. Ann Arbor, MI: University of Michigan Press.

Reinisch, Charlotte, and Parkinson, John (2007) Swiss Landsgemeinden: A deliberative democratic evaluation of two outdoor parliaments. European Consortium for Political Research Joint Sessions. Helsinki.

Resnik, Judith, and Curtis, Dennis E. (2011) *Representing Justice: The Creation and Fragility of Courts in Democracies*. New Haven, CT: Yale University Press.

Reynolds, Andrew (2002) *The Architecture of Democracy: Constitutional Design, Conflict Management and Democracy*. Oxford: Oxford University Press.

Reynolds, David (2007) *Summits: Six Meetings that Shaped the Twentieth Century*. New York: Basic Books.

Ridout, Nicholas (2013) *Passionate Amateurs: Theatre, Communism, and Love*. Ann Arbor, MI: University of Michigan Press.

Roach, Joe (2007) *It*. Ann Arbor, MI: University of Michigan Press.

Rokem, Freddie (2009) *Philosophers and Thespians: Thinking Performance*. Palo Alto, CA: Stanford University Press.

Rose, Gillian (1999) Performing space. In: Massey, Doreen, Allen, John, and Sarre, Philip (eds), *Human Geography Today*. Cambridge: Polity Press. 247–59.

Rosenblatt, Gemma (2007) From one of us to one of them: The socialisation of new MPs. *Parliamentary Affairs*, 60(3), 510–17.

Ross, Fiona (2003) *Bearing Witness: Women and the Truth and Reconciliation Commission in South Africa*. London: Pluto Press.

Rousseau, Jean-Jacques (1960) *Politics and the Arts: Letter to M. D'Alembert on the Theatre*. Tr. A. Bloom. Ithaca, NY: Cornell University Press.

Rowan, Rory (2010) *Geographies of the Kettle: Containment, Spectacle and Counter-Strategy*, 16 Dec., <http://criticallegalthinking.com/2010/12/16/geographies-of-the-kettle-containment-spectacle-counter-strategy> [accessed Aug. 2013].

Roy, Anupama (2005) *Gendered Citizenship: Historical and Conceptual Explorations*. New Delhi: Orient Longmann.

Saalfeld, T., and Müller, W. C. (1997) Roles in legislative studies: A theoretical introduction. *Journal of Legislative Studies*, 3(1), 1–16.

Sachs, Albie (1983) *Images of a Revolution: Mural Art in Mozambique*. Harare: Zimbabwe Publishing House.

Sagart (1922) How to deal with the unmarried mother. *Irish Ecclesiastical Record*, 145–53.

Said, Edward. (1978) *Orientalism*. London: Routledge & Kegan Paul.

Sanders, Lynn (1997) Against deliberation. *Political Theory*, 25(3), 347–76.

Sanders, Mark (2007) *Ambiguities of Witnessing: Law and Literature in the Time of a Truth Commission*. Stanford, CA: Stanford University Press.

Sangari, Kumkum, and Ved, Sudesh (1990) *Recasting Women: Essays in Colonial History*. Rutgers, NJ: Rutgers University Press.

Santner, Eric L. (2006) *On Creaturely Life: Rilke, Benjamin, Sebald*. Chicago, IL, and London: University of Chicago Press.

Sardar, Ziauddin, and Davies, Merryl Wyn (2003) *Why do People Hate America?* London: Disinformation Press.

Saturday Nation (2013) MPs change law to alter Truth report, by *Nation* Reporter. Nairobi, 7 Dec.

Sauter, Willmar (2000) *The Theatrical Event: Dynamics of Performance and Perception*. Iowa City, IA: University of Iowa Press.

Saward, Michael (2003) Enacting democracy. *Political Studies*, 51(1), 161–79.

Saward, Michael (2006) The representative claim. *Contemporary Political Theory*, 5, 297–318.

Saward, Michael (2010) *The Representative Claim*. Oxford: Oxford University Press.

Scallon, Kevin (2011) *Reparation and Repentance March 2010: A Eucharistic Prayer Service for Ireland in Response to the Invitation of Pope Benedict XVI*. Dublin: Veritas Publications.

Schechner, Richard (2003) *Performance Theory*. 2nd edn. London: Routledge.

Schechner, Richard (2013) *Performance Studies: An Introduction*. 3rd edn. Abingdon, Oxon: Routledge.

Schrager Lang, Amy, and Lang/Levitsky, Daniel (eds) (2012) *Dreaming in Public: Building the Occupy Movement*. Oxford: New Internationalist Publications.

Schudson, Michael (1999) *The Good Citizen: A History of American Civic Life*. Cambridge, MA: Harvard University Press.

Sedgwick, Eve Kosofsky (2008) *Epistemology of the Closet*. 2nd edn. Berkeley, CA: University of California.

Šehić, Faruk (2008) *Apokalipsa iz recicle bina*. Sarajevo: Buybook.

Sennett, Richard (2002) *The Fall of Public Man*. London: Penguin.

SHAEF (1945) Flow chart: Inside an Assembly Centre for United Nations DPs. Displaced Persons Branch G-5 SHAEF. The National Archives, Kew, F 945/591.

Shaw, Kara (2009) *Political Theory and Indigeneity: Sovereignty and the Limits of the Political*. New York: Routledge.
Shaw, Rosalind (2007) Memory frictions: Localizing the truth and reconciliation commission in Sierra Leone. *International Journal of Transitional Justice*, 1(2), 183–207.
Shehata, S. S (1992) The politics of laughter: Nasser, Sadat, and Mubarek in Egyptian political jokes. *Folklore*, 103(1), 75–91.
Shils, Edward, and Young, Michael (1953) The meaning of the coronation. *Sociological Review*, 1(2), 63–81.
Simone, Jeanne (n.d.) *ACCUEIL*, <http://www.villagedecirque.com/2r2cms> [accessed Jan. 2014].
Simone, Jeanne (n.d.) Le Parfum des pneus. *Daily Motion,* <http://www.dailymotion.com/video/xhvwti_arts-de-la-rue-cie-jeanne-simone-le-parfum-des-pneus_creation> [accessed Jan. 2014].
Simpson, David (1992) Lying, liars and language. *Philosophy and Phenomenological Research*, 52(3), 623–39.
Singleton, Brian (2013) ANU Productions and site-specific performance: The politics of space and place. In: Walsh, Fintan (ed.), *'That Was Us': Contemporary Irish Theatre and Performance*. London: Oberon.
Smith, Graham (2009) *Democratic Innovations*. Cambridge: Cambridge University Press.
Smith, James M. (2007) *Ireland's Magdalene Laundries and the Nation's Architecture of Containment*. Manchester: Manchester University Press.
Sollors, Werner (1996) *Theories of Ethnicity: A Classical Reader*. New York: New York University Press.
Soule, Sarah, and Davenport, Christian (2009) Velvet glove, iron fist, or even hand? Protest policing in the United States, 1960–1990. *Mobilization*, 14(1), 1–22.
Souweine, Isaac (2005) Naked protest and the politics of personalism. In: Narula, Monica, Sengupta, Sengupta, Bagchi, Jeebesh, Lovink, Geert, Liang, Lawrence, and Vohra, Smriti (eds), *Sarai Reader 05: Bare Acts*. Delhi: Sarai Programme, 526–36.
Spary, C. (2010) Disrupting rituals of debate in the Indian Parliament. *Journal of Legislative Studies*, 16(4), 338–51.
Spary, C., and Rai, S. M. (2013) Disruptive democracy: Analysing legislative protest. Special issue of *Democratization* 20(3), 385–391.
Spencer, Jonathan (1997) Post-colonialism and the political imagination. *Journal of the Royal Anthropological Institute*, 3(1), 1–19.
Spragens, Thomas A. (1990) *Reason and Democracy*. Durham, NC: Duke University Press.
Stallabrass, Julian (2006) Spectacle and terror. *New Left Review*. 37 (Jan.—Feb.), 87–106.
Stanley, Elizabeth (2001) Evaluating the Truth and Reconciliation Commission. *Journal of Modern African Studies*, 39(3), 525–46.
Stan's Cafe (n.d.) *Of All the People in All the World*, <http://www.stanscafe.co.uk/project-of-all-the-people.html> [accessed Jan. 2014].
Stephens, Angharad Closs (2008) Community, time, security: The persistence of nationalism in Judith Butler's *Precarious Lives*. Globalization, Difference and Human Security Conference. Osaka University, Japan, 12–14 March.
Stephens, Angharad Closs (2010) Citizenship without community: Time, design, and the city. *Citizenship Studies*, 14(1), 31–46.
Stone, Deborah (2002) *Policy Paradox: The Art of Political Decision Making*. Revised edn. New York: Norton.
Street, John (2001) *Mass Media, Politics and Democracy*. Basingstoke: Palgrave.

Strøm, K., 1997. Rules, reasons and routines: Legislative roles in parliamentary democracies. *Journal of Legislative Studies*, 3(1), 155–74.

Sunstein, Cass (2002) The law of group polarization. *Journal of Political Philosophy*, 10(2), 175–95.

Szymborska, Wisława (1998) *Poems New and Collected*. Orlando, FL: Harcourt.

Taylor, Astra, Gessen, Keith, and editors from n+1, Dissent, Triple Canopy and the New Inquiry (2011) *Occupy! Scenes from Occupied America*. London and New York: Verso.

Taylor, Charles (2011) Why we need a radical redefinition of secularism. In: Mendieta, Eduardo, and VanAntwerpen, Jonathan (eds), *The Power of Religion in the Public Sphere*. New York: Columbia University Press.

Taylor, Diana (1998) Making a spectacle: The mothers of the Plaza de Mayo. In: Cohen-Cruz, Jan (ed.), *Radical Street Performance*. London and New York: Routledge, 74–85.

Taylor, Diana (2003) *The Archive and the Repertoire: Performing Cultural Memory in the Americas*. Durham, NC, and London: Duke University Press.

The Sultan's Elephant (n.d.) *The Sultan's Elephant*, <http://www.artichoke.uk.com/events/the_sultans_elephant> [accessed Jan. 2014].

Thomas, John Christopher (2004) *Footwashing in John 13 and the Johannine Community*. Edinburgh: T. & T. Clark.

Thompson, Dennis F. (2008) Deliberative democratic theory and empirical political science. *Review of Political Science*. 11, 497–520.

Thomson, George (1946) *Aeschylus and Athens: A Study in the Social Origins of Drama*. 2nd edn. London: Lawrence & Wishart.

Tilly, Charles (2004) *Contention and Democracy in Europe, 1650–2000*. Cambridge: Cambridge University Press.

Tilly, Charles (2008) *Contentious Performances*. Cambridge: Cambridge University Press.

Tillyard, E. M. W. (1943) *The Elizabethan World Picture*. London: Chatto & Windus.

TJRC [Truth, Justice and Reconciliation Commission] (2013) *Report of the Truth, Justice and Reconciliation Commission*, vol. 1. Nairobi: TJRC.

Toibin, Colm (1985) *Seeing is Believing*. Montrath: Pilgrim Press.

Turner, V. W. (1970). *The Forest of Symbols: Aspects of Ndembu Ritual*. Ithaca, NY: Cornell University Press.

Turner, Victor (1974) *Dramas, Fields, and Metaphors: Symbolic Action in Human Society*. Ithaca, NY: Cornell University Press.

Tutu, Desmond (1999) *No Future Without Forgiveness*. London: Rider.

Tyler, Imogen, and Marciniak, Katarzyna (2013) Immigrant protest: Introduction. *Citizenship Studies*, 17(2), 143–56.

Vatican (2000a) *Day of Pardon*, 12 March, <http://www.vatican.va/jubilee_2000/jubilevents/events_day_pardon_en.htm> [accessed Sept. 2013].

Vatican (2000b) *Universal Prayer*, <http://www.vatican.va/news_services/liturgy/documents/ns_lit_doc_20000312_prayer-day-pardon_en.html> [accessed Sept. 2013].

Vatican (2000c) *Day of Pardon Presentation*, <http://www.vatican.va/news_services/liturgy/documents/ns_lit_doc_20000312_presentation-day-pardon_e> [accessed Sept. 2013].

Verba, Sidney (1965) If, as Lipsitz thinks, political science is to save our souls, God help us! *American Political Science Review*, 62, 576–7.

Vernant, Jean-Pierre (1974) *Myth and Society in Ancient Greece*. Tr. Lloyd, Janet. Andover: Harvester Press.

Virmani, Arundhati (2008) *A National Flag for India: Rituals, Nationalism, and the Politics of Sentiment*. New Delhi: Orient Longman.

Waddington, David (1992) *Contemporary Issues in Public Disorder*. London: Routledge.

246 Bibliography

Walker, Greg (1998) *The Politics of Performance in Early Renaissance Drama*. Cambridge: Cambridge University Press.
Walker, Peter (2012) Protester receives Olympics asbo. *Guardian*, 17 April, <http://www.theguardian.com/society/2012/apr/17/protester-receives-olympic-asbo> [accessed Aug. 2013].
Walker, Rob B. J. (1990) International relations/world politics. Unpublished paper.
Walker, Rob B. J. (2007) Closing comments. BISA Security, Aesthetics, and Visual Culture Workshop. Queens University, Belfast, 10 Nov.
Walzer, Michael (1967) On the role of symbolism in political thought. *Political Science Quarterly*, 82(2), 191–204.
Warner, Michael (2002) *Publics and Counterpublics*. New York: Zone Books.
Warner, S. J. (1945) Letter to Lt Col. E. M. Hammer, 20 July. FO 945/557. The National Archives, Kew.
Warner, W. Lloyd (1959) *The Living and the Dead: A Study of the Symbolic Life of Americans*. New Haven, CT: Yale University Press.
Waylen, Georgina (2010) Researching ritual and the symbolic in parliaments: An institutionalist perspective. *Journal of Legislative Studies*, 16(3), 352–65.
Webb, Nicky (ed.) (2006) *Four Magical Days in May: How an Elephant Captured the Heart of a City*. London: Artichoke Trust.
Weber, Cynthia (1999) *Faking it: US Hegemony in a 'Post-Phallic' Era*. Minneapolis, MN: University of Minnesota Press.
Weber, Cynthia (2006) *Imagining America at War: Politics, Morality, Film*. London: Routledge.
Weber, Cynthia (2007) 'I am an American': Portraits of post-9/11 US citizens. 11 Sept., <http://www.opendemocracy.net/article/democracy_power/america_power_world/citizen_identity> [accessed Feb. 2014].
Weber, Cynthia (2008) Designing safe citizens. *Citizenship Studies*, 12(2), 125–42.
Weber, Cynthia (2011) *'I am an American': Filming the Fear of Difference*. Bristol: Intellect Books.
Weiner, Tim (2008) *Legacy of Ashes: The History of the CIA*. New York: Anchor Books.
Welchman, Lynn, and Hossain, Sara (2005) Introduction: 'Honour', rights and wrongs. In: Welchman, Lynn, and Hossain, Sara (eds), *Honour*. London: Zedbooks.
Wertenbaker, Timberlake (2001) *Credible Witness*. London: Faber Plays.
Weschler, Lawrence (2006) Preface. In: Reuter, Laurel (ed.), *Los Desaparecidos/The Disappeared*. Milan: Charta.
Whitehead, Laurence (1999) The drama of democratization. *Journal of Democracy*, 10(4), 84–98.
Wickstrom, Mauyra (2012) *Performance in the Blockades of Neoliberalism*. Basingstoke: Palgrave.
Wigley, Mark (2002) Insecurity by design. In: Sorkin, Michael, and Zukin, Sharon (eds), *After the World Trade Centre: Rethinking New York City*. New York: Routledge.
Wilentz, Sean (ed.) (1985) *Rites of Power: Symbolism, Ritual and Politics since the Middle Ages*. Philadelphia: University of Pennsylvania Press.
Wiles, David (2011) *Theatre and Citizenship: The History of a Practice*. Cambridge: Cambridge University Press.
Willett, John (1977) *The Theatre of Bertolt Brecht: A Study from Eight Aspects*. 3rd edn. London: Eyre Methuen.
Wilson, Francesca M. (1947) *Aftermath: France, Germany, Austria, Yugoslavia 1945 and 1946*. West Drayton, Middlesex, and New York: Penguin Books.

Wilson, Richard A. (2001) *The Politics of Truth and Reconciliation in South Africa: Legitimizing the Post-Apartheid State*. Cambridge: Cambridge University Press.

Winkler, John, and Zeitlin, Froma (1990) *Nothing to Do with Dionysus? Athenian Drama in its Social Context*. Princeton, NJ: Princeton University Press.

Wise, David, and Ross, Thomas (1964) *The Invisible Government*. New York: Random House.

Wright, Tony, and Gamble, Andrew (1999) Commentary: Reforming the Lords (again). *Political Quarterly*, 70(3), 249–53.

Young, Iris Marion (1990) *Justice and the Politics of Difference*. Princeton, NJ: Princeton University Press.

Young, Iris Marion (1997) Unruly categories: A critique of Nancy Fraser's dual systems theory. *New Left Review*, 1/222 (March–April), 147–60.

Young, Iris Marion (2000) *Inclusion and Democracy*. Oxford: Oxford University Press.

Young, Iris Marion (2000) *Justice and the Politics of Difference*. Princeton, NJ: Princeton University Press.

Young, Iris Marion (2001) Activist challenges to deliberative democracy. *Political Theory*, 29(5), 670–90.

Younge, Gary (2011) Who knows where the occupations are going – it's just great to be moving. *Guardian*, 6 Nov., <http://www.theguardian.com/commentisfree/2011/nov/06/knows-occupations-going-great-moving> [accessed Aug. 2013].

Žižek, Slavoj (1994) *The Metastases of Enjoyment: On Women and Causality*. New York: Verso.

Žižek, Slavoj (2009) *Violence*. London: Profile.

Žižek, Slavoj (2011) Occupy first: Demands come later. 26 Oct. <http://www.theguardian.com/commentisfree/2011/oct/26/occupy-protesters-bill-clinton> [accessed Aug. 2014].

Zuckerman, Ethan (2011) The first Twitter revolution? *Foreign Policy*, 14 Jan., <http://www.foreignpolicy.com/articles/2011/01/14/the_first_twitter_revolution> [accessed Feb. 2014].

Index

7/7 bombings, London 39–40, 139–40
9/11 aftermath: citizenships and nationalisms 51–64; missing persons 139–41

abortion, Ireland 67–8
Abse, Leo 211
Abu Ghraib, images of torture 82
activists, arrests of 129
adversely mentioned persons (AMPs) hearings, Kenya 174
Agamben, Georgio 15, 36, 41, 81; 'bare life' 14, 83–7; form-of-life 87, 88, 91; power 152
Ahmed, Sara 62, 65, 75
Alexander, Jeffrey C. 102, 103, 154
Alsultany, Evelyn 51, 53, 54, 55, 64
American Advertising Council 51–6, 61–4
'Americanness' 51–64
Anderson, Benedict 156, 157
Andreas, Peter, *Blue Helmets and Black Markets* 80
'animatives' vs. 'performatives', Taylor 11
Anu Productions 69, 73, 79, 186
apartheid, South Africa 163–4, 169
Arellano, Elvira 57, *58*, 62, 64
Arellano, Saul *59*, 60, 62
Argentina, the disappeared 137–8, 143–5
Aristotle, rhetoric 3, 5, 6, 13, 101
army deserter, story of 60
Ashley, Richard K. 55
audiences, democratic 21–5
Austin, J.L., *How to Do Things with Words* 224
Author, The (Crouch) 47–8

Badiou, Alain 34–5
Balibar, Etienne 14–15, 36, 42–4

'bare life' 14, 83–7
Barth, Karl 194
Baumann, Gerd 160
Beckett, Samuel 6
Bell, Catherine 192
Bellaby, Ross 200
belonging and citizenship 14, 37, 45, 110, 158–9
Bergen, Jeremy 189
Bhabha, Homi 65
Bitzer, Lloyd 100, 101
blackmail, susceptibility of gay spies to 204, 205, 207, 210, 211, 212, 213
Blair, Tony 39
Blau, Herbert 13
Bloch, Maurice 185, 196–7
Blue Boy, The (Cannon and Keegan) 186
Blue Helmets and Black Markets (Andreas) 80
Blunt, Anthony 210–11
Boal, Augusto 6
bombings, London 39–40, 139–40
Boone, Pat 65
Boraine, Alex 163
border issues, Mexico 57–60
Bosnian War (1992–6) 14, 15, 80
Bourdieu, Pierre 12, 76
Brahm, Eric 180–1
'breaking out', Butler 82, 83
Brecht, Bertolt 6, 43
Brown, Wendy 35
Burke, Edmund 20
Burke, Kenneth 25, 28–9; *Grammar of Motives, A* 3
Bush, George W. 56
Butler, Judith 8–9, 63, 130, 131–2, 146, 153; 'breaking out' 82, 83; *Gender Trouble* 159

Cambridge Five 210
Cannon, Feidlim, *Blue Boy, The* 186
Carlson, Eric Stener 147; *I Remember Julia* 144
Carson, Thomas 199
Catholic Church: and motherhood in Irish culture 67–78; sexual abuse scandal 2, 16–17, 68, 185–96
Causey, Mathew, *Performance, Identity and the Neo-Political Subject* 8
Cavarero, Adriana 145
Celermajer, Danielle 188
ceremony in Parliament 5, 7, 129, 148–55, 156–61
Chambers, Simone 98–9
Chomsky, Noam 199
Church of Fear, The (Schlingensief) 91
CIA collusion 205
Cicero 100
citizenship 34–49; 'I am an American' advertising campaign 51–64; street art and storytelling 106–19; through performance 158–9
class prejudice, unmarried mothers 74–5
Clastres, Pierre 95
Cohen, Jean 22
cold war politics 198–215
community, different notions of 137
confession of sins 187–9, 191
Coriolanus (Shakespeare) 93–4, 96–7
'counterpublics' 42, 219–20, 223
'critical difference', Johnson 51–2, 62
critical grammars 217–25
Cronin, Anne 64
Crouch, Tim, *Author, The* 47–8

'Day of Pardon', Vatican 187–9
de Certeau 112
Debord, Guy, Situationist movement 6
deception and espionage 198–215
democracy: ideas of Claude Lefort 120; and parliaments 148–51; the people as 'subject' of 104; performance of 14–15, 19–33; radical 108–10, 116, 118, 119; representation 12–13; synonymous with politics 119; worksites of 42–3
Derrida, Jacques 13, 65–6, 203, 218–19
Devane, R. S. 74, 75
Diklić, D. 81, 85, 88, 90
disappeared people 137–8, 143–5
displaced persons, post-war Europe 141–3
Do You Remember Sarajevo? (film) 88–9, 90–1, 92
Dolan, Jill 194

Dollimore, Jonathan 5
Donia, Robert 87–8
Dorfman, Ariel 145–6
Dryzek, John 20
Dunsire, Andrew 33
Durkheim, Emile 154–6

Edelman, Joshua 16–17
Edgar, David, *Testing the Echo* 45–6, 48
Edkins Jenny 10, 11, 14, 16
elections: Kenya 166–7, 180; post-election violence 179
Elizabethan World Picture, The (Tillyard) 5
Elstub, Stephen 24
'emancipated spectator', Rancière 114
Epistemology of the Closet (Sedgwick) 206
espionage 198–215
Evreinov, Nikolai 89, 90

Facebook revolutions 28
Farrell, Thomas 101–2
Fatayi-Williams, Anthony 140
Fatayi-Williams, Marie 140, 141
Ferriter, Diarmuid 74
films: post-9/11 documentaries 60–3; Sarajevo Film Festival 81–92
Fine, John 87–8
Finlayson, Alan 16
Fish, Stanley 184
Fitzpatrick, Lisa 15
Flynn, Gerald Mannix, *James X* 186
footwashing ritual 194
forgiveness, sought by church 187, 188, 189, 192–3, 195
'form-of-life' (Agamben) 87, 88, 91
Fortes, Meyer 94–5
Fortier, Anne-Marie 56
Foucault, Michel 137, 143, 156, 159
Fraser, Nancy 8–9
Freire, Paulo 113

Gender Advertisements (Goffman) 154
gender roles 68–9, 157, 159
Gender Trouble (Butler) 159
Goffman, Erving 80, 155; *Gender Advertisements* 154
Goldhill, Simon 5
government, invisible 213–15
Grammar of Motives, A (Burke) 3
Greenblatt, Stephen 5

Habermas, Jürgen 17, 187, 196; *Structural Transformation of the Public Sphere* 183–4

Haedicke, Susan C. 15
Hajer, Maarten 21, 25, 32
Hallward, Peter 12
Hancox, Dan 126–7
Harding, James M. 17, 220
Harvey, David 124, 132
Haskins, Ekaterina V. 100
hearings: homosexuals in US government, 1950s 204–9; TJRC, Kenya 162–82
Herek, Gregory 214–15
'hidden opposites' 224
Hillenkoetter, Admiral Roscoe 207–9, 212, 213, 214, 215–16
Hobsbawm, Eric 123, 148; *Invention of Tradition, The* 156
homosexuality, 1950s US Government 198–214
Hong Kong, 1 July marches 31, 33
Honig, Bonnie 104–5
Horn, Eva 199–201, 202, 203, 205, 206, 209
How to Do Things with Words (Austin) 224
Howard, Jean E. 5
Hulme, Kathryn 142
human statistics, grains of rice representing 46
Hunt, William 87–8

I Remember Julia (Carlson) 144
identity politics 8–9, 13, 34–5; differences, staging of 44–5
immigration issues, Mexican people 57–60
India, Parliament *151*
infanticide 68, 74
intelligence agencies, intentional deception by 198–215
International Criminal Court (ICC) 179–80
Invention of Tradition, The (Hobsbawm and Ranger) 156
Invisible Government (Wise and Ross) 213–14
Ireland: mother figure in Irish culture 67–78; sexual abuse scandal 183–96
Isin, Engin 40
Isocrates 100

Jacob, Archdeacon William 190
James X (Flynn) 186
Jenkins, Simon 122
Jestrovic, Silvija 15
Johnson, Barbara, 'critical difference' 51–2, 62
Johnson, David K. 208; *The Lavender Scare* 207

Kant, Immanuel 97–8
Kear, Adrian 10, 11, 135, 136, 146
Keegan, Gary, *Blue Boy, The* 186
Keilen, Sean 5
Kennedy, John F. 96
Kennedy, Margaret 190–1
Kenny, Enda 195
Kenya, Republic of, TJRC 162–80
Kershaw, Baz 160
Kertzer, David 151, 153
Kester, Grant H. 112
kettling 127–8
Kingdon, John W. 22
Kiplagat, Bethuel 167, 177–8
Krabill, Ron 182
Kreševljakovic, Nihad 87–92

Laclau, Ernesto 104, 108–9
Laundry (Lowe) 15, 69–78, 186
Lavender Scare, The (Johnson) 207
Lefebvre, Henri 125–6
Lefort, Claude 120
legitimacy, political 221–3
Lehmann, Hans-Thies 8, 43–4, 45, 47, 77; *Postdramatisches Theater* 35
Lennon, T. 189
lies, lying, political secrecy 17, 198–209, 212–13
Liturgy of Lament and Repentance, Dublin 192–5
'Logics of Political Secrecy' (essay, Horn) 202
London 2005 bombings, missing persons 139–41
Lowe, Louise 73; *Laundry* 15, 69–78, 186
Lowie, Robert 95
Luddy, Maria 67, 74
Lukes, Stephen 6, 155–6, 159
Lupton, Julia Reinhard 5–6
Lynch, Gabrielle 16, 167–8, 177, 178, 179

McCarthyism 207
Macchia, Frank 194
McDowell, Phil *59*, 60
McEachern, Charmaine 163–4
MACSAS (Minister and Clergy Sexual Abuse Survivors) 190–2
Magdalene Laundries, Dublin 15, 69, 71, 74, 75, 77, 186
Malik, Kenan 39–40
Mandela, Nelson 178
Manhatten, 9/11 attacks, missing persons 139
March, James G. 160

Marciniak, Katarzyna 57
Martin, Archbishop Diarmuid 192, 193
mass media 164–5
Matus, José 57, 58
Mbembe, Achille 7
Metastases of Enjoyment (Žižek) 82
Mexico-US border, immigrant protests 57–60
Meyer, Edgar 53, 61
missing persons 134–5, 137–40, 142–7
Moore, Simon 129
morality: homosexuality 207, 208; and lying 198–9; unmarried mothers 75
mothers: of missing children, Buenos Aires 143–4; unmarried, historical treatment of, Ireland 69–78
Mothers of the Disappeared, Argentina 131
Mouffe, Chantal 109, 110
Mouton de Vapeur (*Les Quiétils*) 108, *109*
multiculturalism 37, 38–40
Munk, Erika 88

Nagel, Joanne 75
naked life 83–8
Ndege, Bernard, testimony of 175
new institutionalism 149–50, 160
Newly, Glen 208
Nield, Sophie 15–16
Nietzsche, Friedrich 198

Oakeshott, Michael 34, 48
Occupy movement 121–5, 128, 130–3, 224
Of All the People in World, installation 46–7
Oliver, Kelly 77
Olson, Johan P. 160
O'Malley, Cardinal Sean 192
O'Neill, John 20
Orgel, Stephen 5
Osborne, John, *Patriot for Me, A* 17, 205–6, 209–10, 211–12, 213, 215
Osborne, Robin 5
Owens, Patricia 87, 88

paradox of politics 104–5
Parfum des Pneus, Le (*The Perfume of Tyres*) 109, *112*
Parkinson, John 14
parliaments 148–51
Pašović, Haris 81, 83, 85, 89–90
Patriot for Me, A (Osborne) 17, 205–6, 209–10, 211–12, 213, 215
Pearson, Mike 134, 136

Performance, Identity and the Neo-Political Subject (Causey and Walsh) 8
Performance Studies 9–10
Phelan, Peggy 134, 135, 146
Plato 5, 6, 13, 97, 100, 102, 103
police orders 145, 146, 147
political rituals 155–6
politics, performative approaches to 20–1
Polletta, Francesca 120
Pope John Paul II, 'Day of Pardon' mass 187–90
Postdramatisches Theater (Lehmann) 35
posters of missing people 137, 139–40, 141, 147
Protection of Human Life During Pregnancy Bill (2013) 67
protests: Occupy movement 121–5, 128, 130–3, 224; policing of 126–30; ritualisation of 30–1
public order, dramaturgy of 121–32
Public Service Announcements (PSAs), American Ad Council 15, 52–6; alternative 'I am an American' project 56–64
public sphere 23, 130–2, 183–4, 185

Quiétils, Les (Mouton de Vapeur) 108, *109*

Rabkin, Norman 96–7
radical democratic citizenship 110
Rai, Shirin, M. 10, 12, 16
Rancière, Jacques 9, 12, 103, 106–7, 108–9, 110–11, 113–14, 118–19
Ranger, Terence 148; *Invention of Tradition, The* 156
Read, Alan 8, 49
Rebellato, Dan 47
Red Cross, tracing of missing persons 142–3
Redgrave, Vanessa 88
Redl, Colonel Alfred 17, 201–10, 212–15
Reinelt, Janelle 2, 10, 14–15
religion, role of in post-secular state 183–5
representation 12–13
resistance, Sarajevo 80–8
rhetoric 6, 7, 16, 20; Aristotle 101; Isocrates 100; performance of political 150; plebiscitary 98–9; of protection 84–5
Ridout, Nicholas 5, 49–50
ritual, political 148–61
ritualisation of protests 30–1
Roach, Joseph 10, 115

Roman Catholicism *see* Catholic Church
Ross, Thomas 215; *Invisible Government* 213–14
Rousseau, Jean-Jacques 224
Rowan, Rory 128
Roy, Anupama 37, 38
Royal Court Theatre, London 205–6, 209–11
Royal de Luxe 109–10, 114, 116, 117, 119
royalty, protests against 129

Sagart 74–5
Sanders, Lynn 21
Sarajevo, siege of 80–92
Saward, Mike 17, 159
Schechner, Richard 135–6
Schlingensief, Christoph, *Church of Fear, The* 91
Schudson, Michael 23
scripts, democratic 29–31
Second World War, displaced persons 138–40
'secrecy effect' 203, 209, 211–12, 220
Sedgwick, Eve Kosofsky 213; *Epistemology of the Closet* 206
Šehić, Faruk 86
seige of Sarajevo, bare life vs. theatricality 80–92
self-definition, Taylor 185
sexual abuse scandal, Catholic Church, Ireland 185–96
'sexual jihadists' 65
Sexual Offences Act (1967) 211–12
Shakespeare scholarship 5–6
'silent majority' 36–7, 49
Simone, Jeanne 109–10, 111, 114, 119
Simpson, David 198, 200, 215
Sinfield, Alan 5
sins, confession of, Catholic Church 187–9
social coherence 154–6, 158
'social dramas', Turner 186
social identity/solidarity 185
social media: role in uprisings 28; TJRC coverage 175
songs, role of 185
South Africa: Parliament *150*; TRCs 162–5, 175, 177–8, 182
sovereign grammars 217–25
sovereignty 36, 55, 61; authoritative government 195, 196; the people's popular 104
'space of appearance', public sphere as 130
space, grammars of 220–1
Special Group, invisible government 214

speeches: ceremonial 95–6; political 195; rhetorical 100
spies, espionage, lies and state secrets 198–215
Spragens, Thomas 20
staging, democratic 25–9
Stan's Café (theatre company) 46, 48
state ceremonies 5, 7, 129, 148–55, 156–61
state security, espionage 198–215
Stone, Deborah 21
storytelling, street art 106–20
Structural Transformation of the Public Sphere (Habermas) 183–4
Sultan's Elephant (Royal de Luxe) 109–10, 114–18
Sunstein, Cass 26
symbolic violence 76
symphysiotomy 66, 78
Szymborska Wisława 138–9

Tahrir Square *see* Occupy movement
Taylor, Charles, 'self-definition' 185
Taylor, Diana 131, 134; 'animatives' vs. 'performatives' 11
Testing the Echo (Edgar) 45, 46, 48
Thomson, George 5
Tiananmen Square massacre, commemoration 31
Tilly, Charles 20
Tillyard, E. M. W., *Elizabethan World Picture, The* 5
time, grammars of 220–1
traditions, invented 156–8
Truth, Justice and Reconciliation Commission (TJRC), Kenya 166–82
Turner, Victor 158; 'social dramas' 186
Tutu, Desmond 177–8
Tyler, Imogen 57

UK Parliament, security *152*
United States: 1950s hearings on Redl case 207–9; 'I am an American' Ad Council PSA 51–64; Wall Street occupation 121–2, 123, 125, 132
unmarried mothers, Irish Sate 69, 74–8
uprisings, Middle Eastern 28

Vatican: 'Day of Pardon' service 187–9; Irish government's defiance 195
Virgin Mary 72, 75

Waddington, David 126
Waki Commission, post-election violence 179

Walker, Rob B. J. 53, 55, 61, 63
Wall Street, Occupy movement 121–2, 123, 125, 132
Walsh, Fintan, *Performance, Identity and the Neo-Political Subject* 8
Walzer, Michael 6
War on Terror 56, 57, 61, 62, 129
Warner, Michael 42
Warner, S. J. 142–3
Weber, Cynthia 15, 219
Whitehead, Laurence 20
Wickstrom, Maurya 41, 49
Wigley, Mark 139
Wiles, David 5
Winkler, John 5
Wise, David 215; *Invisible Government* 213–14

women: abortion 188; clerical sexual exploitation of 190–2; hearings, Kenya 173–4; Magdalene Laundries, Ireland 67–78; *see also* mothers
Wood, Patricia 40
'worksites of democracy', theatre as 41–4

'X Case' (1992), Irish abortion laws 67–8

Yarker, James 46
Young, Iris Marion 8–9, 21, 37–8
Younge, Gary 130

Zapatistas (the 'faceless'), Occupy movement 131
Zeitlin, Froma 5
Žižek, Slavoj 69, 76, 130; *Metastases of Enjoyment* 82

9780415716505